Abraham Lincoln
and
Jefferson Davis

Two Stories

by

Thomas Dixon

Bandanna Books · 2017 · Santa Barbara

Abraham Lincoln and Jefferson Davis copyright © 2017 Bandanna Books
by Thomas Dixon. Cover art. ISBN 978-0-942208-91-7

SHAKESPEARE DIRECTORS PLAYBOOK SERIES
Hamlet   Merchant of Venice   Twelfth Night   Romeo and Juliet
Taming of the Shrew   A Midsummer Night's Dream   Henry V
As You Like It   Richard III   Much Ado About Nothing   Othello
Macbeth   Antony and Cleopatra   King Lear   Julius Caesar

HISTORY
Mitos y Leyendas/Myths and Legends of Mexico (Bilingual)
The Beechers Through the 19th Century
Uncle Tom's Cabin, Harriet Beecher Stowe
Dred, Harriet Beecher Stowe
The Deserted Village, Ossian, Babylonian Captivity

SCHOOLING AND LANGUAGE
Don't Panic: Procrastinator's Guide to Writing a Term Paper
First Person Intense   Art of Writing (Stevenson)
How to Write... (Poe)   How to Tell a Story (Twain)
How to See a Play (Burton)   Write It Right (Bierce)
The Gospel According to Tolstoy   Gandhi on the Gita
The Everlasting Gospel, Blake   Italian for Opera Lovers
French for Food Lovers   Doctorese for the imPatient
Yiddish, You Say. Nu?   Deadword Dictionary   Ghazals of Ghalib

TEACHERS ONLY
(Q & A, glossaries, critical comments)
Areopagitica   Apology of Socrates, & Crito   Sappho
Leaves of Grass (1855), Whitman   Uncle Tom's Cabin, H.B. Stowe

OTHER
The First Detective: 3 Stories. Poe   Hadji Murad, Tolstoy
Frankenstein, Mary Shelley   Surfing, Jack London   Ski, Doyle
The Martian Testament, Eight 2 Two

Mudborn Press and Beta Books are imprints of Bandanna Books

BETA BOOKS
Eleanore Hill : The Family Secret, Last American Housewife,
Period Pieces, The Gingerbread Girl

INTRODUCTION

The author Thomas Dixon was born just as the War Between the States was entering its final stages, but that history was to haunt him throughout his life. He made it come to life most famously in *The Clansman*, which became, in D.W. Griffith's hands, a classic silent film, *The Birth of a Nation*, an epic of the rise of the Confederacy.

Even as a Southerner, Dixon was able to articulate in this first piece about Lincoln, the subtleties of Lincoln's depth and compassion, what drove him and how he accomplished so much in his few years as a wartime President, despite opposition from several sides. We see examples of Lincoln's personal approach, even when he was always keeping in mind the ultimate and harder task of reconciliation of the Northern states with the estranged South. During the combat, some Northern states had even been pondering their own secession.

The first piece is set as a play, focused on Lincoln, first as a boy, then as President. A counterpoint of Jefferson Davis and his responses is set next in the play, to give the broader perspective of the issues and the major players.

The longer story, beginning on p. 89, is Dixon's extended portrait of Jefferson Davis. Like Lincoln, in some ways Jefferson Davis was an unlikely leader for the newly formed government. The Prologue shows a politician in the making, but little expectation that he might find himself in charge of life and death for millions of people.

Dixon's personalized narrative sets events in motion on the field, and in the offices of power, revealing the human side of difficult decision-making, complex and contradictory issues that had to be settled, sometimes without hesitation. Once the conflict had erupted on the battlefield, the options were simpler—but much more difficult was finding a path to reach a satisfactory resolution. After years of struggle, with the enormous investment in lives lost and property destroyed on both sides, idealism had taken its toll.

Jefferson Davis, thrust into the role of President of the

Confederacy, had no ready playbook to follow. Politicians and generals gave conflicting advice or demands, newspapers sniped at Davis no matter what decision he made, or didn't make. Uniting the various states into a single nation was, in some people's minds, driven by an even greater dream. A secret society, the Knights of the Golden Circle, envisioned a whole community around the Caribbean, from Mexico to the edge of South America to Cuba based on the institution of slavery. That vision was to vanish as the Southern states scrambled to defend their way of life, based, as Vice President Alexander Stephens stated, on the "cornerstone" of the institution of slavery.

Sasha Newborn
August 2017

Abraham Lincoln

A MAN OF THE PEOPLE

Thomas Dixon

While the popular conception of Lincoln as the Liberator of the Slave is true historically, there is a deeper view of his life and character. He was the savior, if not the real creator, of the American Union of free Democratic States. His proclamation of emancipation was purely an incident of war. The first policy of his administration was to save the Union. To this fact we owe a united Nation today. It is this truth of history which I try to make a living reality in my play.

The scenes relating to the issues of our National life have been drawn from authentic records. The plot of the action is based on the letter of Colonel John Nicolay to Major Hay, dated August 25, 1864, in which the following opening paragraph is found:

> Hell is to pay. The New York politicians have got a stampede on that is about to swamp everything. Raymond and the National Committee are here today. R. thinks a Commission to Richmond is about the only salt to save us; while the President sees and says it would be utter ruination. The matter is now undergoing consultation. Weak-kneed damned fools are in the movement for a new candidate to supplant the President. Everything is darkness, doubt, and discouragement.

No liberty has been taken with an essential detail of history in the development of the action except to slightly shift the dates of two incidents for dramatic unity. In neither case does the change of date affect the validity of the scene as used.

Thomas Dixon

Contents

Prologue: The Lincoln cabin in the woods of Indiana, 1820	7
Act I: In the President's room, the morning of August 23, 1864	14
Act II: The same, that evening	43
Act III: Scene 1. Jefferson Davis' room three days later, in Richmond. Morning	65
Scene 2. Same as Acts I and II	75
Epilogue—Victory. The Platform of the second Inauguration, March 4, 1865, before the Capitol at Washington	84

Cast of Characters

Abe: a boy of ten
Sarah: his sister
Tom **Lincoln**: his father
Nancy: his mother
The Doctor: an old-fashioned pioneer

Prologue Scene

The rough-hewn log cabin of Tom Lincoln is seen in the center surrounded by the forest wilderness of Southern Indiana, 1820.

The cabin door is cut in level with the ground. There is no shutter to the door and no window to the cabin.

Right and Left of the door opening are rude benches of split logs. On the walls are stretched a coon and a small bear, squirrel and muskrat skins. In the foreground on the right is seen an old-fashioned wash pot set on three stones. Near the wash pot is fixed in the ground a pole, on the top of which are hung six gourds cut for martin swallows to nest in. Beside it are a rude bench and two wash tubs. On the left is a crude settee made of a split log with legs set in augur holes and a rough back made of saplings. An old-fashioned doctor's saddle-bags hang across the back of the settee. The trees are walnut, beech and oak—undergrowth of dogwood, sumac and wild grapevines. These vines, festooned over the cabin, give a sinister impression. A creek winds down through the hills behind the cabin.

At curtain rise: Sarah is seen softly tiptoeing toward the cabin door. She pauses, listens and slowly peeps inside. She listens again and then slips away and calls.

Sarah: Abe! Abe!

[Sarah goes back to the door and peeps in and runs to the gate]

Abe: Ma's awake now!

[She returns to the door, peeps in again and runs once more to the gate]

Sarah: He's feelin' her pulse! Come on in—don't stay out there in the woods....

[Abe enters slowly]

Abe: What does he say?

Sarah: He ain't said nothin' yet.

Abe: He's a dumb doctor, anyhow. I couldn't get him to say a word comin', last night.

Sarah: Well, he's here now, and there's his saddle-bags full of medicine. You've been ridin' all night—you look terrible tired! Go to bed and sleep a little.

Abe: I can't—while Ma's so sick—I'm afraid to go to sleep.

Sarah: Why?

Abe: You know why—Sarah.

Sarah: Ah, she ain't goin' to die now. She's talkin' to the doctor—lie down just a little while and get to sleep before the sun comes up or ye can't sleep— [Pleading] —come on.

Abe: No—I'm scared—the plague's killin' folks every day—and nobody knows what to do for 'em.

[The Doctor and Tom enter from the cabin and come down slowly— the Doctor seems to be debating his course of action]

   [*Eagerly to Doctor*]

You can do somethin' for her, Doctor?

Doctor: [*Hesitates*] Yes—Get me a clean towel and a bowl.

Abe: Run, Sarah—quick.

Sarah: [*Running to cabin*] Yes—I'll get 'em.

[The Doctor opens his saddle-bags, takes out his lancet and examines its keen point]

Tom: What are ye goin' ter do with that knife?

Doctor: Bleed her, of course—it's the only thing to do— [Starts toward cabin]

Abe: [*To his father*] Don't let him do it!

Doctor: What's that?

Tom: You shan't bleed her—I don't know nothin' 'bout doctorin'—but I know that'll kill her.

Doctor: I've a notion to give you the worst cussin' you ever had in your life, Tom Lincoln...

Tom: 'Twouldn't do no good—Doctor.

Doctor: [*Throwing his arms up*] 'Twould do me good! I've rode all night— thirty-five miles—from my home in Kentucky across the Ohio, into this wilderness, just for you to insult me.

Tom: I didn't mean to.

Doctor: Well, you're doin' it—and I'd give ye the cussin' that'ud pay me for my trouble comin' up here—if I hadn't heard what you've been doin' for your neighbors, in this plague. There's no doctor in thirty miles— You've been the doctor and nurse—mother and father to 'em all. And when they die, you go into the woods, cut down a tree, rip out the boards, make the coffin, dig the grave and lower the dead with a prayer—I'd like to cuss you, Tom Lincoln—but I can't—damn ye!

Tom: I'm sorry, Doctor—but I just couldn't let ye bleed her.

Doctor: All right—goodbye.

[With a snort of anger, the Doctor throws his lancet into his saddlebags, snaps them together, and starts for the gate]

Abe: [*Following the Doctor to gate*] Doctor—.

Doctor: What do ye want?

Abe: [*Seizing his hand*] Please don't go—I'm mighty sorry we made ye mad—I didn't go to do it—you see— [He falters] I love my Ma so, I just couldn't see ye cut her arm open. And Pa didn't mean to hurt yer feelin's—won't ye stay and help us? Can't ye do somethin' else for her? [*Pauses*] I'll pay ye! I'll work for ye a whole—year.

Doctor: You'd work for me a year?

Abe: [*Eagerly*] I'll work for ye five years if you'll just save her—just save her life—that's all—don't go—please, don't.

Doctor: [*The Doctor slips his arm around the boy, draws him close and holds him a moment*] You're a good boy, Abe.

Abe: You'll stay?

Doctor: I'd stay and do something if I could, Sonny, but to tell ye the truth, I don't know what to do—I'm not quite sure I'm right about the bleedin', or I'd stay and make you both help me— [He pauses] But I'm not sure! I'm not sure! And I don't know what else to do—I've got no medicine—so I can't stay. All I can tell ye is to keep her warm—and give her everything good to eat that she can take—she's in God's hands—Goodbye.

[The Doctor hurries through the gate—and leaves Abe and Tom gazing forlornly after him, as Sarah comes from the house]

Sarah: I've got the towel and bowl all ready— [*Pauses*] What's the matter? [*Looks around*] Where's the doctor?

Abe: He's gone.

Sarah: Gone?

Tom: Yes.

[**Nancy** enters by door of cabin]

>[*Nancy's sudden appearance in the door swings Abe around with a quick cry of pain. The sun is tinging the eastern sky with the splendor of an Indian Summer morning. The mother's figure in blue homespun suggests against the dark background of the cabin door the coming of a spirit from the unseen world. She pauses a moment in the doorway and smiles at her son*]

Abe: Oh, Ma, you mustn't.

Tom: [*Following*] Nancy!

Nancy: I'm better, I'm a lot better.

Abe: You're too sick to come out here, Ma.

Nancy: [*Smiling*]

I can walk—as well as you can,—see.

[She sways slightly toward the settee]

Abe: But the Doctor says you must keep warm.

Nancy: Well—I have on the warm stockings that Sarah knit for me and the coon skin moccasins you made—don't you see, I'm better now?

Abe: [*Joyfully*] Look, Pa, she's better!

Sarah: Yes—she's better!

Tom: [*Alarmed*] Don't try to walk—set down, honey!

Nancy: [*Sinking on bench*] Yes—I will.

[The boy comes closer, staring eagerly into his mother's face]

Nancy: Come closer, my boy.

>[**Abe** *kneels at her feet*]

Tom: I'm a feared of this, Nancy—you better let me git a hot rock and wrap it up for your feet.

Nancy: Yes, Tom—and bring me the Bible. I want Abe to read to me.

>[*Tom goes into the cabin worried over her*]

Abe: Feel all right, Ma?

Nancy: [*She nods and breathes deeply—her eyes alight*] I wanted to see the sun rise through the trees! You remember the day you cut down your first tree to begin the clearing and the sunlight came through the hole you'd made to the sky.

Abe: Yes—I remember.

Nancy: You called me to come and see it.

Abe: [*In a whisper*] Yes.

Nancy: I was proud that morning as I saw you stand with your ax on that big log—anything my boy starts to do—he does— [*Pauses*] Your father taught you to use the ax and. [*Turns and looks at Abe*] Your father's a good man, my son—kind-hearted and true and everybody likes him. They made him road supervisor of his township in Kentucky once. If he could read and write he would have gone to the legislature.

> [*Tom enters from the cabin with the rock and Bible, he crosses to Nancy, and Abe takes the rock and puts it under her feet—Sarah kneels and helps him. Nancy's hand drops on the bench. Tom picks up her hand, and the chill of it worries him*]

> [**Abe** *and Sarah rise*]

Nancy: Read to me, son—I like to hear your voice.

Abe: [*Brightly*] All right—what?

Nancy: The Twenty-third Psalm.

> [**Abe** *looks for the place*]

I love to hear you read, my boy. It means that you can do what any other man can—it means so much!

Abe: [*Reads*] The Lord is my shepherd—I shall not want. He maketh me to lie down in green pastures. He leadeth me beside still waters. He restoreth my soul. He leadeth me in the paths of righteousness for his name's sake.

Nancy: [*In a whisper*] Yea, tho' I walk through the valley of the shadow of death, I will fear no evil, for thou art with me.

[**Abe** stops, looks up at his mother in amazement]

Abe: Ma.

Nancy: Remember always, my boy, that God is with you! He is in the day and the night. He is in the sun and the wind, the trees and the grass—and not a sparrow falls to the ground without He knows. You recollect the year you put up those gourds there— [*She points to the pole*] for your martins? You cried when they circled away in the fall.

[*Abe nods*]

I told you God would send them back in the spring, didn't I? [*She laughs softly*] You said that He'd forget to tell them and they'd never find the way—but they came—didn't they?

Abe: Yes, Ma, and I know now they'll come again next spring.

Nancy: So—I want you never again to doubt God, my boy, and I want you never to doubt yourself. Your bare feet, your ragged clothes, how poor you are—this is nothing! It doesn't count here—it's what you feel, it's what you believe—it's what you see that counts! I've taught you to read and write, and now you can do anything! If God takes me. [*She pauses exhausted*]

Abe: But you mustn't say that, Ma!

Nancy: "The judgments of the Lord are true and righteous altogether!"

Abe: No! no, Ma! Don't talk that way! You'll give up if you do!

Nancy: If He calls, my son, then my work is done—and you can do all I've tried and failed to do.

Abe: [*Alarmed*] Had she better talk so much, Pa. [*Stoops to fix her feet*]

Tom: [*Feeling her hand*] Nancy!

Nancy: Just a minute more, Tom! Don't let him know yet—you know!

Tom: [*With upward look of faith*] Yes, I know.

[*To Abe*]

It's all right—boy.

Nancy: Come back close, my son, I want to tell you something I saw last night! I had a dream—the same one I had the night before you were born. You had grown a man—strong and brave—wise and gentle. The people hung on your words, and did you homage. But you remembered this cabin here in the deep woods and you were humble. I walked with you between two white pillars. It was still and solemn, in there. Outside I could hear the people calling your name. You bowed low and whispered in my ear: "This is all yours, my Mother. I bought it for you with my life. All that I am I owe to you—"

[*Her voice sinks to a whisper that is half a laugh of religious ecstasy*]

Abe: [*Joyfully*] See how she's smilin'—Pa! She's getting well—I tell you!

Tom: [*Whispering*] Don't ye understand, boy?

Abe: No—what?

Sarah: What—what is it?

Tom: [*In deep religious awe*] Look—look at her eyes! She's not telling ye a dream—she's looking through the gates of Heaven.

Abe: No—no—no!

Tom: It's death—boy—it's come—Lord, God, have mercy.

[**Abe** *springs to his feet and stares in anguish, as Tom falls on his knees beside Nancy. Nancy's hand rests gently on Tom's shaggy head, while he sobs. With her other hand she feels for Abe's and holds it feebly*]

Nancy: Be good to your Father,— [*She pauses and breathes with difficulty*] In the days to come, he will be the child and you the man.

Abe: Yes.

Nancy: And love your sister.

[*Abe nods*]

If dark hours come, my spirit will be watching, my son—and I'll help you if I can.

Abe: Yes, I know it!

Nancy: And remember that you can be a great man in this free country if you only say—I will.

[*Nancy's body sinks in death as the boy lifts his face illumined by the light of a great purpose*]

Abe: Yes, Ma,—I will!

CURTAIN

ACT I

<u>Cast of Characters</u>

Abraham Lincoln, the President
Mrs. Lincoln, his wife
Colonel Nicolay, his Secretary.
Edward, The Doorman.
Edwin M. Stanton, Secretary of War.
Gen. Geo. B. McClellan, Lincoln's Rival.
Captain Vaughn of the U.S. Army.
Betty Winter, his Sweetheart.
Thaddeus Stevens, Leader of Congress.
Henry Raymond, Editor of the *New York Times*.
John R. Gilmore of the New York *Tribune*.
Colonel Jacquess , a Methodist Clergyman.
Jefferson Davis, President of the Confederacy.
Judah P. Benjamin, his Secretary of State.
Judge Robert Ould, Commissioner of Exchange.
Robert E. Lee, Commanding General.
A sister, who begs for her brother's life.
A **Congressman** who demands a hearing.
A little girl from Virginia.
A mother with a baby.
A woman who has lost two sons.
A telegraph operator in the White House.
A doorman at Richmond.
Committeemen, Soldiers, and Guards

Set Scene: The President's room in the White House, August 23, 1864. A flat desk left center. At right a long table and chairs. Doors open right and left. Large windows open center. Beside the center window stands an upright desk. In one corner, a rack with map rollers and folios of maps on the floor and leaning against the wall.

At Curtain Rise: Colonel Nicolay, the President's Secretary, is seen writing before an enormous pile of mail. He reads a letter and throws it down in disgust. Reads another and hurls it into the waste basket. He rises—turns back to the desk and hurls an armful of the letters into the corner on the floor and removes enough letters to clear a space for his Chief to write.

[*Edward enters dragging a mail bag*]

Nicolay: [*Calling to The Doorman*] Edward!

Edward: Yes, sir.

Nicolay: Hold that door tight this morning.

Edward: Tight as a drum, sir.

Nicolay: If any men of importance try to crowd in before their time.

Edward: I'll look out for them, sir—here's another bag of letters, Colonel Nicolay.

Nicolay: Another?

Edward: And there's two more outside.

Nicolay: My God!

Edward: Don't blame me, sir—I didn't write 'em.

Nicolay: No, I'll vouch for your loyalty to the President.

Edward: Where'll I put these?

Nicolay: Throw the bag in the corner—there's no room on his desk now.

Edward: [*Obeying*] Yes, sir—

[*Edward throws the bag in the corner of the room where Nicolay has already piled the letters from the desk, and turns to Nicolay. He watches Nicolay destroying letters for a moment*]

Nicolay: Well, Edward?

Edward: Will you tell me one thing, Colonel Nicolay?

Nicolay: If I can.

Edward: What do they say in these letters to the President? I've served through four administrations—I've never seen such piles of letters in the White House before.

Nicolay: Well, Edward—these letters ask two things of Abraham

Lincoln: That he dismiss General Grant from command of the Army.

Edward: The idiots.

Nicolay: And stop the war today—August 23, 1864,—make peace—peace at any price—today.

Edward: God save us! After nearly four years—quit, with nothing settled?

Nicolay: That's what these letters demand.

Edward: You couldn't believe it— No wonder his eyes sink back in his head, an' he looks as if he were seeing ghosts. [*Pauses and starts*]

Nicolay: Watch out for that door, Edward.

>[*Edward bows, and exits to door leading to the main corridor. Nicolay returns to his task of reading the letters—one he tosses into the basket wearily—one he crumples in anger and hurls into the basket*]

Nicolay: The fools!

>[*He is absorbed in a letter when Mrs. Lincoln enters in a state of nervous excitement. He rises quickly, and goes to meet her*]

What is it, Mrs. Lincoln?

Mrs. Lincoln: I have just heard that the Republican National Committee is in Washington!

Nicolay: They are.

Mrs. Lincoln: In conference at Senator Winter's house?

Nicolay: Yes.

Mrs. Lincoln: What do they want?

Nicolay: There are ugly rumors.

Mrs. Lincoln: What? What? What?

Nicolay: I can't discuss it, Madam, until the Chief knows.

Mrs. Lincoln: Mr. Lincoln doesn't know.

Nicolay: Not yet. He will, this morning. They've just sent a demand to me that he see them before his public reception begins.

Mrs. Lincoln: You've heard something—you know something—tell me—I can't endure the suspense.

Nicolay: Only rumors—and they're too ugly to put into words—they're incredible.

Mrs. Lincoln: All the same, you believe them— [Impetuously] What have you heard?

Nicolay: [*Shakes his head*] The Chief wouldn't like it if I talk, before he knows. I'll tell you a few things I'm thinking in plain English—if you'd like to hear.

Mrs. Lincoln: You can't make it too plain to suit me.

Nicolay: In my opinion, the devil is to pay. Weak-kneed fools are deserting the Chief. Every man who loves Abraham Lincoln must get off his coat now and fight. He is the only man who can save this Nation today, and he's too big and generous to be trusted alone with wolves.

Mrs. Lincoln: What can you mean? The Republican National Committee have no power over the President of the United States.

Nicolay: No, Madam— But they have certain powers over the Nominee of their party.

Mrs. Lincoln: But Mr. Lincoln is already the nominee of his party for the second term ... chosen two months ago—and the election is but eight weeks off—what do you mean?

[*Edward enters*]

Edward: Miss Betty Winter to see you, Ma'am.

Mrs. Lincoln: How fortunate—they're at her father's house!

Nicolay: Yes.

Mrs. Lincoln: Show her right in here, Edward.

Edward: Yes, Madam.

Mrs. Lincoln: [*To Nicolay*] And she's loyal to Mr. Lincoln.

Edward: [*At door left*] Right this way,—Miss Betty.

[*Betty enters—a young woman 25 years old—poised, cultured, charming*]

Mrs. Lincoln: [Meeting Betty] Welcome—my child.

Betty: You're always so kind!

Nicolay: Excuse me, ladies—while I go out and get rid of some of these people waiting to see the President.

[*Nicolay exits*]

Mrs. Lincoln: Tell me, dear, you've heard something—the Republican National Committee are at your father's.

Betty: They were there—they've adjourned to Thaddeus Stevens' house across the street from us— They were locked in with father for two hours.

Mrs. Lincoln: Locked in?

Betty: [*Nods*] With the keyhole chinked up!

Mrs. Lincoln: And you didn't get a hint of what they're up to?

Betty: Not the faintest.

Mrs. Lincoln: Oh, Betty—they're discussing me.

Betty: They didn't mention your name.

Mrs. Lincoln: How do you know?

Betty: Well—I did hear a little! I could hear from the next room when they got excited! It's Abraham Lincoln they're discussing—not his wife.

Mrs. Lincoln: You're sure?

Betty: Sure! It sounded like a regular dog fight—with one big brute howling— [*Imitates*] —the President's name above the din.

Mrs. Lincoln: But, you can't be sure, my dear.

Betty: What on earth could they be discussing you for?

Mrs. Lincoln: My loyalty, of course—you know that my brothers are in the Southern Army, fighting the Union. Fools have accused me of giving them important secrets of the Government. When I hate them for all they have done to me and mine!

Betty: But my dear Mrs. Lincoln—no one believes such lies about you now—not even in this bitter campaign—it's absurd.

Mrs. Lincoln: [*Hesitates*] That is not the real thing I'm afraid of, child—it's something worse—I'm going to take you into my confidence now—may I?

Betty: I'll be tickled to death with the honor!

Mrs. Lincoln: And I'm going to ask you to help me.

Betty: I'll be in the Cabinet next!

Mrs. Lincoln: The truth is, I owe A. T. Stewart and Company an enormous bill for dresses—$60,000.

Betty: Sixty thousand—oh, my Lord! That's worse than mine!

Mrs. Lincoln: I had to get them! The world said the White House would be disgraced by my awkward husband's regime—I've shown them better! But I just couldn't tell Mr. Lincoln. He has no idea of the cost of clothes. If these jackals have found out and attack him on my account, the thought of it will kill me.

Betty: But you know he'd defend you against any one who dares attack you.

Mrs. Lincoln: Yes, dear—but it would hurt him so to hear it from their brutal lips. I want you to find out from your father, if they know.

Betty: And if they know?

Mrs. Lincoln: Get here before they do, and I'll head them off—I'll tell Mr. Lincoln first.

Betty: [*Smiling*] On one condition—that you help me.

Mrs. Lincoln: Anything you ask.

Betty: I've promised my fiancé that I would get an appointment for him to see the President on something very important.

Mrs. Lincoln: Mr. Lincoln will be here in a few minutes. I'll have him see your sweetheart first.

Betty: But—it's a personal matter and he doesn't wish to come to a public reception. He wants an hour alone— Could you get it for him, tonight?

Mrs. Lincoln: I—think—so.

Betty: You'll try?

Mrs. Lincoln: I'll do it, child—certainly! You're one loyal friend we have in that crowd of wolves on the Capitol Hill.

Betty: All right, I'll find out if they're discussing politics or your dressmaker's bill.

    [*Betty hurries to the door, followed by Mrs. Lincoln*]

Mrs. Lincoln: God bless you, child.

    [*Nicolay enters by the other door*]

Mrs. Lincoln: Hurry!

Betty: If it's dresses—I'll beat them to the White House!

    [*Betty exits*]

Nicolay: The President is coming, Madam.

Mrs. Lincoln: I'm going. But I may want to see him before that Committee—in case I send in—see that he comes, will you?

Nicolay: I'll try to manage it. The friends of the Chief may call on you for some inside work, Madam.

Mrs. Lincoln: [*Eagerly*] I'll do my part, never fear!

> [*Mrs. Lincoln exits and Nicolay hastily arranges his desk and stands at attention as Lincoln enters*]

> [*Lincoln crosses the room with long nervous stride, reaches his desk, looks at the pile of letters and shakes his head wearily*]

Lincoln: Sorry for you, John, with all these letters on your hands. [*Laughs*] You have to work!

Nicolay: I'm trying to get them out of your way, sir.

Lincoln: Thank you—you know the ones I want to see.

Nicolay: Yes, sir.

Lincoln: [*Softly*] And don't forget that no man or woman can be turned from that door, who comes here to ask for the saving of a human life. [*Pauses*] There's a firing squad shooting a boy down in Virginia this morning! [Shakes his head] I hope I didn't do wrong to let them. Somehow I could not find an excuse to save him. [*Sighs*] The Generals are all after me about my pardons.

Nicolay: The Secretary of War is out there now, champing his bit, to head you off on some of them, I think.

Lincoln: Don't let old Mars in yet. He's no business here at this hour. Let him paw a hole in the ground. [*Pauses*] Any news from the front, this morning?

Nicolay: [*Handing him a telegram*] From General Grant's lines—only this, sir.

Lincoln: [*Reads*] "Confederate Cavalry raiders capture a Brigadier General and fifty army mules."—Too bad—rush a regiment after the mules—they're worth $200 a piece—Jeff Davis can have my Brigadier General!

Nicolay: [*Laughs*] Yes, sir—and this came in code from Sherman.

> [Hands Lincoln another telegram]

Lincoln: [*Eagerly*] Word from Sherman! Good! [Reads] —"Scouts report

Hood's trenches before Atlanta are impregnable—carefully considering a flank movement—but as yet, I cannot find the position or strength of Hood's second line—"W. T. Sherman. [*Pauses*] Grant's deadlocked with Lee at Petersburg—If-Sherman-could-only-give-us-Atlanta! [*Pauses*] I've a notion to telegraph Sherman an order direct!

Nicolay: I wouldn't go over General Grant's head, sir, with a military order—he's sensitive.

Lincoln: It might make trouble—Grant might resent my interference with his plan of campaign.

Nicolay: It would have to be filed in the War Department.

Lincoln: Yes—I know. Anything else?

Nicolay: [*Handing him a large document*] Baker's full report of the secret service on the Copperhead Societies— He asks for the immediate arrest of their leaders—and I think he's right.

Lincoln: [*Shakes his head*] It won't do—it won't do just now—it's an ugly business—too ugly for haste—I'll look it over carefully. [*Lays the report on his desk*] I'm ready now to see the people.

Nicolay: The Republican National Committee are in town, sir.

Lincoln: What on earth are they doing here?

Nicolay: That's what everybody's asking.

Lincoln: They should be in their States, leading the Party to victory— What do they want?

Nicolay: To see you.

Lincoln: Umph!

Nicolay: Henry Raymond, their Chairman, is with them, and has just sent word demanding a hearing before your public reception this morning.

Lincoln: Make the appointment later. They're all distinguished men. They can wait while the humbler people have their turn. I came up here from the wilderness. I know what it means to have the great rush by me. [*Laughs*] No—I'll see the common folks first.

Nicolay: I think you'd better see this Committee right away, sir.

Lincoln: Why? What have you heard?

Nicolay: Some ugly rumors.

Lincoln: Spare me the rumors! We've enough of them flying around Washington to poison us all. They can only wish me to hedge on some of my principles in this crisis. I've made all the campaign statements I'm going to make. I've faith in the good sense of the people. I'm going to plant my feet squarely on that faith and wait the verdict of this election.

Nicolay: You won't see the Committee now?

Lincoln: No! I'll take my bath of public opinion first. I want to see real men and women and feel their hearts beat close to mine. It tones me up for the day's work—let them in.

[Stanton bursts into the room in a towering rage]

Stanton: Mr. President, I've been kept waiting! *[Confronting Nicolay]*

[Nicolay turns away and laughs]

Nicolay! How dare you keep me waiting in an anteroom, while you talk to the President! I want you to understand, sir, that as Secretary of War, I've the right to enter this room at any hour, day or night, announced or unannounced, and by God, I'm going to exercise that privilege! [Stanton paces the floor furiously]

Lincoln: *[Laughing]* Well, you're here now, and it's all right, Stanton—Easy! Easy, or we'll have to put some rocks in your pocket to hold you down. What can I do?

Stanton: Mr. President, I've come here this morning to make a square issue with you on the abuse of the pardoning power which you are making daily.

Lincoln: As Chief Magistrate of the people, I have been clothed with that power, Stanton.

Stanton: [Angrily] You have no right to exercise it under the present conditions! Discipline in our armies must be maintained. You are hamstringing me and every General in the field—by suspending the death penalty of our Courts-Martial. Men are deserting in thousands and we've got to put a stop to it.

Lincoln: That's what I say! Bring to me the traitors who are causing them to desert, and see what I'll do to them!

Stanton: You can't evade the issue I'm making, sir! You'll be asked this morning to pardon a deserter. I call a halt here and now—will you stop today the use of this pardoning power?

Lincoln: I've got to hear both sides—it's my solemn duty.

Stanton: All right, I'm done. There's my resignation as your Secretary of War—Goodbye!

> [*Stanton strides angrily to the door and Lincoln speaks as he puts his hand on the knob*]

Lincoln: Wait a minute.

Stanton: It's no use.

Lincoln: Come back here. I've something to say to you.

> [*Stanton returns*]

Stanton: You're wasting your breath.

Lincoln: Stanton, I appointed you Secretary of War against the advice of every man about me. You were a cantankerous Democrat and my enemy. You had said the meanest things about me that were ever spoken in Washington—and that's putting it pretty strong. You called me a low clown—the original gorilla. In spite of all this, I saw your great qualities! I saw that you were absolutely fearless and absolutely honest, that your nerves were made of steel and your capacity for work was boundless. Even in your passions and hatreds, you showed a loyalty to the Union that rose above the parties and creeds of a lifetime. I like men of your strong personality. They stand between a nation and hell. And so, I appointed you, my bitter foe, to my cabinet. I've never regretted it for a minute in these years of blood and anguish. You've made the best Secretary of War this country ever had. In spite of your mean traits and your awful profanity, I've learned to love you! Now, you've resigned, and done your duty, as you see it. I've accepted your resignation, conscripted you again, and reappointed you!

> [*Pauses and strokes his shoulder*]

Go back to your desk and stick to the rules—that's your business; and I'll keep right on here tempering Justice with Mercy when I get a chance.

Stanton: [*Gazing at him a moment hopelessly*] Well,—I suppose I'll have to try! [*Snorts*]

But—I'm—damned—if—you—interfere—with—me—again!

[*Stanton hurries to the door*]

Lincoln: All right now— But look here, Stanton— [*Stanton pauses*] If I have to send over a pardon or two to you this morning…

Stanton: Hell fire!

Lincoln: Easy—easy now! You'll know they're very urgent, and will admit of no delay on account of red tape.

Stanton: [*Throws his hands up in wild gesture of despair*] Oh, my God!

[*Stanton exits*]

Lincoln: John, the old Fox was trying to head me off, wasn't he? Get them in here quick—who's the first in turn?

Nicolay: A young lady to plead for the life of her brother.

Lincoln: Bring her in!

[*As Nicolay goes to the door, Lincoln follows to meet the young woman. She enters, a forlorn little figure with baby face and blonde hair. She is plainly dressed in homespun cloth and does not wear hoopskirts. The President greets her with the utmost deference*]

[Taking both her hands] My dear young lady—I'm glad to see you—good old Pennsylvania Dutch! I knew you before you spoke—my folks came down to Virginia from there, in the old Colonial days.

The Sister: [*Overcome*] Oh—Meester—Presiden—you are so goot to me—you are so kind— [*Pauses overcome*] I haf no speech.

Lincoln: Come now, tell me in your own way what I can do to help you.

The Sister: Oh—Meester Presiden—you can do all—you can do any t'ing—und I am so happy to see you—I cannot begin.

Lincoln: [*Soothing her*] Take your time, little girl—all the others will have to wait on you now.

The Sister: Ya-ya—it is my turn now—ya, und I must hurry. You see, it's mine brudder—he ist just von leetle poy, Meester Presiden—von leetle poy with curly hair like mine— [She chokes]

Lincoln: [*Taking her hand*] And what happened to him, my dear?

The Sister: Vell, you see he lif wid me in Pennsylvania—ve are all alone to-gedder—und he lef me und go into der armee—und von bad man he giv him a leetle book vot tell him to desert und go home to his peoples—I haf dot leetle book, Meester Presiden. [*She hands him the book*] Und my brudder he's such a leetle poy, he read und he tink vot ze book say is so, und he leef ze armee und come home und kiss me und say, 'I vill take care of you now, mein seester—" [Breaks down] Und zey come und take heem, und now he is to be shot— [*She chokes*]

[Lincoln reads the title of the little book]

Lincoln: "Why Should Brothers Fight?" "By Richard Vaughan"—an old Copperhead leader I'll warrant! [*Pauses*] And you came to me, all alone, little girl?

The Sister: Ya—I haf no friens here.

Lincoln: Your **Congressman** does not know of this?

[*Nicolay begins to make out the pardon*]

The Sister: I do not know ze Congress-man—mein leetle brudder is all I haf.

Lincoln: Alone, friendless—with no **Congressman** to speak for you! Well, little girl, you don't need anybody to speak for you—you speak for yourself—you're good and honest and love your brother—and by jings, you don't wear hoopskirts—I'm sorry to rile old Stanton again— [*Laughs*] But I'm going to pardon your brother!

The Sister: [*Seizes and kisses his hand*] Oh—Meester Presiden—I praise ze good God.

Lincoln: There! There! Now, don't do that, you'll have me crying in a minute and John Nicolay here will see me.

The Sister: Ya! Meester Nicolay—won't mind—he so kind to me too.

[*Nicolay has prepared the pardon and the President signs and hands it to her*]

The Sister: [*Seizing the pardon*] Wiz all my heart!

Lincoln: [*To Nicolay*] Send her to Stanton, and tell him to rush that order to stay the execution. They shall not shoot this poor boy, ignorant of our laws, but if he can find the man who put that little book [*Holds up book*] into his hand, advising desertion—I'll hang him on a gallows forty cubits high!

[*He lays the booklet on his desk*]

[Nicolay writes on the back of the pardon]

The Sister: [Joyfully]

Mein brudder he vill go back und he vill be von goot poy for you, Meester Presiden.

Lincoln: Yes, I know he will, my child, I know he will. Goodbye, and God bless you.

The Sister: Und God bless you, Meester Presiden!

[Nicolay pauses at the door and gives orders to The Doorman]

Nicolay: Edward, take her to the War Office with this message.

Edward: Yes, sir.

Congressman: I demand to see the President at once.

Nicolay: I can't admit you, Mr. **Congressman**, just now.

Congressman: [*Forcing his way in*] I demand it, sir.

[Lincoln crosses to the door]

Lincoln: What is it, John.

Congressman: Mr. President, I have been here three times! I demand the right to see you—to ask the pardon of one of my constituents.

Lincoln: All right! Out with it!

Congressman: He is one of the solid citizens of Massachusetts; a slave trader whose ship has been confiscated. He has spent five years in prison, and cannot pay the heavy fine in money imposed— He is not a bad man at heart.

Lincoln: And he wants me to pardon him—this slave-trader!

Congressman: I ask it as a matter of justice—he has paid the penalty— five long years in prison.

Lincoln: [*Laughs*] I might pardon a murderer from old Massachusetts, she's done glorious service in this war—but a man who can make a business of going to Africa and robbing her of helpless men, women and children and selling them into bondage! [*He pauses and stiffens*] —before that man can have liberty by any act of mine, he can stay in jail and rot!

Nicolay: [*To the Congressman*] Now, you've got it!

Congressman: [*Crestfallen*] Yes—I heard it.

Lincoln: [*Turning back to his desk, and examining his papers*] Good— Bring in the next one, John!

> [*As Nicolay exits with the Congressman who continues to talk in loud tones, a sweet little girl of twelve slips by and reaches the President's desk unannounced. The President has taken his seat and is writing. While the President continues to write, the little girl slips close and watches him wistfully. He lifts his head, sees her, and smiles*]

Why, what a wee girl—and you got in here all by yourself?

Virginia: I slipped in when no one was looking.

Lincoln: Did you? What did you do that for?

Virginia: I was afraid they wouldn't let me in, if they knew what I wanted.

Lincoln: [*Tenderly*] And what do you want?

Virginia: If you please, sir—a pass to go through the lines to Virginia— my brother's there—he was shot in the last battle—and I want to see him.

Lincoln: Of course, you do—and you shall too.

> [*He seizes his pen, writes a pass and hands it to her*]

Virginia: [*Breathlessly*] Oh, thank you—thank you!

Lincoln: [*Casually placing his hand on her head*] Of course, you're loyal?

> [*Virginia's lips quiver, she hesitates, looks up into his face through dimmed eyes, and her slender body stiffens as she slowly speaks*]

Virginia: Yes—loyal—with all my heart—to Virginia!

> [*The trembling little fingers hand the pass back as the tears roll down her cheeks. Lincoln looks away to hide from her his own emotion, stoops and takes her hand in his. His voice is low and tender and full of feeling*]

Lincoln: I know what it cost you to say that, child. You're a brave little girl! And I'll love you always for this glimpse you've given me of a great spirit and a great people. That's why I can't let the South go— They can't leave this Union. We need them— Now I can trust you?

Virginia: [*Eagerly*] Yes, sir!

> [*Nicolay enters with a young mother and baby*

and hesitates at sight of the little girl]

Lincoln: Come on in, John—it's all right. I'm about through with this young lady— [*Nicolay brings the young mother to the desk and Lincoln takes Virginia down stage*] Come down here, dear, so old man Nicolay can't hear us—he mightn't understand. [*He sits on a chair and draws the girl close*] You see, I understand you—and can trust you implicitly. Now if I give you back this and let you go—will you promise me that no word shall pass your lips of what you've seen inside our lines?

Virginia: Oh, yes—I promise!

Lincoln: [*Handing her the pass*] May God speed the day, child, when your people and mine shall no longer be enemies.

Virginia: Thank you, sir!

Lincoln: Run now!

[*Virginia exits. At the door she throws him a kiss*]

[*Lincoln comes quickly to the mother and greets her cheerily*]

Well, little mother, what's the matter? [*She hesitates and appeals to Nicolay*]

Nicolay: Tell him yourself.

The Mother: [*Trembling*] If you please, sir, we ain't been married but a little over a year, and my husband's never seen the baby.

Lincoln: That's too bad.

The Mother: He's in the army and I couldn't stand it any longer—so I came down to Washington to get a pass to take the baby to him. But he wouldn't let me have it at the War Office.

Lincoln: [*Laughs*] I'll bet old Mars wouldn't—Phew! [*Pauses and turns to Nicolay*] What do you say, John—let's send her down?

Nicolay: The strictest orders have been issued to allow no more women to go to the front.

Lincoln: Humph! Well, I'll tell you what we can do—give her husband a leave of absence, and let him come up here to see them!

The Mother: [*Laughing and crying*] You don't mind my laughing, do you? I just can't help it—I can't stop! I can't stop laughing!

Lincoln: Laugh and cry as much as you please—but tell me where are you stopping?

The Mother: Nowhere yet, sir.

Lincoln: How's that?

The Mother: I went straight from the depot to the War Office and then I just walked the street blind with crying till I made up my mind to come here.

Lincoln: We'll fix that then! Nicolay will write you an order that will take you and your baby to a good hospital and care for you till your husband comes—and fix it so he can stay here a week with you.

The Mother: [*Laughs*] I just can't thank you! I'm so happy, all I can do is to laugh!

Lincoln: Laugh on, little mother—and off with you now—clear out!

[*The mother goes out laughing*]

[*Nicolay shows the little mother out and returns to Lincoln*]

Nicolay: The deputation of colored men whom you asked to come this morning are waiting, sir—will you see them now?

Lincoln: At once.

[*Lincoln turns to his desk and takes up a document containing his plan of Colonization and examines it as Nicolay and three well-dressed colored men enter. They are typical Africans*]

First Negro: [*Bowing deferentially*] Mr. President!

Second Negro: [*Tenderly*] Our Father Abraham.

Third Negro: [*With religious feeling*] We salute our Savior!

Lincoln: Welcome, my friends. I have sent for you this morning to place in your hands a copy of my plan for colonization and to ask your help.

First Negro: Yes, sir.

[*The ebony faces with their cream white teeth showing in smiles and their wide rolling eyes make a striking contrast to the rugged face and poise of the President*]

Lincoln: Your race is suffering, in my judgment, the greatest wrong inflicted on any people. But even when you cease to be slaves, you are yet far removed from being placed on an equality with the white race. On this broad continent, not a single man of your race is made the equal of a single man of ours.

First Negro: It's so—yes, it's so!

Lincoln: Go where you are treated best and the ban is still upon you. I cannot alter it if I would. It is better for us both, therefore, to be separated. For the sake of your people you should sacrifice something of your present comfort.

First Negro: Let our great leader show us the way.

Lincoln: The Colony of Liberia is an old one, and it is open to you. I am now arranging to open another in Central America. You are intelligent and know that success does not so much depend on external help as on self-reliance. If you will engage in the enterprise I will spend the money Congress has entrusted to me for this purpose. I ask you to consider it seriously, not for yourselves merely, nor for your race and ours for the present time, *but for the good of mankind.*

First Negro: We will, sir!

Lincoln: The practical thing I want to ascertain is whether I can get a number of able-bodied men with their wives and children to go at once—men who "can cut their own fodder" so to speak? Take this plan, show it to your people. [*Hands the document to the First Negro*] — and find this out for me.

First Negro: We'll do our best.

Third Negro: [*Bowing out with religious ecstasy*] Praise God forever for our Savior-Leader!

> [*Nicolay ushers out the three Negroes and shows in a stately black-robed figure in mourning for her dead. She walks quietly to the President and extends her hand with a gracious smile*]

The Woman: Perhaps I've done wrong to take up your time.

Lincoln: My time belongs to the people, Madam.

The Woman: I've come to you, Mr. President, under an impulse I could not resist. Mr. Stoddard, your third Secretary, is my friend. He told me this morning that all night the sound of your footfall came from this room. He heard it at nine, at ten, at eleven. At midnight the Secretary of War left the door ajar and the steady tramp came with heavier sound. The last thing he heard at three was the muffled beat upstairs. The guard said it had not stopped at daylight. I saw you staggering alone under a Nation's sorrow and I wondered if you had been given the vision to see the dawn of a new life for our people. I know I'm looking into the eyes of the man whose word can stop this war and divide the Union—I have come to tell you that I lost my first born son at Fredericksburg—a lad of twenty. [She pauses and Lincoln bends and presses her hand] May God help you in your trials, Mr. President, as he has helped me in mine.

Lincoln: [*Startled*] You lost your first born at Fredericksburg and come to say this to me?

The Woman: And I've been praying for you, day and night since.

Lincoln: [*Softly*] Will you say that again, Madam.

The Woman: I have been praying for you, day and night, and I've come this morning to bring you this message—Be strong and courageous, and God will bring the Nation through!

Lincoln: You say this to me—standing beside the grave of your son?

The Woman: And beside the cot of my other boy of sixteen who was dangerously wounded in General Grant's last battle. I am proud of two such sons to lay on the altar of my country. I had to tell you that I'm praying for you.

[*Lincoln closes both hands over hers and holds them a moment in silence*]

Lincoln: [*With upward gaze*] How strange that you should come to me in this black hour with such a message. I've often wondered if the soul of my mother were not speaking to me! The day she died in the woods of Indiana, she told me that if dark hours came, her spirit would be watching, and she'd help me if she could! While you were talking to me—I got the tremor of her voice and the quiver of her lips—how strange! [*Looking down into her face*] Thank you, Madam! You have brought me medicine for both body and soul.

[*Lincoln presses her hand again and she quietly goes as he gazes after her*]

[Nicolay starts to follow her to the door—Lincoln lifts his hand] John, I'm rested now—I'm ready for any work!

Nicolay: The National Committee have just arrived, sir.

Lincoln: All right—let them in!

[*Lincoln resumes his place beside his desk and the Committee headed by Henry Raymond, Editor of the New York Times, enter and solemnly range themselves about the President*]

[*To Henry Raymond—taking his hand formally*]

Raymond, this is an unexpected honor you and your Committee do me. I thought you were at your desk in the *Times* office pouring hot shot into the flanks of our enemies, and the boys were all at home fighting for the victory that must be ours on the first Tuesday in November. Not that you're unwelcome. You are the leaders of public opinion. The people rule this country, and I am their servant—what is it?

Raymond: You may be sure, Mr. President, that our mission is of the gravest importance. These gentlemen have brought such startling reports from their several states as to the bitterness and closeness of the fight, that they have reached a unanimous conclusion.

Lincoln: And that is?

Raymond: That with your personality and record against General McClellan's, your Democratic opponent—the election for us is lost.

Lincoln: Your statement is blunt. But, as I have been renominated for a second term, my administration has been endorsed by our party, and the election is only eight weeks off—there is but one conclusion possible—and that is, that you should roll up your sleeves and get to work.

Raymond: The National Committee, Mr. President, has reached a different conclusion.

Lincoln: Yes?

Raymond: In view of your unpopularity, in view of the criticism of your policies, and your conduct of the war—they have decided to ask you to withdraw from the ticket and permit them to name a new candidate.

Lincoln: [*Springing to his feet*] What!

Raymond: I have stated it bluntly.

Lincoln: And this is your unanimous verdict, gentlemen?

All: Yes.

Lincoln: [*Paces the floor a moment and then faces the Committee*] It surpasses human belief! Future generations will hold it incredible, that you, my party leaders, should heap this insult upon the man who led you to your first and only victory. That you should come here today to ask me to quit under fire, to sacrifice without a blow all I hold worth fighting for on this earth!

Raymond: The Committee made their request solely on the ground of patriotic duty—and ask you for the sacrifice upon the same grounds. They have found it impossible to defend your policies.

Lincoln: [*Brusquely*] What policies?

Raymond: Understand me, Mr. President—I am telling you the conclusion of this Committee.

Lincoln: All right, Raymond—fire away—spare me the oratory, please—just give me the plain reasons, one at a time, why you wish me to get off the ticket.

Raymond: The first policy found indefensible has been your handling of the border slave states of Maryland, Kentucky and Missouri. You have not yet declared the slaves free in these states, the only ones in which you actually have the power to do so—at all.

Lincoln: The first policy of my Administration has been to save for the Union the great border states—for the simple reason—with these border slave states, we have such a balance of power that the Union may be saved! Without these states, the Union cannot be saved! Therefore in my Proclamation of Emancipation, I purposely did not raise the question of the right or wrong of slavery. If slavery is not wrong, nothing is wrong. But the Constitution of the United States, which I have sworn to uphold in the border states of Maryland, Kentucky and Missouri, guarantees to their people the right to hold slaves if they choose.

Raymond: But why pat on the back the slaveholder of Maryland and strike at the slaveholder of South Carolina?

Lincoln: Because Maryland is loyal to the Union, and South Carolina is fighting it. My Proclamation was not a sermon on the rights of man—black or white. It was an act of war—a blow aimed at the heart of the seceding South to break its wealth and power, end the war, and save the Union. I know the spell of State loyalty in the South, gentlemen. I was born there. Many a mother in Richmond wept the day our flag fell from their Capitol. But they brushed their tears away and sent their sons to the front the next day, to fight that flag—in the name of Virginia! So would thousands of mothers in these border slave states, if I put them to the test. In God's own time slavery will be destroyed. I have saved these states for our cause by conciliation and compromise. I will not apologize for this act. [*He lifts his hand to stop interruption*] My paramount object is to save the Union, and not, either to save or destroy slavery. If I could save the Union, without freeing a slave, I would do it. And if I could save it by freeing all the slaves, I would do it. And if I could save it by freeing some and leaving others alone, I would also do that. What I do about slavery and the colored race, I do because I believe it helps to save this Union! [*Pauses and faces his accusers*] I'll test this question right here—will the three Committeemen from Kentucky, Missouri and Maryland stand up for a minute?

[*The three Committeemen rise*]

Will the gentleman from Kentucky tell me what would have been the effect if I had included his state in my proclamation freeing the slaves?

The Kentucky Committeeman: The state would have seceded from the Union, sir.

Lincoln: Just so, and in Missouri?

The Missouri Committeeman: The Legislature would have joined the Confederacy within twenty-four hours.

Lincoln: And Maryland?

The Maryland Committeeman: Maryland would have promptly cut the railroads leading into Washington, isolated the Capital and joined the South.

Lincoln: And with the loss of our Capital, Europe, eager to strike, would have recognized the Confederacy, would they not?

The Maryland Committeeman: Undoubtedly, sir.

Lincoln: So I hold.

The Maryland Committeeman: Our State believed you when you said in your Inaugural: "I have no purpose directly or indirectly to interfere with the institution of slavery in the states where it exists!"

Lincoln: Then you three gentlemen, at least, are with me on this issue?

All Three: Yes! Yes! Yes!

Lincoln: I thought so.

[*To Raymond*]

What next?

Raymond: Your plan to colonize the Negro race as expressed in your Proclamation of Emancipation and in the bill which you have had passed through Congress has hurt your best friends.

Lincoln: And why should it? My views on that subject were known to all men before you nominated me first in Chicago, four years ago. I said then that I believed there is a sharp physical difference between the white and black races, and I have always linked colonization with freedom. The Negro cannot remain in a free democracy unless we absorb him into our social and political life. Therefore, we must colonize him. We owe it to ourselves, we owe it to future generations—above all, we owe it to the Negro himself. He was brought here by cruel force. At our own expense, therefore, we should return him to the home of his fathers, and build there a free republic for his children. We should give him our language and our ideals, and we should give him millions of our money, until he can stand alone. We must face this problem squarely now.

Raymond: Yet you compromise on other issues.

Lincoln: Only because I must to save the Union. Trim and hedge on this issue, and future generations will feel their way back to it through blood and tears. I have always held that the happiness and progress of this Union of Free Democratic States will be secure only in the separation of the white and black races, and I will not eat my words!.

[*Pauses*]

—the next charge in your bill of indictment, gentlemen?

Raymond: I now present the Hon. Thaddeus Stevens, leader of Congress, the representative of the radical wing of our party, who have split our organization by nominating another candidate for President—Mr. Stevens will give their views.

Stevens: [*Pompously to the Committee*] The radical wing of the party, gentlemen, has been the only creative force within it—and is the only thing that gives it an excuse for being today.

Lincoln: [*Firmly*] Which means that you think that I am superfluous and always have been—I thank you—proceed!

Stevens: We denounce first your policy of reconstruction in the South as weak and vacillating—a civil and military failure. As the army advances, the South should be held as conquered soil, its civilization torn up by the roots, the property of the Southern white people confiscated and given to the negroes. The ballot must be taken from the whites and given to their slaves. We demand this just vengeance and we will be content with nothing less!

Lincoln: Stevens, I greet with shame your demands! Surely the vastness of this war, its grim battles, its heroism, its anguish, its sublime earnestness, should sink all schemes of revenge. Before the grandeur of its simple story our children will walk with uncovered heads. Conquered soil! The South has never been out of this Union. Secession was null and void from the beginning. I say to the South now, as I have always said: "Come back home! You can have peace at any moment, by simply laying down your arms and submitting to the National Authority." When the South lies crushed at our feet, God's vengeance shall be enough.

Stevens: The life of our party, sir, demands that the Negro be given the ballot and made the ruler of the South. This is not vengeance. It is justice—it is patriotism.

Lincoln: The Nation cannot be healed until the South is healed. Let the gulf be closed in which we bury strifes and hatreds. The good sense of our people will never consent to your scheme of vengeance.

Stevens: The people have no sense! And a new fool is born every second.

Lincoln: I have an abiding faith in their honesty and good purpose. I have trusted the people before, and they have not failed me.

Stevens: Bah!

Lincoln: I can't tell you, Stevens, how your venomous plans sicken me. I'd rather work with you than fight you, if it's possible. But the line is drawn now—we've got to fight—and I'm not afraid of you.

Stevens: You had better listen.

Lincoln: I'll suffer my right arm to be severed from my body before I'll sign one measure of revenge on a brave, fallen foe!

Stevens: I have always known you had a sneaking admiration for the South!

Lincoln: I love the South—it is a part of this Union! And when the curse of slavery is lifted, it should be the garden spot of the world—I love every foot of its soil—every hill and valley, and every man, woman and child in it. I am an American!

Stevens: The kind of an American that makes the election of your opponent, General George B. McClellan, a certainty.

Lincoln: Well, who would you put in my place?

[He faces Raymond and Stevens, and dead silence follows]

Come on—out with his name!

[They remain silent]

You can't name him? Let me try to nominate him for you— On a platform of proscription and revenge, the hanging of rebel leaders, the confiscation of the property of the white people of the South and its bestowment upon the negroes, the taking of the ballot from the whites and setting their slaves to rule over them—on this program I resign as your candidate and nominate for President, the Hon. Thaddeus Stevens.

The Committee: *[In a wild uproar]* No! No! No! Not by a damn sight! To hell with Stevens!

[Lincoln quietly laughs and Stevens angrily lifts his hand to quiet them]

Stevens: Now that you've had your joke—let me remind you that the radical wing of the Republican Party has already named General John C. Fremont against you.

Lincoln: *[To the Committee]* What say you, gentlemen? Shall I resign in favor of the bolter who attempted to dictate to you your platform and your candidate before your convention met? Do you ask me to resign in favor of General Fremont?

The Committee: No! No! Down with the bolter! To the devil with Fremont. No! No! No! Damnation—no.

[Raymond quiets the uproar]

Stevens: I am not asking you to nominate Fremont. We split the party and named Fremont because we wouldn't have you. Get off the ticket and we will withdraw Fremont and put up a man who can be elected! Whatever the chances of General Fremont at this moment the election of McClellan on a Democratic Copperhead Platform is conceded by your own party councils. McClellan is even now choosing his Cabinet.

Lincoln: They say it is not wise to count chickens before they're hatched—we still have our chance!

Stevens: You have no chance! You have already been weighed and found wanting! In the Congressional election, what happened?—your majorities were wiped out. Maine cut you down from nineteen thousand to four! The Democrats swept Ohio. Indiana deserted us. In Pennsylvania even, we lost by four thousand. New York elected Horatio Seymour against us. New Jersey turned you down. Wisconsin was a tie. In your own state of Illinois, the Democrats won by seventeen thousand!

Lincoln: Even so, Stevens—the ballots in this election have not yet been counted! My faith in the ultimate good sense of the people is unshaken. You can fool some of the people all the time. You can fool all of the people sometimes. But you can't fool all the people all the time!

Stevens: That's why we ask you to get off the ticket! You are today the most unpopular man who ever sat in the Presidential chair. For the first time in our history the effigy of a living President—your effigy—has been publicly burned in the streets of American towns and cities, amid the curses and jeers of the men who elected you! Your administration is a failure—your conduct of the war a series of blunders.

Lincoln: *[Brusquely]* For example.

Stevens: *[Furiously]* For one thing—you have never yet chosen a successful

General. The South has not changed Commanders since Jeff Davis appointed Robert E. Lee. In thirty days of the last campaign in a series of massacres, Lee has killed and wounded sixty-two thousand of our men—more than he himself commanded—and Grant has only reached the point where McClellan stood in 1862. He could have marched there by McClellan's old line without the loss of a man. Washington is piled with the wounded, the dying and the dead. Your mail is choked with letters demanding the removal of this butcher as our Commander, and you refuse—why?

Lincoln: [*Smiling calmly*] Well, now that you've really let off steam, I think you'll feel better, Stevens!

Stevens: I demand, sir, an answer to my question—why have you not removed Grant?

Lincoln: [*Quickly*] Because I can't spare him! He is the one General we have developed who knows how to fight—his business is not to reach any particular spot where McClellan stood. McClellan was generally standing somewhere—he was a great engineer—of the stationary type— Grant is a fighter. His business is to find and destroy Lee's army—and his sledge hammer blows are winning this war!

Stevens: Winning—is he? And yet Lee sends a division under Jubal Early and reconquers the Valley of Virginia—invades Maryland and Pennsylvania, throws his shells into Washington and burns the home of one of your Cabinet.

Lincoln: And if old Jubal Early had been a little earlier, he would have burned Washington, too—but thank God, Grant got here in time—didn't he? What have you got to say to that?

Stevens: That Lee's strategy has been superb, his moral victory complete! He holds Grant by the throat while he invades the North, and shells our Capitol—a feat that not one of your generals has yet done for Richmond in four years—and still you cling to Grant!

Lincoln: [*Angrily*] Now, I'm going to talk plain English to you, Stevens. You're an Abolitionist, and you can't do Grant justice. Your crowd demanded his removal after the battle of Shiloh—and you made it so hot for me then, I had to appoint General Halleck his superior, to save him for the country. You can't forget that Grant is a Democrat, and therefore he may vote for McClellan against our party, in this election!

Stevens: I've heard that he is for McClellan.

Lincoln: Exactly! And you can't forget that his wife is a Southern woman whose dowry was in Slaves, and therefore at this moment, Grant is constructively a slaveholder, whose slaves I have not freed.

Stevens: I protest.

Lincoln: It's no use—I know the process of your mind—I can see the wheels go round inside! You tell me that the star of Grant has set in a welter of blood before Lee's army. I do not believe it. I know that miles of hospital barracks are the witnesses of our agony. I know that every city, town and village is in mourning. From these stricken homes there has arisen a storm of protest against the new leader of the army. The word butcher is bandied from lip to lip. They tell me that Grant is merely a bulldog fighter—that he can win only as long as thousands are poured into his ranks to take the place of the dead—They tell me that he has no genius, no strategy, no skill. My reply to this is simple but unanswerable. We must fight to win. Grant is the ablest general we have developed. His losses are appalling—but the struggle is on now to the bitter end! Our resources are exhaustless. The South cannot replace her fallen soldiers—and therefore her losses are fatal! If we continue to fight, five millions cannot whip twenty millions—the end is certain—and we're now locked in the last death grapple before—*Victory*!

Stevens: It's a waste of time to talk!

Lincoln: I've thought so from the first, but I've tried to be polite.

Stevens: [*Trying to go*] Good day, sir!

Lincoln: [*Cordially*] Good day, Stevens. [*Pauses*] You know this meeting reminds me of what happened in Illinois once.

Stevens: [*Throwing up his hands in anger*] I won't hear it, sir! You and your stories are sending this country to hell—it's not more than a mile from there now!

Lincoln: I believe it is just a mile from here to the Capitol where you sit!

Stevens: [*Going in rage*] Damnation! [*Stevens goes muttering furiously*]

Raymond: You will consider our request, Mr. President?

Lincoln: Raymond, this is the most brutal insult ever offered to a man in my position in the history of this country. I'm going to waive the insult and give your request my earnest thought. If I can save the Union—that's the only question—that's the only question!

Raymond: You will give us your answer today?

Lincoln: [*Firmly*] No. I must have time to think. As I've listened to you, the conviction grows on me that the life of the Union may be bound with mine now, and I'm not going to give up—without a fight.

Raymond: [*Brusquely*] We cannot leave Washington without your answer, Mr. President.

Lincoln: You'll get it in due time.

Raymond: The time is short.

Lincoln: It may be long enough yet, to save the Nation.

Raymond: [*Firmly*] The Committee must take definite action before we leave—we will give you ten days to decide.

Lincoln: I understand. Good day, gentlemen!

All: [Bowing out] Good day, Mr. President.

> [*Lincoln stands erect, with Nicolay watching them go in silence. When the last man is gone, he turns to Nicolay*]

Lincoln: It's infamous, John! Infamous!

> [*Mrs. Lincoln enters hurriedly*]

Don't tell her the nasty things old Thad said to me. It will hurt her.

Nicolay: Of course not.

Mrs. Lincoln: [*Tensely*] What is it, Father—what did they say?

> [*He pauses and she presses him tremblingly*]

What did they say? What did they say?

Lincoln: [*With dreamy look*] They told me in plain English that I am the most unpopular man in the United States—that my conduct of the war is a series of blunders, my administration a failure!

Mrs. Lincoln: [*Relieved*] Oh!—is that all!

Lincoln: What more?

Mrs. Lincoln: I thought they had something important to tell you.

Lincoln: [*Laughs*] Oh!.

Mrs. Lincoln: That is of no importance, because it's a lie.

Lincoln: But, if they believe it, and millions of people believe it.

Mrs. Lincoln: Well, they won't. I've something important to ask of you—Betty Winter's in my room and wants to bring her lover here to see you alone for an hour tonight.

Lincoln: I'll see Miss Betty Winter any time—she is my good friend—make it nine o'clock.

Mrs. Lincoln: [*Going*] At nine—don't forget now!

Lincoln: I'll not.

   [*Mrs. Lincoln exits*]

 John, is General McClellan at home?

Nicolay: I saw him today, sir.

Lincoln: Go to his house immediately and tell him I want to see him here at eight o'clock tonight. Say that it's a matter of the gravest importance—both to him and to the country—he can't refuse.

Nicolay: Yes, sir.

Lincoln: Say to General McClellan that I would come to him but for the fact that it would attract attention which I wish to avoid. It will be the best for both that this meeting should not be known. Ask him to come in a closed carriage. Assure him that you will meet him at the door and he will see no one but me.

Nicolay: You can't take me into your confidence, Chief?

Lincoln: [*Pauses*] Partly—I'm going to put McClellan to the supreme test, John. If he will make me one pledge on the Copperhead issue which I will ask of him, I'll name for this Committee a candidate they're not looking for—I'll give them the surprise of their life—so help me God!

Nicolay: I don't think the General will give that pledge, sir.

Lincoln: [Gazing upward and folding his arms] I wonder!—I wonder if he will!

   [*Nicolay exits*]

 I wonder if he will.

CURTAIN

ACT II

Set Scene: The same as Act I at a quarter to eight the same evening.

At Curtain Rise: Edward, the old Doorman, is straightening the furniture in the room. He clumsily clears the floor of a litter of letters and places them in the corner with the unopened bag. He draws the heavy draperies of the windows and adjusts them so that no ray of light can reach the outside. Mrs. Lincoln enters and watches him fix the draperies.

Mrs. Lincoln: [*Speaking suddenly*] Edward!
Edward: [*Jumping in fright*] Yes, Madam!
Mrs. Lincoln: What on earth are you doing in here?
Edward: [*In terror of Mrs. Lincoln*] Just—er drawin'—er the curtains, Madam.
Mrs. Lincoln: [*Sternly*] These curtains haven't been drawn in a year.
Edward: [*Stammering*] I-don't-think-they-have-either.
Mrs. Lincoln: You know they haven't!
Edward: [*Gulping wind*] Yes'm.
Mrs. Lincoln: Who told you to draw them?
Edward: Colonel Nicolay!
Mrs. Lincoln: Where is he?
Edward: Downstairs, on the door.
Mrs. Lincoln: In your place?
Edward: Yes'm.
Mrs. Lincoln: While you're up here acting as house maid?
Edward: [*Embarrassed*] Well, so it seems, Madam.
Mrs. Lincoln: [*Sternly*] What does this mean?
Edward: I do not know, Madam.
Mrs. Lincoln: [*Sarcastically*] And you haven't the slightest idea—I suppose?
Edward: Not the slightest. My experience as Doorman of the White House has taught me that my first duty is to obey the orders of my Chief.

Mrs. Lincoln: Mr. Lincoln asked you to remain on duty here tonight?

Edward: [*Bows*] Asked me as a particular personal favor to him, that I remain on duty until eight o'clock and dismiss all the other White House attendants.

Mrs. Lincoln: The guard has been dismissed!

Edward: Yes, Madam, both of them—inside and out.

Mrs. Lincoln: Ask Colonel Nicolay to come here.

Edward: [*Hesitates*] Yes'm.

Mrs. Lincoln: [*Sharply*] Quick!

Edward: [*Jumps*] Right away, Madam!

> [*Mrs. Lincoln quickly examines the President's desk, looking for a memorandum of his appointments—she finds a pad and reads*]

Mrs. Lincoln: At eight o'clock — . At nine o'clock, Miss Betty Winter.

> [*Nicolay enters hurriedly*]

Nicolay: What is it, Madam?

Mrs. Lincoln: Who has this mysterious appointment with the President at eight o'clock—the name is blank.

Nicolay: I am forbidden to discuss it with any one.

Mrs. Lincoln: [*Angrily*] Indeed!

Nicolay: I am sorry.

Mrs. Lincoln: Do you know who is coming?

Nicolay: Yes.

Mrs. Lincoln: Do you know the subject for discussion at this meeting?

Nicolay: I wish to God I did.

> [*Lincoln enters and glances at his wife in surprise*]

Lincoln: Will you go back to the door, John.

Nicolay: At once—sir.

Lincoln: And tell Edward I'm much obliged to him for staying, but he can go now.

Nicolay: Yes, sir.

Lincoln: See that he goes before our visitor arrives. I have asked him to say nothing about this appointment.

Nicolay: You can trust him implicitly, sir.

[*Nicolay exits*]

Mrs. Lincoln: But, you can't trust your wife, tonight, it seems.

Lincoln: [*Whimsically*] Well, you know you're a woman, Mother.

Mrs. Lincoln: [*Angrily*] Thank God.

Lincoln: Amen! So say I!

Mrs. Lincoln: You're afraid to tell me—who this man is?

Lincoln: I may tell you tomorrow.

Mrs. Lincoln: When—you've-made-some-fatal-blunder.

Lincoln: I'll make no mistake this time.

Mrs. Lincoln: Then why are you afraid of my woman's intuition.

Lincoln: [*Smiling*] I'm not afraid of your intuition, Mother.

Mrs. Lincoln: Thank you.

Lincoln: I didn't say it!. [*Laughs*] —But you know you do talk too much sometimes!

Mrs. Lincoln: [*Angrily*] And I'm going to say something to you now. I thought this morning that you would treat those scoundrels with the contempt they deserve when they dared to ask you to sacrifice yourself and the cause of the Union to the ambitions of some traitor behind them.

Lincoln: No! No! They're honest in what they say.

Mrs. Lincoln: [*Furious*] You're too good and simple for this world! Don't you know that some schemer is behind all this?

Lincoln: Maybe— It's not a crime, Mother, for a man to aspire to high office, if the bee's in his bonnet. You know I've felt it tickle me lots of times.

Mrs. Lincoln: Don't—don't—don't say such foolish things. You need a guardian. You kept three men in your Cabinet who used their position to try to climb into the Presidency over your head. And you didn't kick them out.

Lincoln: The country needed them.

Mrs. Lincoln: [*With earnest dignity*] The country needs you—you are the man, and the only man who has the simple common sense to save this Union first, and settle all other questions afterwards.

Lincoln: That may be so—too.

Mrs. Lincoln: Tell me one thing—is the man who has this appointment at eight the traitor whom Raymond's Committee is trying to put in your place?

Lincoln: No! Yet—if there is anywhere a better man who can render the country a greater service than I can, he ought to be in my place.

Mrs. Lincoln: But don't you see that it isn't really the man who can give the greater service who will win in such a treacherous fight? It's the liar and the hypocrite who may win.

Lincoln: I have no right in such an hour to think of my own ambitions. My personal desire for a second term is the biggest thing in my life, God knows.

> [*He pauses as his voice breaks—he struggles a moment and lifts his hand as if to throw off an obsession with a determined smile*]

And yet, my personal desire is a petty thing! My duty today is the biggest thing in the world!

Mrs. Lincoln: You won't take my advice and send these men about their business?

Lincoln: Mary, I've got to fight this thing out alone, with myself and God.

Mrs. Lincoln: I sometimes think, Father, that you're the stubbornest man the Lord ever made!

Lincoln: I've got to be—to do this job.

> [*Mrs. Lincoln exits*]

> [*Lincoln paces the floor with his arms locked behind him in tense thought*]

> [*Nicolay enters*]

Nicolay: The carriage is approaching, sir.

Lincoln: The coast is clear?

Nicolay: Yes. Edward has gone. [*He pauses*] You, of course, realize, Chief, the importance of a cool head in dealing with McClellan.

Lincoln: I won't lose my temper, John.

Nicolay: McClellan may lose his.

Lincoln: I'll watch out. [*Looking over his desk*] That report of Baker's on the Copperhead Societies.

Nicolay: [*Pointing*] Under that paper weight, sir.

Lincoln: Oh, yes, I see. [*Picks up report, glances at it, and lays it back on his desk*] I'm ready—bring him in. See that we are not interrupted, and when he goes, I'll not need you any more tonight. I'll let in the young people myself, at nine o'clock.

Nicolay: Yes, sir.

> [*Nicolay exits and Lincoln returns to his desk and writes*]
>
> [*Nicolay enters with General McClellan. The General is thirty-eight years old, dressed in a uniform of immaculate cut, flashing with gold. While his figure is short and stocky, in striking contrast to the President, he is a man of commanding appearance, and gives one the impression of a born leader of men. He enters with quick military precision and salutes with studied formality the President as his superior officer. The President answers his salute, as Nicolay exits*]

Lincoln: I suggest, General McClellan, that we forget for the moment that I am the Commander in Chief of the Army and Navy—and we have a little heart to heart talk in a perfectly informal way.

McClellan: [*Stiffening*] May I enquire, Mr. President, at once, to what I owe this extraordinary summons?

Lincoln: [*Cordially*] Will you be seated, General?

McClellan: Thank you, I prefer to stand. [*Angrily*] What right have you to send for me or ask anything, after the foul injustice with which you have treated me as Commanding General.

Lincoln: [*Interrupting*] Just a moment—I have not treated you with injustice—I have treated you with more than justice. I have treated you with the generous faith and love of a father for a wayward boy.

McClellan: Really!

Lincoln: I have. When I appointed you to the chief command of our Army, you were but thirty-four years old. I did it against the bitterest opposition of my party leaders. They told me you were a pro-Slavery Democrat—a political meddler, and that you were opposed to me on every issue before the people. I refused to listen. I asked but one question: Is McClellan the man to whip the new army into a mighty fighting machine, and hurl it against the Confederacy? I said to them: 'I don't care what his religion is, or his politics may be. The question is, not whether I shall save the Union—but that the Union shall be saved. My future and the future of my party can take care of themselves'—and I appointed you.

McClellan: And forced me to march against Richmond before I was ready!

Lincoln: I ordered you to move, because it was necessary to forestall a great tragedy. Your army of 180,000 men had gone into winter quarters around a glittering camp over which a young Napoleon presided. Fools about you daily advised that you proclaim the end of the Republic and establish yourself as Dictator. You do not deny this?

McClellan: No. The fact is well known. Besides, Stanton, your Secretary of War, was at that time my attorney, and he knew.

Lincoln: Exactly. I took the bull by the horns and ordered your grand army to move on Richmond. When you failed and retreated, I refused to dismiss you against the fierce protest of my Cabinet. I left you in command of half our men and appointed General Pope to lead the other half.

McClellan: [*Sneeringly*] And he led them to overwhelming disaster at the second battle of Manassas.

Lincoln: [*Quickly*] For which disaster, you must share the blame. You were ordered to join Pope. You didn't move. Pope was broken by a deliberate design, that was little short of treason, sir. But instead of agreeing to the demand for your trial by court martial, I did the most unpopular act of my life. I reappointed you to the chief command of the whole army—defied public opinion, and faced a storm of abuse in my party councils.

McClellan: And when I led that superb, reorganized army to our first victory at Antietam, you removed me from my command before I could win my campaign.

Lincoln: I removed you from your command because, after you had cut Lee's army to pieces, and he had but 23,000 men left, and you had 75,000—three to one—you lay down on your arms and allowed Lee to escape across the river without a blow—while Jeb.

Stuart with his cavalry once more insulted you by riding around your army. Come now, can't we leave to posterity to settle the merits of our controversy over the command of armies? Can't you believe me today, when I tell you with God as my witness, that I have never allowed a personal motive to enter into a single appointment or removal which I have made?

McClellan: I cannot believe it.

Lincoln: In spite of the fact that when I reappointed you to the chief command of the army after the disaster to Pope, you thought that my messenger was an officer with a warrant for your arrest! You still say no?

McClellan: I still say no—you had to do it—and you know that you had to reappoint me.

Lincoln: Well, I'll not pretend that I didn't understand the seriousness of that hour. The Army was behind you, to a man! I sounded the officers, I sounded the men. They were against me and with you. If the leaders had dared risk their necks on a revolution, they might have won and set up a Dictatorship!

McClellan: Just so!

Lincoln: This power over men which you possess, General McClellan, is a marvelous thing. It is a dangerous force. It can be used to create a Nation, or destroy one. Because you held this power over your men, I honestly believed you were the ablest General in sight, and I called you back to your high position.

McClellan: [*With a smile*] Very kind!

Lincoln: You had to win or lose at Antietam. If you had won I was vindicated, and your success would have been mine! But when Lee's army escaped, you lost the power over the imagination of your men, the threat of a Dictatorship had passed—the supremacy of the civil government was restored, and I removed you from command.

McClellan: [*Angrily*] I repeat that your act was one of foul injustice!

Lincoln: [*Cordially*] All right then. I've given you my side. Granted for the sake of argument that I have treated you unfairly, I'm going to put you to a supreme test. I am going to propose, on a certain condition, to the man whom I have wronged, an amazing thing.

McClellan: Hence the secrecy with which I am summoned!

Lincoln: Yes. I have just written out on this sheet of paper. [*Takes up the sheet*] and addressed to Henry Raymond, Chairman of our National Committee, my resignation as a Candidate for the Presidency for a second term—and I will give it to him tonight, if you will agree to take my place and save the Union?

McClellan: [*Overwhelmed with excitement*] What-can-you-mean?

Lincoln: Exactly what I've said.

McClellan: [*Paces the floor trembling*] And your conditions?

Lincoln: Very simple. Agree to preside tomorrow night at a great Democratic Union Mass Meeting in New York, and boldly put yourself at the head of that wing of your party which stands for the preservation of the Union.

McClellan: And you?

Lincoln: I will withdraw from the race, secure your endorsement, or prevent my party from naming a successor, take the stump for you and guarantee your election.

McClellan: [*Studies Lincoln a moment with suspicion*] You are in earnest?

Lincoln: I was never more so.

McClellan: And there is no string to this offer?

Lincoln: On my word of honor. [*Dreamily*] It is needless for me to say that I came into this office with high ambitions to serve my country. My dream of glory may be at an end and I have left only the agony and the tears.

> [*He pauses, breathes deeply, and struggles with his emotions, recovers himself, and goes on wistfully*]

I did want a chance to stay here for another term to see the sun shine again, to heal my country's wounds, and show all the people, North, South, East and West, that I love them. But I can't risk the chances of this election—if you and I can come to a perfect understanding, and you agree to take my place upon the solemn pledge to save the Union without division. I've made up my mind to this, because I have on my desk here a report from our Secret Service [*Pauses and picks up the report*] showing that the Copperhead Societies are of your party and are thoroughly organized in every state of the North—that they demand an immediate peace and will accept a division of the Union.

McClellan: [*Interrupting*] What has this to do with me, may I ask?

Lincoln: [*Evenly*] This report shows that they propose to end the war on the night of the election by a revolutionary uprising which will result in the recognition of the Confederacy. I am now being urged to arrest their leaders. [*He pauses and watches McClellan closely*] I shall answer no. Let sleeping dogs lie. One revolution at a time. If the Union candidate wins the election, they won't dare to rise. If he loses, it's all over anyhow—and it makes no difference what they do.

McClellan: A sensible decision.

Lincoln: I'm glad you agree with it. Now the Democratic Convention meets in Chicago next week—you have no opposition. Your nomination will be unanimous. The question is,—what will they do on the issue of the war? The leaders of the Copperhead Societies are now in touch with the rebel government in Richmond.

McClellan: That's a large statement, sir—even about Copperhead Societies.

Lincoln: I have the proofs in this document. [*Touches Baker's report*] My fear is, that they may get complete control of your Convention.

McClellan: [*Angrily*] Indeed?

Lincoln: I have heard the ugly rumor that they are counting on you.

McClellan: [*Advancing*] Stop!

Lincoln: [*Going to meet McClellan and holding his gaze firmly*] Well?

McClellan: No man can couple the word Treason with my name, sir!

Lincoln: Have I done so?

McClellan: You are insinuating it!

Lincoln: Am I?

McClellan: I demand a retraction!

Lincoln: [*Smiling*] Then, I apologize for my careless expressions. I am glad to see you meet the ugly subject in this way! I have never believed you a traitor to the Union. That's why I sent for you tonight. Will you denounce these men publicly at a Union Mass Meeting, and let me resign and take the stump for you?

McClellan: [*Hesitates*] I am sure of this election without your help, sir!

Lincoln: You can't be.

McClellan: A straw vote was taken yesterday in the Carver Hospital. The wounded soldiers gave me three votes to your one. Straws show which way the wind is blowing. I know that your party is divided—that John C. Fremont has split your organization, and is daily gaining ground—that unless he retires, you can't be elected! Your party is in a hopeless panic—and my election is conceded. Yet, you ask me allow you to dictate the policy of my administration!

Lincoln: [*Evenly and pressingly*] Will you denounce these conspirators within your party?

McClellan: No! When I need your advice on any public utterance, I'll let you know.

Lincoln: Will you preside over this Union Meeting?

McClellan: [*Firmly*] Never! I'll do my best to save my country, but in my own way without suggestion or assistance from you.

Lincoln: [*With firm conviction*] Then, sir, you are committed by your pledges to the possible division of this Union! I suspected it—but I had hoped for the best—good night!

[*The General bows stiffly and leaves the President standing in sorrowful silence, his deep eyes staring into space, seeing nothing as Nicolay enters*]

[*Pausing, and looking up*] I thought you'd gone?

Nicolay: I hope there may be something else I can do for you, sir?

Lincoln: Yes—there is.

Nicolay: What?

Lincoln: Bear witness with me to this, the blackest hour of my life—I have touched the depths of despair. [*Springs to his feet*] But I can't give up—there's too much at stake!

Nicolay: Corruption, intrigue and malice are doing their work, Chief—but you can't be beaten! Unless you should give up!

Lincoln: Well! I won't give up!

Nicolay: McClellan refused the pledge you asked?

Lincoln: Yes. He is bound hand and foot to the Copperhead leaders who will control his convention.

Nicolay: I thought so.

Lincoln: John, if I could win one man out of the inner councils of the Copperhead orders—one man who really loves his country.

Nicolay: Can a Copperhead love his country?

Lincoln: Why not? A rattlesnake might love his own fence corner! There are plenty of honest misguided men among them. I have been studying Baker's report this afternoon— If I could just get hold of one Copperhead who knows the signs and passwords of their inner council, I've worked out *a plan that can win this fight!*

Nicolay: [*Suddenly*] The very man may be on the way here at this moment!

Lincoln: [*Eagerly*] What's that?

Nicolay: [*Thinking*] Miss Winter is due here with her lover—a young Captain of Grant's Army. [*Pauses*]

Lincoln: Well?

Nicolay: [*Slowly*] In view of the attempts to take your life—I made some inquiries today about him—I knew the White House would be without guards tonight. [*Pauses*]

Lincoln: Yes—yes—go on! What about him?

Nicolay: He was on McClellan's staff at one time.

Lincoln: That's promising!

Nicolay: He's a McClellan man—then.

Lincoln: Beyond a doubt.

Nicolay: In the hospital the past two months he has heard a lot of bitter talk.

Lincoln: [*Quickly*] And may have joined The Knights of the Golden Circle!

Nicolay: It's almost a certainty.

Lincoln: Of course. Their infernal agents haunt our hospitals daily, and pour their poison into every open wound.

Nicolay: Prove to this boy tonight that these men are liars.

Lincoln: If he'll listen.

Nicolay: He's got to listen! He comes to ask of you a great favor.

Lincoln: I wonder what?

Nicolay: I couldn't find out. But you can use the opportunity to gain his confidence. He is engaged to a girl who is Mrs. Lincoln's intimate friend—a girl who admires and trusts you. You can win him, Chief, if you only try!

Lincoln: [*With excited emphasis*] Don't you worry—I'm going to try! [*Pauses*] — You wait and show them in. I'll report to Mother my talk with McClellan. She'll be uneasy about it. I'll be back in a minute.

Nicolay: All right, sir.

> [*Lincoln exits*]

> [*Nicolay watches him go with deep sympathy, shaking his head as Betty and Vaughan enter*] Oh, Miss Winter.

Betty: Captain Vaughan,—Colonel Nicolay.

Nicolay: [*Studying Vaughan*] Pleased to meet you, Captain—the President will be back in a moment. He has just stepped in to speak to Mrs. Lincoln. He is expecting you—make yourselves at home.

Betty: Thank you, Colonel.

> [*Nicolay exits*]

What's the matter, dear?

Vaughan: Nothing—nothing.

Betty: But your arm is trembling— I didn't realize you're so weak—I keep forgetting that you're just out of the hospital.

Vaughan: Oh—I'm all right.

Betty: I'm afraid of the strain of this interview! [*Pauses*] —You've never told me, dear—for what was your father imprisoned?

Vaughan: [*Deliberately*] He made a speech against the war in our town in Missouri and printed it in a pamphlet.

Betty: Oh—for making and circulating seditious writing.

Vaughan: Technically, yes—in reality for exercising the right of free speech on a policy of the government.

Betty: It may be very serious. [*Pauses*] —I've an idea! Let me stay and help you.

Vaughan: But I may have something to say that a girl's ears should not hear.

Betty: Please don't say it! You differ with the President in politics. You must say nothing to offend him.

Vaughan: I'll not! I think I love my country as well as I love my father.

Betty: Let me stay!

Vaughan: You mustn't—I don't need a chaperone.

Betty: But you may need a friend.

Vaughan: [*Bitterly*] He does wield a terrible power, doesn't he?

Betty: Yes—with the tenderness and love of a father.

Vaughan: [*Lightly*] All right, dear, run along now, see Mrs. Lincoln and get the President to come.

Betty: Can't I stay and help you?

Vaughan: No, no.

Betty: It means so much to me now!

[*She nestles in his arms and Vaughan kisses her*]

Vaughan: I'll know how to plead my cause.

Betty: All right—good luck. I'm sure you'll win.

[*Betty exits*]

[*Vaughan walks to the door leading to the Lincoln Apartments, and listens a moment, and walks to the President's desk. His eye rests on the worn copy of the Bible which Lincoln always kept on his desk. He gazes at the thumbed pages in amazement*]

Vaughan: The Bible—My God! [*Turns its leaves*] And every page thumbed! [*He continues to turn the leaves of the Bible*]

[*The sound of Lincoln's voice is heard outside talking to Mrs. Lincoln*]

Lincoln: [*Outside*] Go back, and talk to Miss Betty!

[*Vaughan quickly places the Bible back on his desk and takes his stand near the door to the hall, as if he had just entered. Lincoln enters from the other door, still talking to his wife who follows him*]

Don't worry, Mother! Who cares for a few old dresses more or less in these times! But if I'd known they cost that much, I'd taken a second look at them and tried to get my money's worth!

Mrs. Lincoln: You're sure it won't influence your decision?

Lincoln: Not a bit! If we stay here—it'll be all right. We can skimp a little. If we don't stay—the old sign still swings on the door in Springfield—Billy Herndon's waiting for me and the law business will be better than ever. Go back now, and don't worry! It's my business to do all the worrying.

> [*Lincoln closes the door after she goes, and comes down toward the desk, lifts his haggard eyes in a dazed way and looks about the room. Anxiety and suffering again mark his rugged face. He sees Vaughan, and at once throws off the spell of his troubles, advances to meet him and takes his hand*]

I'm glad to see you, my boy—Will you pull up a chair?

> [*Lincoln drops wearily into his chair and his voice has a far-away dreamy expression in its tones while he studies Vaughan carefully*]

And what can I do for you?

Vaughan: My name is Vaughan—the elder son of Dr. Richard Vaughan of Palmyra, Missouri.

Lincoln: [*Thoughtfully*] Vaughan—Richard Vaughan—I've heard that name—But you're one of our boys fighting with Grant's army?

Vaughan: Yes.

Lincoln: [*Looking him over*] You've been very ill, I see—wounded of course?

Vaughan: Yes.

Lincoln: [*Rises, takes Vaughan's hands in both his, and presses it*] There's nothing I won't do for one of our wounded boys—if I can.

Vaughan: Thank you.

Lincoln: What is it?

Vaughan: [*With cold precision*] My mother writes me that my father has been arrested without warrant, is held in prison without bail, and denied the right of trial. [*He pauses, trembling with excitement*]

Lincoln: Go on—my boy.

Vaughan: I have come to ask for justice.

Lincoln: He shall have it.

Vaughan: I ask that he be confronted by his accusers in open court and given a fair trial.

Lincoln: [*Interrupting*] For what was he arrested?

Vaughan: For exercising the right of free speech. In a public address, he denounced the war.

Lincoln: Oh!—And his address was printed?

[*Lincoln picks up the little booklet and looks again at the title page and then at Vaughan*]

Vaughan: He had as much right to print as to speak it.

Lincoln: No, he hadn't. [*Pauses and looks at Vaughan*] You say your father's name is Richard Vaughan?

Vaughan: Yes—Dr. Richard Vaughan—and I ask for him a fair trial confronted by his accusers—I ask for justice—will you grant him this trial?

[*Lincoln lays the pamphlet down on his desk and rises*]

Lincoln: [*Shakes his head*] I cannot! I cannot do it!

[*He folds his arms behind his back and paces the floor, unconscious of the glitter of murder in Vaughan's eyes. Vaughan slowly draws his revolver and is about to lift to fire, when Lincoln suddenly turns and speaks*]

[*With sharp emphasis*]

That little pamphlet, sir, found its way into the ranks and caused a number of soldiers to desert.

Vaughan: Who says this?

Lincoln: I happen to know it! [*Lincoln pauses and shakes his head sorrowfully*] You see, my boy, your house is divided against itself—the symbol of our unhappy country. Of course, I didn't know of this particular case. Such things hurt me so, I refuse to know them unless I must. They tell me that Seward and Stanton have arrested without warrant and hold in jail more than thirty-five thousand men at this moment. I hope the number is exaggerated—still it may be so.

Vaughan: [*Angrily*] It's true—I've learned it since my father's arrest!

Lincoln: [*Tenderly*] But, come now, my son, put yourself in my place! I'm here to save the Union for which you are fighting—for which you have poured out your blood. I've armed two million men and we are spending four millions a day, to fight the South for trying to secede. My opponents, taking advantage of our sorrow, harangue the people and elect hostile legislatures in the Northern states. They were about to pass ordinances of Secession and establish a

Northwestern Confederacy! Shall I fight Secession in the South and merely argue with it here? I was compelled to suspend the civil law, arrest these men and hold them without bail or trial.

Vaughan: You are using the naked power of an emperor then?

Lincoln: [*Shaking his head sadly*] I have been entrusted with that power for a brief term by the people. I am using it sorrowfully but firmly—and I am backed by the prayers of the mothers whose sons are dying for our cause—and the silent millions out there, whom I can't at this moment see—but whom I love and trust.

Vaughan: [*With angry tears*] The Constitution of the Republic guarantees to every freeman the right to trial in open court, confronted by his accusers.

Lincoln: [*Passionately*] But we are fighting a war for the life of the Constitution itself! I did not begin it. Once begun it must be fought to the end and the Nation saved. We must prove now that among freemen there can be no successful appeal from the ballot to the bayonet. To preserve the Constitution of the Republic I must in this crisis strain some of its provisions.

Vaughan: [*In hard tones*] And you will not interfere to give these accused men a trial?

Lincoln: I dare not interfere! The civil law must be suspended for the moment—as the law of life is suspended while the surgeon cuts a cancer out of bleeding flesh! I cannot shoot one soldier for desertion if I allow the man to go free who causes him to desert. [*He pauses, and puts his hands on Vaughan's shoulders*] Don't think, my son, that all the suffering of this war is not mine! Every shell from those guns finds my heart. The tears of widows and orphans—all, the blue and the gray—are mine! For we are equally responsible for this war! When I came here from the West, I found a panic-stricken North, strangling with the poison of Secession. Our fathers had only dreamed a Union—they never lived to see it. The North had threatened Secession for thirty years. Horace Greeley in his great paper on the day of my inauguration was telling the millions who hung on his word as the oracle from Heaven, that Secession was inevitable! "Therefore let our erring sisters of the South go!" was his daily cry. I could not have prevented this war, nor could Jefferson Davis. We are in the grip of mighty forces sweeping in from the centuries. We are fighting the battle of the ages. [*He pauses again*] But our country's worth it, my boy, if we can only save it! Out of this agony will be born a united people. There has never been a democracy in this world because there's never been one without the shadow of a slave. We must build a real Government of the people, by the people, for the people. It's not the question merely of four million black slaves. It's a question of the life of freemen yet unborn. I hear the tread of these coming millions. Their destiny is in your hands and mine. A mighty Union of free democratic states without a slave—the hope, refuge and inspiration of the world—a beacon light on the shores of time! [*Pauses*] —There's but one tragedy, that can have no ray of light, and that is that this blood we are now pouring out shall have flowed in vain, and these brave men shall die for naught, that the old curse shall remain, the Union be broken into hostile sections and these battles must be fought again.

> [*He pauses, breathes deeply, and lifts his figure as if to throw off another nightmare and slips his arm around Vaughan*]

My enemies call me a tyrant and usurper! I who came up here from a pioneer's cabin in the wilderness, out of rags and poverty. [*Pauses*] —How well I remember when my mother looked at them and said—"This is nothing—it doesn't count here—it's what you feel—it's what you believe—it's what you see that counts—"

> [*Struggles with his emotions*]

Now I'm going to show you something, my son, and I'll let you be the judge as to whether I'm a tyrant. [*He takes up the booklet and hands it to Vaughan*] Read the title page.

Vaughan: [*Reading in amazement*] "Why Should Brothers Fight?" By Dr. Richard Vaughan.

Lincoln: That pamphlet was taken by his sister from the pocket of a poor ignorant boy, who was sentenced to be shot for desertion tomorrow at sunrise.

Vaughan: No! No!.

Lincoln: I pardoned him this morning.

> [*Vaughan sighs his relief*]

Your father wrote and printed that poison, and has forfeited his life for that boy's act.

Vaughan: [*Trembling*] I know you could order his execution.

Lincoln: I said today that I'd hang such a man on a gallows forty cubits high—but now that I see you trembling. [*He pauses*] I shall not order his execution. I shall only hold him until the war is over, and then let him and all the others go. [*Pauses*] Tyrant and usurper they call me! And I'm the humblest man who walks the earth tonight!

Vaughan: [*Slowly sinking to a seat and covering his face with his hands in a cry of despair*] Oh,— my God!

Lincoln: [*Bending in sorrowful amazement and touching Vaughan's head*] Why, what's the matter, my boy? I'm the only man to despair. You're just a Captain in the army. You have only to obey your superior officer. If to be the head of hell is as hard as what I've had to undergo here, I could find it in my heart to pity Satan himself. And if there's a man outside of perdition who suffers more than I do, I pity him!

Vaughan: [*Springing to his feet and throwing his hands up in anguish*] You don't understand! You don't understand!

Lincoln: Understand—what?

Vaughan: [*Impetuously*] When I lay in the hospital suffering from my wounds, I received the letter telling me of my father's imprisonment. I must have gone mad—for when you refused tonight to give him a trial—I started to—kill—you— Oh, my God! [*Breaks down*]

Lincoln: To kill me! You are the second man to try it. He'll get me the next time—I who envy the dead their rest! [*Laughs*] What a strange thing this life of ours! [*Pauses*] Why didn't you do it?

Vaughan: Because, for the first time you made me see things as they are, and I got a glimpse of the inside.

Lincoln: [*Eagerly*] Then, I won—didn't I?

Vaughan: Yes—and I can never forgive myself the thought of harming you!

Lincoln: [*Ignoring his grief*] If I've won you, I can win others, if I only get their ear and make them know as you know! All I need is a little time! And I'm going to fight for it now. [*With quick uplift of spirit*] I've told you the truth and the truth has turned a murderer into my friend!

If only the people can know—can have time to think, I'll win—I'll win! Look here—I've won you now?

Vaughan: [*Eagerly*] Just give me a chance to prove it!

[*Lincoln studies Vaughan thoughtfully*]

Lincoln: You doubtless said many bitter things in Washington?

Vaughan: Many of them.

Lincoln: Then, you were approached by the leaders of a Copperhead Secret Order called The Knights of the Golden Circle—were you not?

Vaughan: Yes!

Lincoln: I thought so. [*Cautiously*] You—joined the Order?

Vaughan: [*Hesitates*] I joined, and I'm one of their officers.

Lincoln: [*Carefully*] Of their inner council?

Vaughan: Yes.

Lincoln: You—know—all their signs and passwords?

Vaughan: Every one.

Lincoln: [*With sudden deep excitement*] Young man, you may have thought you came here tonight with murder in your heart—but Almighty God sent you for a different purpose!

Vaughan: What do you mean?

Lincoln: You'll stand by me now, through thick and thin?

Vaughan: [*Passionately*] I'd count it an honor to die for you!

Lincoln: Well, I'm going to ask you to do something harder than that for a man of sensitive honor. These Copperhead traitors took advantage of your illness and grief over your father to inveigle you into a scheme of high treason.

Vaughan: What!

Lincoln: You believed their purpose to be patriotic—didn't you?

Vaughan: Of course.

Lincoln: [*Seizing Baker's Report*] This document from Baker's Office contains the original order of their Chief for an uprising on the night of the election.

Vaughan: Uprising for what?

Lincoln: To overturn the Government, recognize the Confederacy, and divide the Union.

Vaughan: Is it possible!

Lincoln: You know—after what has passed between us tonight—that I speak the truth.

Vaughan: Yes!

Lincoln: You came in here to demand a trial for your father—and find him in reality justly condemned to death. I have pardoned him. I want you to atone for his wrongs and your own tragic mistake, by placing yourself with the signs and passwords of that Society at my disposal. You have been basely deceived and betrayed—will you do it?

Vaughan: If my country calls—yes—and I'll thank God for the chance to atone!

Lincoln: Good! You are the one man on earth tonight whom I need and didn't think I could get! I'm going to send you on a dangerous mission. I need two things to carry this election and save the Union—a single victory in the field to lift our people out of the dumps, and a word from Jefferson Davis that there can be no peace save in division! I know Davis. We were both born in Kentucky, on almost the same day. He holds that position. But the peace party of the North refuse to believe it. They say he will compromise. Now I've sent two men down there—Colonel Jacquess , a Methodist clergyman, of our hospital service, and John R. Gilmore of the *Tribune*, old Greeley's paper. They go as private citizens of the North, who desire peace. They are to draw Davis out, and get his declaration for me. Technically, they are spies—for they have no credentials. They may be imprisoned or executed. They passed through our lines but twenty miles from Richmond, seven days ago. I haven't been able to hear from them. The silence is ominous.

Vaughan: And you wish me to find out what has happened to them?

Lincoln: [*Eagerly*] I want another man in Richmond, quick—whose identity will be unknown—a man who can win the confidence of Judah P. Benjamin, Davis' Secretary of State, who is preventing my interview with the Confederate President. Benjamin is the ablest and by far the most dangerous man in the South today. I know from this document on my desk [*touches Baker's Report*] that he is in close touch with the Copperhead Societies of the North—if his keen mind is not actually directing them. You have their signs and passwords. It seems too good to be true! If you carry to Benjamin a special report of this planned uprising, you can gain his confidence, and persuade him to let my men see Davis. If you can only get through the lines and reach him before being arrested!

Vaughan: I've a brother in General Lee's army—sir—for whom I've often been mistaken before the war.

Lincoln: That's great!

Vaughan: He is an officer too—a First Lieutenant.

Lincoln: Fine! Before you go, confer with Baker. He will give you the names of our agents in Richmond and decide on your disguise. He will probably put you in Confederate uniform and make out in your brother's name a rebel leave of absence to use in an emergency. You are a Southern man. Your accent is perfect. Your chances of success great. I want you to leave within an hour. [*He writes on two cards*]

Vaughan: In five minutes, if you wish.

Lincoln: If you can get for Jacquess and Gilmore a hearing and they are allowed to return and tell their story, all right—your work in Richmond is done. But if they are imprisoned or executed, report this fact and Mr. Davis' answer, and it will be doubly effective—you understand?

Vaughan: Perfectly, sir.

Lincoln: That's your first job. Your next will be to get a special message through from inside the Confederacy to General Sherman, who is laying siege to Atlanta. [*Takes up telegram*] This message from him, received this morning, says that he has as yet been unable to locate and count up Hood's second line of defense which he must fight in a flank movement. Take the train from Richmond to Atlanta. Keep your eyes open every foot of the way. Find out from inside, the position of this second line, and the number of regiments holding it. Make no mistake about it. Break through to Sherman, and report to him.

Vaughan: A tough job, sir—but I believe I can do it.

Lincoln: That's the way to talk, my boy! When you reach General Sherman, you will deliver to him a verbal message—I'll give you a sign that will identify you. This is the big thing I'm sending you to do. I could telegraph my order direct to Sherman, but it would have to be filed in the War Office, and might offend General Grant. As an officer, you understand that.

Vaughan: Clearly, sir.

Lincoln: For this reason I'm sending you on this urgent and dangerous business. Tell General Sherman for me, that if he can take Atlanta at once, the blow will lift our people from despair, carry the election, and save the Union! I send by you the order for him to strike. If he wins, the order will remain a secret—the credit shall all be his! If he strikes and loses, I'll publish my order and take the blame on myself.—You think you can do this?

Vaughan: [*Quietly*] I'll do it—or I'll die trying, sir.

Lincoln: [*Writing on the back of his card*] All right, take this card to Stanton's Office and tell him what I've told you. Ask him to arrange to send you by boat to Aquia, Virginia, by horse from there. This card to Baker's Office—Return here for your papers, and say goodbye to your sweetheart.

Vaughan: At once, sir.

Lincoln: My boy—I trust you implicitly! My mother's God has been talking to me since you entered this room! You've lifted my spirit to the heights!

> [*Vaughan exits*]

CURTAIN

ACT III

Scene I

Set Scene: Jefferson Davis' room in the Confederate Capitol at Richmond, two days later. A long table is on the right. Two small tables on left. Doors right and left, and mantel center.

At Curtain Rise: A Doorman in Confederate uniform arranges the chairs about a long table as if for a Cabinet Meeting.

   [Benjamin enters]

Benjamin: Mr. Davis has not yet arrived?

The Doorman: Not yet, Mr. Benjamin—I am expecting him at ten o'clock—it's now a quarter of.

Benjamin: I've asked a young man to wait in your room for me—has he come?

The Doorman: He's there now—sir.

Benjamin: You've talked with him freely?

The Doorman: *[Laughs]* Oh, yes, sir—we've been swappin' yarns for half an hour.

Benjamin: I thought so—that's why I asked him to wait in your room.

The Doorman: Well, I always try to be sociable!

Benjamin: I know! Did you get much out of him?

The Doorman: Why, how—how do ye mean?

Benjamin: Find out anything about his people—where he came from, where he's going to—what he's doing in Richmond?

The Doorman: Oh, no, sir! He's full of fun—he kept me laughin' most o' the time.

Benjamin: I see! *[Laughs]* He knows his business. Show him in.

The Doorman: Yes, sir.

   [Benjamin seats himself at one of the small tables at left and examines his

schedule for the day's work. The Doorman opens the door and shows Vaughan in, dressed in Confederate uniform. Benjamin rises and greets him cordially]

Benjamin: Good morning, young man. [*Gives Vaughan the Sign of the Knights of the Golden Circle*]

Vaughan: [*Returns Sign*] Good morning, Mr. Benjamin—I hope you've rested well?

Benjamin: Not so well as usual—the truth is I've been wrestling all night with the problem of Jacquess and Gilmore. I've confirmed your view that they have given their real names. Gilmore is a reporter of the New York *Tribune* and Colonel Jacquess is a Methodist clergyman well known in the hospital service, in fact famous for his kindly treatment of Southern prisoners.

Vaughan: Just as I told you.

Benjamin: I've allowed the Commissioner of Exchange who has been holding them in custody to bring them here this morning.

Vaughan: Good!

Benjamin: Last night, I made up my mind to take your advice and to let them see Mr. Davis.

Vaughan: I'm glad.

Benjamin: This morning I'm puzzling over it!

Vaughan: [*Showing his disappointment*] Why?

Benjamin: I agree with you that we could use the interview for our own purposes. But the trouble is, Mr. Davis is soft-hearted sometimes. He may refuse to take my advice. He may let these men go.

Vaughan: You surely can depend on his allowing you to hold them in Libby Prison until after the election?

Benjamin: I'm not sure of it. If he takes a notion to let them go—he's as stubborn as a mule.

Vaughan: All right—Let me be present at the interview and take notes. If Mr. Davis makes an important declaration about peace and lets them go, I'll beat them to the North and give your version of the interview first!

Benjamin: [*Hesitating*] I might do that—yes!

Vaughan: I could not only head off any injury from their report, but I could give it a twist that would make it a boomerang on Lincoln.

[Benjamin hesitates while Vaughan watches him breathlessly]

Benjamin: *[Thinking]* You could act as my special secretary for the meeting and take shorthand notes—or pretend to.

Vaughan: I take shorthand. I've been a reporter in Washington.

Benjamin: Then it would be easy.

Vaughan: No matter what is said, I can make a report that will harden the purpose of our Societies to swing the uprising on the night of the election.

Benjamin: You are sure the order for the revolt against the Lincoln Government has been issued?

Vaughan: Absolutely sure.

Benjamin: I know they have discussed it and may have decided to do it, but are the actual preparations under way?

Vaughan: In every Lodge of the Knights of the Golden Circle, the command is now on record. Our forces are being drilled. I have read the original order with the signature of the Commander.

Benjamin: *[Elated]* It's great news you've brought us, young man—great news! *[Benjamin hesitates and Vaughan watches him]* All right, we'll risk it!

[Vaughan shows his secret joy and deep excitement]

These men are Lincoln's spies beyond a doubt—but we'll dig out of them all the information possible, and then use them for our purpose.

[The Doorman enters]

The Doorman: Judge Ould, the Commissioner of Exchange.

[Ould enters]

Ould: Our visitors are outside, Mr. Benjamin.

Benjamin: You understand, Judge Ould, that these men are prisoners of war in your charge as Exchange Commissioner?

Ould: I am painfully aware of that fact, sir—and the responsibility is not to my liking.

Benjamin: While in Richmond, they are to be held under the strictest guard and on no conditions allowed a liberty except by my order, or the order of the President.

Ould: I can trust them here with you, I hope, for half an hour?

Benjamin: You can. Show them in.

> [*Vaughan takes his seat at the small table near Benjamin who gives him a note book and he prepares to take notes. Ould re-enters conducting Jacquess and Gilmore*]

Ould: Colonel James F. Jacquess and Mr. John R. Gilmore. Mr. Secretary of State.

> [*Ould bows and exits, while Benjamin advances with marked cordiality to greet his visitors. He does not shake hands but bows politely*]

Benjamin: I am delighted to see you, gentlemen—pray be seated.

> [*The two men sit and Gilmore shoots at Vaughan a look of startled recognition which Vaughan fails to return*]

You bring overtures from your Government I trust.

Jacquess: No, sir, we bring no overtures.

Gilmore: We have no authority from our Government.

Jacquess: We have come simply as private citizens to know what terms will be acceptable to Mr. Davis for ending the war?

Benjamin: You are acquainted with Mr. Lincoln's views, however?

Jacquess: One of us is fully.

Benjamin: I supposed so. May I ask, did Mr. Lincoln in any way authorize you to come here?

Gilmore: No, sir. We came on his pass through the lines, of course, but not by his request.

Jacquess: We came, Mr. Benjamin, simply as men and Christians, not as diplomats, hoping in a frank talk with Mr. Davis to discover some way by which this war may be stopped.

Benjamin: On my advice, gentlemen, Mr. Davis will see you.

Jacquess and **Gilmore**: Thank you.

Benjamin: I think he is here now.

> [*Benjamin exits*]

Gilmore: [*In low tones to Vaughan*] What are you doing here?

Vaughan: Writing! I don't know you.

Gilmore: The hell you don't!

Vaughan: No!

Gilmore: We worked on the same paper in Washington, once.

Vaughan: Never saw you before.

Gilmore: Get-word-through-will you! We're in a trap!

Vaughan: Shut your damned trap! or we'll both make our breakfast on lead at sunrise tomorrow morning! Get back to your seat!

> [*The sound of approaching steps are heard. Benjamin enters as Gilmore drops into his seat*]

Benjamin: Gentlemen: The President of the Confederate States of America!

> [*Davis enters and bows to his visitors, who rise. His figure is about five foot ten and quite thin. His features are typically the Southern scholar and thinker with angular cheeks and high cheek bones. His iron gray hair is long and thick and inclined to curl at the ends. His whiskers are thin and trimmed farmer fashion, on the lower end of his strong chin. His eyes flash with strong vitality. His forehead is broad, his mouth strong. He wears a brown suit of foreign cloth which fits him perfectly. His shoulders slightly droop. His manner is easy and graceful, his voice charming and cultured*]

Davis: I am glad to meet you, gentlemen. You are very welcome to Richmond.

Gilmore: We thank you, Mr. Davis.

Davis: Mr. Benjamin tells me that you have asked to see me. [*He pauses and waits for his visitors to finish the sentence*]

Jacquess: Yes, sir. Our people want Peace. Your people do. We have come to ask how it may be brought about?

Davis: Very simply. Withdraw your armies from the South, let us alone and Peace comes at once.

Jacquess: But we cannot let you alone so long as you seek to divide the Union.

Davis: I know. You deny us, what you exact for yourselves—the right of self-government.

Jacquess: Even so, Mr. Davis, we cannot fight forever. The war must end sometime. We must finally agree on something. Can we not find the basis of agreement now, and stop this slaughter?

[*Vaughan takes notes rapidly*]

Davis: I wish peace as much as you do. I deplore bloodshed. But I feel that not one drop of this blood is on my hands. I can look up to God and say this. I tried to avert this war. I saw it coming and for twelve years I worked day and night to prevent it. The North was mad and blind and would not let us govern ourselves, and now it must go on until the last man of this generation falls in his tracks and their children seize their muskets and fight our battle—unless you acknowledge our right to self-government. We are not fighting for Slavery. We are fighting for independence and that or extermination we will have.

Jacquess: [*Protesting*] We have no wish to exterminate the South! But we must crush your armies. Is it not already nearly done? Grant has shut you up in Richmond, and Sherman is before Atlanta.

Davis: [*Laughs*] You don't seem to understand the situation! We're not exactly shut up in Richmond yet. If your papers tell the truth, it is your Capitol that is in danger, not ours. Lee's front has never yet been broken. He holds Grant, invades the North and shells Washington. Sherman, to be sure, is before Atlanta. But suppose he is? His position is a dangerous one. The further he goes from his base of supplies, the more disastrous defeat must be. And his defeat may be at hand.

Jacquess: And yet, the odds are overwhelmingly against you. How can you hope for success in the end?

Davis: My friend, the South stands for a principle—their equal rights under the Constitution which their fathers created. This country has always been a Republic of Republics—not an Empire. We are fighting for the right of local self-government which we won from the tyrants of the old world. The states of the Union have always been sovereign. We never paused to figure on success or failure, sir. Five million Southern freemen drew their sword against twenty millions because their rights had been invaded.

Jacquess: And yet, Mr. Davis, you know as well as I that five millions cannot hold out forever against twenty. Have we not reached the end?

Davis: Hardly! Do you think there are twenty millions in the North still determined to crush us? If so, let me tell you that I am better informed on the present situation inside your lines than you are. The North at this moment is hopelessly divided, sir.

[Benjamin exchanges signs with Vaughan]

Jacquess : The dispute then with your government is narrowed to this—union—or disunion?

Davis: Let us say independence or subjugation. We mean to govern ourselves. We will hold this principle if we have to see every Southern plantation sacked and every city in flames.

[Jacquess and Gilmore rise. Vaughan catches Gilmore's eye]

Jacquess: I am sorry, sir.

[Davis takes Jacquess' hand in both his in the same way Lincoln did]

Davis: I respect your character, Colonel Jacquess and your motives and I wish you well—every good wish possible consistent with the interests of the Confederacy. [*He presses Gilmore's hand and follows them to the door*]

Jacquess: Thank you.

Davis: [*At door*] And say to Mr. Lincoln that I shall be pleased to receive proposals for peace direct from him, at any time, on the basis of our independence. It will be useless to approach me with any other.

[Jacquess and Gilmore exit and Ould reenters]

Ould: [*To Davis*] And shall I conduct these gentlemen back to Grant's lines?

Benjamin: [*Quickly*] No, these men are spies straight from Lincoln's desk. It's the slyest trick the old fox has ever tried to play on us. He knows that McClellan's election on a peace platform is a certainty. He's after ammunition for this campaign. We dare not play into his hands! Our very life may depend on it! Make no mistake—these men must be locked up tonight and shot at sunrise.

Ould: [*Shakes his head*] I wouldn't do it if I were you.

Benjamin: Why?

Ould: For one reason this.

[*Ould unfolds a note*] Ben Butler sent this note to me by their hands. It was sealed. Read it.

Davis: [*Interrupting*] Just a moment. [*To the Doorman*] General Lee is in the War Office—ask him if he can see me for a few minutes, please.

[*The Doorman bows and exits*]

Go on, gentlemen.

Ould: [*To Benjamin—handing him the note*] Read it!

Benjamin: [*Reading*] "If these men do not return to my lines within ten days, I shall demand them, and if you don't produce them—I'll execute two for one."(Signed) B.F. Butler." [*Angrily*] Bluff! Bluff!

Davis: He's a beast. He'll do it.

Benjamin: All right! Let him try it! Two can play that game. We can execute four for one.

Davis: I don't like these bloody reprisals. There's no end, once we begin.

Benjamin: The decision is yours, sir.

Davis: I reserve my decision. I'll give it to you presently. I want a word with General Lee—first—if you will give me this room.

Benjamin: Certainly, we'll retire until you're ready. This way.

[*Benjamin conducts Vaughan and Ould into the room right—opposite the door through which Jacquess and Gilmore made their exit.—The Doorman enters and announces*]

The Doorman: General Lee!

Davis: [*Advances cordially and takes Lee's hand in both of his*] Thank you, General. I wish to consult you first on a peculiar matter—of small importance from one point of view—of tremendous importance from another. Two men have been passed into our lines to sound me on the question of Peace. I have just talked with them. I am certain—so is Benjamin—that they come straight from Lincoln though they have no credentials. Benjamin demands their execution—Judge Ould protests. Are they spies?

Lee: Technically, yes—morally, no.

Davis: Thank you. Before I decide whether to let these men go with a message to the North, I must ask you one or two questions.

Lee: At your service, sir.

Davis: How long can you hold Grant?

Lee: Certainly a year—unless.

Davis: Yes?

Lee: Unless Atlanta falls.

Davis: And then?

Lee: If General Hood fails to hold Atlanta, Sherman can cut the South in two and my supplies fail. My men are living now on parched corn. If Sherman takes Atlanta, I cannot get the corn.

Davis: What is the spirit of your men at this moment, General?

Lee: A more formidable force was never set in motion than the army I command, sir. They are our stark fighters—men who individually or in the mass can be depended on for any feat of arms in the power of mortals to accomplish. I know them from experience. They will blanch at nothing—yet they must have food.

Davis: You shall have it. But after one year—then what?

Lee: It's solely a question of manpower, sir. I must have more men.

Davis: And you suggest?

Lee: That you immediately begin to arm and drill 500,000 negroes for my command.

Davis: And you think they would make good soldiers?

Lee: Led by their old masters—they'll fight—to a man.

Davis: It would be necessary to give each black volunteer his freedom?

Lee: Of course. I, as you know, freed my own slaves before entering the service of the South. It is one of the ironies of Fate that I am supposed to be fighting for slavery—I who refuse to own a slave and my opponent General Grant is through his wife's estate a slaveholder. Slavery is doomed, sir. It can never survive this tragedy. The Legislature of Virginia came within one vote of freeing her slaves, years ago.

Davis: I know. But the great Gulf States and South Carolina with their majority of Negro population will never agree to the arming of half a million slaves.

Lee: And you will allow Mississippi, Louisiana, and South Carolina to defeat a plan necessary to save the life of the Confederacy?

Davis: The States are sovereign, General Lee—for this principle we are fighting.

Lee: Then I think it may be time to ask ourselves, heart to heart, the question whether the Confederacy, as organized, does not carry within its own body the seeds of death? The rights of a state must somewhere yield to the supreme power of a nation. The Negro will make a brave soldier, and he can save the South. Will you use him?

Davis: I'll consider your suggestion, General, but I can't see it—I can't see it now. I won't detain you longer.

> [*General Lee salutes and exits—Davis goes to the opposite door—opens it and calls*]

I am ready, gentlemen.

> [*Ould, Benjamin and Vaughan reenter*]

Benjamin: You have decided?

Davis: Yes. [*He sits and writes a pass*] It is probably a bad business for us.

Benjamin: There can be no doubt about that, sir.

Davis: But it would alienate many of our Northern friends if we held these men. I have decided to let them go. Give them this pass. [*Hands pass to Ould*] Show them through the hospitals and Libby Prison and conduct them back to General Grant's lines.

Ould: You have acted wisely, sir.

Benjamin: [*With deep feeling to Vaughan*] He has made exactly the blunder I feared.

Vaughan: [*With elation*] We'll hope for the best, sir! With the twist I'll give the news.

CURTAIN

Scene II

Set Scene: The same as Acts I and II, except that a small table has been placed down center on the side near Lincoln's desk. A telegraph instrument has been installed on this table.

At Curtain Rise: At rise, the audience sees only Lincoln and Operator, the lights gradually rise until full day shows the entire room. It is the morning of September 3, 1864.

Lincoln: [*Bending over the key*] Try to get Atlanta again, my boy.

> [*The Operator tries again and again to get Atlanta*]

Operator: It's no use, sir.

Lincoln: We don't seem to have any luck, do we? My messenger should have reached Sherman! He must be there now. He must be there—he can't be lost! [*Laughs forlornly*] Two whole days I've listened to that thing click.

> [*The Operator calls Atlanta, with a peculiar loud call*]

Is that the word Atlanta you're clicking off?

Operator: Yes, sir—calling—over this wire we have a direct connection today. The trouble is Sherman's old headquarters don't answer either.

Lincoln: Call Atlanta again. Do it slowly. I want to learn it—Uncle Billy.

> [*The Operator clicks off each letter in the Morse Code, spelling it slowly*]

Must be there by this time!

Operator: A—T—L—A—N—T—A— G—A— Atlanta, Ga.

Lincoln: Once more.

> [*The Operator repeats the call and Lincoln follows it repeating after him*]

I want to catch that as quick as you do—when it comes! [Aside] Oh, my God, why don't it come!—Why don't it come!

> [*Nicolay enters*]

Nicolay: The time's up. Raymond and his damned Committee are here, sir, and insist on your final answer at once.

Lincoln: Hold them back awhile. We're bound to hear something today. I promised them my decision this morning, I know—but I'm still full of foolish hopes.

Nicolay: They are not foolish hopes, Chief!

Lincoln: This machine here seems to think they are. The darn fool thing will talk one way but won't chirp the other.

Nicolay: What shall I tell them?

Lincoln: [*Listening at the instrument*] Anything—tell them a funny story! [*Listening*] They need a laugh—the bunch of undertakers! Waiting for me to deliver my corpse to them!—Restless, because I haven't given it up sooner!

> [*The sharp click of the telegraph receiver catches his ear and he starts to the table*]

No—that wasn't it. [*Turns again to Nicolay*] Tell them positively, I will see them within half an hour.

> [*Nicolay exits and Lincoln returns to his vigil by the telegraph table*]

How close can you get to Atlanta over the Chattanooga line?

Operator: Twenty miles out is the last station that answers and he don't know what's the matter with the line.

Lincoln: Strange—we got closer than that yesterday—Sherman's on the move....

> [*Betty enters timidly*]

That's certain. [*Looking up*] Come right in, Miss Betty—I know what you want.

Betty: Nothing yet from General Sherman?

Lincoln: Nothing.

Betty: And no message of any kind from John since he left?

Lincoln: Not yet.

Betty: Why—why hasn't he reported?

Lincoln: [*Hopefully*] I'm sure—remember, sure to a moral certainty—that he left Richmond safely.

Betty: [*Eagerly*] You have a message then?

Lincoln: Indirectly.

Betty: Oh.

Lincoln: [*To Edward at door*] Edward, ask Mr. Gilmore to step in here a minute.

Edward: Yes, sir.

Lincoln: Gilmore's report ought to be worth half a million votes for me—it may be worth something to you.

[*Gilmore enters*]

Gilmore, did you see a handsome young fellow in Confederate uniform taking notes at your interview with Davis.

Gilmore: Yes, sir, and I knew him too.

Betty: [*Eagerly*] It was Captain Vaughan?

Gilmore: Sure! He denied it, of course, but I knew him all right.

Betty: He was well?

Gilmore: I never saw him looking better. He was scared stiff, of course, and so were we.

Betty: Thank you!

Lincoln: That'll do, Gilmore. I wish you'd help Nicolay choke that Committee off a little while—and you come with them when they break in—will you?

Gilmore: Gladly, Mr. President.

[*Gilmore exits*]

Lincoln: [*To Betty lightly*] Now you've had some good news.

Betty: [*Forlornly*] How long since any word came from General Sherman?

Lincoln: Two days. I know the hole where he went in at. But I can't tell where the old varmint's going to come out.

Betty: [*Chokes*] If he ever comes out!

Lincoln: Oh! He'll come out.

[*He stops and listens at the telegraph instrument again, and sighs in disappointment*]

He'll come out somewhere—It's a habit Uncle Billy has.

Betty: [*Hopelessly*] They've no news at the War Department either.

Lincoln: No news is generally good news from Sherman.

[Betty turns away to hide her tears and Lincoln follows her with tender pleading]

Come, come, my dear—these tears won't do! You've got to help me now!

[Betty brushes the tears away]

I may have sent your lover to his death. I know that! But he went with a smile on his face and a great joy in his heart for the service he was doing his country.

Betty: Yes—I know—I know—I'm proud of the honor you did him.

Lincoln: *[Whispering]* Give me a little lift, then. *[Pauses]* I'm just whistling to keep up my courage! *[He pauses again in an agony of suffering]* I know that he got to Atlanta. *[Pauses]* Sherman has disappeared!

Betty: Forgive me—I forgot. You're going to win. I feel it. I know it!

Lincoln: That's the way to talk! That's the way I'm talking to myself though I'm scared within an inch of my life.

[He pauses and goes over to the Operator—Betty following]

Say, boy—can't you beat it a little harder and make the blame thing talk for us?

Operator: I wish I could, sir.

Lincoln: Try him again—

[The Operator calls Atlanta and pauses—Lincoln and Betty bend over with breathless suspense. The instrument gives one click—Lincoln starts. The instrument stops]

Didn't the thing start to answer? *[The Operator shakes his head]*

Call the War Office and ask Stanton to step over here—My God—why can't we hear!

Betty: *[Wistfully]* I'm not going to cry again—but I just want to ask one question—you won't mind?

Lincoln: As many as you like!

Betty: He—he—had to enter Atlanta a spy, didn't he? *[Sobs and catches herself]*

Lincoln: Yes—of course.

Betty: Well, if he should be captured—could—they execute him without our knowing it?

Lincoln: They might—but he's a very bright young man! He'll be too smart for them.

Betty: [*Hopelessly*] I don't know—I don't know!

Lincoln: Now listen! I'm going to tell you something—I know! I've a sort of second sight that tells me things sometimes, my dear. After the battle of Gettysburg I saw General Daniel E. Sickles in the hospital. They told me that he was mortally wounded and could not possibly live. I told General Sickles that he would live and get well, and he did! I saw his living body that day at work in health and strength as plainly as I see you! We have not heard from Captain Vaughan yet, but it will come! He has reached Atlanta. The General got my message. I know that. I felt it flash through the air from his soul to mine! I can see you and your lover at this moment seated side by side smiling and happy.

Betty: [*In awe*] You—see—this!

Lincoln: [*In dreamy tones*] As plainly as I see the sunlight dancing on the leaves outside that window now.

> [*Stanton enters and Lincoln turns to meet him eagerly*]

Stanton: You've no news?

Lincoln: I sent for you, to ask that.

Stanton: Nothing.

Lincoln: [*In low tones*] What does it mean?

Stanton: A storm swept Atlanta yesterday—the wires may be all down.

Lincoln: You think that's it?

Stanton: No—I don't.

Lincoln: Neither do I.

Stanton: Something big has happened! Sherman has either taken Atlanta or Hood has cut his communications and his army may be imperiled.

Lincoln: [*His head droops*] That's what I think too—God help us!

> [*The sharp click of the telegraph instrument causes him to start quickly, cross to the table and listen. The committee headed by Raymond and Stevens crowd through the door against the protests of Nicolay*]

Nicolay: I promised you an answer in half an hour, gentleman!—you must wait.

Raymond: Not another minute!

Stevens: [*Waving a telegram*] The matter is too urgent!

Lincoln: All right—John—let 'em in—I'm ready.

Raymond: We have just heard a most painful and startling piece of news from the War Department.

Lincoln: [*To Stanton*] War Department. [*Low voice*] —What is it, Stanton?

Stanton: Something I didn't believe and wouldn't repeat to you.

Lincoln: [*Whispering to Operator*] Pull for me, boy, pull for me—keep picking at that thing!

Stevens: [*Triumphantly*] You were advised to withhold the new draft of men until after the election! Well, read that copy of a telegram from New York, just received by General Halleck, sir! [*Offers telegram to Lincoln and he refuses to take it*]

Lincoln: I don't want to read it, Stevens. Your face is enough for me. It must be bad, or you wouldn't be so happy. You're almost smiling!

Stevens: Read it!

Lincoln: [*Ignoring the proffered telegram*] You know, Stevens, you remind of an old farmer I knew in Illinois.

> [*The committee gather around Lincoln eager for the story, glancing at Stevens*]

Stevens: Go on, give 'em the joke. It's your funeral—not mine!

Lincoln: [*Facing the committee*] This old farmer raised the biggest hog ever seen in the county. He was so fat the news of his size spread over the country and people came from far and near to see this wonder in pork. A stranger came up one day and asked the farmer to see him. The old man said: "Wal I've got sech a animal an' he's the biggest one I ever seed. I'll say that. But so many folks are comin' here pesterin' me to look at him, I've decided to charge a shillin' a look." The stranger put his hand in his pocket, pulled out the money, paid the shilling, stared at the old man, turned and walked away. The farmer called after him—"Hi—there—ain't yer goin' ter see the hog?" "No"—the fellow answered—"I've seen you! I've got my money's worth."

> [*All laugh except Stevens. During the laugh Lincoln bends over the telegraph instrument—in low tones*]

How goes it, boy? How goes it? [*The Operator shakes his head*] Not a click?

[*Operator shakes his head again—and Lincoln's face contracts in suffering*]

Stevens: Just a minute, Mr. President,—I'll give you the telegram if you won't read it.

Lincoln: Fire away, Stevens, if it makes you happy.

Stevens: [*Reading*] "New York, Sept. 3, 1864." "The Federal authorities have just discovered a nation-wide conspiracy to resist by force of arms the new draft. It will be necessary for General Grant to detach half his army from Lee's front immediately to put down this counter revolution. Send these soldiers without delay to our great cities." The signature is in code.

Raymond: It's the blackest news yet, sir—and it's true.

Stevens: You must realize that we cannot delay a moment in placing another man at the head of the ticket. [*There is a moment of dead silence while all watch Lincoln's face. Suddenly the sharp click of the telegraph instrument begins to spell the word A-T-lanta. Lincoln starts—his face flashing with excitement*]

Lincoln: What's that? [*He follows breathlessly the spelling of the full word—his face expressing his joy*]

Operator: Mr. President—It's come! It's here!

[*Lincoln rushes to the table, the crowd following*]

It's for you, sir!

Lincoln: Out with it, boy, word for word as you get it!

Operator: [*Click-click*] Atlanta. [*Click-click*] Georgia. [*Click-click-click*] September 3, 1864.

Lincoln: Glory to God!

Operator: [*Click-click*] —Atlanta [*Click-click*] —is ours. [*Click—click—click*] and fairly won—W. T. Sherman.

Lincoln: O my soul, lift up thy head! [*To Betty*] Go tell Mother, quick, tell her to come here!

[*Betty exits running*]

Nicolay: Three cheers for General William Tecumseh Sherman!

All shout: Sherman! Sherman! Sherman! [*When the shout dies away Lincoln lifts his head solemnly and cries*]

Lincoln: Unto thee, O God, we give all the praise now and forever more!

[*Mrs. Lincoln enters with Betty and rushes to meet*

the President. He takes her in his arms]

    Mother! It's all right!—Uncle Billy's there!

Mrs. Lincoln: You'll never doubt again?

Lincoln: Never! [*Turning to the committee*] My friends! A poem is singing in my heart!

"Mine eyes have seen the glory of the coming of the Lord!

He is trampling out the vintage where the grapes of wrath are stored:

He has loosed the fateful lightning of His terrible swift sword—

His truth is marching on!

"He has sounded forth the trumpet that shall never call retreat!

He is sifting out the hearts of men before His judgment seat:

Oh! Be swift my soul to answer Him! Be jubilant my feet!

Our God is marching on!"

Stanton: That draft will be all right, Stevens! Now all together! [*Stanton leads and all sing*] [*Lincoln listens with bowed head*]

We are coming, Father Abraham, three hundred thousand more,

 From Mississippi's winding stream and from New England's shore;

We leave our plows and workshop, our wives and children dear,

With hearts too full for utterance, with but a single tear,

We dare not look behind us but steadfastly before,

We are coming, Father Abraham, three hundred thousand more!

Chorus

We are coming, we are coming, our Union to restore!

 We are coming, Father Abraham, three hundred thousand more,

 We are coming, Father Abraham, three hundred thousand more!

Lincoln: And remember, gentlemen, U.S. Grant sent Sherman on that mission. You know I didn't remove him! Well, Raymond, what say you, now!

Raymond: It's glorious. It's a miracle! Lee's army can't survive. The end is sure! McClellan is beaten—the Union is saved!

Lincoln: What say you all?

A Committeeman: Your triumph is sure!

Another Committeeman: You'll sweep the nation, sir!

Nicolay: Three cheers for the old President and three cheers for the new!

All: Lincoln! Lincoln! Lincoln! [*All join except Stevens, whose face remains a mask*]

Lincoln: Come on, Stevens, smile! Take a chance. It may kill you, but my Lord, man, take a chance!

Stevens: You're not elected yet, sir—and such levity ill becomes a Nation's Chief in these tragic hours.

Lincoln: [*Laughs*] If I couldn't laugh I'd have died long ago at this job!

CURTAIN

EPILOGUE

Set Scene: The great pillars of the Capitol at Washington fill the entire stage from arch to arch. In the foreground stands the platform on which the Justices of the Supreme Court of the United States, headed by Salmon P. Chase, Chief Justice, are grouped about the President, who is delivering his Second Inaugural. John Vaughan beside Betty Winter is conspicuously leading the applause.

At Curtain Rise: The President is reading his Inaugural. A great burst of cheering follows the sentence he is closing before the curtain rises:

Lincoln: [*Before rise*] Shall we discern therein any departure from those divine attributes which the believers in a living God always ascribe to Him? [*Applause as curtain rises*] Fondly do we hope—fervently do we pray—that this mighty scourge of war may speedily pass away. Yet, if God wills that it continue until all the wealth piled by the bondman's two hundred and fifty years of unrequited toil shall be sunk, and until every drop of blood drawn with the lash shall be paid by another drawn with the sword, as was said three thousand years ago, so still it must be said, "The judgments of the Lord are true and righteous altogether."

[*Applause*]

With malice toward none; with charity for all; with firmness in the right, as God gives us to see the right, let us strive on to finish the work we are in; to bind up the nation's wounds; to care for him who shall have borne the battle, and for his widow, and his orphan—to do all which may achieve and cherish a just and lasting peace among ourselves and all nations.

[*Fade out with the light on Lincoln's face as he utters the last word*]

CURTAIN

Jefferson Davis

a Victim of History

Thomas Dixon

To the brave who died for what they believed to be right

> Fold up the banners! Smelt the guns!
> Love rules. Her gentle purpose runs.
> A mighty mother turns in tears
> The pages of her battle years
> Lamenting all her fallen sons!
> *Thompson*

Introduction

The story of Jefferson Davis in many ways parallels that of Abraham Lincoln. Both seemed ill-prepared for the tasks they faced immediately on gaining their leadership positions, yet both exhibited the extraordinary capacity to combine high principles with unprecedented, often unpopular, administrative decisions that would ultimately result in millions of deaths in battle, disease, or execution. And, once started, how could this intolerable situation be brought to an end?

The forces of history within this new nation tested the idea of self-government. If not a king, who then would write the laws and enforce them—the Nation or the States? In other words, how "united" was the United States going to be? In the "land of the free," who was going to be free?

Thomas Dixon's perspective in this story gives insight into the impetus that led the Southern States to secede from a government dominated by the Northern States that were on a course to abolish the practice of slavery within the United States. By seceding, they would no longer be subject to that impending decision.

Some in the North, the Copperheads, were quite satisfied with that outcome, even to the extent of considering their own secession from the no-longer "United" States.

The new Republican Party, however, the party of Lincoln, won the 1860 election. But even before Lincoln was sworn in as President, the Southern States made their move, separately seceding, and then forming a Confederacy of those states. Jefferson Davis was installed as the leader, given the task of welding together this new entity while simultaneously preparing a war machine for the expected conflict.

Who was this Jefferson Davis? Dixon starts the narrative early in Davis' life.

Sasha Newborn

Preface

In the historical romance which I have woven of the dramatic events of the life of Jefferson Davis I have drawn his real character unobscured by passion or prejudice. Forced by his people to lead their cause, his genius created an engine of war so terrible in its power that through it five million Southerners, without money, without a market, without credit, withstood for four years the shock of twenty million men of their own blood and of equal daring, backed by boundless resources.

The achievement is without a parallel in history, and adds new glory to the records of our race.

The scenes have all been drawn from authentic records in my possession. I have not at any point taken a liberty with an essential detail of history.

Thomas Dixon

CONTENTS

The Prologue

1 Kidnapped	95
2 The Wilderness	100
3 The Hermitage	103
4 The Monastery Bells	106
5 Home	112
6 Rebellion	115
7 Life	121
8 Love	130
9 War	134
10 Romance	138
11 The Fairy Bells	143
12 Truth	146

The Story

1 The Curtain Rises	150
2 The Parting	161
3 A Midnight Session	175
4 A Friendly Warning	180
5 Boy and Girl	182
6 God's Will	186
7 The Best Man Wins	190
8 The Storm Center	194
9 The Old Regime	201
10 The Gauge of Battle	209
11 Jennie's Vision	217
12 A Little Cloud	223
13 The Closing of the Ranks	225
14 Richmond in Gala Dress	235
15 The House on Church Hill	243

16 The Flower-Decked Tent	248
17 The Fatal Victory	253
18 The Aftermath	267
19 Socola's Problem	279
20 The Anaconda	286
21 Gathering Clouds	289
22 Jennie's Recruit	298
23 The Fatal Blunder	303
24 The Sleeping Lioness	311
25 The Bombardment	318
26 The Irreparable Loss	335
27 The Light that Failed	342
28 The Snare of the Fowler	350
29 The Panic in Richmond	358
30 The Deliverance	369
31 Love and War	377
32 The Path of Glory	380
33 The Accusation	397
34 The Turn of the Tide	403
35 Suspicion	414
36 The Fatal Deed	417
37 The Raiders	423
38 The Discovery	429
39 The Conspirators	442
40 In Sight of Victory	448
41 The Fall of Richmond	457
42 The Capture	465
43 The Victor	476
44 Prison Bars	478
45 The Master Mind	485
46 The Torture	489
47 Vindication	493

Leading Characters of the Story

The Prologue
    1814-1853
Lt. Jefferson Davis, Of the U. S. Army.
Joseph E. Davis, His Big Brother.
Colonel Zachary Taylor, "Old Rough and Ready."
Sarah Knox Taylor, His Daughter.
James Pemberton, A Faithful Slave.
The Story
    1860-1867
Hon. Roger Barton, An Original Secessionist.
Jennie, His Daughter.
Dick Welford, A Confederate Soldier.
Joseph Holt, A Renegade Southerner.
Henrico Socola, A Soldier of Fortune.
The President, Of the Confederacy.
Mrs. Davis, His Wife.
Burton Harrison, His Secretary.
Joseph E. Johnston, A Master of Retreat.
P. G.T. Beauregard, The First Hero.
Stonewall Jackson, Of the "Foot Cavalry."
Robert E. Lee, The Southern Commander.
U. S. Grant, The Bull Dog Fighter.
Nelson A. Miles, A Jailer.
John C. Underwood, A Reconstruction Judge.

PROLOGUE

1: KIDNAPPED

The hot sun of the South was sinking in red glow through the giant tree-tops of a Mississippi forest beyond the village of Woodville. A slender girl stood in the pathway watching a boy of seven trudge manfully away beside his stalwart brother.

Her lips trembled and eyes filled with tears.

"Wait—wait!" she cried.

With a sudden bound she snatched him to her heart.

"Don't, Polly—you hurt!" the little fellow faltered, looking at her with a feeling of sudden fear. "Why did you squeeze me so hard?"

"You shouldn't have done that, honey," the big brother frowned.

"I know," the sister pleaded, "but I couldn't help it."

"What are you crying about?" the boy questioned.

Again the girl's arm stole around his neck.

"What's the matter with her, Big Brother?" he asked with a brave attempt at scorn.

The man slowly loosened the sister's arms.

"I'm just going home with you, ain't I?" the child went on, with a quiver in his voice.

The older brother led him to a fallen log, sat down, and held his hands.

"No, Boy," he said quietly. "I'd as well tell you the truth now. I'm going to send you to Kentucky to a wonderful school, taught by learned men from the Old World—wise monks who know everything. You want to go to a real school, don't you?"

"But my Mamma don't know—"

"That's just it, Boy. We can't tell her. She wouldn't let you go."

"Why?"

"Well, she's a good Baptist, and it's a long, long way to the St. Thomas monastery."

"How far?"

"A thousand miles, through these big woods—"

The blue eyes dimmed.

"I want to see my Mamma before I go—" his voice broke.

The man shook his head.

"No, Boy; it won't do. You're her baby—"

The dark head sank with a cry.

"I want to see her!"

"Come, come, Jeff Davis, you're going to be a soldier. Remember you're the son of a soldier who fought under General Washington and won our freedom. You're named after Thomas Jefferson, the great President. Your three brothers have just come home from New Orleans. Under Old Hickory we drove the British back into their ships and sent 'em flying home to England. The son of a soldier—the brother of soldiers—can't cry—"

"I will if I want to!"

"All right!" the man laughed—"I'll hold my hat and you can cry it full—"

He removed his hat and held it smilingly under the boy's firm little chin. The childish lips tightened and the cheeks flushed with anger. His bare toes began to dig holes in the soft rich earth. The appeal to his soldier blood had struck into the pride of his heart and the insult of a hat full of tears had hurt.

At last, he found his tongue:

"Does Pa know I'm goin'?"

"Yes. He thinks you're a very small boy to go so far, but knows it's for the best."

"That's why he kissed me when I left?"

"Yes."

"I thought it was funny," he murmured with a half sob; "he never kissed me before—"

"He's quiet and reserved, Boy, but he's wise and good and loves you. He's had a hard time out here in the wilderness fighting his way with a wife and ten children. He never had a chance to get an education and the children didn't either. Some of us are too old now. There's time for you. We're going to stand aside and let you pass. You're our baby brother, and we love you."

The child's hand slowly stole into the rough one of the man.

"And I love you, Big Brother—" the little voice faltered, "and all the others, too, and that's-why-I'm-not-goin'!"

"I'm so glad!" The girl clapped her hands and laughed.

"Polly!—"

"Well, I am, and I don't care what you say. He's too little to go so far and you know he is—"

The man grasped her hand and whispered:

"Hush!"

The brother slipped his arm around the Boy and drew him on his knee. He waited a moment until the hard lines at the corners of the firm mouth had relaxed under the pressure of his caress, pushed the tangled hair back from his forehead and looked into the fine blue-gray eyes. His voice was tender and his speech slow.

"You must make up your mind to go, Boy. I don't want to force you. I like to see your eyes flash when you say you won't go. You've got the stuff in you that real men are made of. That's why it's worth while to send you. I've seen that since you could toddle about the house and stamp your feet when things didn't suit you. Now, listen to me. I've made a vow to God that you shall have as good a chance as any man to make your way to the top. We're going to be the greatest nation in the world. I saw it in the red flash of guns that day at New Orleans as I lay there in the trench and watched the long lines of Red Coats go down before us. Just a lot of raw recruits with old flintlocks! The men who charged us, the picked veterans of England's grand army. But we cut 'em to pieces, Boy! I fired a cannon loaded with grape shot that mowed a lane straight through 'em. It must have killed two hundred men. They burned our Capitol at Washington and the Federalist traitors at Hartford were firin' on us in the rear, but Old Hickory showed the world that we could lick England with one hand tied behind our back. And we did it. We drove 'em like sheep—drove 'em into the sea.

"There's but one name on every lip in this country now, Boy, and that's Old Hickory. He'd be President next time—but for one thing,—just one thing—he didn't have a chance to learn when he was a boy. He's not educated."

The brother paused, and a dreamy look came into his eyes. "We may make him President anyhow. But if he'd been educated—there wouldn't be any if or and about it. Washington and Jefferson and Madison belong to the rich and powerful class. Jackson is a yeoman like your father. But he'd be President, Boy, if he'd been educated! Nothing could stop him. Don't you see this is your country? This is a poor man's world. All you have to do is to train your mind. You've got to do this—you understand—you've got to do it—"

The man paused suddenly and looked into the Boy's wondering eyes. He had forgotten the child's rebellion. The young pioneer of the wilderness was talking to himself. Again he had seen a vision.

He seized the Boy's arms:

"Don't you see, Boy, don't you?"

The child's mouth hardened again:

"No, I don't. I'm just a little boy. I love my Mamma. She's good and sweet to me and I'm not going to leave her—"

Again Polly laughed.

A smile slowly played about the brother's lips and eyes. He must show his trump card.

"But you don't know what I've got for you—"

"What?"

"Something you've always wanted to have for your own—"

"A pony?"

The man slowly rose:

"Come out to the big road—"

The Boy seized his sister's hand:

"Polly, let's see!"

The girl's eyes grew dim:

"Oh, Jeff, I know you're goin'!"

"No—we'll just see what it is—come on!"

In five minutes they emerged from the deep woods into the clearing around a cabin. Beside the roadway stood a horse and pony, both bridled and saddled.

The swift feet of the Boy flew across the opening, the sister wide-eyed and trembling, close on his heels. He threw his arms around the pony's neck and stroked his head with gentle touch. The pony pressed his mouth against the Boy's cheek in friendly response.

"Did you see him kiss me, Polly?" he cried tremblingly.

"Yes, I saw him," was the solemn response.

"Isn't he a beauty? Look, Polly—he's got a white spot on every foot and one in his forehead and black as a coal all over—and Oh—what a saddle—a red belt and red martingales!"

He touched the saddle lovingly and circled the pony's neck with his arms.

The brother smiled again:

"Well, what do you think of that?"

The Boy was trembling now from head to foot, his heart in his throat as he slowly asked:

"You mean that—you'll—give—him—to me—for—all my own?"

"If you'll be a good boy, go to school and work hard—yes."

"All right, Big Brother," was the quick answer, "I'll go. Help me on him quick, and let me try him!"

The Boy lifted his bare foot into the strong hand, sprang into the saddle, bounded down the road, wheeled, flew back and leaped to the ground.

"He's a dandy!"

Polly dropped her head and started home, making a brave fight to keep back the tears. Halfway across the clearing she gave up in a long pitiful wail.

The Boy, busy with his pony, had not missed her. In a moment he was by her side, his arms about her neck.

"Don't cry, Polly honey, I'll be back before long," he pleaded.

The only answer was a sob:

"Goodbye, Jeff—"

Her hands slowly slipped through his.

"Goodbye, Polly—"

He watched her go with quivering lips, and as the little figure slowly faded into the shadows of the woods he called in broken accents:

"Kiss Mamma for me—and tell her I wanted to go back and say goodbye—but Joe wouldn't let me!"

"Yes, honey!"

"And you—watch out for that old drunk man we saw once in the woods, Polly!"

"Yes!"

"Don't let him get you—"

"No—I won't—good—goodbye!"

"Goodbye—"

The last goodbye stuck in the Boy's throat, but he lifted his blue eyes, saw his pony and smiled through the tears.

2. THE WILDERNESS

A journey of a thousand miles through the unbroken wilderness—the home of the Choctaw and Chickasaw Indian Nations and all on his own beautiful pony! It was no time for tears.

The Boy's soul leaped for joy.

The party was a delightful one. Major Hinds, a veteran of General Jackson's campaign, the commander of the famous Mississippi Dragoons at the battle of New Orleans, was the leader, accompanied by his wife, her sister and niece, and best of all a boy his own age, the Major's little son Howell.

Howell also was riding a pony. He was a nice enough pony, of course, as ponies went, but couldn't compare with his own. He made up his mind to race the first chance they got, and show those pretty white heels to his rival. He was just dying to tell him how fast they could beat the ground—but he'd wait and surprise the party.

A negro maid accompanied the ladies and a stalwart black man rode a pack-mule laden with tents, blankets and a cooking outfit. They stopped at houses when one could be reached at nightfall. If not, they camped in the woods beneath the towering trees. There was no need of the tents unless it rained. So dense was the foliage that only here and there a bright star peeped through, or a moonbeam shot its silvery thread to the ground. The Indians were all friendly. It was the boast of the Choctaws that no man of their breed had ever shed the blood of a white man.

For days they followed the course of the majestic river rolling its yellow flood to the sea and watched the lazy flat and keel boats drift slowly down to New Orleans bearing the wealth of the new Western World. The men who had manned these rude craft were slowly tramping on foot back to their homes in the North. Their boats could not stem the tide for the return trip. Every day they passed these weary walkers. The Boy was sorry they couldn't ride. His pony's step was so firm and quick and strong.

He raced with Howell the first day and beat him so far there was no fun in it. He never challenged his rival again. He was the guest of Major Hinds on this trip. It would be rude. But he slipped out in the dark that night, and hugged his pony:

"You're the finest horse that ever was!" he whispered.

"Of course I am!" the pony laughed.

"I love you—"

"And I love you," was the quick response as the warm nose touched his cheek.

In the second week, they reached the first stand, "Folsoms'," on the border of the Choctaw Nation. These stands were log cabins occupied by squaw men—whites who had married Indian women. They must pass three more of these stands the Major said—the "Leflores," known as the first and second French camps, and the one at the crossing of the Tennessee River, which had the unusual distinction of being kept by a half-breed Chickasaw Indian.

Here, weary, footsore travelers stopped to rest and refresh themselves—and many dropped and died miles from those they loved. The little graveyard with its rude, wooden-marked mounds the Boy saw with a dull ache in his heart.

And then the first bitter pang of homesickness came. He wondered if his sweet mother were well. He wondered what she said when they told her he had gone. He knew she had cried. What if she were dead and he could never see her again? He sat down on a log, buried his face in his hands and tried to cry the ache out of his heart. He felt that he must turn back or die. But it wouldn't do. He had promised his Big Brother. He rose, brushed the tears away, fed and watered his pony and tenderly rubbed down every inch of his beautiful black skin. He forgot the ache in his new-found love and the strength which had come into his boy's soul from the sense of kinship with Nature which this beautiful dumb four-footed friend had brought him. No man could be friendless or forsaken who possessed the love of a horse. His horse knew and loved him. He said it in a hundred ways. His wide, deep, lustrous eyes, shining with intelligence, had told him! So had the touch of his big warm mouth in many a friendly pony kiss. His pony could laugh, too. He had seen the smiles flicker about his mouth and eyes as he pretended to bite his bare legs. How could any human being be cruel or mean to a horse! His pony had given him new courage and conscious power. He was the master of Nature now when they flew along the trail through the deep woods. His horse had given him wings.

He looked up into the star-sown sky, and promised God to be kind and gentle to all the dumb world for the love of the beautiful friend He had given.

3: THE HERMITAGE

At the last stand on the banks of the winding Tennessee, the Major sat up late in eager discussion about Old Hickory with an enthusiastic Tennesseean. The ladies had retired, and the Boy listened with quiet eagerness to the talk.

"Waal, we're goin' ter make Andrew Jackson President anyhow, Major!" the Tennesseean drawled.

"I'm afraid they'll beat us," the Major answered, with a shake of his head.

"How'll they beat us when we git ready ter make the fight?"

"Old Hickory says himself, he ain't fit—"

"I reckon we know more about that than he does," persisted the man from Tennessee.

"The aristocrats don't think so—"

"What t'ell they got agin him? Ain't he the biggest man in this country today? Didn't he lick Spain and England both at Pensacola and didn't he finish the Red Coats at New Orleans—"

"They say his education's poor—"

"He knowed enough to make this country cock o' the walk—what more do they want—damn 'em!"

"They say he swears—"

The Tennesseean roared:

"Waal, if all the cussin' men vote fur him—he'll sho be elected!"

"The real trouble—" the Major said thoughtfully, "is what the scandal-mongers keep saying about his wife—"

"He's killed one son-of-a-gun about that already, an' they better let him alone—"

"That's just it, my friend: he killed that skunk in a duel and it's not the only one he has fought either. Old Hickory's got the temper of the devil."

"Waal, thar ain't nothin' in them lies about his wife—"

The Major lifted his hand and moved closer:

"There's just enough truth at the bottom of it all to give the liars the chance they need to talk forever—"

"I never knowed thar wuz ary grain er truth in hit, at all—"

"There is, though," the Major interrupted, "and that's where we're going to have a big fight on our hands when it comes to the rub. This Lewis Robards, her first husband, was a quarrelsome cuss. Every man that looked at his wife, he swore was after her, and if she lifted her eyes, he was sure she was guilty. There was no divorce law in Virginia and Robards petitioned the Legislature to pass an Act of Divorce in his favor. The dog swore in this petition that his wife had deserted him and was living with Andrew Jackson. He was boarding with her mother, the widow Donelson. The Legislature passed the Act, but it only authorized the Courts of the Territory of Kentucky to try the case, and grant the divorce if the facts were proven.

"Robards never went to Court with it for over two years, and Jackson, under the impression that the Legislature had given the divorce, married Rachel Robards at Natchez in August, 1791.

"Two years later, the skunk slips into Court and gets his divorce!

"As quick as Old Hickory heard this, he married her over again. There was a mighty hullabaloo kicked up about it by the politicians. They tried to run Jackson out of the country—the little pups who were afraid of him. He challenged the leader of this pack of hounds, and shot him dead—"

"Served him right, too," broke in the Tennesseean, removing his pipe, with a nod of his shaggy head.

"But it don't help him on the way to Washington!" The Major grunted, suddenly rising and dismissing the subject for the night.

The Boy's curiosity was kindled to see the great man whose name had filled the world.

The distance to Nashville was quickly covered. The Major pressed straight through the town without pause and drew rein at the General's gate.

The welcome they received from their distinguished host was so simple, so genuine, so real, the Boy's heart went out in loyal admiration.

The house was a big rambling structure of logs, in front of which stood a stately grove of magnificent forest trees. Behind it stretched the grain and cotton fields.

Nothing could surpass the unaffected and perfect courtesy with which the General welcomed his guests. The tall, stately figure, moving with the unconscious grace of perfect manhood, needed no rules of a dancing master for his guidance. He had sprung from the common people, but he was a born leader and ruler of men.

The Boy listened with keen ears to hear him rip out one of those terrible oaths of which so much had been said. His speech was gentle and kind, and he asked a blessing at every meal exactly as his own quiet, dignified father at home. In all the three weeks they remained his guests not an oath or an ugly word fell from his lips. The Boy wondered how people could tell such lies.

The General liked boys, too. It was easy to see that. He gave hours of his time to the games and sports of his adopted son, Andrew Jackson, Jr., and his two little guests. He got up contests of all sorts. They raced their ponies. They ran and jumped. They played marbles. They followed the hounds. And always with them as friend and counselor, the General, gentle, kind, considerate. The only thing he prohibited was wrestling.

"No, boys," he said with a frown. "That's not a good sport for high spirited youth. To feel the hand of a rival on your body may lead to a fight."

The deep-set eyes flashed with the memory of his own hot blooded boyhood and young manhood.

The General's wife won the Boy's whole heart from the moment he saw her.

"How could they tell such lies!" he kept repeating with boyish indignation. Pure and sweet as the face of his own mother was hers. Loving, unselfish, tender and thoughtful, she moved through her house with the gentle step of a ministering angel. The knightly deference with which the General attended her slightest wish, stirred the Boy's imagination. He could see him standing erect, pistol in hand, in the gray dawn of the morning on which he faced the enemy who had slandered her. He could see the big firm hand grip the pistol's handle in a clasp of steel as he waited the signal of Death. He wondered what sort of wound Dickenson's bullet had made in the General's breast. Anyhow, it had not been fatal. His enemy lived but a few hours.

He set his lips firmly, and repeated the Tennesseean's verdict:

"Served him right, too."

The Boy left the Hermitage under the spell of Old Hickory's personality for life. He had seen a great man.

4: THE MONASTERY BELLS

The journey from Nashville to Springfield, Kentucky, was quick and uneventful. Long before the spire of St. Thomas' church loomed on the horizon, they passed through the wide, fertile fields of the Dominican monks. The grim figure of a black friar was directing the harvest of a sea of golden-yellow wheat. His workmen were sleek negro slaves. Herds of fat cattle grazed on the hills. A flock of a thousand sheep were nipping the fresh sweet grass in the valley. They passed a big flour mill, whose lazy wheel swung in rhythmic unison with the laughing waters of the creek that watered the rich valley. The monks were vowed to poverty and self-denial. But their Order was rich in slaves and land, in mills and herds and flocks and generous harvests.

As the sun sank in a smother of purple and red behind the hills, they saw the church and monastery. The bells were chanting their call to evening prayer.

The Boy held his breath in silent ecstasy. He had never heard anything like it before. It was wonderful—those sweet notes echoing over hill and valley in the solemn hush of the gathering twilight.

They waited for the priests to emerge from the chapel before making their presence known. Through the open windows the deep solemn throb of the organ pealed. The soul of the Boy rose enchanted on new wings whose power he had never dreamed. Hidden depths were sounded of whose existence he could not know. There was no organ in the little bare log church the Baptists had built near his father's farm in Mississippi. His father and mother were Baptists and of course he was going to be a Baptist some day. But why didn't they have stained glass windows like those through which he saw the light now streaming—wonderful flashing lights, whose colors seemed to pour from the soul of the organ. And why didn't they have a great organ?

He was going to like these Roman Catholics. He wondered what his mother would say to that?

It all seemed so familiar, too. Where had he heard those bells?

Where had he heard the peal of that organ and seen the flash of those gorgeous lights? In the sky at sunset perhaps, and in the rumble of the storm. Maybe in dreams—and now they had come true.

In a few months, he found himself the only Protestant boy in school and the smallest of all the scholars. The monks were kind. They seemed somehow to love him better than the others. Father Wallace reminded him of his big brother. He was so gentle.

The Boy made up his mind to join the Catholic Church and went straight to Father Wilson, the venerable head of the college.

The old man smiled pleasantly:

"And why do you wish this, my son?"

"Oh, it's so much more beautiful than the Baptist Church. Besides it's so much easier—"

"Indeed?"

"Yes, sir. The Baptists have such a hard time getting religion. They seek and mourn so long—"

"Really?"

"Indeed they do—yes, sir—I've seen stubborn sinners mourn all summer in three protracted meetings and then not come through!"

"And you don't like that sort of penance?"

"No, sir. I've always dreaded it. And the worst thing is the new converts have to stand right up in church before all the crowd and tell their experience out loud. I'd hate that—"

"And you like our ways better?"

"A great deal better. The Catholics manage things so nicely. All you have to do is to go to church, learn the catechism and the good priests do all the rest—"

"Oh—I see!"

"Yes, sir."

Father Wilson laid his wrinkled hand tenderly on the Boy's head:

"You are very, very young, my son, and you are growing rapidly. What you really need is good Catholic food. Sit down and have a piece of bread and cheese with me."

The Boy sat down and ate the offered bread and cheese in silence.

"I can't join, Father Wilson?" he asked at last.

The priest smiled again:

"No, my son."

"You don't like me, Father?" the boy asked wistfully.

"We like you very much, sir. But we are responsible for the trust your father and mother have put in us. In God's own time when you are older and know the full meaning of your act, I should be glad—but not this way."

The Boy was so small, in fact, that a fine old priest in pity for his tender years had a little bed put in his own room for him to watch the light and shadows in eager young eyes when homesickness threatened. And then he talked of the wonders and glory of Rome on her seven hills by the Tiber, of the Coliseum, the death of Christian martyrs in the arena—of the splendors of St. Peter's, beside whose glory all other churches pale into insignificance. He lifted the curtain of history and gave the child's mind flashes of the Old World whose pageants stretch down the ages into the mists of eternity.

Of books, the Boy learned little—but the monks kindled a light in his soul the years could not dim.

To the other students the old man was not so gentle. They were tougher and he set their tasks accordingly. They rebelled at last and decided on revenge. The plot was hatched and all in readiness for its execution. The only problem was how to put the light out in his room.

The Boy held the key to the citadel. He was on the inside. He could blow the candle out and the thing was done. He refused at first, but the rebels crowded around him and appealed to his sense of loyalty.

"They can force you to sleep in his room," pleaded the ringleader, "but, by Gimminy, that don't make you a monk, does it?"

"No, of course not—"

"You're one of us—stand by us. You didn't ask to sleep in his old room, did you?"

"No."

"Well, you're there—the right man in the right place, in the nick of time. Will you stand by us?"

"What do you want me to do?"

"Just blow out the candle—that's all—we'll do the rest. Will you do it?"

The Boy hesitated, smiled and said:

"Yes—when everything's quiet."

The old man had gone to bed and began to snore. The Boy rose noiselessly and blew the candle out.

Instantly from the darkness without, poured a volley of cabbage heads, squashes, potatoes and biscuits. Not a word was spoken, but the charge of the light brigade was swift and terrible.

The Boy pulled the cover over his head and waited for the storm to pass.

When the light was lit and search made, not a culprit could be found. They were all in bed sound asleep. The only one awake was the Boy in the little bed on which lay scattered potatoes, biscuits and cabbage.

The priest drew him from under the cover. His face was stern—the firm mouth rigid with anger.

"Did you know they were going to do that, sir?" he asked.

The Boy trembled but held his tongue.

"Answer me, sir!"

"I didn't know just what they were going to do—"

"You knew they were up to something?"

"Yes!"

"And you didn't tell me?"

"No."

"Why?"

"I couldn't be a traitor, sir."

"To those young rascals—no—but you could betray me—"

"I'm not a monk, Father—"

"Tell me what you know at once, sir, before I thrash you."

"I don't know much," the Boy slowly answered, "and I can't tell you that."

There was a final ring in the tones with which he ended the sentence. The culprit must be punished. It was out of the question that he should whip him—this quiet, gentle, bright little fellow he had grown to love. He was turned over to another—an old monk of fine face and voice full of persuasive music.

He took the Boy by the hand and led him up the last flight of stairs to the top of the house and into a tiny bare room. The only piece of furniture was an ominous looking cot in the middle of the floor. The Boy had not read the history of the Spanish Inquisition, but it required no great learning in history or philosophy to guess the use of that machine.

There was no terror in the blue eyes. Their light grew hard with resolution. The monk to whom he had been delivered for punishment was the one of all the monastery who had the kindliest, gentlest face. The Boy had always thought him one of his best friends.

Yet, without a word, he laid the culprit face downward on the strange leather couch and drew the straps around his slim body. He had dreamed of mercy, but all hope vanished now. He held his breath and set his lips to receive the blow—the first he had ever felt.

The monk took the switch in his hand and hesitated. He loved the bright, handsome lad. The task was harder than he thought.

He knelt beside the cot and put his hand on the dark little head:

"I hate to strike you, my son—"

"Don't then, Father," was the eager answer.

"I've always had a very tender spot in my heart for you. Tell me what you know and it'll be all right."

"I can't—"

"No matter how little, and I'll let you off."

"Will you?"

"I promise."

"I know one thing," the Boy said with a smile.

"Yes?"

"I know who blew out the light."

"Good!"

"If I tell you that much, you'll let me off?"

"Yes, my son."

The little head wagged doubtfully:

"Honest, now, Father?"

"I give you my solemn word."

"I blew it out!"

The fine old face twitched with suppressed laughter as he loosed the straps, sat down on the cot and drew the youngster in his lap.

"You're a bright chap, my son. You'll go far in this world some day. A great diplomat perhaps, but the road you've started on tonight can only lead you at last into a blind alley. You know now that I love you, don't you?"

"Yes, Father."

"Come now, my Boy, there's too much strength and character in those fine eyes and that splendid square chin and jaw for you to let roistering fools lead you by the nose. You wouldn't have gotten into that devilment if they hadn't persuaded you—now would you?"

"No."

"All right. Use the brain and heart God has given you. Don't let fools use it for their own ends. Do your own thinking. Be your own man. Stand on your own bottom."

And then, in low tones, the fine old face glowing with enthusiasm, the monk talked to his little friend of Truth and Right, of Character and Principle, of Love and God, until the tears began to slowly steal down the rosy cheeks. A new resolution fixed itself in the Boy's soul. He would live his own life. No other human being should do it for him.

5: HOME

The mother's heart rebelled at last. She would not be put off longer. Her baby had been gone two years. She refused point blank to listen to any further argument.

Charles Green, the young Mississippian, studying law in Kentucky, and acting as the Boy's guardian, was notified to bring him at the end of the spring term.

On a glorious day in June they left Bardstown for Louisville, to take the new steamboat line for home. These wonderful boats were the marvels of their day. Their names conveyed but a hint of the awe they inspired. The fleet of three vessels bore the titles, Volcano, Vesuvius and Ætna. And the sparks that flew heavenward from their black chimneys were far more impressive to the people who crowded the shores than the smoke and lava of old Vesuvius to the lazy loungers of Naples.

The Boy saw his pony safely housed on board the Ætna, and amid the clang of bells and the scream of whistles, the floating wonder swung out from her wharf into the yellow tide of the Ohio.

Scores of people crowded her decks for the pleasure of a ride ten miles down the river to return in their carriages.

The Captain of the Ætna, Robinson DeHart, held the Boy in a spell by his lofty manners. He had been a sailor on board an ocean-going brig. To him the landing of his vessel was an event, no matter how often the stop was made, whether to put off a single passenger, or take on a regiment. In fact, he never landed the Ætna, even to take on a cord of wood, without the use of his enormous speaking trumpet and his big brass spy-glass.

A beautiful, slow, uneventful voyage on the Father of Waters landed the Boy in safety at the Woodville stopping-place. He leaped down the gang-plank with a shout and clasped his Big Brother's hand.

"My, my, but you've grown, Boy!"

"Haven't I?"

"Won't little mother be surprised and glad?"

"Let's fool her," the Boy cried. "Let me go up by myself and she won't know me!"

"All right—we'll try."

The brother stopped at the village and the young stranger walked alone to his father's house. How beautiful it all seemed—the big log house with the cabins clustering around it! A horse neighed at the barn and a colt answered from the field.

He walked boldly up to the porch and just inside the door sat his lovely mother. She had been one of the most beautiful girls in all South Carolina in her day, his father had often said. She was beautiful still. She had known what happiness was. She was the mother of ten strong children—five boys and five girls—and her heart was young with their joys and hopes. A smile was playing about her fine mouth. She was dreaming perhaps of his coming.

The Boy cleared his throat with a deep manly note and spoke in studied careless tones:

"Seen any stray horses around here, ma'am?"

The mother's eyes flashed as she sprang through the doorway and snatched him to her heart with a cry of joy:

"No—but I see a stray Boy! Oh, my darling, my baby, my heart!"

And then words failed. She loosed her hold and held him at arm's length, tried to say something, but only clasped him again and cried for joy.

"Please, Ma, let me have him!" Polly pleaded.

And then he clasped his sister in a long, voiceless hug—loosed her and caught her again:

"I missed you, Polly, dear!" he sighed.

When all the others had been greeted, he turned to his mother:

"Where's Pa?"

"Down in the field with the colts."

"I'll go find him!"

With a bound he was off. He wondered what his silent, undemonstrative father would do. He had always felt that he was a man of deep emotion for all his self-control.

He saw him in the field, walked along the edge of the woods, and suddenly came before him without warning. The father's lips trembled. He stooped without a word, clasped the Boy in his arms and kissed him again and again.

The youngster couldn't help wondering why a strong man

should kiss so big a boy. The mother—yes—but his father, a man—no.

It was sweet, this home-coming to those who loved deepest. Somehow the monastery, its bells, its organ, its jeweled windows, and its kindly black-robed priests seemed far away and unreal now—only a dream that had passed.

6: REBELLION

The mother's breakdown was not allowed to stop the Boy's education. Both father and older brother were determined on this. They would use the schools at home now.

He was sent to the County Academy in the fall. The Boy didn't like it. After the easy life with the kindly old monks at St. Thomas, this academy was not only cheap and coarse and uninteresting, but the teacher had no sense. He gave lessons so long and hard it was impossible to memorize them.

The Boy complained to the teacher. A lesson of the same length was promptly given again. The rebel showed the teacher he was wrong by failing to know it.

"I'll thrash you, sir!" was the stern answer.

The Boy would not take that from such a fool. He rose in his wrath, went home and poured out the indignant story of his wrongs.

The father was a man of few words, but the long silence which followed gave a feeling of vague uneasiness. He was never dictatorial to his children, but meant what he said. His voice was quiet and persuasive when he finally spoke.

"Of course, my son, you will have to choose for yourself whether you will work with your hands only, or with your head and hands. You can't be an idler, I need more cotton pickers. You don't like school, try the cotton, I'll give you work."

The Boy flushed and looked at his father keenly. It was no joke. He meant exactly what he had said, and a boy with any sand in his gizzard couldn't back down.

"All right, sir," was the firm answer. "I'll begin in the morning."

He went forth to his task with grim determination. The sun of early September had just risen and it was already hot as he bent to work. Cotton picking looked easy from a distance. When you got at it, things somehow were different. A task of everlasting monotony, this bending from boll to boll along the endless rows! He never realized before how long the cotton rows were. There was a little stop at the end before turning and selecting the next, but these rows seemed to stretch away into eternity.

Three hours at it, and he was mortally tired. His back ached in a dull hopeless pain. He lifted his head and gazed longingly toward the school he had scorned.

"What a fool!" he sighed. "But I'll stick to it. I can do what any nigger can."

He looked curiously at the slaves who worked without apparent effort. Not one of them seemed the least bit tired. He could get used to it, too. After all, this breath of the open world was better than being cooped up in a stuffy old schoolhouse with a fool to set impossible tasks.

"Pooh! I'll show my father!" he exclaimed.

The negroes broke into a plantation song. Jim Pemberton, the leader, sang each stanza in a clear fine tenor that rang over the field and echoed through the deep woods. The others joined in the chorus and after the last verse repeated in low sweet notes that died away so softly it was impossible to tell the moment the song had ceased.

The music was beautiful, but it was impossible for him to join in their singing. He couldn't lower himself to an equality with black slaves. This cotton picking seemed part of their scheme of life. Their strong black bodies swayed in a sort of rhythmic movement even when they were not singing. Somehow his body didn't fit into the scheme. His back ached and ached. No matter. He had chosen, and he would show them he had a man's spirit inside a boy's breast.

At noon the ache had worn away and he felt a sense of joy in conquering the pain.

He ate his dinner in silence and wondered what Polly was thinking about at school. Girl-like, she had cried and begged him to go back.

With a cheerful wave of his hand to his mother, he returned to the field before the negroes, strapped the bag on his shoulder and bent again to his task. The afternoon was long. It seemed at three o'clock there could be no end to it and still those long, long rows of white fleece stretched on and on into eternity—all alike in dull, tiresome monotony.

He whistled to keep up his courage.

The negroes whispered to one another and smiled as they looked his way. He paid no attention.

By four o'clock, the weariness had become a habit and at sundown he felt stronger than at dawn. He swung the bag over his back and started to the weighing place.

"Pooh—it's easy!" he said with scorn.

The negroes crowded around his pile of cotton.

"Dat Boy is sho one cotton-picker!" cried Jim Pemberton, regarding him with grinning admiration.

"Of course, I can pick cotton if I want to—"

"But ye raly don't wanter?" Jim grinned.

"Sure I do. I'm sick of school."

Jim laughed aloud and, coming close, whispered insinuatingly:

"I'se sho sick er pickin' cotton, an' when yer quits de job—"

"I'm not going to quit—"

"Yassah, yassah?—I understan' dat—but de pint is, when yer do quit, don't fergit Jim, Marse Jeff. I likes you. You got de spunk. I wants ter be yo' man."

The appeal touched the Boy's pride. He answered with quiet dignity:

"All right, James—"

Jim lifted his head and walled his eyes:

"Des listen at him call me Jeemes! I knows a real marster when I sees him!"

That night, the father asked no questions and made no comment on the fact that he had picked a hundred and ten pounds of cotton—as much as any man in the field. His deciding to work with his hands had apparently been accepted as final.

This thing of deciding life for himself was a serious business. It would be very silly to jump into a career with slaves, coarse and degrading, just because a fool happened to be teaching at the County Academy. He must think this thing over. Tired as he was, he lay awake until eleven o'clock, thinking, thinking for himself.

It was lonesome work, too, this thinking for himself.

If his father had only done the thinking for him, it would have been so much easier to accept his decision and then rebel if he didn't like it.

He returned to the field next morning with renewed determination. Through the long, hot, interminable day he bent and fought the battle in silence. His back ached worse than the first day.

Every muscle in his finely strung little body was bruised and sore and on fire.

He began to ask if his father were right. Wasn't a man a double fool who had brains and refused to use them?

An idiot could pick cotton when the bag was fastened on his back. All he needed was one hand. All he had to do was to bend, hour after hour, day after day, until it became the habit of life and the ache stopped.

He could see this now, for himself. He smiled at the quiet wisdom of his father. He certainly knew how to manage boys. He must acknowledge that. He was quiet and considerate about it, too. He didn't dictate. He only suggested things for consideration and choice. It was easy to meet the views of that kind of a father. He treated a boy with the dignity of a man.

When the cotton was weighed, the Boy faced his father: "I've thought it all over, sir, and I'd like to go back to school."

"All right, my son, you can return in the morning."

He made no comment. He indulged in no smile at the Boy's expense. He received his decision with the serious dignity of a judge of the Supreme Court of Life.

The rebellion ended for all time. Teachers and schools took on a new meaning. A lesson was no longer a hard task set by a heartless fool who had been accidentally placed in a position of power. School meant the training of his mind for a higher and more useful life.

Progress now was steady. The next year a new teacher came, a real teacher, the Rev. John Shaw from Boston, Massachusetts—a man of even temper, just, gentle, a profound scholar with a mind whose contagious enthusiasm drew the spirits of the young as a magnet.

The Boy learned more under his guidance within a year than in all his life before, and next full was ready to enter Transylvania University at Lexington, Kentucky.

The polite, handsome boy from Mississippi who had served an apprenticeship with his father's negroes in a cotton field, gave the professors no trouble. Good-natured, prudent, joyous, kind, manly, he attended to his lessons and his own business. He neither gambled nor drank, nor mingled with the rowdy set. He had come there for something else.

He had just passed his examinations for the Senior class in July, 1824, when the first great sorrow came. The wise father whom he had grown to love and reverence died in his sixty-eighth year.

His thoughtful Big Brother came in person to tell him and break the blow with new ambitions and new hopes. He had secured an appointment from President Monroe as a cadet to West Point from the State of Mississippi.

And then began the four years of stern discipline that makes a soldier and fits him to command men.

But once in those busy years did the gay spirit within rise in rebellion, to learn wisdom in the bitterness of experience.

With Emile Laserre, his jolly Creole friend from Louisiana, he slipped down to Bennie Haven's on a frolic—taking French leave, of course. The alarm was given of the approach of an instructor, and the two culprits bolted for the barracks at breakneck speed through pitch darkness. Scrambling madly through the woods, there was a sudden cry, a crash and silence. He had fallen sixty feet over a precipice to the banks of the Hudson. Young Laserre crawled carefully to the edge of the rock, peered over and called through the darkness:

"Are you dead, Jeff?"

He was suffering too much to laugh, though he determined to give an Irishman's reply to that question, if it killed him. He managed to wheeze back the answer:

"Not dead—but spachless!"

Many were the temptations of rebellion from the friends he loved in the years that followed, but never again did he yield. Somehow the thing didn't work in his case.

There was one professor who put his decision of obedience to the supreme test. For some reason this particular instructor took a violent dislike to the tall, dignified young Southerner. Perhaps because he was more anxious to have the love of his cadet friends than the approval of his teachers. Perhaps from some hidden spring of character within the teacher which antagonized the firm will and strong personality of the student who dared to do his own thinking. From whatever cause, it was plain to all that the professor sought opportunities to insult and browbeat the cadet he could not provoke into open rebellion.

The professor was lecturing the class on presence of mind as the supreme requisite of a successful soldier. He paused, and looked directly at his young enemy:

"Of course, there are some who will always be confused and wanting in an emergency—not from cowardice, but from the mediocre nature of their minds."

The insult was direct and intended. He hoped to provoke an outburst which would bring punishment, if not disgrace.

The cadet's lips merely tightened and the steel from the depths of his blue eyes flashed into his enemy's for a moment. He would bide his time.

Three days later, in a building crowded with students, the professor was teaching the class the process of making fire-balls.

The room was a storehouse of explosives and the ball suddenly burst into flames.

Cadet Davis saw it first and calmly turned to his tormentor:

"The fire-ball has ignited, sir,—what shall I do?"

The professor dashed for the door:

"Run! Run for your lives!"

The cadet snatched the fire-ball from the floor, dashed it through the window and calmly walked out.

He had saved many lives and the building from destruction. His revenge was complete and sweet. But deeper and sweeter than his triumph over an enemy was the consciousness that he was master of himself. He had learned life's profoundest lesson.

7: LIFE

On his graduation, the Second Lieutenant of Infantry, from the State of Mississippi, barely twenty years old, reported for duty to the Jefferson Barracks at St. Louis.

He was ordered to the frontier to extend the boundaries of the growing Republic—now accompanied by his faithful body servant, James Pemberton.

The Fort, situated on the Wisconsin River, was the northern limit of the Illinois tribe of Indians, and the starting point of all raids against the Iroquois who still held the rich lands around the village of Chicago.

The Boy Lieutenant was the first lumberman to put axe into the virgin forests of Wisconsin. He was sent into the wilderness with a detachment for cutting timber to enlarge the Fort.

Under the direction of two voyageurs he embarked in a little open boat and began the perilous journey.

The first day out his courage and presence of mind were put to quick test.

The Indians suddenly appeared on the shore and demanded a trade for tobacco. The little party rowed to the bank and began to parley. A guide's keen eyes saw through their smooth palaver the hostile purpose of a bloody surprise and warned the commander. The order to push into the river and pull for their lives was instantly given.

With savage yells the Indians sprang into their canoes and gave chase.

It was ten to one and they were sure of their prey. The chance of escape from such strong, swift rowers in light bark canoes was slight. The low fierce cries of victory and the joyous shout of coming torture rang over the waters.

The Indians gained rapidly.

The young Lieutenant's eye measured the distance between them and saw the race was hopeless. With quick command he ordered a huge blanket stretched in the bow for a sail. The wind was blowing a furious gale and might swamp their tiny craft. It was drowning or death by torture. The commander's choice was instantaneous.

The frail boat plunged suddenly forward, swayed and surged from side to side through the angry, swirling waters, settled at last, and drew steadily away from the maddened savages.

With a curious smile, the boyish commander stood in the stern and watched the black swarm of yelling devils fade in the distance.

He was thinking of his old professor at West Point. His insult had been the one thing in life to which he owed most. He could see that clearly now. His heart went out in a wave of gratitude to his enemy. Our enemies are always our best friends when we have eyes to see.

The winter following he was ordered down to Winnebago.

The village of Chicago was the nearest center of civilization. The only way of reaching it was by wagon, and the journey consumed three months.

There was much gambling in the long still nights, and some drinking. In lieu of the excitement of the gaming table, he took his fun in breaking and riding wild horses, and hairbreadth escapes were the order of his daily exercise. It was gambling, perhaps, but it developed the muscles of mind and body.

His success with horses was remarkable. No animal that man has broken to his use is keener to recognize a master and flout a coward than the horse. No coward has ever been able to do anything with a spirited horse.

He was wrestling one day with a particularly vicious specimen, to the terror and anguish of Jim Pemberton.

"For de Lawd's sake, Marse Jeff, let dat debbil go!"

"No, James, not yet—"

"He ain't no count, no how—"

"All the more reason why I should be his master, not he be mine."

The horse was possessed of seven devils. He jumped and plunged and bucked, wheeled and reared and walked on his hind legs in mad effort to throw his cool rider. The moment he reared, the Lieutenant dropped his feet from the stirrups and leaned close to the brute's trembling, angry head. At last in one supreme effort the beast threw himself straight into the air and fell backwards, with the savage purpose of crushing his tormentor beneath his body.

With a quiet laugh, the young officer slipped from the saddle and allowed him to thump himself a crashing blow. As the horse sprang to his feet to run, the Lieutenant leaped lightly into the saddle and the fight was over.

"Well, for de Lawd, did ye ebber see de beat er dat!" Jim Pemberton cried with laughing admiration.

Scarcely a week passed without its dangerous excursions against the Pawnees, Comanches and other hostile tribes of Indians. The friendly tribes, too, were everlastingly changing to hostiles in a night. Death rode in the saddle with every man who left a fortified post in these early days of our national life.

The Lieutenant was ordered on a peculiarly long and daring raid into hostile territory, and twice barely escaped a massacre. Their errand accomplished, and leisurely returning to the Fort, they suddenly met a large party of Indians.

The Lieutenant shot a swift glance at their leader and saluted him with friendly uplifted hand:

"Can you tell us the way to the Fort, Chief?"

The tall brave placed himself squarely in the path and pointed in the wrong direction.

Instantly the Lieutenant spurred his horse squarely on the savage, grasped him by the hair, dragged him a hundred yards and flung him into the bushes. The assault was so sudden, so unexpected, so daring, the whole band was completely cowed, and the soldiers rode by without attack.

Nor was the Indian the only enemy to test the youngster's mettle. The pioneer soldiers of the rank and file in these turbulent days had minds of their own which they sometimes dared to use.

The Lieutenant had no beard. His smooth, handsome face, clear blue eyes, fresh color and gay laughter, gave the impression of a boy of nineteen, when by the calendar he could boast of twenty-one.

A big strapping, bearded soldier, employed in building the Fort, had proven himself the terror of his fellow workmen. He was a man of enormous strength and gave full rein to an ugly, quarrelsome disposition.

His eyes rested with decided disapproval on the graceful young master of horses.

"I'll whip that baby-faced Lieutenant," he coolly announced to his satellites, "if ever he opens his jaw to me—watch me if I don't. What does he know about work?"

The men reported the threat to the Lieutenant. The next day without a moment's hesitation, in quiet tones, he gave his first order to the giant:

"Put that piece of dressed scantling beside the window—"

The man deliberately lifted a rough board and placed it.

"The rough board won't do," said the even voice. "It must be a dressed scantling."

The soldier threw him an insolent laugh, and stooped to take up a board exactly like the one he had laid down.

The baby-faced Lieutenant suddenly seized a club, knocked him down, and beat him until he yelled for quarter.

The soldiers had watched the clash at first with grins and winks and nudges, betting on their giant. His strength was invincible. When the unexpected happened, and they saw the slender, plucky youngster standing over the form of the fallen brave, they raised a lusty shout for him.

When the giant scrambled to his feet, the victor said with a smile:

"This has been a fight, man to man, and I'm satisfied. I'll not report it officially."

The big one grinned sheepishly and respectfully offered his hand:

"You're all right, Lieutenant. I made a mistake. I beg your pardon. You're the kind of a commander I've always liked."

Again the soldiers gave a shout. No man under him ever again presumed on his beardless face. He had only to make his orders known to have them instantly obeyed.

Jim Pemberton had watched the little drama of officer and man with an ugly light gleaming in his eyes. The young master had not seen him. That night in his quarters Jim quietly said:

"I'd a killed him ef he'd a laid his big claws on you, Marse Jeff."

"Would you, James?"

"Dat I would, sah."

Nothing more was said. But a new bond was sealed between master and man.

While at Fort Crawford, the Lieutenant had been ordered up

the Yellow River to build a saw mill. He had handled the neighboring Indians with such friendly skill and won their good will so completely, he was adopted by their chief as a brother of the tribe. An old Indian woman bent with age traveled a hundred miles to the Fort to warn the "Little Chief" of a coming attack of hostile bands. Her warning was unheeded by the new commander and a massacre followed.

The success of this attack raised the war spirit of the entire frontier and gave the soldiers a winter of exceptional danger and hardship. The country in every direction swarmed with red warriors on the warpath. The weather was intensely cold, and his Southern blood suffered agonies unknown to his companions. Often wet to the skin and compelled to remain in the saddle, the exposure at last brought on pneumonia. For months he lay in his bed, directing, as best he could, the work of his men.

James Pemberton lifted his weak, emaciated form in his arms as if he were a child. The black man carried his money, his sword and pistols. At any moment, day or night, he could have stepped from the door into the wilderness and been free. He was free. He loved the man he served. With tireless patience and tenderness, he nursed him back from the shadows of death into life again.

On recovering from this illness, the Lieutenant faced a new commander at the head of his regiment—a man destined to set in motion the greatest event of his life.

Colonel Zachary Taylor had been promoted to the command of the First Infantry on the death of Colonel Morgan. Already he had earned the title that would become the slogan of his followers in the campaign which made him President. "Old Rough and Ready" at this time was in the prime of his vigorous manhood.

Colonel Taylor sent the Lieutenant on an ugly, important mission.

Four hundred pioneers had taken possession of the lead mines at Dubuque against the protest of the Indians whose rights had been ignored. The Lieutenant and fifty men were commissioned to eject the miners. To a man, they were heavily armed. They believed they were being cheated of their rights of discovery by the red tape of governmental interference. They had sworn to resist any effort to drive them out of these mines. Most of them were men of the higher types of Western adventurer. The Lieutenant liked these hardy sons of his own race, and determined not to use force against them if it could be avoided.

He crossed the river to announce his official instructions, and was met by a squad of daring, resolute fellows, armed and ready for a fight.

Their leader, a tall, red-headed, serious-looking man, opened the conference with scant ceremony. Looking the youthful officer squarely in the eye, he slowly drawled:

"Young man, we have defied the gov'ment once befo' when they sent their boys up here to steal our mines. Now, ef yer know when yer well off, you'll let honest white men alone and quit sidin' with Injuns—"

There was no mistaking his accent. He meant war.

The Lieutenant's answer came in quick, even, tones:

"The United States Government has ordered your removal, gentlemen. My business as a soldier is to obey. I shall be sorry to use force. But I'll do it, if it's necessary. I suggest a private interview with your leader—" he nodded to the red-headed man.

"Sure!"

"Talk it over!"

"All right."

The men from all sides gave their approval. The leader hesitated a moment, and measured the tall, straight young officer. He didn't like this wrestle at close quarters with those penetrating eyes and the trained mind behind them. But with a toss of his red locks he muttered:

"All right, fire away—you can talk your head off, for all the good it'll do ye."

They walked off together a few yards and sat down.

With the friendliest smile the Lieutenant extended his hand:

"Before we begin our chat, let's shake hands?"

"Certain—shore—"

The brawny hand clasped his.

"I want you to know," the young officer continued earnestly, "my real feelings toward you and your men. I've been out here four years with you fellows, pushing the flag into the wilderness, and the more I see of you the better I like you. I know real men when I see them. You're strong, generous, brave, and you do things. You're building a great republic on this frontier of the world. I've known your hospitality. You've had little education in the schools, but you're trained for this big work in the only school that counts out here—the School of Danger and Struggle and Experience—"

The brawny hand was lifted in a helpless sort of protest:

"Look a here, Boy, you're goin' ter bamboozle me, I kin jist feel it in my bones—"

"On the other hand," the Lieutenant continued eagerly, "I assure you I am going to treat you and your friends with the profoundest respect. It's due you. Let's reason this thing out. You've taken up these mines under the old right of first discovery—"

"Yes, and they're ours, too,"—the lean jaws came together with a snap.

"So I say. But it will take a little time and a little patience to establish your claims. The Indian, you know, holds the first rights to this land—"

"T'ell with Injuns!"

"Even so, isn't it better to first settle their claims and avoid war?"

"Mebbe so."

"And you know we can't settle with the Indians while you hold by force the mines they claim as the owners of the soil—"

The leader scratched his head and rose with sudden resolution:

"Come on, and tell this to the boys."

The leader escorted the Lieutenant to the crowd, and commanded them to hear him. His speech was interrupted at first by angry exclamations, but at its close there was respectful silence. The fight was won without a blow.

The new Colonel was much pleased at the successful ending of the dangerous job. He had received the orders to eject these miners with a wry face. That the work had been done without bloodshed had lifted a load from his mind.

The Lieutenant was honored on the night of his return by an invitation to dine with Colonel Taylor's family. They had been settled in the crowded quarters of the Fort during his absence—the wife, three daughters and a little son.

The Lieutenant's curiosity was but mildly roused at the thought of meeting the girls. In the lofty ways of youth, he had put marriage out of his mind. A soldier should not marry. He had given his whole soul to his country, its flag and its service. He would be agreeable to the ladies, of course, in deference to his commander and the honor he was receiving at his hands.

The dinner was a success. The mother was charming and gracious in her welcome. Something in her ways recalled his own mother.

She extended her hand with a genial smile, and took his breath with her first remark:

"I've quite fallen in love with you, sir, because of a story I heard of your West Point career—"

"Not in pity for my fall over the cliff, I hope," he answered gravely.

The mother's voice dropped to a whisper:

"No,—your friend Albert Sydney Johnston told me that you saved a large part of your allowance and sent it home to your mother—"

The young officer's lips trembled, and he looked away for a moment:

"But she sent it back to me, madam."

"Yes, until you wrote that she hurt you by not keeping it—"

To relieve his evident embarrassment, the mother introduced him in rapid succession to her daughters, the eldest Anne, the second Sarah Knox, the youngest Elizabeth. Richard, the handsome little boy, had introduced himself. He had liked the Lieutenant from the first.

He had been so surprised by the mother's possession of one of the sweetest secrets of his schoolboy life, and had blushed so furiously over it, he had scarcely noticed the girls, merely bowing in his confusion.

It was not until they were seated at the table and the dinner had fairly begun, that he became conscious of the charm of the second daughter, who sat directly opposite.

Her beauty was not dazzling, but in fifteen minutes she had completely absorbed his attention. It was impossible, of course, not to look at her. She sat squarely before him. There was no embarrassment in the frank, honest curiosity with which she returned his gaze.

The thing that first impressed him was the frankness of a winsome personality. He listened with keen attention to her voice. There was no simper, no affectation, no posing. She was just herself. He found himself analyzing her character. Refined—yes. Intelligent— beyond a doubt. She talked with her father in a quiet, authoritative way which left no doubt on that score. Graceful, tender, sincere, too—

her tones to her impulsive brother and her younger sister proved that. And a will of her own she had. The firmly set, full lips were eloquent of character. He liked that above all things in a woman. He couldn't stand a simpering doll.

"Sing for us, Sarah!" her brother said impulsively, as they rose from the table.

"Certainly, Dick, if you wish it."

There was no holding back for urging. No mock modesty. No foolishness in her answer. It was straight, affectionate, responsive, open hearted, generous—just like his own sweet little sister Polly when he had asked of her a favor.

And then, he blushed to find himself staring at her in a sort of dreamy reverie. He hoped her music would not spoil the impression her personality had made. This had happened once in his life. He could never talk to the girl again, after he had heard her sing. The memory of it was a nightmare.

He watched her tune the guitar with a sense of silly dread. The tuning finished, she turned to her brother and asked with a smile:

"And what shall I sing, Sir Richard?"

"The one I love best—'Fairy Bells.'"

When the first line with its sweet accompaniment floated out from the porch on the balmy air of the June evening, the Lieutenant's fears had vanished. Never had he heard a song whose trembling melody so found his inmost soul. It set the Fairy Bells ringing in the deep woods of his far-away Mississippi home. He could see the fairy ringing them—her beautiful hair streaming in the moonlight, a smile on her lips, the joy and beauty of eternal youth in every movement of her exquisite form.

When the last note had died softly away, he leaned close and before he knew what he was doing, whispered:

"Glorious, Miss Sarah!"

"You like it very much?" she asked.

"It's divine."

"My favorite, too."

All night the "Fairy Bells" rang in his heart. For the first time in life, he failed to sleep. He listened entranced until dawn.

8: LOVE

In the swift weeks which followed, life blossomed with new and wonderful meaning.

In the stern years on the plains, the young officer had known but one motive of action—duty. He was an exile from home and its comforts, friends and the haunts of civilized man for his country's sake. He had come to plant her flag on the farthest frontier and push it farther against all corners.

In the struggle against the snows of winter and the pestilence of the summer wilderness, he had fought Nature with the dogged determination of the soldier. Snow meant winter quarters, the spring marching and fighting. The hills were breastworks. The night brought dreams of strategy and surprise. The grass and flowers were symbols of a nation's wealth and the prophecy of war.

By a strange magic, the coming of a girl had transformed the world. He had seen the strategic value of these hills and valleys often before. He had not dreamed of their beauty. The mists that hung over the ragged lines of the western horizon were no longer fogs that might conceal an army. They were the folds of a huge veil which Nature was softly drawing over the face of a beautiful bride. Why had he not seen this before?

The awful silence of the plains from which he had fled to books had suddenly become God's great whispering gallery. He listened with joyous awe and reverence.

The stars had been his guides by night to find the trail. He had merely lifted his eyes to make the reckoning. He had never seen before the crystal flash from their jeweled depths.

He looked into the eyes of the graceful young rider by his side and longed to tell her of this miracle wrought in his soul. But he hesitated. She was too dignified and self-possessed. It would be silly when put into words.

But the world today was too beautiful to hurry through it. He just couldn't.

"Let's stop on this hill and watch the sunset, Miss Sarah?" he suggested.

"I'd love to," was the simple answer.

With a light laugh, she sprang from the saddle. They touched the ground at the same moment.

He looked at her with undisguised admiration.

"You're a wonderful rider," he said.

"A soldier's daughter must be—it's part of her life."

He tied their horses to the low hanging limbs of a cluster of scrub trees, and found a seat on the bowlders which the Indians had set for a landmark on the lonely hilltop.

Westward the plains stretched, a silent ocean of green, luscious grass.

"What's that dark spot in the valley?" the girl eagerly asked.

"Watch it a moment—"

They sat in silence for five minutes.

"Why, it's moving!" she cried.

"Yes."

"How curious—"

"An illusion?" he suggested.

"Nonsense, I'm not dreaming."

"I've been dreaming a lot lately—"

A smile played about the corners of her fine mouth. But she ignored the hint.

"Tell me," she cried; "you studied the sciences at West Point, what does it mean?"

"Look closely. Any fifteen-year-old boy of the plains could explain it."

"Am I so ignorant?" she laughed.

"No," he answered soberly, "our eyes just refuse to see things at which we are looking until the voice within reveals. The eyes of a hunter could make no mistake about such a spot—particularly if it moved."

"It might be a passing cloud—"

"There's none in the sky."

"Tell me!" she pleaded.

"A herd of buffalo."

"That big black field! It must be ten acres—"

The man laughed at her ignorance with a sudden longing in his heart to help and protect her.

"Ten acres! Look again. They are twenty miles away. The herd is packed so densely, the ground is invisible. They cover a thousand acres."

"Impossible—"

"I assure you, it's true. They were once even more plentiful. But we're pushing them back with the Indians into the sunset. And they, too, will fade away into the twilight at last—"

He stopped suddenly. He had almost spoken a sentence that would have committed him beyond retreat. It was just on his lips to say:

"I didn't take such tender views of Indians and buffaloes until I met you!"

For the life of him he couldn't make the girl out. Her voice was music. Her laughter contagious. And yet she was reserved. About her personality hung a spell which forbade familiarity. Flirting was a pastime in the army. But it had never appealed to him. He was not so sure about her when she laughed.

And then her father worried him. The fiery old Southerner had the temper of the devil when roused. He could see that this second daughter was his favorite. He had caught a look of unreasonable anger and jealousy in his eye only that afternoon when they rode away together.

Still he must risk it. He had really suggested this sunset scene for that purpose. The field was his own choosing. Only a coward could run now.

He managed at last to get his lips to work.

"Since you came, Miss Sarah—I've been seeing life at a new angle—" he paused awkwardly.

The red blood mounted to her cheeks.

"You have given me new eyes—"

She turned her head away. There was no mistaking the tremor of his tones. She was too honest to simper and pretend. Her heart was pounding so loudly she wondered if he could hear.

He fumbled nervously with his glove, glanced at her from the corner of his eye, and his voice sank to a whisper:

"I—I love you, Sarah!"

She turned slowly and looked at him through dimmed eyes:

"And I love you—"

She paused, brushed a tear from her cheek, and with sweet reproach quietly added:

"Why didn't you tell me sooner? We've lost so many beautiful days that might have been perfect—"

He suddenly stooped and kissed her full lips.

"We'll not lose any more—"

"The world is beautiful, isn't it, dear!" she said, nestling closer.

"Since I see with your eyes—yes. It was only a place to fight in, before. Now it's a fairy world, and these wild flowers that cover the plains only grow to make a carpet for the feet of the girl I love—"

"A fairy world—yes—" she whispered, "it's been just that to me since I first sang the 'Fairy Bells' for you—"

"I'll never love another song as that," he said reverently.

"Nor I," was the low response. "My heart will beat to its music forever—it just means you, now—"

For a long time they sat without words, holding each other's hand. The sun hung a glowing ball of fire on the rim of the far-away hills, and the shadows of the valley deepened into twilight.

"How wonderful the silence of the plains!" the lover sighed.

"It used to oppress me."

The man nodded.

"And now, I hear the beat of angels' wings and know that God is near—"

"Because we love—" and she laughed for joy.

Again they sat in sweet, brooding silence.

A horseman rode over the hilltop in the glow of the fading sun. From its summit, he lifted his hand and waved a salute. They looked below, and in the doorway of a cabin, a young mother stood, a babe in her arms answering with hand uplifted high above her child.

"What does it matter, dear," she whispered, "a cabin or a palace!"

9: WAR

Side by side through the still white light of the full moon they rode home, in each heart the glow of the wonder and joy of Love's first revelation. Words were an intrusion. The eyes of the soul were seeing now the hidden things of life.

The gleam of the lights at the Fort brought them sharply out of dreamland into the world of fact.

"You must see my father tonight, dear," she said eagerly.

"Must I, tonight?"

"It's best."

"I'd rather face a hundred Red Men in war paint."

A merry laugh was her answer as she leaned close:

"Don't be silly, he likes you."

"But he loves you."

"Of course, and for that reason my happiness will be his."

"God knows, I hope so," was the doleful response. "But if I must, I must. I'll see him."

A quick kiss in the friendly shadows and she was gone.

He walked alone an hour after supper, screwing up his courage to the point of bearding the Colonel in his den. He fumbled the doorbell at last, his heart in his throat.

Old Rough and Ready was not inclined to help him in his embarrassment. Never had he seen the lines of his strong jaw harder or more set than when he grunted:

"Sit down, sir. Don't stand there staring. I'm not on inspection."

The perspiration started on his forehead and he moistened his dry lips.

"I beg your pardon, Colonel. I was a little flustered. I've—a—something—on—my mind—"

"Out with it!"

"I—I—I'm in love with Miss Sarah."

"You don't say?"

"Y-yes, sir."

"Well, it's no news to me. The whole family have been enjoying the affair for some time. I suppose you're asking—or think you're asking—for my daughter's hand in marriage?"

"That's it—yes, sir—exactly."

"I guessed as much. I'm glad to tell you, young man, that I've always had the kindliest feelings for you personally—"

"Thank you, sir—"

"And the warmest admiration for your talents as an officer. You're a good soldier. You have brains. You have executive ability. You're a leader of men. You'll go far in your profession—"

"Thank you, sir—"

"And that's why I don't like you as a son-in-law."

"W—Wha—"

"I love my daughter, and I want her to be happy in a real home with a real husband and children by her side. A soldier's life is a dog's life. I've pitied the poor girl who gave up her home for me. Many a bitter tear has she shed over my absence, in torturing dread of the next letter from the frontier—"

He paused and sprang to his feet:

"A hundred times I've sworn no daughter of mine should ever marry a soldier! The better the soldier, the more reason she should not marry him—"

"But, sir—"

"There's no 'but' about it!" the Colonel thundered. "You're asking me to let you murder my girl, that's all—but it's life. I'll have to give my consent and wish you good luck, long life, and all the happiness you can get out of a soldier's lot."

The Colonel extended his hand and the Lieutenant grasped it with grateful eagerness.

The days that followed were red lettered in the calendar of life.

And then it came—a crash of thunder out of the clear sky—the thing he had somehow felt and dreaded.

A petty court-martial was called to adjust a question of army discipline. The court was composed of Z. Taylor, Colonel Commanding, Major Thomas F. Smith, a fiery-tempered gay officer of the old army, Lieutenant Jefferson Davis, and the new Second Lieutenant who had just arrived from the Jefferson Barracks at St. Louis.

The army regulations required that each officer sitting in court-martial should be in full uniform. The new arrival from St. Louis had come without his uniform. His trunk had miscarried and was returned to the Jefferson Barracks.

He rose with embarrassment:

"I must beg the pardon of the Court, Colonel," he began cautiously, "for not appearing in my uniform. As it is in St. Louis I respectfully ask to be excused today from wearing it."

The old Colonel scowled. It was just like a young fool to wish to sit in solemn judgment on a fellow officer—in his shirt sleeves. If he had asked to be excused from serving on the Court—yes—he could accept his excuse and let him go. But this insolence was unbearable. The Colonel glanced over the Court before putting the question to a vote. Smith was his enemy. Whichever way he voted as President, the Major could be depended on to go against his decision. There was a feud between those two hot-tempered fire-eaters which had lasted for years. He glanced at his future son-in-law with a smile of assured victory. Tom Smith would vote against him, but the trembling youngster who had quailed before him that night asking for his daughter's hand was practically in the family. He smiled at the certainty of downing Smith once more.

In a voice, whose tones left nothing to the imagination of the presumptuous Second Lieutenant, the Colonel growled:

"Gentlemen, we are asked to allow an officer to sit in the formal judgment of a court-martial without uniform—I put the question to a vote and cast mine. No!"

"I vote yes!" shouted the Major.

The Colonel did not condescend to look his way. He knew what that vote was before he heard it. He bent his piercing eyes on his future son-in-law:

"Lieutenant Davis?"

There was just a moment's hesitation. The Lieutenant smiled at his embarrassed young fellow officer and mildly answered:

"I think, Colonel, in view of the distance to St. Louis, we may excuse the young man for the first offense—I vote—yes."

The old Colonel stared at him in speechless amazement. Smith grinned.

The Colonel's face grew purple with rage. He was just able to gasp his words during the progress of the trial. It was brief, and when it ended and the rest had gone, he faced the Lieutenant with blazing eyes:

"How dare you, sir, vote with that damned fool against me?"

"Why, I never thought to hurt you, Colonel—"

"No? And what did you think?"

"I only thought of relieving the evident embarrassment of a young officer—"

"You did, eh?—no thought of me or my feelings, of my wishes. You're a hell of a son-in-law, you are—"

He paused for breath and choked with rage no words could express. When at last his tongue found speech, he swore in oaths more expressive and profound than modern man has ever dreamed. He damned the Court. He damned Tom Smith. He damned the Second Lieutenant. He damned the regiment. He damned the Government that created it. He damned the Indians that called it to the plains. He damned the world and all in it, and all things under it. But, particularly and specifically, he damned the young ass who dared to flaunt his feelings and opinions after smiling in his face at his house, for days and weeks and months.

Finally, facing the blushing Lieutenant, his eyes flashing indignant scorn, he shouted:

"No man who votes with a damned fool like Tom Smith, can marry my daughter!"

"Colonel, I protest," pleaded the heartsick lover.

"I forbid you to ever put your foot inside my quarters again!"

"Colonel—"

"Silence, sir! I forbid you to ever speak to my daughter again!"

"But, Colonel—"

"I repudiate you and all yours. I wipe you from the map. You don't exist. I don't know you. I never knew you. Get out of my sight!"

The tall, slender form slowly straightened and a look of cold pride shot from the depths of his blue eyes. Without a word he turned and left.

10: ROMANCE

Black Hawk was leading his red warriors in a great uprising. A wave of fierce excitement swept the frontier. There was stern work now for men to do and women must wait alone.

The regiment marched to the front. The Colonel as a man was freezingly formal with the Lieutenant. As an officer, he knew his worth and relied on it in every emergency. The State of Illinois had raised two companies of raw recruits to join in subduing the Indians. The Colonel sent his most efficient subordinate to swear in the new soldiers. On the morning of the muster, there appeared before the tall Lieutenant, a man full three inches taller, and famous in his county as the gawkiest, slab-sidest, homeliest, best-natured fellow in the State. He was dressed in a suit of blue jeans.

In slow, pleasing drawl, he announced:

"I am the Captain, of this company—"

And he waved his long arm toward the crowd of his countrymen on the right.

Lieutenant Jefferson Davis promptly administered to Abraham Lincoln his first oath to support the Constitution and laws of the United States.

Two men destined to immortal fame had met and passed with scarcely a glance at each other. The young army officer was too much of a gentleman to mark the ill-fitting blue jeans of the awkward captain of militia. Great events, after all, make men great. Only the eye of God could foresee the coming tragedy in which these two would play their mighty roles.

At the end of the brief struggle on the frontier, Black Hawk's people were scattered to the four winds and the brave old warrior, with a handful of his men, sought Colonel Taylor's command to surrender.

Again, the Colonel sent his most accomplished officer, the Lieutenant whom he had forbidden to enter his house,—to treat with the fallen Chief.

The Lieutenant received with kindly words the broken-hearted warrior, his two sons and sixty braves, and conducted them at once as prisoners of war to the barracks at St. Louis.

The cholera was raging at Rock Island, and on the boat two of the Indian prisoners were seized with the fatal disease. The Lieutenant, at the risk of his life, personally ministered to their needs. The two stricken men made known to the commander in broken words and signs that they had sworn an oath of eternal friendship. In pleading tones the stronger said:

"We beg the good Chief to put us ashore that hand in hand we may go to the happy hunting grounds together."

Near the first little settlement their prayer was granted.

The young officer turned to his boat with a sigh as he saw the red warriors slip their arms about each other and slowly sink to the ground to die alone and unattended.

Old Black Hawk sat in silent, stolid indifference to his fate until the curious settlers began to crowd on the boat and stare at his misery.

The Lieutenant interfered with sharp decision.

"Push those men back, Corporal!" he ordered angrily.

The crowd was roughly pushed back and the Lieutenant took Black Hawk kindly by the arm and led him into a reserved apartment where he was free from vulgar eyes.

The old man's lips tightened. He gazed at the officer steadily and spoke in measured tones:

"The young war Chief treats me with much kindness. He is good and brave. He puts himself in my place and sees all that I suffer. With him I am much pleased."

The Lieutenant bowed and left him under the protection of the guard. Courtesy to a fallen foe in the old days was the first obligation of an officer and a gentleman.

In the autumn, Colonel Taylor again sent his Lieutenant on a distant duty—this time one of peculiar danger. He was ordered to Louisville and Lexington on recruiting service. And the cholera was known to be epidemic but a few miles from Lexington.

The goodbye scene that night at the lovers' trysting place, the little tent reception-room of the McCreas', was long and tender and solemn.

"Oh, I feel dreadful about this trip, dear," his sweetheart kept repeating with pitiful despair that refused to be comforted.

"You must be brave, my own," he answered with a frown. "A soldier's business is to die. I am a soldier. I go where duty calls—"

"To battle—yes—but this black pestilence that comes in the night—I'm afraid—I just can't help it—I'm afraid. I've always had a horror of such things. I've a presentiment that you'll die that way—"

"Presentiments and dreams go by opposites. I'll live to a ripe old age—"

She looked up into his face with a tender smile:

"You think so?"

"Yes, why not?"

"Well—I've something to tell you—"

She paused and the man bent low.

"What?"

"I've made a vow to God—" the voice stopped with a sob—"that if He will only send you safely back to me this time—I'll wait no longer on my father's whim—I am yours—"

The lover clasped her trembling form to his heart.

"Goodbye, dearest," he said at last. "I wish to go with that promise ringing in my soul."

Ten days after he reached Lexington, the cholera broke out, and hundreds fled. He stood by his men, watched their diet, nursed the sick, and buried the dead. He helped the carpenter make the coffins and reverently bore the victims to their graves. No fear was in his soul. Love was chanting the anthem of Life.

A strange new light was burning in the eyes of the woman he loved on the day he returned in safety.

She seized his hand and spoke with decision:

"Come with me."

Her father was standing at the gate. She faced him, holding defiantly the hand of her lover.

The old man saw and understood. His jaw was set with sullen determination and his face hardened.

"We have waited two long years," she began softly. "We have been patient and hopeful, but you have given no sign. My lover's character is beyond reproach, and I am proud of him. I am sorry to cross you, Father, but I've made up my mind, I am going to marry him now."

The Colonel turned in silence and slowly walked into the house.

Captain McCrea engaged a stateroom for her on the boat for Louisville.

The lovers planned to meet at her aunt's, the Colonel's oldest sister. The tearful good-bys had been said to Mother and sisters and brother.

The Colonel had not spoken, but he had business on the boat before she cast her lines from the shore.

The daughter drew him into her stateroom and slipped her arms around his neck. Few words were spoken and they were broken.

"Please, Father—please?—I love you—please—"

"No."

"I'm no longer a child. I'm a woman. You're a real man and you know I could have no respect for myself if I should yield my life's happiness to a whim—"

The old Colonel stroked her shoulder:

"I understand. You're a chip off the old block. You're just as stubborn as I am. And—I—won't—eat—my—words."

With firm hand, he drew away and hurried from the boat.

The Taylor clan of Kentucky gathered for the wedding in force. The romance appealed to their fancy. They loved their high-spirited, self-poised little kinswoman and they liked the tall, modest, young officer she had chosen for her husband. The stern old Colonel was not there, but his brother and his three sisters and all their tribe made merry at the wedding feast.

On the deck of the lazy river steamer, the bride and groom slowly drifted down the moonlit shimmering way to the fields of Mississippi.

The bride nestled close to her lover's side in the long sweet silences too deep for words.

He took her hand in his at last, and said tenderly:

"I've something very important to tell you now, my dear—"

"I'm not afraid—"

"You trust me implicitly?"

"Perfectly—"

"You have given up all for me," he went on evenly, "I'll show your father what I can do for you—"

"You love me—it's enough."

"No. I have resigned my commission in the army. I have given up my career. We'll live only for each other now and build our nest in the far sunny South beyond the frost line."

A little smothered cry was her answer. And then her head slowly sank with a sob on his breast.

11: THE FAIRY BELLS

They built their home on the banks of the great river where the tide sweeps in graceful curve, all but completing the circle of an enchanted isle.

From the little flower-veiled porch through festoons of lacing boughs gleamed the waters of the huge curved mirror held by Nature's hand. The music from the decks of the steamers floated up on the soft air until music and perfume of flowers seemed one.

In the cool of the morning, on swift, high-bred horses, they rode side by side along the river's towering bluff and laughed in sheer joy at their foolish happiness. In the waning afternoon, hand in hand, they walked the sunlit fields and paused at dusk to hear the songs of slaves. The happiness of lovers is contagious. It sets the hearts of slaves to singing.

In the white solemn splendor of the Southern moon they strolled through enchanted paths of scented roses. On the rustic seat beneath a magnolia in full second bloom they listened to the song of a mockingbird whose mate had built her nest in the rose trellis beside their door. They could count the beat of his bird heart night after night as he sang the glory of his love and the beauty of his coming brood of young.

"You are happy, dearest?" the lover sighed.

"In heaven,—I am with you."

"And it shall be forever."

"Forever!"

"The old life of blood and strife—it seems an ugly dream."

"Except for the sweet days when you were near."

"This only is life, my own, to hold your hand, and walk the way together, to build, not to destroy, to make flowers bloom, birds and slaves sing, to create, not kill—production is communion with God. We live now in His peace that passeth understanding!"

A long silence followed. An owl in a distant tree top gave a shrill plaintive cry. The bride nestled closer and he felt her shiver.

"You are chill, dearest?" he murmured.

"Just a little."

"We're forgetting the late August night winds—"

"No—no—it's nothing—I'm just a wee bit afraid of an owl, that's all."

A dark figure slowly approached and stood with uncovered head.

"What is it, James?" the master asked.

"It's too late, sir, for you and the mistis to be out in dis air—it's chill an' fever time—"

"Thank you, James—we'll go in at once."

When the faithful footfall had died away, the lover lifted his bride in his arms and carried her in, while she softly laughed and clung to his strong young shoulders.

It came with swift, sure tread, the silent white figure of the Pestilence that walks in Tropic Splendor.

The lover laughed the doctor's fears to scorn and the old man was brave and cheerful in the presence of youth and happiness.

James Pemberton followed him to the gate and held his horse's bridle with a tremor in his black hand.

"You don't think, doctor—" he paused, afraid to say the thing—"you don't think my young mistis gwine ter die?"

"She's very ill, Jim—it's an even fight for life."

"Ef she do—hit'll kill my young marster—"

"Soldiers can't die that way—no—"

"Yassah—but dey ain't been married but three months, sah, an' he des worship de very groun' her little foot walks on—she des can't die—she too young an' putty, sah—hit des natchally can't be—"

The doctor's gray head slowly moved as if in remembrance of tragic scenes.

"Death loves a shining mark sometimes!"

He turned to the slave in tones of warning:

"Watch your master closely—"

"My marster—sah!"

"He'll go down next—"

"Yassah—yassah!"

Two days later, the strong man collapsed with a crash that took even the experienced old doctor by surprise. An iron will had bent over the bedside of his bride and fought with grim defiance the battle with unseen foe until the last ounce of strength had gone.

In his delirium they moved him to another room and he awoke to find himself in a prison cell on a desert island a thousand miles from the mate he adored.

He watched his jailers and at last his hour came. The tired guard beside his prison pallet slept. With fevered stealth he rose and with the strength of a giant, bent the bars of his cage and crawled and fought his way over hill and valley, rocks and mountains, back to the bedside of his beloved.

He paused in rapture at the door. She was sitting up in bed, the pillows propped behind her back, singing their favorite song—"Fairy Bells." How soft and weirdly sweet her voice—its notes so far away and plaintive—never had she sung so divinely!

He held his breath lest a word or quiver of its melody should be lost. And then he slipped his strong arms about her and looked into her eyes shining with unearthly beauty.

"You have come at last, my own!" she sighed. "I knew the Bells would call you—"

"Yes—dearest—and I'll never leave you again—they took me away a wounded prisoner of war—but I broke the bars and came when I heard you call—"

"Look," she whispered, pointing with the slender blue-veined finger, "there she is, in the doorway again with her baby in her arms, waving at sunset to her lover on the hill?—what does it matter, a cabin or a palace!"

The shining eyes grew dim, the figure drooped, and a wild piteous cry came from the lover's fevered lips:

"Lord God of Love and Pity— she's dying!— Help— Help— Help!"

His faithful servant, worn with watching day and night, heard the cry, rushed to his side and caught his fainting form, as the light of the world faded.

12: TRUTH

They nursed him slowly back into life again, the loving heart of the older brother guiding the arm of his faithful slave.

He refused to live at first.

"It's no use, Joe," he cried with bitter despair. "Life isn't worth the struggle any more. I'm tired, I just want to rest—by her side—that's all."

"I know, Boy, how you feel. But you must live. Duty calls. Great events are stirring the world. You've a man's part to play—"

"I won't play it. I'm done with ambition. I'm done with strife. The game's not worth the candle. I've lived the only life worth living, and it's finished."

Little by little, each day, the brother slowly rebuilt in the stricken soul the will to live. Before he was able to walk, he lifted the frail form in his arms, carried him into his big library, and seated him in an arm-chair before a fire of glowing logs.

With a sweep of his arm about the room toward the crowded shelves he began in earnest tones:

"You're going to live with me now, Boy. We love each other with the love of strong men. I need your help and companionship in my study. You had the advantage of a college career—I didn't. We'll master here these records of the world's life. We'll seek wisdom in the history and experience of man. What do you know of the treasures buried in those big volumes? Our young men go to school and plunge into life with a mere smattering. Do you know the history of your own country, how it was discovered, how its colonies grew, how its battles were fought against overwhelming and impossible odds? How its great Constitution grew in the hands of inspired leaders, who builded better than they knew a chart for the guidance of man. Do you know the history of the mind of man? Do you know the story of those ragged bleeding feet—of the great thinkers of the ages who have found the path of truth through blood and tears and then walked its way to the stake, to the block and the gallows? Come with me into the big world of the past—read, study, think, and gird yourself with power! We're just entering on the struggle that means life or death to our Republic. I believe as I believe in God, that we have set a beacon light on the shores of the world that will guide the human race to its mightiest achievements—unless we fail to keep its lantern trimmed and bright.

"The poison of indolence is in our blood—the tendency to centralized tyranny. We are but a few years removed from its curse. As we grow in years, the temptation to make Washington the gilded Capital of an Empire becomes more and more apparent. Unless we control this tendency to lapse into the past, we are lost and the story of our fallen Republic will be but one more added to the failures of history. Unless we can preserve the sovereignty of our States, the Union will become an Empire, not a Republic of republics. It's a difficult thing for men to govern themselves, though they can do it better than anyone else has ever done it for them. We are making this wonderful experiment here in the new world. The fate of unborn millions hangs on its success. You're done with self and self-seeking. Ambition is a dream that is passed. Good! Lay your life in unselfish sacrifice on the altar of your country. Only the man who has given up ambition is fit for great leadership. He alone dares to seek and know and speak the Truth!"

The tired spirit rose with a new view of human life, its aim and purpose. For eight years he buried himself in the library on his brother's estate. Through the long winter nights the two brilliant minds fought over in friendly contests the battles of the ages until the passion for Truth grew into the one purpose of a great soul.

When the first rumblings of the storm that was to shake a continent broke over the Republic, he stepped forth to take his place in the world of action—the best equipped, most thoroughly trained, most perfectly poised man who had ever entered the arena of American politics.

His rise was brilliant and unprecedented. In his first contest he met the foremost orator of the age, Sergeant Prentiss, and vanquished him on his own ground. In two years he took his seat in Congress, the favorite son of Mississippi.

He had scarcely begun his career, as a lawmaker, when war was declared against Mexico. He resigned his high office, raised a regiment and once more found himself a soldier under the orders of stern old Zachary Taylor.

On his first battle field at the head of his Mississippi regiment, he planted the flag of the Republic on the Grand Plaza of Monterey. And in the supreme crisis of the battle of Buena Vista, with the blood streaming from his wounds, he led his men in a charge against overwhelming odds, turned the tide from defeat to victory and gave the Presidency to the man who had denied to him his daughter's hand.

He hobbled back on crutches to his brother's home in Mississippi amid the shouts and frenzied acclaim of a proud and grateful people. Within three years from the day he entered public life, he took his seat in the Senate Chamber of the United States beside Clay, Calhoun and Webster, the peer of any man within its walls, and with the conscious power of Knowledge and Truth, girded himself for the coming struggle of giants.

The Story

1: THE CURTAIN RISES

"For the Lord's sake, Jennie—"

Dick Welford paused at the bottom of a range of steps which wound up the capitol hill from Pennsylvania Avenue.

The girl standing at the top stamped her foot imperiously.

"Hurry—hurry!"

"I won't—"

"Then I'll leave you!"

The boy laughed.

"You don't dare. It's barely sunup—still dark in spots—the boogers'll get you—"

With a grin he deliberately sat down.

"Dick Welford, you're the laziest white man I ever saw in my life—We won't get a seat, I tell you—"

"We can stand up."

"We won't even get our noses in the door—"

"You don't think these old Senators get up at daylight, do you?"

"They didn't go to bed last night—"

"I'll bet they didn't!" Dick laughed.

"I know one that didn't anyhow—"

"Who?"

"Senator Davis."

"How do you know?"

"Spent the night there. Father stayed so late, Mrs. Davis put me to bed. Regular procession all night long! And among his visitors the Blackest Republican of them all—"

"Old Abe run over from Illinois to say goodbye?"

"No, but his right hand man Seward did—"

"Sly old snuff-dipping hypocrite—"

"Anyhow, he's the brains of his party."

"And he called on Jeff Davis last night?"

"Not the first time either. Mrs. Davis told me that when the Senator was so ill with neuralgia and came near losing his sight, Seward came every day, sat in the darkened room and talked for hours to his enemy—"

"That's because he's a Black Republican. Their ways are dark. They like rooms with the shades pulled down—"

"Anyhow he likes Mr. Davis."

"Well, it's goodbye to the old Union—how many Senators are going today?"

"Yulee and Mallory from Florida, Clay and Fitzpatrick from Alabama and Senator Davis—"

"All in a day?"

"Yes—"

"Jennie, they'll talk their heads off. It'll be three o'clock before the first one finishes. We'll die. Let's go to Mt. Vernon—"

"Dick Welford, I'm ashamed of you. You've no patriotism at all—"

"And I just proposed a pilgrimage to the home of George Washington!"

"You don't care what happens in the Senate Chamber today—"

"No—I don't."

The boy's lazy figure slowly rose, mounted the steps, paused and looked down into the tense eager young face.

"You really want to know," he began slowly, "why speaking tires me now?"

"Yes—why?"

"Because it's a waste of breath—we're going to fight!"

The girl flushed with excitement.

"Who told you? What have you heard? Who said so?"

A dreamy look in the boy's eyes deepened.

"Nobody's told me. I just know. It's in the air. A wild duck knows when to go north. A bluebird knows when to move south. It's in the air. That's the way I know—" his voice dropped. "Let's go to Mt. Vernon and spend the day, Jennie—"

The girl looked up sharply. The low persuasive tones were unmistakable.

The faintest flush mantled her cheeks.

"No—I wouldn't miss those speeches for anything. You promised to take me to the Senate gallery. Come on."

With a quick bound the boy scaled the next flight of steps and looked down at her laughing:

"All right, why don't you come on!"

With a frown she sprang up the stone stairs and he caught her step with a sudden military salute. They walked in silence for a few minutes.

"What's the matter with you today, Dick Welford?"

"Why, Miss Jennie Barton?"

"I never saw you quite so foolish."

"Maybe it's because I never saw you quite so pretty—"

The little figure stiffened with dignity.

"That will do now, sir—"

"Yessum!"

She threw him a look of quiet scorn as they picked their way through the piles of building material for the unfinished dome of the Capitol and mounted the steps.

Barely half past seven o'clock and the crowds were pouring into the Senate Chamber, its cloak rooms and galleries. Within thirty minutes after they had found seats opposite the diplomatic gallery every inch of space in the great hall was jammed and packed.

Southern women and their escorts outnumbered the others five to one. The Southern wing of official Washington was out in force.

The tense electric atmosphere was oppressive.

The men and women whose eager anxious faces looked down on the circular rows of senatorial chairs and desks were painfully conscious that they were witnessing the final scene of a great historical era.

What the future might hold God alone could know. Their fathers had dreamed a beautiful dream—"E Pluribus Unum"—one out of many. The Union had yet to be realized as an historical fact. The discordant elements out of which our Constitution had been strangely wrought had fought their way at last into two irreconcilable hostile sections, the very structure of whose civilization rested on antagonistic conceptions of life and government.

The Northern Senators were in their seats with grave faces long before the last straggling Southerner picked his way into the Chamber bowing and smiling and apologizing to the ladies on whose richly embroidered dresses he must step or give up the journey.

For weeks the pretense of polite formalities between parties had been unconsciously dropped. Men no longer bowed and smirked and passed the time of day with shallow words.

With heads erect, they glanced at each other and passed on. And if they spoke, it was with taunt, insult and challenge.

Jennie's keen eyes rested on two vacant chairs on the floor of the Senate—every seat was crowded save these two.

She pressed Dick's arm.

"See—the vacant seats of South Carolina!"

"They're not vacant," the boy drawled.

"They are—look—"

"I see a white figure in each—"

"Nonsense!"

"We're going to have war, I tell you! Death sits in those chairs today, Jennie—"

"Sh—don't talk like that—"

The boy laughed.

"I'm not afraid, you know—just a sort of second sight—maybe it means I'll be killed—"

* * * * *

South Carolina had felt no forebodings on the day her Convention had recalled those Senators. Kiett the eloquent leader of the Convention sprang to his feet, his face flaming with passion that was half delirium as he shouted:

"This day is the culmination of long years of bitterness, of suffering and of struggle. We are performing a great deed, which holds in its magic not only the stirring present, it embraces the ages yet to come. I am content with what has been done today. I shall be content with it tomorrow. We have lowered the body of the old Union to its last resting place. We drop the flag over its grave."

When the vote was announced, without a single dissenting voice, the crowd rose to their feet with a shout of applause which shook the building to its foundations. It died away at last only to rise again with redoubled fury.

Alabama, Mississippi, Georgia and Florida had followed in rapid succession, Louisiana's Convention was to meet on the twenty-sixth, Texas on February first. On this the twenty-first day of January the Senators from Florida, Mississippi and Alabama had announced their farewell addresses to the Old Union.

The girl's eyes swept the crowded tiers of the galleries packed with beautifully gowned Southern women. Every glove, fan, handkerchief, bonnet or dress—every dainty stocking and filmy piece of lingerie had been imported direct from the fashion centers of Europe. Gowns of priceless lace and velvets had been woven to order in the looms of Genoa, Venice and Brussels.

The South was rich.

And yet not one of her representatives held his office in Washington because of his money. Her ruling classes were without exception an aristocracy of brains—yet they were distinctly an aristocracy.

The election of Abraham Lincoln was more than a threat to confiscate three thousand millions of dollars which the South had invested in slaves. The homely rail splitter from the West was the prophecy of a new social order which threatened the foundations of the modern world. He himself was all unconscious of this fact. And yet this big reality was the secret of the electric tension which strangled men into silence and threw over the scene the sense of ominous foreboding.

The debates in Congress during the tempestuous session had been utterly insincere and without meaning. The real leaders knew that the time for discussion had passed. Two absolutely irreconcilable moral principles had clashed and the Republic was squarely and hopelessly broken into two vast sectional divisions on the issue.

Beyond the fierce and uncompromising hatred of Slavery which had grown into a consuming passion throughout the North and had resulted in the election of Lincoln as a purely sectional candidate—behind and underneath this apparent moral rage lay a bigger and far more elemental fact—the growing consciousness of the laboring man that the earth and the fullness thereof were his.

And bigger than the fear of the confiscation of their property and the destruction of the Constitution their fathers had created loomed before the Southern mind the Specter of a new democracy at the touch of whose fetid breath the soul of culture and refinement they believed must die. In the vulgar ranks of this democracy must march sooner or later four million negroes but yesterday from the jungles of Africa.

This greater issue was felt but dimly by the leaders on either side but it was realized with sufficient clearness to make compromise impossible.

In vain did the aged and the feeble plead once more for compromise. Real men no longer wished it.

The day of reckoning had come. The seeds of this tragedy were planted in the foundation structure of the Republic.

The Union of our fathers, for all the high-sounding phrases of its Declaration of Independence was not a democracy. It was from the beginning an aristocratic republic founded squarely on African Slavery.

And the degraded position assigned to the man who labored with his hands was recognized in our organic law.

The Constitution itself was the work of a rich and powerful group of leaders in each State, and its provisions were a compromise of conflicting sectional property interests.

The world had moved from 1789 to 1861.

The North was unconsciously lifting the banner of a mighty revolution. The South was clinging with the desperation of despair to the faith of its fathers.

The North was the world of steam and electricity, of new ideas, of progress. The South still believed in the divine inspiration of the men who founded the Republic. They must believe in it, for their racial life depended on it. Four million negroes could not be loosed among five million Southern white people and two such races live side by side under the principles of a pure democracy. Had this issue been put to them in the beginning not one Southern State would have entered the Union.

The Northern workingman, with steam and electricity bringing North and South into closer and closer touch, answered this cry of fear from the South with the ultimatum of democracy:

"This Nation cannot endure half slave and half free!"

Back of all the mouthings of demagogues and the billingsgate of sectionalists lay this elemental fact—a democracy against a republic.

Nor could the sword of the Sections settle such an issue. The sectional sword could only settle an issue which grew out of it— whether a group of States holding a common interest in this conflict of principles could combine for their own peace and safety, leave the old Union, form a new one and settle it in their own way.

The North said no—the South said yes. This conviction bigger than party platforms was the brooding terror which brought the sense of tragedy to young and old, the learned and the unlearned—that made young men see visions and maids dream of mighty deeds.

* * * * *

The Southern boy's eyes had again rested on the vacant chairs of the Senators from South Carolina with a set look in their depths.

The crowd turned with sudden stir to the door of the Senate Chamber.

"Look," Jennie cried, "that's Mrs. Clem Clay of Alabama—how pale and beautiful she is! The Senator's going to make the speech of his life today. She's scared—Ah, that dress, that dress—isn't it a dream? Did you ever see such a piece of velvet—and—do look at that dear little gold hand holding the skirt up just high enough to see the exquisite lace on her petticoat—"

"Where's the golden hand—I don't see it?" Dick broke in skeptically.

"Don't you see the chain hanging from her waist?"

"Yes, I see that."

"Follow it with your eye and you'll see the hand. The Bayard sisters introduced them from Paris, you know."

The boy had ceased to listen to Jennie's chatter. His eye had suddenly rested on a group of three men seated in the diplomatic gallery—one evidently of high official position by the deference paid him. The man on the left of the official was young, handsome, slender, and pulled the corners of his mustache with a slow lazy touch of his graceful hand. His eyes were fixed on Jennie with a steady gaze. The Minister from Sardinia, of the Court of Victor Emmanuel, sat on the right, bowing and gesticulating with an enthusiasm out of all proportion to the importance of the conversation.

Behind this group sat a fourth man who leaned forward occasionally and whispered to the official. His face was in shadow and the only thing Dick could see was the thick dark brown beard which covered his regular features and a pair of piercing black eyes.

"For heaven's sake, Jennie," the boy cried at last, "who is that villain in the Diplomatic gallery?"

"Where?"

"In the corner there on the right."

"Oh, that's the Sardinian Minister—King Victor Emmanuel's new drummer of trade for Genoa. He's getting ahead of the French, too."

"No—no, I don't mean that little rat. I mean the big fellow with the heavy jaw and a face like a rattlesnake. He's trying to charm you too."

Jennie laughed.

"Silly! That's the new Secretary of War, Joseph Holt."

"A scoundrel, if God ever made one—"

"Because he looks at me?"

"No—that shows his good taste. It's the way he looks at you and moves his crooked mouth and the way he bends his big flat head forward."

"Rubbish—he's a loyal Southerner—and if we have to fight he'll be with us."

"Yes—he—will!"

"Of course, he will. He's careful now. He's in old Buck's cabinet. Wait and see. He called on Mr. Davis last night."

"That's nothing—so did old Seward—"

"Different—Seward's a Black Republican from New York—Holt's a Southern Democrat from Mississippi."

"And who's the young knight by his side with the dear little mustache to which he seems so attached?"

Jennie looked in silence for a moment.

"I never saw him before. He's handsome, isn't he?"

"Looks to me like a young black snake just shed his skin waiting for that old adder to show him how to strike."

"Dick—"

"God save the Queen! They're coming here—they're coming for you—"

The Secretary of War had nodded in recognition of Jennie, risen suddenly, and moved toward the gallery exit with his slender companion.

"Nonsense, Dick—he only bowed because he saw me staring—"

"He's bringing that mustache to meet you—"

The boy turned with a scowl toward the door of their gallery and saw the Secretary of War slowly making his way through the crowd to their seats.

"I told you so—"

Jennie blushed and smiled in friendly response to the Secretary's awkward effort at Southern politeness.

"Miss Barton, may I ask a little favor of you?"

"Certainly, Mr. Holt. Allow me to introduce my friend, Mr. Welford of Virginia."

The Secretary bowed stiffly and Dick nodded his head with indifference.

"The Italian Minister with whom I've just been talking wishes the honor of an introduction for his Secretary. Miss Jennie, will you meet him?"

"Certainly—"

"He's looking forward to the possible new Empire of the South," Holt whispered, "and proposes at an early day to forestall the French—"

Dick threw him a look of scorn as he returned to the door and rose with a scowl.

"I'll go out and get fresh air."

"Don't go—"

"I can't breathe in here. Two's company and three's a crowd."

She seized his arm:

"Please sit down, Dick."

"I'll be back directly—"

In spite of her protest he bounded up the steps of the gallery, turned sharply to the right, avoided the intruders and disappeared in the crowd.

The Secretary of War bowed again:

"Miss Barton, permit me to introduce to you Signor Henrico Socola, Secretary to His Excellency, the Minister of Sardinia."

The slender figure bent low with an easy grace.

"Pleased to meet you, Signor Socola," Jennie responded, lifting the heavy lashes from her lustrous brown eyes with the slightest challenge to his.

"The pleasure is all mine, Mad'moiselle," he gravely replied.

"You'll excuse me now if I hurry on?" the Secretary said, again bowing and disappearing in the crowd.

"Mr. Holt tells me, Miss Barton, that you know every Senator on the floor."

"Yes. My father has been in Congress and the Senate for twenty years."

"You'll explain the drama to me today when the curtain rises?"

"If I can."

"I'll be so much obliged—" he paused and the even white teeth smiled pleasantly. "I'm pretty well up on American history but confess a little puzzled today. Your Southern Senators are really going to surrender their power here without a struggle?"

"What do you mean?" the girl asked with a slight frown.

"That your Democratic party has still a majority in both the House and the Senate. If the Southern members simply sit still in their places, the incoming administration of Abraham Lincoln will be absolutely powerless. The new President cannot even call a cabinet to his side without their consent."

"The North has elected their President," Jennie answered with decision.

"The South scorns to stoop to the dishonor of cheating them out of it. They've won the election. They can have it. The South will go and build a government of her own—as we built this one—"

"And fight twenty-three million people of the North?"

"If forced to—yes!"

"With the certainty of an uprising of your slaves at home?"

Jennie laughed.

"Our slaves would fight for us if we'd let them—"

A curious smile twitched the lips of the Italian.

"You speak with great confidence, Miss Barton!"

"Yes. I know what I'm talking about."

The keen eyes watched her from the shadows of the straight thick brows.

"And your Senators who took a solemn oath in entering this Chamber to support the Constitution will leave their seats in violation of that oath?"

The Southern girl flushed, turned with quick purpose to answer, laughed and said with winning frankness:

"You don't mind if I give you my father's answer in his own words? I know them by heart—"

"By all means."

"An oath to support the Constitution of the United States does not bind the man who takes it to support an administration elected by a mob whose purpose is to subvert the Constitution!"

"Oh,—I see," was the quiet response.

"You speak English with perfection, Signor!" Jennie said with a smile.

"Yes, Mad'moiselle, I've spent my life in the Diplomatic service."

He bowed gravely, lifted his head and caught the smile on the lips of the Secretary of War standing in the shadows of the doorway of the Diplomatic gallery.

The stately figure of John C. Breckinridge, the Vice-President, suddenly mounted the dais and his piercing eyes swept the assembly. He rapped for order and the silence which followed was as the hush of death.

"The curtain rises on our drama, Mad'moiselle," the smooth even voice said.

"Sh!" the girl whispered.

2: THE PARTING

The breathless galleries leaned forward to catch the slightest sound from the arena below.

One by one the Senators from the seceding Southern States rose and renounced their allegiance to the United States in obedience to the voice of their people.

With each solemn exit the women of the galleries grew hysterical, waved their perfumed handkerchiefs and shouted their approval with cries of sympathy and admiration.

David Yulee, Stephen K. Mallory and Benjamin Fitzpatrick had each closed his portfolio and with slow measured tread marched down the crowded aisle and out of the Chamber never again to enter its doors.

All eyes were focused now on the brilliant young Senator from Alabama, Clement C. Clay, Jr. It was understood that he had prepared an eloquent defense of his action and would voice the passionate feeling of the masses of the Southern people in this his last utterance in the crumbling temple of the old Republic.

He rose in his place, lifted his strong head with its leonine locks and broad, high forehead, paused a moment and began his speech in the clear steady tones of the trained orator, master of himself, his theme and his audience. The Northern Senators met his gaze with scorn and he answered with a look of bold defiance.

The formal announcement of the secession of his State he made in brief sharp sentences and plunged at once into the reasons for their solemn act.

"Forty-two years ago, Alabama was admitted into the Union," he declared in ringing tones. "She entered it as she goes out, with the Republic convulsed by the hostility of the North to her domestic institutions. Not a decade has passed, not a year has elapsed since her birth as a State that has not been marked by the steady and insolent growth of the mob violence of the North which has demanded the confiscation of her property and the destruction of the foundations of her civilization.

"Who are the leaders of these mobs who seek thus to overthrow the Constitution? Who are these hypocrites who claim the championship of freedom and the moral leadership of the world?

"The men who sold their own slaves to us because they could not use them with profit in a northern climate; the men who built and manned every American slave ship that ever sailed the seas; the sons of old Peter Faneuil of Boston who built Faneuil Hall, their cradle of liberty, out of the profits of slave ships whose trade the Southern people had forbidden by law; the men who have flooded Congress for two generations with petitions to dissolve the Union; the men who threatened to secede with the addition of every foot of territory we have added to our Republic!

"These are the men who have denied to the manhood of the South Christian Communion because they could not endure what they have been pleased to style the moral leprosy of Slavery! These are the men who refuse us permission to sojourn or even pass through the sacred precincts of a Northern State and dare to carry our servants with us. These are the men who deny to the South equal rights in the lands of the West bought by Southern blood and brains and added to our inheritance against their furious protests. These are the men who burn the sacred charters of American Liberty in their public squares, and inscribe on their banners the foul motto:

"'The Constitution is an agreement with Death, a covenant with Hell.'

"These are the men who dare to call us traitors! These are the men who have deliberately passed laws in fourteen Northern States nullifying the provisions of the Constitution of the Union which they have sworn to defend and enforce—"

The speaker paused and lifted high above his head a little morocco bound volume.

"Here in the presence of Almighty God—the God of our fathers, and these witnesses, I read its solemn provisions which the laws of fourteen Northern States have brazenly and openly defied!"

He opened the little book and slowly read:

"Article 4, Section 2.

"No person held to service of labor in one State, under the laws thereof, escaping into another, shall in consequence of any law or regulation therein, be discharged from such service or labor—but shall be delivered up on claim of the party to whom such service or labor may be due.'"

He turned suddenly to the Northern Senators:

"Your States have not only repudiated the Constitution you have sworn to uphold, but your emissaries have invaded the peaceful South and sought to lay it waste with fire and sword and servile insurrection. You have murdered Southern men who have dared demand their rights on Northern soil. You have invaded the borders of Southern States, burned their dwellings and murdered their people. You have proclaimed John Brown, the criminal maniac who sought to murder innocent and helpless men, women and children in Virginia, a hero and martyr and then denounced us in your popular meetings, your religious and legislative assemblies as habitual violators of the laws of God and the rights of humanity! You have exerted all the moral and physical agencies that human ingenuity can devise or a devil's malice employ to heap odium and infamy upon us and make the very name of the South a by-word of hissing and of scorn throughout the civilized world—"

He paused overcome with emotion and lifted his hand to stay the burst of applause from the galleries.

"We have borne all this for long years and might have borne it many more under the assurance of our Northern friends that such fanaticism does not represent the true heart of the Northern people. But the fallacy of these promises and the folly of our hopes have been too clearly proven in the late election. The platform of the political party on which you have swept every Northern State and elected a sectional President is a foul libel upon our character and a declaration of open war on the lives and property of the Southern people.

"In defiance of the Constitution which protects our rights your mob has decreed the confiscation of three thousand million dollars' worth of our property. If we claim the protection of our common law, your mob solemnly burns the Constitution in your public squares and denounces it as 'an agreement with Death and covenant with Hell.' We appeal to the Supreme Court of the Republic and when its Judges unanimously sustain our position on every point, your mob cries:

"'Down with the Supreme Court of the United States!'

"You have not only insulted us as unchristian and heathen, you have proclaimed that four million ignorant negroes but yesterday taken from the savagery of cannibal Africa are our equals and entitled to share in the solemn rights of American citizenship. Your declaration is an open summons that they rise in insurrection with the knife in one hand and the torch in the other.

"Your mob has declared the South outlawed, branded with ignominy, consigned to execration and ultimate destruction. Your mob has decreed the death of Slavery and sends the new President to execute their decree.

"All right—kill Slavery and then what? Kill Slavery and what will you do with its corpse? Who shall deliver us from the body of this death? We are not leaving this Hall to fight for the Institution of African Slavery. The grim specter of a degraded and mongrel citizenship which lies back of your mob's program of confiscation is the force that is driving the Southern people out of the Union to find peace and safety. Whatever may be the sins of Slavery in the South they are as nothing when compared to the degradation of your life which must follow their violent emancipation. The Southern white man is slowly lifting the African out of barbarism into the light of Christian civilization. In our own good time we will emancipate him and start him on a new life beyond the boundaries of our Republic. Whatever may be the differences of opinion in the South on the institution of slavery—there is no difference and there has never been on one point—it was true yesterday—it is true today—it will be true tomorrow—Slavery is the only modus vivendi by which two such races as the Negro and the Aryan can live side by side in a free democracy with equality the law of its life—"

Again a burst of tumultuous applause swept the gallery.

"The issue is clear cut and terrible in its simplicity—the South stands on the faith of our fathers who created this Republic. The South stands for Constitutional freedom under the forms of established law. The North has lifted the red flag of revolution and proclaims the irresponsible despotism of an enthroned mob!

"For a generation your school mistresses have been training your boys to hate us and arming them to fight us. Make no mistake about this movement today. We who go are but the servants of those who sent us. They now recall their ambassadors, and we obey their sovereign will. Make no mistake about it. They are not a brave and rash people, deluded by bad men, who are attempting in an illegal way to wreck the Union. They seek peace and safety outside driven by the Rebellion against Law and Order within.

"Are we more or less than men? Can we love our enemies and bless them that curse and revile us? Are we devoid of the sensibilities, the sentiments, the passions, the reason, and the instincts of mankind? Have we no pride, no honor, no sense of shame, no reverence for our ancestors, no care for posterity, no love for home, or family or friends? Must we quail before the onion breath of an enthroned mob, confess our baseness, discredit the fame of our sires, degrade our children, abandon our homes, flee from our country and dishonor ourselves—all for the sake of a Union whose Constitution you have publicly burned and whose Supreme Court you have spit upon?

"Shall we consent to live under an administration controlled by those who not only deny us justice and equality and brand us as infamous, but boldly proclaim their purpose to rob us of our property and destroy our civilization?

"The freemen of Alabama have proclaimed to the world they will not. In their sovereign power they have recalled me. As their servant I go!"

With a wave of his hand in an imperious gesture of defiance to the silent Senators of the North, amid a scene of unparalleled passion, the speaker turned to his seat, gathered his books and papers and strode with quick firm step down the aisle.

Jennie had leaped to her feet and stood clapping her hands in a frenzy of excitement, unconscious of the existence of the strangely quiet young man by her side.

He rose and stood smiling into her flushed face as she gasped:

"A wonderful speech—wasn't it?"

"They say the South has never lacked audacity, Miss Barton. I'm wondering if they are really going to make good such words with deeds."

He spoke with a cold detachment that chilled and angered the impulsive girl. A hot answer was on her lips when she remembered suddenly that he was a foreigner.

"Of course, Signor, you cannot understand our feelings!"

"On the other hand, I assure you, I do—I'm just wondering in a cold intellectual way whether the oratorical temperament—the temperament of passion, of righteous wrath of the explosive type which we have just witnessed, will win in the trial by fire which war will bring—"

"You doubt our courage?" she interrupted, with a slight curve of the proud little lips.

"Far from it—I assure you! I'm only wondering if it has the sullen, dogged, staying qualities these stolid Northern men down there have exhibited while they listened—"

The girl threw him a quick surprised look and he stopped. His voice had unconsciously taken the tones of a soliloquy.

"I beg your pardon, Miss Barton," he said, with sudden swing to the polite tones of society. "I'm annoying you with my foreign speculations—"

A sudden murmur swept the galleries and all eyes were turned on the tall slender figure of Jefferson Davis as he slowly entered the Senate Chamber.

"Who is it?" Socola asked.

"Senator Davis—you don't know him?"

"I have never seen him before. He has been quite ill I hear."

"Yes. He's been in bed for the past week suffering agonies from neuralgia. He lost the sight of one of his eyes from chronic pain caused by exposure in the service of his country in the northwest."

"Really—I didn't know that."

"He was compelled to remain in a darkened room for months the past year to save the sight of his remaining eye."

"That accounts for my not having seen him before."

Socola followed the straight military figure with painful interest as he slowly moved toward his seat greeting with evident weakness his colleagues as he passed. He was astonished beyond measure at the personality of the famous leader of the "Southern Conspirators" of whom he had heard so much. He was the last man in all the crowd he would have singled out for such a role. The face was too refined, too spiritual, too purely intellectual for the man of revolution. His high forehead, straight nose, thin compressed lips and pointed chin belonged to the poet and dreamer rather than the man of action. The hollow cheek bones and deeply furrowed mouth told of suffering so acute the sympathy of every observer was instantly won.

In spite of evident suffering his carriage was erect, dignified, and graceful. The one trait which fastened the attention from the first and held it was the remarkable intensity of expression which clothed his thin muscular face.

"You like him?" Jennie ventured at last.

"I can't say, Miss Barton," was the slowly measured answer. "He is a remarkably interesting man. I'm surprised and puzzled—"

"Surprised and puzzled at what?"

"Well, you see I know his history. The diplomatist makes it his business to know the facts in the lives of the leaders of a nation to whose Government he is accredited. Mr. Davis spent four years at West Point. He gave seven years of his life to the service of the army in the West. He carried your flag to victory in Mexico and hobbled home on crutches. He was one of your greatest Secretaries of War. He sent George B. McClellan and Robert E. Lee to the Crimea to master European warfare, organized and developed your army, changed the model of your arms, introduced the rifled musket and the minie ball. He explored your Western Empire and surveyed the lines of the great continental railways you are going to build to the Pacific Ocean. He planned and built your system of waterworks in the city of Washington and superintends now the extension of the Capitol building which will make it the most imposing public structure in the world. He has never stooped to play the part of a demagogue. He has never sought an office higher than the role of Senator which fits his character and temperament. His mind has always been busy dreaming of the imperial future of your widening Republic. His eye has seen the vision of its extension to the Arctic on the north and the jungles of Panama on the south. Why should such a man deliberately come into this chamber today before this assembled crowd and commit hari-kari?"

"He's a true son of the South!" Jennie Barton proudly answered.

"Even so, how can he do the astounding thing he proposes to carry out today? His record shows that passionate devotion to the Union has been the very breath of his life. I've memorized one of his outbursts as a model of your English language—"

Jennie laughed.

"I never heard of his Union speeches, I'm sure!"

"Strange that your people have forgotten them. Listen: 'From sire to son has descended the love of the Union in our hearts, as in our history are mingled the names of Concord and Camden, of Yorktown and Saratoga, of New Orleans and Bunker Hill. Together they form a monument to the common glory of our common country. Where is the Southern man who would wish that monument less by one Northern name that constitutes the mass? Who, standing on the ground made sacred by the blood of Warren, could allow sectional feeling to curb his enthusiasm as he looks upon that obelisk which rises a monument to freedom's and his country's triumph, and stands a type of the time, the men and the event it commemorates; built of material that mocks the waves of time, without niche or molding for parasite or creeping thing to rest upon, pointing like a finger to the sky to raise man's thoughts to high and noble deeds!'"

Socola paused and turned his dark eyes on Jennie's upturned face.

"How can the man who made that speech in Boston do this mad deed today?"

"Senator Clay has given the answer," was the girl's quick reply.

"For Senator Clay, yes—the fiery, impulsive, passionate child of emotion. But this thin hollow-cheeked student, thinker and philosopher, who spoke the thrilling words I quote—he should belong to the order of the Prophet and the Seer—the greatest leaders and teachers of history."

"We believe he does, Signor!" was the quick answer. "Look—he's going to speak—you'll hear him now."

Jennie leaned forward, her thoughtful little chin in both hands, as a silence so intense it was pain fell suddenly on the hushed assembly.

The face of the Southern leader was chalk white in its pallor. His first sentences were weak and scarcely reached beyond the circle of his immediate hearers. His physician had forbidden him to leave his room. The iron will had risen to perform a solemn duty. The Senators leaned forward in their arm-chairs fearful of losing a word.

He paused as if for breath and gazed a moment on the upturned faces with the look of lingering tenderness which the dying cast on those upon whom they gaze for the last time.

His figure suddenly rose to its full height, as if the soul within had thrust the feeble body aside to speak its message. His words, full, clear and musical rang to the furthest listener craning his neck through the jammed doorways of the galleries. Never was the music of the human voice more profoundly appealing. Unshed tears were in its throbbing tones.

There was no straining for effect—no outburst of emotion. The impression which reached the audience was the sense of restraint and the consciousness of his unlimited reserve power. Back of the simple clean-cut words which fell in musical cadence from his white lips was the certainty that he was only speaking a small part of what he felt, saw and knew. He neither stormed nor raved and yet he filled the hearts of his hearers with unspeakable passion.

He turned suddenly and bent his piercing single eye on the Northern Senators:

"I hope none who hear me will confound my position with the advocacy of the right of a State to remain in the Union and disregard its Constitutional obligations by the nullification of the law—"

A sudden cheer swept the tense galleries. The sergeant-at-arms called for order. The cheer rose again. The Vice-President rapped for silence and threatened to close the galleries. The speaker lifted his hand and commanded silence.

"It was because of his deep attachment to the Union—his determination to find some remedy for existing ills short of a severance of the ties which bound South Carolina to the other States—that John C. Calhoun advocated the doctrine of nullification which he proclaimed to be peaceful and within the limits of State power.

"Secession belongs to a different class of remedies. It is to be justified upon the basis that the States are sovereign. There was a time when none denied it. The phrase 'to execute the laws' General Jackson applied to a State refusing to obey the law while yet a member of the Union. You may make war on a foreign state. If it be the purpose of gentlemen—"

He paused and again his eagle eye swept the tiers of Northern Senators.

"You may make war against a State which has withdrawn from the Union; but there are no laws of the United States to be executed within the limits of a seceded State—"

Seward leaned forward in his seat and shook his head in grave dissent. The speaker bent his gaze directly upon his great antagonist and spoke with strange regretful tenderness.

"A State finding herself in a condition in which Mississippi has judged she is—in which her safety requires that she should provide for the maintenance of her rights out of the Union—surrenders all the benefits (and they are known to be many), deprives herself of all the advantages (and they are known to be great), severs all the ties of affections (and they are close and enduring) which have bound her to the Union; and thus divesting herself of every benefit—taking upon herself every burden—she claims to be exempt from any power to execute the laws of the United States within her limits.

"When Massachusetts was arraigned before the bar of the Senate for her refusal to permit the execution of the laws of the United States within her borders, my opinion was the same then as now. Her State is sovereign. She never delegated to the Federal Government the power to drive her by force. And when she chooses to take the last step which separates her from the Union, it is her right to go!—"

Another electric wave swept the crowd that burst into applause. The speaker lifted his long arm with an impatient gesture. "And I would not vote one dollar nor one man to coerce her back into unwilling submission. I would say to her—'God speed in the memory of the kind associations which once existed between her and her sister States.'

"It has been a conviction of pressing necessity—a belief that we are to be deprived in the Union of the rights which our fathers bequeathed us—which has brought Mississippi to her present decision.

"You have invoked the sacred Declaration of Independence as the basis of an attack upon her social order. The Declaration of Independence is to be construed by the circumstances and purposes for which it was made. It was written by a Southern planter and slave owner. The Colonies were declaring their independence from foreign tyranny—were asserting in the language of Jefferson, 'that no man was born booted and spurred to ride over the rest of mankind; that men were created equal'—meaning the men of their American political community; that there was no divine right to rule; that no man could inherit the right to govern; that there were no classes by which power and place descended from father to son; but that all stations were equally within the grasp of each member of the body politic. These were the principles they announced.

"They had no reference to a slave. The same document denounced George III for the crime of attempting to stir their slaves to insurrection, as John Brown attempted at Harper's Ferry. If their Declaration of Independence announced that negroes were free and the equals of English citizens how could the Prince be arraigned for daring to raise servile insurrection among them? And how should this be named among the high crimes of George III which caused the Colonies to sever their connection with the Mother country?

"If slaves were declared our equals how did it happen that in the organic law of the Union they were given a lower caste and their population allowed (and that only through the dominant race) a basis of three-fifths representation in Congress? So stands the compact of Union which binds us together.

"We stand upon the principles on which our Government was founded!—"

The sentence rang clear and thrilling as the peal of a trumpet. The effect was electric. The galleries leaped to their feet, and cheered.

Jennie turned to the silent diplomat.

"Isn't he glorious!"

"He stirs the hearts of men"—was the even answer.

Around them were unmistakable evidences. Women were weeping hysterically and men embracing one another in silence and tears.

Again the Senator's hand was lifted high in command for silence and again he faced Seward and his Northern colleagues with figure tense, erect.

"When you repudiate these principles, and when you deny to us the right to withdraw from a Government which, thus perverted, threatens to destroy our rights, we but tread the path of our fathers when we proclaim our independence and take the hazard!"

Again a cheer and shout which the Vice-President's gavel could not quell. When the murmur at last died away the speaker's voice had dropped to low appealing tenderness.

"We do this, Senators, not in hostility to others, not to injure any section of our common country, not for our own pecuniary benefit, but from the high and solemn motive of defending and protecting the rights we inherited, which we will transmit unshorn to our children. We seek outside the Union that peace, with dignity and honor, which we can no longer find within.

"I trust I find myself a type of the general feeling of my constituents towards yours. I am sure I feel no hostility toward you, Senators from the North—"

He paused and swept the Northern tiers with a look of tender appeal.

"I am sure there is not one of you, whatever sharp discussion there may have been between us, to whom I cannot now say in the presence of my God, I wish you well!"

Seward turned his head from the speaker, his eyes dimmed—the scheming diplomat and unscrupulous politician lost in the heart of the man for the moment.

"Such I am sure is the feeling of the people whom I represent toward those whom you represent. I but express their desire when I say I hope and they hope for peaceful relations with you, though we must part—"

He paused as if to suppress emotions too deep for words while a silence, intense and suffocating, held the crowd in a spell. The speaker's voice dropped to still lower and softer notes of persuasive tenderness as each rounded word of the next sentence fell slowly from the thin lips.

"If war must come, we can only invoke the God of our fathers, who delivered us from the power of the lion, to protect us from the ravages of the bear, and putting our trust in Him and in our firm hearts and strong arms we will vindicate the right as best we may—"

No cheer greeted this solemn utterance. In the pause which followed, the speaker deliberately gazed over the familiar faces of his Northern opponents and continued with a suppressed intensity of feeling that gripped his bitterest foe.

"In the course of my service here, associated at different times with a great variety of Senators, I see now around me some with whom I have served long. There have been points of collision, but, whatever offense there has been to me, I leave here. I carry with me no hostile remembrance. For whatever offense I may have given which has not been redressed, or for which satisfaction has not been demanded, I have, Senators, in this solemn hour of our parting to offer you my apology—"

The low musical voice died softly away in the silence of tears.

A woman sobbed aloud.

Socola bent toward his trembling companion and whispered: "Who is she?"

Jennie brushed the tears from her brown eyes before replying:

"The Senator's wife. She's heart-broken over it all—didn't sleep a wink all night. I've been looking for her to faint every minute."

The leader closed his portfolio. His hollow cheeks, thin lips and white drawn face were clothed with an expression of sorrow beyond words as he slowly turned and left the scene of his life's triumphs.

The spell of his eloquence at last thrown off the crowd once more dissolved into hostile lowering groups.

Stern old Zack Chandler of Michigan collided with Jennie's father in the cloak room, his eyes red with wrath.

"Well, Barton," he growled, "after the damned insolence of that scene if the North don't fight, I'll be much mistaken—"

"You generally are, sir," Barton retorted.

"If they don't fight, by the living God, I'll leave this country and join another nation—the Comanche Indians preferred to this Government."

Barton glanced at his opponent and his heavy jaw closed with a snap.

"I trust, Senator," he said with deliberate venom, "you will not carry out that resolution—the Comanche Indians have already suffered too much from contact with the whites!"

Dick Welford heard the shot and gripped the fierce old Southerner's hand as Chandler turned on his heel and disappeared with an oath.

"You got him that time, Senator!"

Barton laughed with boyish glee.

"I did, didn't I? Sometimes we can only think of our best things when it's too late. But by Gimminy I got the old rascal this time, didn't I?"

"You certainly plugged him—what did you think of the speeches?"

"Clay said something! Davis is too slow. He's got no blood in his veins. I don't like him. He'll pull us back into the Union yet if we don't watch him. He's a reconstructionist at heart. The State of Mississippi is dragging him out of Washington by the heels. He makes me tired. The time for talk has passed. To your tents now, O Israel!"

Dick hurried to the gallery and watched Socola talking in his graceful Italian way with Jennie. He had hated this elegant foreigner the moment he had laid eyes on him. He made up his mind to declare himself before another sun set.

He ignored the Italian's existence.

"You are ready, Miss Jennie?"

She took Dick's proffered arm in silence and bowed to Socola who watched them go with a peculiar smile playing about his handsome mouth.

Jennie insisted on stopping at Senator Davis' home to tell his wife of the wonderful power with which his speech had swept the galleries.

The house was still, the library door open. The girl paused on the threshold in awe. The Senator's tall figure was lying prostrate across his desk, his thin hands clasped in prayer, his face buried in his arms. His lips were murmuring words too low to be heard until at last they swelled in sorrowful repetition:

"May God have us in his holy keeping and grant that before it is too late peaceful councils may prevail!"

The girl turned softly and left without a word.

3: A MIDNIGHT SESSION

The Secretary of War invited Socola to join him at the White House after the Cabinet meeting which President Buchanan had called at the unusual hour of ten at night. He had waited for more than two hours in the anteroom and still the Cabinet was in session. Without show of impatience he smoked cigar after cigar, flicked their ashes into the fireplace and listened with an expression of quiet amusement to the storm raging within while the sleet of a January blizzard rattled against the windows with increasing fury.

Once more the question of the little fort in the harbor of Charleston had plunged the discordant Cabinet of the dying administration into the convulsions of a miniature war.

The feeble old President, overwhelmed by the gathering storm, crouched in the corner by the fire. His emaciated figure was shrouded in a ridiculous old dressing-gown. Mentally and physically prostrate he sat shivering while his ministers wrangled.

He rose at last, shambled to the Cabinet table, and leaned his trembling hands on it for support.

"What can I do, gentlemen—what can I do? If Anderson hadn't gone into that fort at night, the State of South Carolina might not have seceded—"

Stanton shook his massive head with an expression of uncontrollable rage. "Great God!"

The President continued in feeble, pleading tones: "Now they tell me that unless Anderson withdraws his troops their presence will provoke bloodshed—"

"Let them fire on him if they dare!" shouted Stanton.

"I cannot plunge my country into fratricidal war. My sands are nearly run. I only ask of God that my sun may not set in a sea of blood—"

He paused and lifted his thin hands, trembling like two withered leaves of aspen in the winter's blast. "What can I do?"

Stanton suddenly sprang from his seat and confronted the shivering old man.

"I'll tell you what you cannot do!"

The President gasped for breath and listened helplessly.

"You can't yield that fort to the conspirators who demand it. Dare to do it, and I tell you, as the Attorney General of the United States, you are guilty of high treason—and by the living God you should be hung!"

The venerable Secretary of the Navy, Isaac Toucey, lifted his hand in protest. Stanton merely threw him a look of scorn, and shouted into the President's face: "Your act could no more be defended than Benedict Arnold's!"

"And what say you, Holt?" the President asked, turning to his heavy-jawed Secretary of War.

"Send a ship to the relief of Sumter within twenty-four hours, and let South Carolina take the consequences—"

"Good!" Stanton cried.

Holt's crooked mouth was drawn in grim lines, and the left-hand corner was twisted into a still lower knot of ugly muscles. His furtive eyes beneath their shaggy brows glanced quickly around the table to see the effect of his patriotic stand.

The President turned to the white-haired Secretary of the Navy: "And you, General Toucey?"

The venerable statesman from Connecticut bowed gravely to his Chief and spoke with quiet dignity. "I would order Anderson to return at once to Fort Moultrie—"

Stanton smashed the table with his big fist.

"And you know that the State of South Carolina has dismantled Fort Moultrie?"

Toucey answered Stanton's bluster with quiet emphasis. "I'm aware of that fact, sir!"

"And it makes no difference?"

"None whatever. Anderson left Fort Moultrie and moved into Fort Sumter without orders—"

A faint smile flickered about the drooping corners of Holt's mouth.

The speaker turned to Holt: "As a matter of fact, he moved into that fort against the positive orders of your predecessor, James B. Floyd, the Secretary of War. As he went there without orders, and against orders, he should be ordered back forthwith—"

With the look of a maddened tiger Stanton flew at him. "And you expect to go back to Connecticut after making that statement?"

"I do, sir—"

"I couldn't believe it."

"And why, pray?"

"I asked the question in good faith, that I might know the character of the people of Connecticut, or your estimate of them."

The old man drew himself up with cold dignity. "I have served the people of my State for over forty years—their **Congressman**, their Attorney General, their Governor, their Senator. I consult no upstart of your feeble record, sir, on any question of principle or policy!"

Stanton quailed a moment beneath the cold scorn of his antagonist, surprised that another man should dare to use his methods of invective.

He lifted his hands with a gesture of contempt. "All I can say is, that if I should dare take that position and return to the State of Pennsylvania, I should expect to be stoned the moment I set foot on her soil, stoned through the State and flung into the river at Pittsburg with a stone around my neck—"

Toucey stared at his opponent.

"And in my opinion they would deserve well of their country for the performance!"

While his Cabinet wrangled, the feeble, old man in the faded wrapper shambled to the window and gazed with watery eyes on the swaying trees of the White House grounds. The sleet had frozen in shining crystals and every limb was hung in diamonds. The wind had risen to hurricane force, howling and shrieking its requiem through the chill darkness. A huge bough broke and fell to the ground with a crash that sent a shiver through his distracted soul.

He turned back to the table to hear their decision. It came with but one dissenting voice, Toucey, Secretary of the Navy.

"A ship be sent at once to the relief of Sumter."

With stubborn terror the President refused to sign the order for an armed vessel. At one o'clock they compromised on the little steamer, Star of the West, and Buchanan agreed that she should attempt to land provisions for Anderson's fifty-odd men.

Holt hurried from the council chamber at one o'clock with a smile of triumph playing about his sinister mouth. His plan had succeeded.

He had worked Stanton as the legal adviser of the President exactly as he had foreseen. The little steamer would test the mettle of the men of South Carolina who were training their batteries on Fort Sumter. If they dared to fire on her—all right—the lines of battle would be drawn.

He seized Socola's arm. "Come with me to the War Office."

Inside, he closed the door, inspected the room in every nook and corner for a possible eavesdropper, seated himself and leaned close to his attentive listener.

"I have established your character now through your connection with the Minister from Sardinia beyond the possibility of any doubt. Your position will not be called in question. You will appear in the South as the representative, unofficial and yet duly accredited, for King Victor Emmanuel. Your purpose will be, of course, the cultivation of friendly relations with the officials of the new Government looking to the day of its coming recognition—you understand?"

"Perfectly—"

"You have absolutely consecrated your life, and every talent, to your country?"

"Body and soul—" The dark eyes flashed with the light of a religious fanatic.

"Good." The Secretary paused and studied his man a moment. "I introduced you to the girl not merely to obtain an invaluable witness to your credentials should they be questioned—but for a double purpose."

Socola nodded.

"I guessed as much."

"She's bright, young, pretty, and you can pass the time pleasantly in her company. The association will place you in a strong position. Her father is a fool—the stormy petrel of Secession. He has the biggest mouth in America, barring none. His mouth is so huge, they'll never find a muzzle big enough if they could get men enough around him to put it on. He's bound to land somewhere high in the councils of the coming Confederacy—"

"There'll be one?"

Holt smiled. "You doubt it?"

"It may be bluster after all."

"Men of the Davis type don't bluster, my boy. They are to meet at Montgomery, Alabama, on February fourth. They'll organize the Cotton States into a Southern Confederacy. If they can win Virginia, North Carolina, Tennessee and Arkansas, they may gobble Maryland, Kentucky, and Missouri—all Slave States. If they get them all—they'll win without a fight, and reconstruct the Union on their own terms; if they don't—well, we'll see what we'll see—"

"And you wish?"

"That you get for me—and get quickly—inside information of what is done and what is proposed to be done at Montgomery. I want the names of every man discussed for high office among them, his chances of appointment, his friends, his enemies—why they are his friends, why they are his enemies. I want their plans, their prospects, their hopes, their fears, and I want this information quickly. You will be supplied with ample funds, and your report must be made to me in person. My tenure of this office will be but a few weeks longer—but you are my personal representative, you understand?"

"Quite."

"Your report must be in person to me, and to me alone."

"I understand, sir."

Socola rose, extended his hand, drew his cloak about his slender shoulders and passed out into the storm, his dark face lighted by a smile as he recalled the winsome face of Jennie Barton.

4: A FRIENDLY WARNING

The withdrawal of the Southern Senators and Representatives from Congress produced in Washington the upheaval of a social earthquake.

An atmosphere of tears and ominous foreboding hung pall-like over the city's social life. Each step in the departure of wives and daughters was a pang.

Carriages drawn by sleek, high-bred horses dashed through the broad streets with excited haste. The black coachman on the box held his reins with a nervous grip that communicated itself to the horses. He had caught the excitement in the quivering social structure of which he was part. What he was really thinking down in the depths of his African soul only God could see. His dark face merely grinned in quick obedience to command.

From every house where these farewells were being said, a weeping woman emerged and waved a last adieu to the tear-stained faces at the window.

Wagons and carts lumbered through the streets on their way to the wharf or station, piled high with baggage.

Hotel-keepers stood in the doorway of their establishments with darkened brows. The glory of the past was departing. The future was a blank.

On the morning after his farewell address to the Senate, a messenger, who refused to give his name, was ushered into the library of Senator Davis.

The stately black butler bowed again with quiet dignity.

"Yo' name, sah? I—failed to catch it?"

The messenger lifted his hand: "No name. Please say to the Senator that I came from an important official with a message of the gravest importance—I wish to see him alone at once—"

The faithful servant eyed his visitor with an ominous look. There was no question of his loyalty to the man he served.

"It's all right, Robert, I'm a friend of Senator Davis."

A moment's hesitation and the black man bowed with deference.

"Yassah—yassah—I tell him right away, sah. You sho' knows me anyhow, sah—"

The Senator was in bed suffering again from facial neuralgia. He rose promptly, dressed hastily but completely and carefully and extended both hands to his visitor.

"You have come to see me at an unusual hour, sir. It must be important—"

"Of the utmost importance, Senator. A high official in the confidence of the President sent me to inform you that Stanton, the Attorney General, is planning to issue a warrant for your arrest for high treason."

"Indeed?"

"You are advised to leave Washington on the first train."

A dry smile flickered about the corners of the Senator's strong mouth.

"Thank you. Please say to my friend that I appreciate the spirit that prompted his message. Ask him to say to Mr. Stanton that I have decided to remain in Washington a week. Nothing would please me better than to submit this issue to the courts for adjustment. He will find me at home every day and at all hours."

5: BOY AND GIRL

From the moment Dick Welford had seen Socola bowing and smiling before Jennie Barton he had hated the man. He hated foreigners on general principles, anyhow. This kind of foreigner he particularly loathed—the slender, nervous type which suggested over-refinement to the point of effeminacy. He had always hated slender, effeminate-looking men of the native breed. This one was doubly offensive because he was an Italian. How any woman with true womanly instincts could tolerate such a spider was more than he could understand.

Jennie Barton had always frankly said that she admired men of his own type. He was six feet one, fair-haired, blue-eyed, and weighed a hundred and ninety-six pounds at twenty-one years of age. He had always felt instinctively that he was exactly the man for Jennie's mate. She was nineteen, dark and slender, a bundle of quick, sensitive, nervous intelligence. Her brown eyes were almost black and her luxuriant hair seemed raven-hued beside his. He had always imagined it nestling beside his big blond head in perfect contentment since the first summer he had spent with Tom Barton at their cottage at the White Sulphur Springs.

He had taken it for granted that she would say yes when he could screw up his courage to speak. She had treated him as if he were already in the family.

"Confound it," he muttered, clenching his big fist, "that's what worries me! Maybe she just thinks of me as one of her brothers!"

It hadn't occurred to him until he saw the light kindle in her eyes at the sight of that smooth-tongued reptilian foreigner. He was on his way now to her house, to put the thing to the test before she could leave Washington. Thank God, the spider was tied down here at the Sardinian Ministry. He hoped Victor Emmanuel would send him as Consul to Shanghai.

Mrs. Barton met him at the door with a motherly smile. "Walk right in the parlor, Dick. It's sweet of you to come so early today. We're all in tears, packing to go. Jennie'll be delighted to see you. Poor child—she's sick over it all."

Mrs. Barton pressed Dick's hand with the softest touch that reassured his fears. The only trouble about Mrs. Barton was she was gentle and friendly to everybody, black and white, old and young, Yankee or Southerner. She was even sorry for old John Brown when they hung him.

"Poor thing, he was crazy," she said tenderly. "They ought to have sent him to the asylum."

Try as he might, he couldn't fling off the impression of tragedy the meeting of Socola with Jennie had produced. He was in a nervous fit to see and tell her of his love. Why the devil hadn't he done so before anyhow? They might have been engaged and ready to be married by this time. They had met when she was sixteen.

Why on earth couldn't he throw off the fool idea that he was going to lose her? His big fist suddenly closed with resolution.

"I'll not lose her! I'll wring that viper's neck—I'll wade through blood and death and the fires of h—"

Just as he was plunging waist deep through the flames of the Pit, she appeared in the door, the picture of wistful, tender beauty.

He rose awkwardly and extended his hand.

"Good morning, Dick!"

"Good morning, Jennie—"

Her hand was hot, her eyes heavy with tears.

"What's the matter?" he asked.

"As if you didn't know—I've been saying goodbye to some of the dearest friends I've ever known. It's terrible. I just feel it's the end of the world—"

He started to say: "Don't worry, Jennie darling, you have me. I love you!" The thought of it made the cold beads of perspiration suddenly stand out on his forehead. It was one thing to think such things—another to say it aloud to a girl with Jennie's serious brown eyes.

She seemed terribly serious this morning and far away somehow. Never had he seen her so utterly lovely. The mood of tender seriousness made her more beautiful than ever. If he only dared to crush her in his arms and laugh the smiles back into her eyes.

When he spoke it was only a commonplace he managed to blurt out: "So you're really going tomorrow?"

"Yes—we've telegraphed the boys to come home from school at

once and join us in Montgomery."

He tried to say it again, but the speech turned out to be political, not personal.

"Of course Virginia'll stand by her Southern sisters, Jennie—"

"Yes—"

"It's just a few old moss-backs holding her. No army will ever march across her soil to fight a Southern State—"

"I hope not."

"Of course not. I'll meet them on the border with one musket anyhow—"

The girl was looking out the window at the slowly drizzling rain and made no answer. He flushed at her apparent indifference to his heroic stand.

"Don't you believe I would?"

"Would what, Dick?" she smiled, recovering herself from her reverie.

It was no use beating about the bush, trying to talk politics. He had to make the plunge. He suddenly took her hand in his.

She threw him a startled look, sat bolt upright, made the faintest effort to draw her hand away, and blushed furiously.

He was in for it now. There was no retreat. He gripped with desperate earnestness, tried to speak, and choked.

He drew a deep breath, tried again and only squeezed her hand harder. The girl began to smile in a sweet, triumphant way. It was nice, this conscious power over a big, stunning six-footer who grasped her hand as a drowning man a straw. The sense of her strength was thrilling.

She looked at him with demure reproach. "Dick!"

He grinned sheepishly and clung to her hand.

"Yes—Jennie—"

"Do you know what you are doing?"

"No—but—I know—what—I'm—trying—to—do—and—I'm—going—to—do—it—" Again his big hand crushed hers.

"You're trying to break every bone in my hand as near as I can make out—I'd like it back when you're through with it—"

He found his tongue at last:

"I—I—can't let you have it back, Jennie, I'm going to keep it forever—"

"Really?"

"Yes—I am. I—I love you—Jennie—don't you love me—just—a—little bit?"

The girl laughed. "No!"

"Not the least—little—tiny—bit?"

"I don't think so—"

The hand slipped through his limp fingers and he stared at her in a hopeless, pitiful way.

Her heart went out in a wave of tender sympathy. She put her hand back in his in a wistful touch.

"I'm sorry, Dick dear, I didn't think you loved me in that way—"

"What did you think I was hanging round you so much for?"

"I knew you liked me, of course. And I like you—but I've never thought seriously about love."

"There's no other fellow?"

"Of course, not—"

"You liked that Socola, didn't you?"

"I liked him—yes—"

"I thought so."

"He's cultured, handsome, interesting—"

"He's a sissy!"

"Dick!"

"A little wizened-faced rat—the spider-snake! I could break his long neck. Yes—you do like him! I saw it when you met him. You're throwing me down because you met him!"

"Dick!"

"But he shan't have you, I tell you—I'll show him I could lick a thousand such sissies with one hand tied behind me."

The girl rose with dignity. "Don't you dare to speak to me like that, sir—"

"You're going to see that fellow again—I'll bet you've got an engagement with him now—tonight—today!"

The slender figure rose. "I'll see him if I please—when I please and where I please and I'll not consult you about it, Dick Welford—Good day!"

Trembling with anger the big, awkward boy turned and stumbled out of the house.

6: GOD'S WILL

Dick Welford had played directly into the hands of his enemy. When Socola called at the Barton home to pay his respects to Miss Jennie and wish them health and happiness and success in their new and dangerous enterprise, he found the girl in a receptive mood. The accusation of interest had stimulated her to her first effort to entertain the self-poised and gentlemanly foreigner.

He turned to Jennie with a winning appeal in his modulated voice: "Will you do me a very great favor, Miss Barton?"

"If I can—certainly," was the quick answer.

"I wish to meet your distinguished father. He is a great Southern leader. I have been commissioned by the Sardinian Ministry to cultivate the acquaintance of the leaders of the Confederacy. I am to make a report direct to the Court of King Emmanuel on the prospects of the South."

Jennie rose with a smile. "With pleasure. I'll call father at once."

Barton was delighted at the announcement.

"Invite him to spend a week with us at Fairview," Jennie suggested.

"Good idea—we'll show him what Southern hospitality means!"

Barton grasped Socola's outstretched hand with enthusiasm. "Permit me," he began in his grand way, "to extend you a welcome to the South. Your King is interested in our movement. It's natural. Europe must reckon with us from the first. Cotton is the real King. We are going to build on this staple an industrial empire whose influence will dominate the world. The sooner the political rulers realize this the better."

Socola bowed. "I quite agree with you, Senator Barton. His Majesty King Victor Emmanuel has great plans for the future. He is profoundly interested in your movement. He does not believe that the map of Italy has yet been fixed. It will be quite easy to convince his brilliant, open mind that the boundaries of this country may be readjusted—"

"I shall be delighted to show you every courtesy within my

power, sir," Barton responded. "You must go South with us tomorrow and spend a week at Fairview, our country estate. You must meet my grand old father and my mother and see the curse of slavery at its worst!" Barton laughed heartily and slipped his arm persuasively about the graceful shoulders of his guest.

"I hadn't thought of being so honored, I assure you—" He paused and looked at Jennie with a timid sort of appeal.

"Come with us—we'll be delighted to have you—"

"I'll enjoy it, I'm sure," he said hesitatingly. "We will reach Montgomery in time for the meeting of the Convention of Seceding States?"

"Certainly," Barton replied. "I'm already elected a delegate from my State. Her secession is but a question of days."

Socola's white, even teeth gleamed in a happy smile. "I'll go with pleasure, Senator. You leave tomorrow?"

"The ten-twenty train for the South. You'll join our party, of course?"

"Of course."

With a graceful bow he hurried home to complete the final preparations for his departure. He walked with quick, strong step. And yet as he approached the door of the little house in the humbler quarter of the city his gait unconsciously slowed down.

He dreaded this last struggle with his mother. But it must come. He entered the modestly furnished sitting room and looked at her calm, sweet face with a sudden sinking. She would be absolutely alone in the world. And yet no harm could befall her. She was the friend of every human being who knew her. It was the agony of this parting he dreaded and the loneliness that would torture her in his absence.

He spoke with forced cheerfulness.

"Well, mater, it's all settled. I leave at ten-twenty tomorrow morning." She rose and placed her hands on his shoulders. The tears blinded her.

"How little I thought when I taught your boyish lips to speak the musical tongue of Italy I was preparing this bitter hour for my soul! I begged your father to resign his consulship at Genoa and brought you home to teach you the great lesson—to love your country and reverence your country's God. And since your father's death the dream of my heart has been to see you a minister, teaching and uplifting the people into a higher and nobler life—"

"That is my aim, mater dear. I am consecrating body, mind and soul to the task now of saving the Union, an inheritance priceless and glorious to millions yet unborn. I'm going to break the chains that bind slaves. I'm going to break the brutal and cruel power of the Southern Tyranny that has been strangling the nation for forty years!"

His eyes flashed with the fire of fanatical enthusiasm. He slipped his arm about his mother's slender waist, drew her to the window and pointed to the unfinished dome of the white, majestic capitol.

"See, mater dear, the sun is bursting through the clouds now and lighting with splendor the marble columns. Last night when the speeches were done and the crowds gone I stood an hour and studied the flawless symmetry of those magnificent wings and over it all the great solemn dome with its myriad gleaming eyes far up in the sky—and I wondered if God meant nothing big or significant to humanity when he breathed the dream of that poem in marble into the souls of our people! I can't believe it, dear. I stood and prayed while I dreamed. I saw in the ragged scaffolding and the big ugly crane swinging from its place in the sky the symbol of our crude beginnings—our ragged past. And then the snow-white vision of the finished building, the most majestic monument ever reared on earth to Freedom and her cause—and I saw the glory of a new Democracy rising from the blood and agony of the past to be the hope and inspiration of the world!

"You hate this masquerade—this battle name I've chosen. Forget this, dear, and see the vision your God has given to me. You've prayed that I might be His minister. And so I am—and so I shall be when danger calls; you dislike this repulsive mission on which I'm entering. Just now it's the one and only thing a brave man can do for his country. Forget that I'm a spy and remember that I'm fitted for a divine service. I speak two languages beside my own. Our people don't study languages. Few men of my culture and endowment will do this dangerous and disagreeable work. I rise on wings at the thought of it!"

The mother's spirit caught at last the divine spark from the soul of the young enthusiast. Her eyes were wide and shining without tears when she slipped both arms about his neck and spoke with deep tenderness.

"You have fully counted the cost, my son?"

"Yes."

"The lying, the cheating, the false pretenses, the assumed name, the trusting hearts you must betray, the men you must kill alone, sometimes to save your own life and serve your country's?"

"It's war, mater dear. I hate its cruelty and its wrongs. I'll do my best in these early days to make it impossible. But if it comes, I'll play the game with my life in my hands, and if I had a hundred lives I'd give them all to my country—my only regret is that I have but one—"

"How strange the ways of God!" the mother broke in. "He planted this love in your soul. He taught it to me and I to you and now it ends in darkness and blood and death—"

"But out of it, dear, must come the greater plan. You believe in God—you must believe this, or else the Devil rules the universe, and there is no God."

The mother drew the young lips down and kissed them tenderly.

"God's will be done, my Boy—it's the bitterness of death to me—but I say it!"

7: THE BEST MAN WINS

Before Socola could purchase his ticket for the South, Senator Barton laid his heavy hand on his shoulder.

"I just ran down, sir, to ask you to wait and go in Senator Davis' party. He has been threatened with arrest by the cowards who are at the present moment in charge of the Government. He can't afford to leave town while there's a chance that so fortunate an event may be pulled off. I have decided to stay until Lincoln's inauguration. My wife and daughter will make you welcome at Fairview. And you'll meet my three boys. I'm sorry I can't be with you."

Socola's masked face showed no trace of disappointment. He merely asked politely: "And the party of Senator Davis will start?"

"A week from today, sir—and my wife and daughter will accompany them—unless—of course—" He laughed heartily. "Unless the great Attorney General, Edwin M. Stanton, decides to arrest him—if he'll only do it!"

Socola nodded carelessly. "I understand, Senator. A week from today. The same hour—the same train."

In a moment he had disappeared in the crowd and hurried to the office of the Secretary of War.

Holt received his announcement with a smile about the corners of his strong, crooked mouth.

"That's lucky. I'd rather you were with Davis ten to one. Amuse yourself for the week by getting all the information possible of their junta here—"

"Barton will stay until the inauguration—"

"Of course—a spy in the camp of the enemy. He could be arrested, but it's not wise under the circumstances—"

"You will not arrest Senator Davis?"

"Nonsense. Stanton's a fool. Nothing would please them better. I've convinced him of that. A wrangle in the courts now over such an issue would postpone its settlement indefinitely. The Supreme Court of the United States has sustained the South on every issue that has been raised. The North is leading a revolution. The South is entrenched behind the law. They can't be ousted by law. It can only be done by the bayonet—"

Holt paused and looked thoughtfully across the Potomac. "Report to me daily—"

Socola silently saluted and left the office with his first feeling of suspicion and repulsion for his Chief. He didn't like the blunt, brutal way this Southern Democrat talked. He couldn't believe in his honesty. Beneath those bushy eyebrows burned a wolf's hunger for office and power. On the surface he was loyal to the Union. He wondered if he were not in reality playing a desperate waiting game, ready at the moment of the crisis to throw his information to either side? The air of Washington reeked with suspicion and double dealing.

"Oh, my Country," he murmured bitterly, "if ever true men were needed!"

He strolled through the street on which Senator Davis and Barton lived directly opposite each other. He would call on Jennie and express his regret that their party had been postponed. At the door he changed his mind. Too much attention at this stage of the game would not be wise. He passed on, glancing at the distinguished-looking group of men who were emerging from the Davis door.

He wondered what was going on in that home? It seemed impossible that Davis should be the leader of a Southern rebellion. Clay or Toombs, yes—but this man with his blood-marked history of devotion to the Union—this man with his proud record of constructive statesmanship as Senator and Secretary of War—it seemed preposterous!

Could he have heard the counsel Davis was giving at that moment to the excited men who made his unpretentious house their Mecca, he would have been still more astonished. For six days and nights with but a few hours snatched for sleep, he implored the excited leaders of Southern opinion to avoid violence, and be patient. The one note of hopefulness in his voice came with the mention of the new President-elect, Abraham Lincoln.

"Mr. Lincoln is a man of friendly, moderate opinions personally," he persistently advised. "He may he able to surround himself with a council of conservative men who will use their power to hold the radical wing of his party in check until by delay we can call a convention of all the States and in this national assembly find a solution short of bloodshed. We must try. We must exhaust every resource before we dream of war. We must accept war only when it is forced upon us by our enemies."

By telegrams and letters to every Southern leader he knew, he urged delay, moderation, postponement of all action.

The week passed and the Cabinet of Buchanan had not dared accept the Southern leader's challenge to arrest and trial.

The Davis party had found their seats in the train for the South. Socola strolled the platform alone, waiting without sign of interest for the hour of departure.

Dick Welford arrived five minutes before the train left and extended his hand to Jennie.

"Forgive me, Jennie!"

With a bright smile she clasped his hand.

"Of course, Dick—I took your silly ravings too seriously."

"No—I was a fool. I'll make up for it. I'll go over now and shake hands with the reptile if you say so—"

"Nonsense—you'll not do anything of the sort. He's nothing to me. He's the guest of the South—that's all."

"Honest now, Jennie—you don't care for any other fellow?"

"Nor for you, either!" she laughed.

"Of course, I know that—but I can keep on trying, can't I?"

"I don't see how I can prevent it!"

Dick grinned good-naturedly and Jennie laughed again.

"You're in for a siege with me, I'll tell you right now."

"It's a free fight, Dick. I'm indifferent to the results."

"Then you don't mind if I win?"

"Not in the least. At the present moment I'm a curious spectator—that's all."

"Lord, I wish I were going with you—"

"I wish so, too—"

"Honest, Jennie?"

"Cross my heart—"

Dick laughed aloud.

"Say—I tell you what I'm going to do!"

"Yes?"

"If Virginia don't secede in ten days—I will. I'll resign my job here with old Hunter and join the Confederacy. I don't like this new clerkship business anyhow—expect me in ten days—"

Before Jennie could answer he turned suddenly and left the car.

At the end of the platform he ran squarely into Socola. He was about to pass without recognition, stopped on an impulse, and extended his hand:

"Fine day, Signor!"

"Beautiful, M'sieur," was the smooth answer.

Dick hesitated.

"I'm afraid I was a little rude the other day?"

"No offense, I'm sure, Mr. Welford—"

"Of course, you can guess I'm in love with Miss Barton—"

"I hadn't speculated on that point!" Socola laughed.

"Well, I've been speculating about you—"

"Indeed?"

"Yes—and I'm going to be honest with you—I don't like you—we're enemies from today. But I'll play the game fair and the best man wins—"

The two held each other's eye steadily for a moment and Socola's white teeth flashed.

"The best man wins, M'sieur!"

8: THE STORM CENTER

Socola hastened, through Jennie, to cultivate the acquaintance of Senator Davis.

"You'll be delighted with Mrs. Davis, too," the girl informed him with enthusiasm. "His second love affair you know—this time, late in life, he married the young accomplished granddaughter of Governor Howell of New Jersey. Their devotion is beautiful—"

The train had barely pulled out of the station before Socola found himself in a delightful conversation with the Senator. To his amazement he discovered that the Southerner was a close student of European statesmanship and well informed on the conditions of modern Italy.

"I am delighted beyond measure, Signor," he said earnestly, "to learn of the interest of your King in the South. I have long felt that Cavour was one of the greatest statesmen and diplomats of the world. His achievement in establishing the Kingdom of Sardinia in the face of the bitter rivalries and ambitions of Europe, to say nothing of the power of Rome, was in itself enough to mark him as the foremost man of his age."

"The King has great ambitions, Senator. Very shortly his title will be King of Italy. He dreams of uniting all Italians."

"And if it is possible, the Piedmontese are the people ordained for leadership in that sublime work—"

He looked thoughtfully out of the window at the Virginia hills and Socola determined to change the conversation. He was fairly well informed of the affairs in the little Kingdom on whose throne young Victor Emmanuel sat, but this man evidently knew the philosophy of its history as well as the facts. A question or two with his keen eye boring through him might lead to an unpleasant situation.

"Your family are all with you, Senator?" he asked pleasantly.

Instantly the clouds lifted from the pale, thoughtful face.

"Yes—I've three darling babies. I wish you to meet Mrs. Davis—come, they are in the next car."

In a moment the statesman had forgotten the storm of

revolution. He was laughing and playing with his children. However stern and high his uncompromising opinions might be on public questions, he was wax in the hands of the two lovely boys who climbed over him and the vivacious little girl who slipped her arms about his neck.

His respite from care was brief. At the first important stop in Virginia a dense crowd had packed the platforms. Their cries throbbed with anything but the spirit of delay and compromise.

"Davis!"

"Hurrah for Jefferson Davis!"

"Speech—speech!"

"Davis!"

"Speech!"

There was something tense and compelling in the tones of these cries. They rang as bugle calls to battle. In their hum and murmur there was more than curiosity—more than the tribute of a people to their leader. There was in the very sound the electric rush of the first crash of the approaching storm. The man inside who had led soldiers to death on battle fields felt it instantly and the smile died on his thin lips. The roar outside his car window was not the cry of a mob echoing the sentiments of a leader. It was the shrill imperial cry of a rising people creating their leaders.

From the moment he bowed his head and lifted his hand over the crowd that greeted him, hopeless sorrow filled his soul.

War was inevitable.

These people did not realize it. But he saw it now in all its tragic import. He had intended to counsel patience, moderation and delay. Before the hot breath of the storm he felt already in his face such advice was a waste of words. He would tell them the simple truth. He could do most good in that way. These fiery, impulsive Southern people were tired of argument, tired of compromise, tired of delay. They were reared in the faith that their States were sovereign. And these Virginians had good reason for their faith. The bankers of Europe had but yesterday refused to buy the bonds of the United States Government unless countersigned by the State of Virginia!

These people not only believed in the sovereignty of their States and their right to withdraw from the Union when they saw fit, but they could not conceive the madness of the remaining States attempting to use force to hold them. They knew, too, that millions of Northern voters were as clear on that point as the people of the South. Their spokesman, Horace Greeley, in The *Tribune* had said again and again:

"If the Southern States are mad enough to withdraw from the Union, they must go. We cannot prevent it. Let our erring sisters go in peace." The people before him believed that Horace Greeley's paper represented the North in this utterance. Davis knew that it was not true. In a flash of clear soul vision he saw the inevitable horror of the coming struggle and determined to tell the people so.

The message he delivered was a distinct shock. He not only told them in tones of deep and tender emotion that war was inevitable, but that it would be long and bloody.

"We'll lick 'em in two months!" a voice yelled in protest and the crowd cheered.

The leader shook his fine head.

"Don't deceive yourselves, my friends. War once begun, no man can predict its end—"

"It won't begin!" another cried.

"You have convinced me today that it is now inevitable."

"The Yankees won't fight!" shouted a big fellow in front.

The speaker bent his gaze on the stalwart figure in remonstrance.

"You never made a worse mistake in your life, my friend. I warn you—I know these Yankees. Once in it they'll fight with grim, dogged, sullen, unyielding courage. We're men of the same blood. They live North, you South—that's all the difference."

At every station the same scene was enacted. The crowd rushed around his car with the sudden sweep of a whirlwind, and left for their homes with grave, thoughtful faces.

By three o'clock in the afternoon he was thoroughly exhausted by the strain. The eager crowds had sapped his last ounce of vitality.

The conductor of the train looked at him with pity and whispered:

"I'll save you at the next station."

The leader smiled his gratitude for the sympathy but wondered how it could be done.

At the next stop, the Senator had just taken his position on the rear platform, lifted his hand for silence and said:

"Friends and fellow citizens—"

The engine suddenly blew off steam with hiss and roar and when it ceased the train pulled out with a jerk amid the shouts and protests of the crowd. The grateful speaker waved his hand in regretful but happy farewell.

The conductor repeated the trick for three stations until the exhausted speaker had recovered his strength and then allowed him a few brief remarks at each stop.

From the moment the train entered the State of Mississippi, grim, earnest men in groups of two, three, four and a dozen stepped on board, saluted their Chief and took their seats.

When the engine pulled into the station at Jackson a full brigade of volunteer soldiers had taken their places in the ranks.

The Governor and state officials met their leader and grasped his hand.

"You have been commissioned, Senator," the Governor began eagerly, "as Major-General in command of the forces of the State of Mississippi. Four Brigadier-Generals have been appointed and await your assignment for duty."

The tall figure of the hero of Buena Vista suddenly stiffened.

"I thank you, Governor, for the high honor conferred on me. No service could be more congenial to my feelings at this moment."

The Governor waved his hand at the crowd of silent waiting men. "Your men are ready—the first question is the purchase of arms. I think a stand of 75,000 will be sufficient for all contingencies?"

The Senator spoke with emphasis:

"The limit of your purchases should be our power to pay—"

"You can't mean it!" the Governor exclaimed.

"I repeat it—the limit of your purchase of arms should be the power to pay. I say this to every State in the South. We shall need all we can get and many more I fear."

The Governor laughed.

"General, you overrate our risks!"

"On the other hand," Davis continued earnestly, "we are sure to underestimate them at every turn."

He paused, overcome with emotion.

"A great war is impending, Governor, whose end no man can foresee. We are not prepared for it. We have no arms, we have no ammunition and we have no establishments to manufacture them. The South has never realized and does not now believe that the North will fight her on the issue of secession. They do not understand the silent growth of the power of centralization which has changed the opinions of the North under the teaching of Abolition fanatics—"

Again he paused, overcome.

"God help us!" he continued. "War is a terrible calamity even when waged against aliens and strangers—our people are mad. They know not what they do!"

The new Commander hurried to Briarfield, his plantation home, to complete his preparations for a long absence.

Socola on a sudden impulse asked the honor of accompanying him. It was granted without question and with cordial hospitality.

It was an opportunity not to be lost. An intimate view of this man in his home might be of the utmost importance. He promised Jennie to hasten to Fairview when he had spent two days at Briarfield. Mrs. Barton was glad of the opportunity to set her house in order for her charming and interesting guest.

The Davis plantation was a distinct shock to his fixed New England ideas of the hellish institution of Slavery.

The devotion of these simple black men and women to their master was not only genuine, it was pathetic. He had never before conceived the abject depths to which a human being might sink in contentment with chains.

And he had come to break chains! These poor ignorant blacks kissed the hand that bound them and called him their best friend.

The man they called master actually moved among them, a minister of love and mercy. He advised the negroes about the care of their families in his long absence. He talked as a Hebrew Patriarch to his children. He urged the younger men and women to look after the old and helpless.

He was particularly solicitous about Bob, the oldest man on the place. Over and over again he enumerated the comforts he thought he might need and made provision to supply them. He sent him enough cochineal flannel for his rheumatism to wrap him four-ply deep. For Rhinah, his wife, he ordered enough flannel blankets for two families.

"Is there anything else you can think of, Uncle Bob?" he asked kindly.

The old man scratched his gray head and hesitated, looked into his master's face, smiled and said:

"I would like one er dem rockin' cheers outen de big house, Marse Jeff.—yassah!"

"Of course, you shall have it. Come right up, you and Rhinah, and pick out the two you like best."

With suppressed laughter Socola watched the old negroes try each chair in the hallway and finally select the two best rockers in the house.

The Southern leader was obviously careworn and unhappy. Socola found his heart unconsciously going out to him in sympathy.

Assuming carefully his attitude of foreign detached interest, the young man sought to draw him out.

"You have given up all hope of adjustment and reunion with the North?" he asked.

"No," was the thoughtful reply, "not until the first blood is spilled."

"Your people must see, Senator, that secession will imperil the existence of their three thousand millions of dollars invested in slaves?"

"Certainly they see it," was the quick answer. "Slavery can never survive the first shot of war, no matter which side wins. If the North wins, we must free them, or else maintain a standing army on our borders for all time. It would be unthinkable. Rivers are bad boundaries. We could have no others. Fools have said and will continue to say that we are fighting to establish a slave empire. Nothing could be further from the truth. We are seeking to find that peace and tranquillity outside the Union we have not been able to enjoy for the past forty years inside. If the Southern States enact a Constitution of their own, they will merely reaffirm the Constitution of their fathers with no essential change. The North is leading a revolution, not the South.

"Not one man in twenty down here owns a slave. The South would never fight to maintain Slavery. We know that it is doomed. We simply demand as the sons of the men who created this Republic, equal rights under its laws. If we fight, it will be for our independence as freemen that we may maintain those rights."

"I must confess, sir," Socola replied with carefully modulated voice, "that I fail to see as a student from without, why, if Slavery is doomed and your leaders realize that fact, a compromise without bloodshed would not be possible?"

"If Slavery were the only issue, it would be possible—although as a proud and sensitive people we propose to be the judge of the time when we see fit to emancipate our slaves. Abolition fanatics, whose fathers sold their slaves to us, can't dictate to the South on such a moral issue."

"I see—your pride is involved."

"Not merely pride—our self-respect. In 1831 before the Northern Abolitionists began their crusade of violence there were one hundred four abolition societies in America—ninety-eight of them in the South and only six in the entire North. But the South grew rich. At the bottom of our whole trouble lies the issue of sectional power. New England threatened to secede from the Union when we added the Territory of Louisiana to our domain, out of which we have carved seven great States. Slavery at that time was not an issue. Sectional rivalry and sectional hatred antedates even our fight against England for our freedom. Washington was compelled to warn his soldiers when they entered New England to avoid the appearance of offense. The Governor of Massachusetts refused to call on George Washington, the first President of the Union, when he visited Boston.

"And mark you, back of the sectional issue looms a vastly bigger one—whether the Union is a Republic of republics or a Centralized Empire. The millions of foreigners who have poured into the North from Europe during the past thirty years, until their white population outnumbers ours four to one, know nothing and care nothing about the Constitution of our fathers. They know nothing and care nothing for the principles on which the Federal Union was founded. They came from empires. They think as their fathers thought in Europe. And they are driving the sons of the old Revolution in the North into the acceptance of the ideas of centralized power. If this tendency continues the President of the United States will become the most autocratic ruler of the world. The South stands for the sovereignty of the States as the only bulwark against the growth of this irresponsible centralized despotism. The Democratic party of the North, thank God, yet stands with us on that issue. Our only possible hope of success in case of war lies in this fact—"

Socola suddenly started.

"Quite so—I see—The North may be divided, the South will be a unit."

"Exactly; they'll fight as one man if they must."

The longer Socola talked with this pale, earnest, self-poised man, the deeper grew the conviction of his utter sincerity, his singleness of purpose, his pure and lofty patriotism. His conception of the man and his aims had completely changed and with this change of estimate came the deeper conviction of the vastness of the tragedy toward which the Nation was being hurled by some hidden, resistless power. He had come into the South with a sense of moral superiority and the consciousness not only of the righteousness of his cause but the certainty that God would swiftly confound the enemies of the Union. He had waked with a shock to the certainty that they were entering the arena of the mightiest conflict of the century.

He girded his soul anew for the role he had chosen to play. The character of this Southern leader held for him an endless fascination. It was part of his mission to study him and he lost no opportunity. The greatest surprise he received during his stay was the day of the election of President at Montgomery. He had expected to be present at this meeting of the Southern Convention but, hearing that it would be held behind closed doors, had been decided on his visit to Briarfield.

A messenger dashed up to the gate, sprang from his horse, hurried into the garden, thrust a telegram into the Senator's hand.

He opened it without haste, and read it slowly. His face went white and he crushed the piece of paper with a sudden gesture of despair. For a moment he forgot his guest, his head was raised as if in prayer and from the depths came the agonizing cry of a soul in mortal anguish:

"Lord, God, if it be possible let this cup pass from me!"

A moment of dazed silence and he turned to Socola. He spoke as a judge pronouncing his own sentence of death. His voice trembled with despair and his lips twitched with pitiful suffering.

"I have been elected President of the Southern Confederacy!"

He handed the telegram to Socola, who scanned it with thrilling interest. He had half expected this announcement from the first. What he could not dream was the remarkable way in which the

Southern leader would receive it.

"You are a foreigner, Signor. I may be permitted to speak freely to you. You are a man of culture and sympathy and you can understand me. As God is my judge, I have neither desired nor expected this position. I took particular pains to forestall and make it impossible. But it has come. I am not a politician. I have never stooped to their tricks. I cannot lie and smile and bend to low chicanery. I hate a fool and I cannot hedge and trim and be all things to all men. I have never been a demagogue. I'm too old to begin. Other men are better suited to this position than I—"

He paused, overcome. Socola studied him with surprise.

"Permit me to say, sir," he ventured disinterestedly, "that such a spirit is evidence that your people have risen to the occasion and that their choice may be an inspiration."

The leader's eye suddenly pierced his guest's.

"God knows what is best. It may be His hand. It may be that I must bow to His will—"

Again he paused and looked wistfully at Socola's youthful face.

"You are young, Signor—you do not know what it is to yield the last ambition of life! I have given all to my country for the past years. I have sacrificed health and wealth and every desire of my soul— peace and contentment here with those I love! When I saw this mighty struggle coming, I feared a tragic end for my people. I fear it now. The man who leads her armies will win immortality no matter what the fate of her cause—I've dreamed of this, Signor—but they've nailed me to the cross!"

He called his negroes together and made them an affectionate speech. They responded with deep expressions of their devotion and their faith. With the greatest sorrow of life darkening his soul he left next day for his inauguration at Montgomery.

9: THE OLD REGIME

Socola left Briarfield with the assurance of the President-elect of the Confederacy that he might spend a week with the Bartons and yet be in ample time for the inauguration at Montgomery.

He boarded the steamer at the Davis landing and floated lazily down to Baton Rouge.

From Briarfield he carried an overwhelming impression of the folly of Slavery from its economic point of view. The thing which amazed his orderly New England mind was the confusion, the waste, the sentimental extravagance, the sheer idiocy of the slave system of labor as contrasted with the free labor of the North.

The one symbol before his vivid imagination was the sight of old Uncle Bob and Aunt Rhinah seated in their rocking chairs gravely listening to the patriarchal farewell of their master. The ancient seers dreamed of Nirvana. These two wonderful old Africans had surely found it in the new world. No wave of trouble could ever roll across their peaceful breasts so long as their lord and master lived. He was their king, their protector, their physician, their almoner, their friend. The burden of life was on his shoulders, not on theirs. Their working days were over. He must feed and clothe, house and care for their worthless bodies unto the end. And the number of these helpless ones were constantly increased.

He marveled at the folly that imagined such a system of labor possible in a real world where the iron laws of economic survival were allowed free play. He ceased to wonder why it still flourished in the South. The South was yet an unsettled jungle of bewildering tropical beauty. One might travel for miles and hundreds of miles without the sight of a single important town. Vast reaches of untouched forests stretched away in all directions. Apparently the foot of man had never pressed them. Rich plantations of thousands of acres were only scratched in spots to yield their marvelous harvests of cotton and cane, of rice and corn.

The idea of defending such a territory, extending over thousands of miles, from the invading hosts of the rich and densely populated

North was preposterous. His heart leaped with the certainty of swift and sure triumph for the Union should the question be submitted to the test of the sword.

As the boat touched her landing at Baton Rouge, Jennie waved her welcome from the shore. The graceful figure of her younger brother stood straight and trim by her side in his new volunteer uniform. Whatever the political leaders might think or do, these Southern people meant to fight. There was no mistaking that fact. With every letter to his Chief in Washington he had made this plain. The deeper he had penetrated the lower South the more overwhelming this conviction had become.

For the moment he put the thought of his tragic mission out of his heart. There was something wonderful in the breath of this early Southern spring. The first week in February and flowers were blooming on every lawn of every embowered cottage and every stately house! The song of birds, the hum of bees, the sweet languor of the perfumed air found his inmost soul. The snows lay cold and still and deathlike over the Northern world.

This was fairyland.

And the Bartons' home on the banks of the river was the last touch that completed the capture of his imagination. Through a vista of overhanging boughs he caught the flash of its white fluted pillars in the distance. The broad verandas were arched with climbing roses. In the center of the sunlit space in front a fountain played, the splash of its cooling waters keeping time to the song of mocking birds in shrubs and trees. In the spacious grounds which swept to the water's edge more than a thousand magnificent trees spread their cooling shade. The white rays of the Southern sun shot through them like silver threads and glowed here and there in the changing, shimmering splotches on the ground.

And everywhere the grinning faces of slowly moving negroes. The very rhythm of their lazy walk seemed a part of the landscape.

This fairy world belonged to his country. His heart went out in renewed devotion. Not one shining Southern star should ever be torn from her diadem! He swore it.

For three days he bathed in the beauty and joy of a Southern home. He saw but little of Jennie. The boys absorbed him. They were eager for news. They plied him with a thousand questions. Tom was going to join the navy, Jimmie and Billy the army. "Would the United States Army stand by the old flag?" Tom asked with painful eagerness.

Socola was non-committal.

"As a rule the sailor is loyal to the flag of his ship. It's the symbol of home, of country, of all he holds dear."

"That's so, too," Tom answered thoughtfully. "Well, we'll build a navy. We built the old one. We can build a new one!"

The last night Socola spent at Fairview was one never to be forgotten. It gave him another picture of the old regime. They sat on the great pillared front porch looking out on the silvery surface of the moonlit river. Jennie's grandfather. Colonel James Barton, a stately man of eighty-five, who had led a regiment with Jefferson Davis in the Mexican War, though at that time long past the age of military service, honored them with his presence to a late hour.

His eyes were failing but his voice was stentorian. Its tones had been developed to even deeper power during the past ten years owing to the deafness of his wife. This beautiful old woman sat softly rocking beside the Colonel, answering in gentle monosyllables the questions he roared into her ears.

To escape the volume of the Colonel's conversation Socola asked Jennie to walk to the river's edge.

They sat down on a bench perched high on the bluff which rose abruptly from the water at the lower end of the grounds. The scene was one of memorable beauty.

He laughed at the folly of his schemes to learn the inner secrets of the South. These people had no secrets. They wore their hearts on their sleeves. He had only to ask a question to receive the answer direct without reserve.

"Your three younger brothers will fight for the South, of course, Miss Jennie?"

"Of course—I only wish I were a man!"

"You have an older brother in New Orleans, I believe?"

"Judge Barton, yes."

"He, too, will enter the army?"

The girl drew a deep breath and hesitated.

"He says he will not. He is bitterly opposed to my father's views."

Socola's eyes sparkled.

"He is for the Union then?"

"Yes."

"He is a man of decided views and character I take it."

"Yes—as firm and unyielding in his position as my father on the other side."

"You will be very bitter towards him if war should come?"

"Bitter?" A little sob caught her voice. "He is my Big Brother. I love him. It would break my heart—that's all—but I'll love him always."

Her tones were music, her loyalty to her own so sweet in its simplicity, so utterly charming, he opened his lips to speak the first words to test her personal attitude toward him. A flirtation would be delightful with such a girl. And Mr. Dick Welford was a fearful temptation. He put the thought out of his heart. She was too good and fine to be made a pawn in such a game. Beside it was utterly unnecessary.

He had gotten exactly the information about this older brother in New Orleans he desired and sat in brooding silence.

Jennie rose suddenly.

"Oh, I forgot—I must go in. My maids are waiting for me, I've an affair to settle between them before they go to bed."

Socola accompanied her to the door and turned again on the lawn to enjoy the white glory of the Southern moon. The lights were still twinkling in the long rows of negro cabins that lined the way to the overseer's house. Through the shadows of the trees he could see the dark figures in the doorways of their cabins silhouetted against the lighted candles in the background.

He strolled leisurely into the lower hall. The door of the library was open. He paused at the scene within. A group of four little negro girls surrounded Jennie. She was reading the Bible to them.

"Can't you say your prayers together tonight?" the young mistress asked.

The kinky heads shook emphatically.

Lucy couldn't say hers with Amy: "'Cause she ain't got no brother and sister to pray for."

Maggie couldn't say hers with Mandy: "'Cause she ain't got no mother and father.'"

So each repeated her prayer alone and stood before their little mistress who sat in judgment on their day's deeds.

Lucy had jabbed a carving knife into Amy's arm in a fit of temper.

Her prayer had made no mention of this important fact. The judge gave a tender lecture on the need of repentance. The little sullen black figure hung back stubbornly for a moment and walled her eyes at her enemy. A sudden burst of tears and they were in each other's arms, crying and begging forgiveness. And then they filed out, one by one.

"Good night, Miss Jennie!"

"Good night!"

"God bless you, Miss Jennie—"

"I'll never be bad no mo'!"

He had come to break the chains that cut through human flesh and he had found this—great God!

For hours he lay awake, dreaming with wide staring eyes of the long blood-stained history of human Slavery and its sharp contrast with the strange travesty of such an institution which the South was giving to the world.

He had barely lost consciousness when he leaped to the floor, roused by loud voices, tramping feet and the flash of weird lights on the lawn. Growls and long calls echoed from point to point on the spacious grounds, hulloes and echoing answers and the tramp of many feet.

Some horrible thing had happened—sudden death, murder or war had broken out. A voice was screaming from the balcony aloft that sounded like the trumpet of the arch-angel calling the end of time.

He listened.

It was old Colonel Barton yelling at the sleepy negroes. In heaven's high name what could they be doing?

Socola dressed hastily and rushed down-stairs. Jennie and the boys appeared almost at the same moment.

"What is it?" Socola asked excitedly. "War has been declared? The slaves have risen?"

Jennie laughed.

"No—no! Grandmamma smells a smell. She thinks something is burning somewhere."

"Oh—"

The whole place, house, yard, grounds, outhouses, swarmed with bellowing negroes. Those that were not bellowing were muttering in sleepy, quarrelsome protest.

And they all carried candles to look for a fire in the dark!

There were at least seventy—two-thirds of them too old or too young to be of any service, but they belonged to the house.

The old Colonel's voice could be heard a mile. In his nightgown he was roaring from the balcony, giving his orders for the busy crowd hunting for fire with their candles flickering in the shadows.

Old Mrs. Barton, serenely deaf, was of course oblivious of the sensation she had created. The loss of her hearing had rendered doubly acute her sense of smell. Candles had to be taken out of her room to be snuffed. Lamps were extinguished only on the portico or on the lawn. Violets she couldn't endure. A tea rose was never allowed in her room. Only one kind of sweet rose would she tolerate at close range.

In the mildest voice she was suggesting places to be searched.

Far out at the negro quarters the candle brigade at length gathered —the flickering lights closing in to a single point one by one.

The smell was found.

A family had been boiling soap—a slave-ridden plantation was a miniature world which must be practically self-supporting. There could be no economy of labor by its scientific division. Around the soap pot the negro woman had swept some woolen rags. They were smoldering there and the faint odor had been wafted to the great house.

Socola couldn't sleep. All night long he could hear that wild commotion—the old Colonel's voice roaring from the balcony and seventy sleepy, good-for-nothing negroes with lighted candles looking for a fire in the dark. When at last he was tired of laughing at the ridiculous picture, his foolish fancy took another turn and fixed itself again on old Bob and Aunt Rhinah in their rocking chairs, swathed in cochineal flannel.

10: THE GAUGE OF BATTLE

Socola found the little town of Montgomery, Alabama, breathing under a suppression of emotion that was little short of uncanny on the day Jefferson Davis was inaugurated President.

The streets were crowded to suffocation and tents were necessary to accommodate the people who could not be housed.

He was surprised at the strange quiet which the spirit of the new President had communicated to the people. There was no loud talk, no braggadocio, no threats, no clamor for war. On the contrary there had suddenly developed an overwhelming desire for a peaceful solution of the crisis.

The Convention which had unanimously elected Jefferson Davis, President, and Alexander H. Stephens, Vice President, had relegated the hot heads and fire eaters to the rear.

Three great agitators had really created the new nation, William L. Yancey of Alabama, Robert Toombs of Georgia and Barnwell Rhett of South Carolina. And they were consumed with ambition for the Presidency.

Toombs was the most commanding figure among the uncompromising advocates of secession in the South—an orator of consummate power, a man of wide learning and magnetic personality. William L. Yancey was as powerful an agitator as ever stirred the souls of an American audience since the foundation of our Republic. Barnwell Rhett of the *Charleston Mercury* was the most influential editor the country had ever produced.

Yet the suddenness with which these fiery leaders were dropped in the hour of crisis was so amazing to the men themselves they had not yet recovered sufficient breath to begin complaints.

Toombs destroyed what chance he ever had by getting drunk at a banquet the night before the Convention met. William L. Yancey's turbulent history ruled him out of consideration. He had killed his father-in-law in a street brawl. Rhett's extreme views had been the bugle call to battle but something more than sound was needed now.

Toombs was dropped even for Vice-President for Alexander H.

Stephens, the man who had pleaded in tears with his State not to secede.

The highest honor had been forced on the one man in all the South who most passionately wished to avoid it.

So acute was the consciousness of tragedy there was scarcely a ripple of applause at public functions where Socola had looked for mad enthusiasm.

The old Constitution had been reenacted with no essential change. The new President had even insisted that the Provisional Congress retain the old flag as their emblem of nationality with only a new battle flag for use in case of war. The Congress over-ruled him at this point with an emphasis which they meant as a rebuke to his tendency to cling to the hope of reconciliation.

It was exactly one o'clock on Monday, February 18, 1861, that Jefferson Davis rose between the towering pillars of the State Capitol in Montgomery and began his inaugural address. It was careful, moderate, statesmanlike, and a model of classic English. The closing sentence swept the crowd.

"It is joyous in the midst of perilous times to look thus upon a people united in heart, whose one purpose of high resolve animates and actuates the whole; where the sacrifices to be made are not weighed in the balance against honor, and right, and liberty and equality." The cheer that greeted his appeal rose and fell again and again the third time with redoubled power and enthusiasm.

The President-elect stepped forward, placed his hand on the open Bible, and took the oath of office. As the last word fell from his white lips cannon thundered a salute from the hill crest and the great silk ensign of the South was slowly lifted by the hand of the granddaughter of President Tyler.

As the breeze unrolled its huge red, white and blue folds against the shining Southern skies the crowd burst into hysterical applause.

A Nation had been born whose history might be brief, but the people who created it and the leader who guided its destiny were the pledge of its immortality.

Socola found no difficulty in possessing himself of every secret of the new Government. What was not proclaimed from the street corners and shouted from the housetops, the newspapers printed in double leads. The new Government had yet to organize its secret service.

The President addressed himself with energy to the task which confronted him. But seven States had yet enrolled in the Confederacy. Of four more he felt sure. The first attempt to coerce a Southern State by force of arms would close the ranks with Virginia, North Carolina, Tennessee and Arkansas by his side. Maryland, Kentucky and Missouri were peopled by the South and the institution of Slavery bound them in a common cause.

And yet the defense of these eleven Southern States with their five million white population and four million blacks was a task to stagger the imagination of the greatest statesman of any age. This vast territory would present an open front on land of more than a thousand miles without a single natural barrier. Its sea coast presented three thousand miles of water front—open to the attack of the navy. This enormous coast of undefended shore was pierced by river after river whose broad, deep waters would carry the gunboats of an enemy into the heart of the South.

The audacity of our fathers in challenging the power of Great Britain was reasonable in comparison with the madness of the South's challenge to the North. Three thousand miles of storm-tossed ocean defended our Revolutionary ancestors from the base of the enemy supplies. Three thousand miles of undefended coast invited the attack of the U. S. Navy, while twenty million Northerners stood with their feet on the borders of the South ready to advance without the possibility of hindrance save the bare breasts of the men who might oppose them.

The difference between the sections in material resources was absurd. The North was rich and powerful. Her engines of war were exhaustless and under perfect control. The railroads of the South were few and poorly equipped, with no work shops from which to renew their equipment when exhausted. The railroad system of the entire country was absolutely dependent on the North for supplies. The Missouri River was connected with the Northern seaboard by the finest system of railways in the world, with a total mileage of over thirty thousand. Its annual tonnage was thirty-six million and its revenue valued at four thousand millions of dollars. The annual value of the manufactures of the North was over two thousand millions, and their machinery was complete for the production of all the material of war. Her ships sailed every sea and she could draw upon the resources of the known world. Her manufacturing power compared to the South was five hundred to one.

No leader in the history of his race was ever confronted by such insuperable difficulties as faced Jefferson Davis.

He had been called to direct the government of a proud, sensitive, jealous people thrown without preparation into a position which threatened their existence, without an army, without arms, or the means to manufacture them, without even powder, or the means to make it, or the material out of which it must be made, without a navy or a single shipyard in which to build one, and three thousand miles of coast to be defended against a navy which had whipped the greatest maritime nation of the world. His genius must meet every difficulty and supply every want or his Confederacy would fall at the first shock of war. The one tremendous and apparently insuperable difficulty in case of war was the lack of a navy. A navy could not be built in a day, or a year or two years, were the resources of the Confederacy boundless. The ships of war now in the possession of the United States were of incalculable power in such a crisis. The South was cut in every quarter by navigable rivers. Many of their waters opened on Northern interiors accessible to great workshops from which new gunboats could be built with rapidity and launched against the South. The Mississippi River, navigable for a thousand miles, flowed through the entire breadth of the Confederacy with its approaches and its mouth in the hands of the North. Both the Tennessee and the Cumberland rivers had their mouths open to Northern frontiers and were navigable in midwinter for transports and gunboats which could pierce the heart of Tennessee and Alabama.

It is not to be wondered at, therefore, that the first purpose of the President of the Confederacy was to secure peace by all means consistent with public honor and the trust imposed on him by the people.

His first official act was the dispatch of Confederate Commissioners to Washington to treat for peace.

The hope that they would be received with courtesy and consideration was a reasonable one. The greatest newspapers of the North were outspoken in their opposition to the use of arms against any State of the Union.

The *New York Tribune*, the creator of Lincoln's party, led in this opposition to the use of force. The *Albany Argus* and the *New York Herald* were equally emphatic. Governor Seymour of New York boldly declared in a great mass meeting his unalterable opposition to coercion. The *Detroit Free Press* suggested that a fire would be poured into the rear of any troops raised to coerce a State. It was already known that Mr. Lincoln would not advocate coercion in his inaugural.

Stephen A. Douglas, leader of the millions of the Northern Democracy, offered a resolution in the Senate of the United States recommending the immediate withdrawal of the garrisons from all forts within the limits of the States which had seceded except those at Key West and Dry Tortugas needful for coaling stations.

"I proclaim boldly," declared the Senator from Illinois, "the policy of those with whom I act. We are for peace!"

Socola reported to his Chief in Washington that nothing was more certain than that Jefferson Davis hoped for reunion, with guarantees against aggression by the stronger section of the Union.

Buchanan had agreed to receive the Southern Commissioners, and sent a message to Congress announcing their presence and their overtures.

The Commissioners found Washington seething with passion and trembling with excitement. Buchanan had collapsed in terror, fearing each hour to hear that his home had been sacked and burned at Wheatland.

But the Southern leaders' hope of peaceful settlement was based on a surer foundation than the shattered nerves of the feeble old man in the White House. Joseph Holt, the Secretary of War, was a Southern Democrat born in Kentucky, and from the State of Mississippi. Holt had called on Davis in Washington and assured him of his loyalty to the South and her people. The President of the Confederacy knew of his consuming personal ambitions and had assured him of his influence to secure generous treatment.

But the Secretary of War had received information from the South. He had studied the situation carefully. He believed his chances of advancement in the North a better risk. The new Government had ignored him in the selection of a Cabinet—and with quick decision he cast his fortunes with the Union. That he had deceived Davis and Clay, to whom he had given his pledge of Southern loyalty, was a matter of no importance, save that these two men, who alone knew his treachery, were marked for his vengeance.

Little could they dream in this hour the strange end toward which Fate was even now hurrying them through the machinations of this sullen, envious Southern renegade.

The Secretary of War placed his big fist on the throat of the trembling President, and the Peace Commissioners could not reach the White House or its councils.

They were forced to await the inauguration of Abraham Lincoln.

Jefferson Davis gave himself body and soul to the task of preparing his over-sanguine, credulous people for the possible tragedy of war.

General Beauregard was ordered to command the forces in South Carolina, and erect batteries for the defense of Charleston and the reduction of Fort Sumter in case of an attempt to reinforce it. This grim fort, in the center of the harbor of the chief Southern Atlantic city, commanded the gateway of the Confederacy. If it should be reinforced, the Confederate Government might be strangled by the fall of Charleston, and the landing of an army even before a blow could be struck.

Captain Raphael Semmes was sent North to buy every gun in the market. He was directed to secure machinery, and skilled workingmen to man it, for the establishment of arsenals and shops, and above all to buy any vessel afloat suitable for offensive or defensive work. Not a single ship of any description could be had, and the intervention of the authorities finally prevented the delivery of a single piece of machinery or the arms he had purchased.

Major Huse was sent to Europe on the third day after the inauguration at Montgomery on a similar mission.

General G.W. Rains was appointed to establish a manufactory for ammunition. His work was an achievement of genius. He created artificial niter beds, from which sufficient saltpeter was obtained, and within a year was furnishing the finest powder.

General Gorgas was appointed Chief of Ordnance. There was but one iron mill in the South which could cast a cannon, and that was the little Tredegar works at Richmond, Virginia. The State of Virginia had voted against secession and it would require the first act of war against her Southern sisters to bring her to their defense.

The widespread belief in the North that the South had secretly prepared for war, was utterly false, and yet the impression was of the utmost importance to the President of the Confederacy. It gave his weak government a fictitious strength, and gave him a brief time in which to prepare his raw recruits for their first battle.

Day and night he prayed for peace at any sacrifice save that of honor. The first bloodshed would be the match in the powder magazine. He pressed his Commissioners in Washington for haste.

The inaugural address of Abraham Lincoln had been so carefully worded, its utterances so conservative and guarded, his expressions of good will toward the South so surprisingly emphatic, that Davis could not believe an act of aggression which would bring bloodshed could be committed by his order.

And yet day dragged after day with no opportunity afforded his Commissioners to treat with the new Administration save through the undignified course of an intermediary. The Southern President ordered that all questions of form or ceremony be waived.

Seward, the Secretary of State, gave to these Commissioners repeated assurances of the peaceful intention of the Government at Washington, and the most positive promise that Fort Sumter would be evacuated. He also declared that no measure would be instituted either by the Executive or Congress changing the situation except on due notice given the Commissioners.

These assurances were accepted by the Confederate President in absolute good faith. And yet early in April the news was flashed to Montgomery that extraordinary preparations were being made in the Northern ports for a military and naval expedition against the South. On April the fifth, sixth and seventh, a fleet of transports and warships with shotted guns, munitions and military supplies sailed for Charleston.

The Commissioners in alarm requested an answer to their proposals. To their amazement they were informed that the President of the United States had already determined to hold no communication with them whatever in any capacity or listen to any proposals they had to make.

On Beauregard's report to them that Anderson was endeavoring to strengthen his position instead of evacuating the Fort, the Commissioners again communicated with Mr. Seward.

The wily Secretary of State assured them that the Government had not receded from his promise. On April seventh Mr. Seward sent them this message:

"Faith as to Sumter fully kept: wait and see."

His war fleet was already on the high seas, their black prows pointed southward, their one hundred and twenty guns full with shot, their battle flags streaming in the sky!

Lincoln's sense of personal honor was too keen to permit this crooked piece of diplomacy to stain the opening of his administration. He dispatched a special messenger to the Governor of South Carolina and gave notice of his purpose to use force if opposed in his intention of supplying Fort Sumter.

On the eve of the day the fleet was scheduled to arrive this notice was delivered. But a storm at sea had delayed the expedition and Beauregard asked the President of the Confederacy for instructions.

His Cabinet was called, and its opinion was unanimous that Fort Sumter must be reduced or the Confederacy dissolved. There was no choice.

Their President rose, his drawn face deadly pale:

"I agree with you, gentlemen. The order of the sailing of the fleet was a declaration of war. The responsibility is on their shoulders, not ours. To juggle for position as to who shall fire the first gun in such an hour is unworthy of a great people and their cause. A deadly weapon has been aimed at our heart. Only a fool would wait until the shot has been fired. The assault has already been made. It is of no importance who shall strike the first blow or fire the first gun."

With quick decision he seized his pen and wrote the order for the reduction of Fort Sumter.

11: JENNIE'S VISION

Wild rumors of bombardment held Charleston in a spell.

Jennie Barton sat alone on the roof of her aunt's house at two o'clock on the morning of April 13. The others had gone to bed, certain that the rumors were false. She had somehow felt the certainty of the crash.

Seated beside the brick coping of the roof she leaned the strong little chin in her hands, waited and watched. Lights were flickering around the shore batteries like fireflies winking in the shadows of deep woods. Her three brothers were there. She might look on their dead faces tomorrow. Her father had rushed to Charleston from Washington at the first news of the sailing of the fleet. He had begged and pleaded with General Beauregard to reduce the Fort immediately, with or without orders from Davis.

"For God's sake, use your discretion as Commanding General and open fire. If that fleet reaches Sumter the cause of the Confederacy is lost. Old Davis is too slow. He's still crying peace, peace, when there is no peace. The war has begun!"

The General calmly shook his head and asked for instructions.

Besides losing her brothers, she might be an orphan tomorrow. Her father was quite capable of an attack on Sumter without orders. And if the bombardment should begin he would probably be roaming over the harbor from fort to fort, superintending the job under the guns of both sides.

"If Anderson does not accept the terms of surrender offered, he will be fired on at four o'clock." Jennie repeated the headlines of the extra with a shiver.

The chimes of St. Michael's struck three. The minutes slowly dragged.

The half hour was sung through the soft balmy air of the Southern spring.

Dick Welford, too, was behind one of those black guns on the shore. How handsome he had looked in his bright new uniform! He was a soldier from the crown of his blond head to the soles of his heavy feet. He had laughed at danger. She had liked him for that. He hadn't posed. He hadn't asked for sympathy or admiration. He just marched to his duty with the quick, firm step of the man who means business.

She was sorry now she hadn't told him how much she liked and admired him. She might not have another chance.

"Nonsense, of course I will!" she murmured with a toss of her brown head.

A dog barked across the street, and a wagon rattled hurriedly over the cobblestones below. A rooster crowed for day.

She looked across the way, and a dark group of whispering women were huddled in a corner on the roof, their gaze fixed on Sumter.

Another wagon rumbled heavily over the cobbles, and another, and another. A blue light flamed from Fort Sumter, blinking at intervals. Anderson was signaling someone. To the fleet that lay on the eastern horizon beyond the bar, perhaps.

The chimes of St. Michael struck the fatal hour of four. Their sweet notes rang clear and soft and musical over the dim housetops just as they had sung to the sleeping world through years of joyous peace.

Jennie sprang to her feet and strained her eyes toward the black lump that was Sumter out in the harbor. She waited with quick beating heart for the first flash of red from the shore batteries. It did not come. Five minutes passed that seemed an hour, and still no sound of war.

Only those wagons were rumbling now at closer intervals—one after the other in quick succession. They were ammunition trains! The crack of the drivers' whips could be heard distinctly, and the cries of the men urging their horses on. The noise became at last a dull, continuous roar.

The chimes from the old church tower again sang the half hour and then it came—a sudden sword leap of red flame on the horizon! A shell rose in the sky, glowing in pale phosphorescent trail, and burst in a flash of blinding flame over the dark lump in the harbor. The flash had illumined the waters and revealed the clear outlines of the casemates with their black mouths of steel gaping through the portholes. A roar of deep, dull thunder shook the world.

Jennie fell on her knees with clasped hands and upturned face. Her lips were not moving, and no sound came from the little dry throat, but from the depths of her heart rose the old, old cry of love.

"Lord have mercy on my darling brothers, and keep them safe—let no harm come to them—and Dick, too—brave and strong!"

The house below was stirring with the rush of hurrying feet in the corridors and the clatter on the narrow stairs that led to the roof. They crowded to the edge and gazed seaward. The hum of voices came now from every house. Women were crying. Some were praying. Men were talking in low, excited tones.

Jennie paid no attention to the people about her. Her eyes were fixed on those tongues of flame that circled Sumter.

Anderson was firing now, his big guns flashing their defiant answer to Beauregard's batteries. Jennie watched the lurid track of his shells with sickening dread.

A man standing beside her in the gray dawn spoke.

"A waste of ammunition!"

The cannon boomed now with the regular throb of a great human pulse. The sobs and excited cries and prayers of women had become a part of the weird scene.

A young mother stood beside Jennie with a baby boy in her arms. He was delighted with the splendid display and the roar of the guns.

He pointed his fingers to the circling shells and cried:

"Ook, mamma, 'ook!"

The mother made no answer. Only with her hungry eyes did she follow their track to the shore. Her mate was there.

The baby clapped his hands and caught the rhythm of the throb and roar of the cannon in his little voice:

"Boom!—Boom!"

The sun rose from the sea, a ball of dull red fire glowing ominously through the haze of smoke that hung in the sky.

Hour after hour the guns pealed, the windows rattled and the earth trembled.

Couriers were dashing into the city with reports from the batteries. Soldiers were marching through the streets. It was reported that the men from the fleet would attempt a landing.

The women rushed to the little iron balcony and watched the troops marching to repel them.

In the first line Jennie saw the tall figure of Dick Welford. He glanced upward, lifted his cap and held it steadily in his hand for four blocks until they turned and swept out of sight.

Jennie was leaning on the rail with tear-dimmed eyes.

"I wonder why that soldier took his hat off?" her aunt asked.

"Yes—I wonder!" was the soft answer.

By three o'clock it was known that not a man had been killed at either of the shore batteries and women began to smile and breathe once more.

The newsboys were screaming an extra.

Jennie hurried into the street and bought one.

In big black headlines she read:

RICHMOND AND WASHINGTON ABLAZE WITH EXCITEMENT!

THE NORTH WILD WITH RAGE

VIRGINIA AND NORTH CAROLINA ARMING TO COME TO OUR RESCUE!

She walked rapidly to the water's edge to get the latest news from the front. A tiny rowboat was deliberately pulling through the harbor squarely under the guns of Sumter. She watched it with amazement, looking each moment to see it disappear beneath the waves. It was probably her foolish father.

With steady, even stroke the boatman pulled for the shore as unconcerned as if he were listening to the rattle of firecrackers on the fourth of July.

To her surprise it proved to be a negro. He tied his boat and deliberately unloaded his supply of vegetables. His stolid, sphinx-like face showed neither fear nor interest.

"Weren't you afraid of Anderson's cannon, uncle?" Jennie asked.

"Nobum—nobum—"

"You might have been blown to pieces—"

"Nobum—Marse Anderson daresn't hit me!"

"Why not?"

"He knows my marster don't 'low nuttin like dat—I'se too val'eble er nigger. Nobum, dey ain't none ob 'em gwine ter pester me, an' I ain't gwine ter meddle wid dem—dey kin des fight hit out twixt 'em—"

Through the long night the steady boom of cannon, and the scream of shells from the shore.

At one o'clock next day the flagstaff was cut down by a solid shot, and Sumter was silent.

At three o'clock a mob surged up the street following Senator Barton, who had just come from the harbor. He was on his way to Beauregard's headquarters.

Anderson had surrendered.

A strange quiet held the city. There was no jubilation, no bonfires, no illuminations to celebrate the victory. A sigh of relief for deliverance from a great danger that had threatened their life—that was all.

The Southern flag was flying now from the battered walls, and the people were content. They were glad that Beauregard had given old Bob Anderson the privilege of saluting his flag and marching out with the honors of war. All they asked was to be let alone.

And they were doubly grateful for the strange Providence that had saved every soldier's life while the walls of the Fort had been hammered into a shapeless mass. No blood had yet been spilled on either side. The President of the Confederacy caught the wonderful news from the wires with a cry of joy.

"Peace may yet be possible!" he exclaimed excitedly. "No blood has been spilled in actual conflict—"

His joy was short lived. A rude awakening was in store.

Dick Welford strolled along the brilliantly lighted "Battery" that night with Jennie's little hand resting on his arm.

"I tell you, Jennie, I was scared!" he was saying with boyish earnestness. "You see a fellow never knows how he's going to come out of a close place like that till he tries it. I had a fine uniform and I'd learned the drill and all that—but I had not smelled brimstone at short range. I didn't know how I'd do under fire. Now I know I'm a worthy descendant of my old Scotch-Irish ancestor who held a British officer before him for a shield and gracefully backed out of danger."

They stopped and gazed over the lazy, shimmering waters of the harbor.

Jennie looked up into his manly face with a glow of pride.

"You're splendid, Dick,—I'm proud of you!"

"Are you?" he asked eagerly.

"Yes. You're just like my brothers."

"Look here now, Jennie," he protested, "Don't you go telling me that you'll be a sister to me. I've got a lot of sisters at home and I don't need any more—"

"I didn't mean it that way, Dick," she responded tenderly. "My brothers are just the finest, bravest men that God ever made in this world—that's what I meant."

"Don't you like me a little?"

"I almost love you tonight—maybe it's our victory—maybe it's the fear that made me pray for you and the boys on that house top the other night—I don't know—"

"Did you pray for me?" he asked softly.

"Yes—"

"I ought to be satisfied with that, but I'm not—I want you! Won't you be mine?"

She smiled into his eager face in a gentle, whimsical way. A half promise to him was just trembling on her lips when Socola's slender, erect figure suddenly crossed the street. He lifted his hat with a genial bow.

Dick ground his teeth in a smothered oath, and Jennie spoke abruptly:

"Come—it's late—we must go in."

Through the long night the girl lay awake with the calm, persistent, smiling face of the foreigner looking into the depths of her brown eyes.

12: A LITTLE CLOUD

The first aggressive act of the President of the Confederacy revealed his alert and far-seeing mind. His keen eye was bent upon the sea, with an instinctive appreciation of the tremendous import of the long Southern coast line.

Without a ship afloat or a single navy yard, by a stroke of his pen he created a fleet destined to sweep the commerce of the North from every sea. His task was to create something out of nothing and how well he did it events swiftly bore their testimony.

The United States Government was the only nation which had refused to join the agreement to abandon the use of letters of marque and reprisal for destroying the unarmed vessels of commerce in time of war. This unfortunate piece of diplomacy gave Jefferson Davis the opportunity to strike his first blow at the power and prestige of the North.

He immediately issued a proclamation offering to issue such letters to any ship that would arm herself and enlist under the ensign of the Confederate navy. The response was quick and the ultimate result the lowering of the flag of the Union from practically every ship of commerce that sailed the ocean.

Gideon Welles conferred with his Chief in Washington and Abraham Lincoln issued a proclamation which at the time created scarcely a ripple of excitement. And yet that order was the most important document which came from the White House during the entire four years of the war.

When the test came sixteen captains, thirty-four commanders and one hundred and eleven midshipmen resigned and cast their fortunes with the South. Not one of them attempted to use his position to surrender a ship.

Small as it was, the entire navy of the United States was practically intact. It comprised ninety ships of war—forty-two of them ready for active service. The majority of the vessels ready for war were steam-propelled craft of the latest improved type.

The United States had been one of the first world powers to

realize the value of steam and rebuild its navy accordingly. In twenty years, practically a new navy had been constructed, ranking in effective power third only to England and France. Within the past five years, the Government had built the steam frigates, Merrimac, Niagara, Colorado, Wabash, Minnesota, and Roanoke. In addition to these twelve powerful steam sloops of war had been commissioned—the Hartford, Brooklyn, Lancaster, Richmond, Narragansett, Dakota, Iroquois, Wyoming, and Seminole. They were of the highest type of construction and compared favorably with the best ships of the world.

These ships at the opening of the war were widely scattered, but their homeward bound streamers were all fluttering in the sky.

President Lincoln in his proclamation ordered the most remarkable blockade in the history of the world. This document declared three thousand miles of Southern coast, from the Virginia Capes to the Rio Grande, closed to the commerce of the world.

The little fleet boldly sailed on its tremendous mission. The smoke of its funnels made but a tiny smudge on the wide, shining Southern skies. But with swift and terrible swirl this cloud, no bigger than a man's hand, grew into a storm whose black shadow shrouded the Southland in gloom.

13: THE CLOSING OF THE RANKS

A wave of fierce anger swept the North. The fall of Sumter was the one topic on every lip. Men stopped their trade, their work, their play and looked about them for the nearest rallying ground of soldiers.

The President of the United States was quick to seize the favorable moment to call for 75,000 volunteers. That these troops were to fight the Confederacy was not questioned for a moment.

The effect of this proclamation on the South was a political earthquake.

In a single day all differences of opinion were sunk in the common cause. A feeling of profound wonder swept every thoughtful man within the Southern States. To this moment, even a majority of those who favored the policy of secession had done so under the belief that it was the surest way of securing redress of grievances and of bringing the Federal Government back to its original Constitutional principles. Many of them believed, and all of their leaders in authority hoped, that a re-formation of the Union would soon take place in peaceful ways on the basis of the new Constitution proclaimed at Montgomery. Many Northern newspapers, led by the *New York Herald*, had advocated this course. The hope of the majority of the Southern people was steadfast that the Union would thus be continued and strengthened, and made more perfect, as it had been in 1789 after the withdrawal of nine States from the Old Union by the adoption of the Constitution of 1787.

Abraham Lincoln's proclamation shattered all hope of such peaceful adjustment.

Thousands of the best men in Virginia and North Carolina had voted against secession. Not one of them, in the face of this proclamation, would dispute longer with their brethren. Whatever they might think about the expediency of withdrawing from the Union, they were absolutely clear on two points. The President of the United States had no power under the charter of our Government to declare war. Congress only could do that. If the Cotton States were out of the Union, his act was illegal because the usurpation of supreme power. If they were yet in the Union, the raising of an army to invade their homes was a plain violation of the Constitution.

The heart of the South beat as one man. The cause of the war had been suddenly shifted to a broader and deeper foundation about which no possible difference could ever again arise in the Southern States.

The demand for soldiers to invade the South was a bugle call to Southern manhood to fight for their liberties and defend their homes. It gave even to the staunchest Union men of the Old South the overt act of an open breach of the Constitution. From the moment Abraham Lincoln proclaimed a war without the act of Congress, from that moment he became a dictator and a despot who deliberately sought to destroy their liberties.

The cause of the South not only meant the defense of their homes from foreign invasion; it became a holy crusade for the reestablishment of Constitutional freedom.

Virginia immediately seceded from the Union by the vote of the same men who had refused to secede but a few weeks before. The old flag fell from its staff on her Capitol and the new symbol of Southern unity was unfurled in its place. As if by magic the new flag fluttered from every hill, housetop and window, while crowds surged through the streets shouting and waving it aloft. Cannon boomed its advent and cheering thousands saluted it.

A great torchlight parade illumined the streets on April 19. In this procession walked the men who a week ago had marched through Franklin Street waving the old flag of the Union and shouting themselves hoarse in their determination to uphold it. They had signed the ordinance of secession with streaming eyes, but they signed it with firm hands, and sent their sons to the muster fields next day.

Augusta County, a Whig and Union center, and Rockingham, an equally strong Democratic Union county, each contributed fifteen hundred soldiers to the new cause. Women not only began to prepare the equipment for their men, but many of them began to arm and practice themselves. Boys from ten to fourteen were daily drilling. In Petersburg three hundred free negroes offered their services to fight or to ditch and dig.

The bitterness of the answers of the Southern Governors

from the Border States yet in the Union amazed the President at Washington.

His demand for troops was refused in tones of scorn and defiance.

Governor Magoffin of Kentucky replied: "The State will furnish no troops for the wicked purpose of subduing her sister Southern States."

Governor Harris telegraphed from Nashville: "The State of Tennessee will not furnish a single man for coercion, but fifty thousand if necessary for the defense of her rights."

The message of Governor Ellis of North Carolina was equally emphatic: "I will be no party to this wicked violation of the laws of our country, and to this war upon the liberties of a free people."

Governor Rector of Arkansas replied: "Your demand adds insult to injury."

Governor Jackson of Missouri was indignant beyond all others: "Your requisition in my judgment is illegal, unconstitutional, and revolutionary—its objects inhuman and diabolical."

Tennessee followed Virginia by seceding on May 6. Arkansas on May 18, and North Carolina by unanimous vote on May 21.

North Carolina had been slow to announce her final separation from the old Union. But she had been prompt in proclaiming her own sovereign rights within her territory when the National Government had dared to call them in question. On the day the President had issued his proclamation she seized Fort Macon at Beaufort. Fort Caswell was taken and garrisoned by her volunteers, and on April 19, the arsenal at Fayetteville was captured without bloodshed. The value of this achievement to the South was incalculable. The Confederacy thus secured sixty-five thousand stand of arms, of which twenty-eight thousand were of the most modern pattern.

Virginia had seceded on April 17 and immediately moved to secure under the resumption of her complete sovereignty all the arms, munitions of war, ship stores and military posts within her borders. Two posts of tremendous importance she attempted to seize at once—the great navy yard at Norfolk and the arsenal and shops at Harper's Ferry. The navy yard contained a magnificent dry dock worth millions, huge ship houses, supplies, ammunition, small arms and cannon, and had lying in its basin several vessels of war, complete and incomplete.

Harper's Ferry contained ten thousand muskets, five thousand rifles and a complete set of machinery for the manufacture of arms capable of turning out two thousand muskets a month.

A force of Virginia volunteers moved on Harper's Ferry. The small Federal garrison asked for a parley, which was granted. In a short time flames were pouring from the armory and arsenal. The garrison had set fire to the buildings and escaped across the railroad bridge into Maryland.

The Virginia troops rushed into the burning buildings, and saved five thousand muskets and three thousand unfinished rifles. The garrison had laid trains of powder to blow up the workshops, but the Virginians extinguished the flames and saved to the South the invaluable machinery for making and repairing muskets and rifles. It was shipped to Fayetteville and Richmond and installed for safety.

The destruction of the navy yard at Norfolk was more complete and irreparable. The dry dock was little damaged, but the destruction of stores and property was enormous. All ships in the harbor were set on fire and scuttled.

Events moved now with swift and terrible certainty.

Massachusetts attempted, on April 19, to send a regiment through the streets of Baltimore to invade the South, and the indignant wrath of her citizens could not be controlled by the mayor or police. The street cars on which they were riding across town to the Camden station were thrown from the tracks. The crowds jammed the streets and shouted their curses in the face of the advancing volunteers. Stones were hurled into their ranks and two soldiers dropped. A volley was poured into the crowd and several fell dead and wounded.

The crowd went mad. Revolvers were drawn and fired point blank into the ranks of the soldiers and those who were unarmed rushed to arm themselves. From Frederic to Smith Streets the firing on both sides continued with the regular crash of battle. Citizens were falling, but even the unarmed men continued to press forward and hurl stones into the ranks of the New Englanders.

The troops began to yield before the determined onslaughts of the infuriated crowds, bewildered and apparently without real commanders. They pressed through the streets, staggering, confused, breaking into a run and turning to fire on their assailants as they retreated.

Harassed, bleeding and exhausted, the regiment at last reached the Baltimore & Ohio station. The fight continued without pause. Volleys of stones were hurled into the cars, shattering windows and paneling. The troops were ordered to lie down on the floors and keep their heads below the line of the windows. Maddened men pressed to the car windows, cursing and yelling their defiance. For half a mile along the tracks the crowd struggled and shouted, piling the rails with new obstructions as fast as policemen could remove them. Through a steady roar of hoots, yells and curses the train at last pulled slowly out, the troops pouring a volley into the crowd.

In this first irregular battle of the sections the Massachusetts regiment lost four killed and thirty-six wounded. The Baltimoreans lost twelve killed and an unknown number wounded.

A wave of tremendous excitement swept the State of Maryland. Bridges on all railroads leading north were immediately burned and the City of Washington cut off from communication with the outside world. Troops were compelled to avoid Baltimore and find transportation by water to Annapolis. Mass meetings were held and speeches of bitter defiance hurled against the Federal Government. The Baltimore Council appropriated five hundred thousand dollars to put the city in a state of defense, though the State had proclaimed its neutrality.

The shrewd, good-natured, even-tempered President at Washington used all his powers of personal diplomacy to pour oil on the troubled waters of Maryland. In the meantime with swift, sure, and merciless tread he moved on the turbulent State with the power of Federal arms. It was impossible to hold the Capital of the Nation with a hostile State separating it from the loyal North.

The steps he took were all clearly unconstitutional, but they were necessary to save the Capital. They were the acts of a dictator, for Congress was not in session, but he dared to act. Troops were suddenly thrown into the city of Baltimore and its streets and heights planted with cannon. The chief of police was arrested and imprisoned, the police board was suspended and the city brought under the rule of drumhead court-martial. The writ of habeas corpus was suspended by Federal authorities in a free and sovereign State whose Legislature had proclaimed its neutrality in the sectional conflict. Blank warrants were issued by military officers and the house of every suspect entered by force and searched. The mayor and his Council were arrested without warrant, held without trial, and imprisoned in a military fortress, and when the Legislature dared to protest, its members were arrested and its session closed by bayonets.

So thoroughly was this work done that within thirty days from the attack on the troops of New England, Maryland's Governor by proclamation called for four regiments of volunteers to assist the Washington Government in the proposed invasion of the South.

In like manner, with hand of steel within a velvet glove, Mr. Lincoln prevented the secession of Kentucky and Missouri. It was done with less violence, but it was done, and these rich and powerful States saved to the Union.

The swift and bloodless conquest of Maryland inspired the North with the most grotesque conception of the war and its outcome.

The British and French Governments had immediately recognized the Confederate States as belligerents under the terms of international law and closed their ports to the armed vessels of both contestants. Mr. Seward, Lincoln's Secretary of State, hastened to assure the nations of Europe that a dissolution of the Union was an absurd impossibility. It had never entered the mind of any candid statesman in America and should be dismissed at once by statesmen in Europe. And yet at this time eleven Southern States, stretching from the James to the Rio Grande, with a population of eight millions, had by solemn act of their Legislatures withdrawn from the Union and their armies were camping within a few miles of the City of Washington.

In all the North not a single statesman or a single newspaper appeared to have any conception of the serious task before them. The fusillades of rant, passion and bombast which filled the air would have been comic but for the grim tragedy which was stalking in their wake.

The "Rebellion" was ridiculed and sneered at in terms that taxed the genius of the writers for words of contempt.

The *New York Tribune*, the greatest and most powerful organ of public opinion in the North, a paper which had boldly from the first proclaimed the right of the South to peaceable secession, was now swept away with the popular fury.

Its editor gravely declared: "The Southern rebellion is nothing more or less than the natural recourse of all mean-spirited and defeated tyrannies to rule or ruin, making of course a wide distinction between the will and the power, for the hanging of traitors is soon to begin before a month is over. The Nations of Europe may rest assured that Jeff Davis and Co. will be swinging from the battlements at Washington, at least by the fourth of July. We spit upon a later and longer deferred justice."

The *New York Times* gave its opinion with equal clearness:

> "Let us make quick work. The Rebellion is an unborn tadpole. Let us not fall into the delusion of mistaking a local commotion for a revolution.
>
> A strong active pull together will do our work in thirty days. We have only to send a column of twenty-five thousand men across the Potomac to Richmond to burn out the rats there; another column of twenty-five thousand to Cairo to seize the Cotton ports of the Mississippi and retain the remaining twenty-five thousand called for by the President at Washington—not because there is any need for them there but because we do not require their services elsewhere."

The staid old *Philadelphia Press* declared:

> "No man of sense can for a moment doubt that all this much-ado-about-nothing will end in a month. The Northern people are invincible. The rebels are a band of ragamuffins who will fly like chaff before the wind on our approach."

The West vied with the East in boastful clamor.

The *Chicago Tribune* shouted from the top of its columns:

> "We insist that the West be allowed the honor of settling this little trouble by herself since she is most interested in its suppression to insure the free navigation of the Mississippi River. Let the East stand aside. This is our war. We can end it successfully in two

months. Illinois can whip the whole South by herself. We insist on the affair being turned over to us."

With prospects of a short war and cheaply earned glory the rage for volunteering was resistless. The war for three months was to be a holiday excursion and every man would return a hero crowned with garlands of flowers, the center of admiring thousands. The blacksmiths of Brooklyn were busy making handcuffs for one of her crack regiments. Each volunteer had sworn to lead at least one captive rebel in chains through the crowded streets in the great parade on their return.

Socola on his arrival at Montgomery from Charleston read these fulminations from the North with amazement and rage. He sent his bitter and emphatic protest against such madness to Holt. The faithful Joseph had been rewarded with an office to his liking. He was now the Judge Advocate General of the United States Army. He turned Socola's letters over to Cameron, the new Secretary of War, who read them with rising wrath.

"The author of those letters," he said with a scowl, "is either a damned fool, or traitor."

Holt's lower lip was thrust out and the lines of his big mouth drawn into a knot.

"I assure you, sir—he is neither. He is absolutely loyal. His patriotism is a religion. He has entered his dangerous and important mission with the zeal of a religious fanatic."

"That accounts for it then—he's insane. I don't care to read any more such twaddle and I won't pay for the services of such a man out of the funds of the War Department."

With the utmost difficulty Holt secured the consent of the Secretary of War to continue Socola's commission for two months longer.

The only consolation the young patriot found in the contemptuous reply his Government made to his solemn warnings was the almost equal fatuity with which the Southern people were now approaching their first test of battle.

Until the proclamation of President Lincoln, both Jefferson Davis and the South had believed in the possibility of a peaceful reconciliation. Even when the proclamation had been made and the wild response of the North had been instantly given, the Southern people refused to believe that the millions of Northern voters who still clung to the old forms of Constitutional Government under the leadership of Stephen A. Douglas would surrender their principles, arm themselves and march to coerce a State at the command of a President against whom they had voted.

Senator Barton, from his new position in the Confederate Senate, scouted the idea of serious war.

"Bah!" he growled to Socola, who was drawing him out. "The Yankees won't fight!"

"That's what they say about you, sir," was the cool response.

"Who ever heard of a race of shopkeepers turning into soldiers?" The Senator laughed. "Such men have no martial prowess! They are unequal to mighty deeds of valor."

The white teeth of the young observer gleamed in a smile.

"On the other hand, Senator, I'm afraid history proves that commercial communities, once aroused, are the most dogged, pugnacious, ambitious and obstinate fighters of the world—Carthage, Venice, Genoa, Holland and England have surely proven this—"

"There's one thing certain," Barton roared. "We'll bring England to her knees if there is a war. Cotton is the King of Commerce, and we hold the key of his empire. The population of England will starve without our cotton. If we need them they've got to come to our rescue, sir!"

Socola did not argue the point. It was amazing how widespread was this idea in the South. He wrote his Government again and again that the whole movement of secession was based on this conception.

There was one man in Washington who read these warnings with keen insight—Gideon Welles, the Secretary of the Navy. The part this quiet, unassuming man was preparing to play in the mighty drama then unfolding its first scene was little known or understood by those who were filling the world with the noise of their bluster.

Jefferson Davis at his desk in Montgomery saw with growing anxiety the confidence of his people in immediate and overwhelming success. In answer to Abraham Lincoln's proclamation calling for 75,000 volunteers to fight the South, he called for 100,000 to defend it. The rage for volunteering in the South was even greater than the North. An army of five hundred thousand men could have been enrolled for any length of service if arms and equipment could have been found. It was utterly impossible to arm and equip one hundred thousand, before the first battle would be fought.

Ambitious Southern boys, raging for the smell of battle, rushed from post to post, begged and pleaded for a place in the ranks. They offered big bounties for the places assigned to men who were lucky enough to be accepted.

The Confederate Congress, to the chagrin of their President, fixed the time of service at six months. Jefferson Davis was apparently the only man in the South who had any conception of the gigantic task before his infant government. He begged and implored his Congress for an enrollment of three years or the end of the war. The Congress laughed at his absurd fears. The utmost they would grant was enlistment for the term of one year.

With grim foreboding but desperate earnestness the President of the Confederacy turned his attention to the organization and equipment of this force with which he was expected to defend the homes of eight million people scattered over a territory of 728,000 square miles, with an open frontier of a thousand miles and three thousand leagues of open sea.

14: RICHMOND IN GALA DRESS

From the moment Virginia seceded from the Union it wan a foregone conclusion that Richmond would be the capital of the new Confederacy—not only because the great Virginian was the Father of the Country and his glorious old Commonwealth the mother of States and Presidents, but because her soil must be the arena of the first great battle.

On May 23, the Provisional Congress at Montgomery adjourned to meet in Richmond on July 20, and Jefferson Davis began his triumphal procession to the new Capital.

Jennie Barton, her impulsive father, the Senator, Mrs Barton, with temper serene and unruffled, and Signor Henrico Socola of the Sardinian Ministry, were in the party. Dick Welford and two boys were already in Virginia with their regiments. Tom was in New Orleans with Raphael Semmes, fitting out the little steamer Sumter for a Confederate cruiser.

Senator Barton had been requested by the new President to act as his aide, and the champion of secession had accepted the honor under protest. It was not of importance commensurate with his abilities, but it was perhaps worthwhile for the moment until a greater field was opened.

The arrangement made Socola's association with Jennie of double importance. As the train whirled through the sunlit fields of the South he found his position by her side more and more agreeable and interesting. She was a girl of remarkable intelligence. He had observed that she was not afraid of silence. Her tongue was not forever going. In fact she seemed disinclined to talk unless she had something to say. He glanced at her from the corners of his dark eyes with a friendly smile.

"You are serious today, Miss Jennie?"

"Yes. I wish I were a man!"

"You'd go to the front, of course?"

"Yes—wouldn't you?"

"For my country—yes—"

He paused a moment and went on carelessly:

"Your older brother, the Judge, will fight for the Union?"

The sensitive lips trembled.

"No—thank God. He has sent my mother word that for her sake and mine he'll not fight his father and younger brothers in battle. He's going to do a braver thing than march to the front. He's going to face his neighbors in New Orleans and stand squarely by his principles."

"It will take a brave man to do that, won't it?"

"The bravest of the brave."

The train was just pulling into a sleepy Southern town, the tracks running straight down the center of its main street. A company was drawn up to salute the new President and cheering thousands had poured in from the surrounding country to do him honor. They cheered themselves hoarse and were still at it when the train slowly started northward. The company which greeted their arrival with arms presented were on board now, chatting, shouting, singing, waving their caps and handkerchiefs to tear-stained women.

The country through which the Presidential party passed had been suddenly transformed into a vast military camp, the whole population war mad.

Every woman from every window of every house in sight of the train waved a handkerchief. The flutter of those white flags never ceased.

The city of Richmond gave their distinguished visitor a noble reception. He was quartered temporarily at the Spotswood Hotel, but the City Council had purchased the handsomest mansion in town at a cost of $40,000 and offered it to him as their token of admiration of his genius.

Mr. Davis was deeply touched by this mark of esteem from Virginia, but sternly refused the gift for himself. He accepted it for the Confederate Government as the official residence of the President.

Socola found the city a mere comfortable village in comparison with New York or Boston or Philadelphia, though five times the size of Montgomery. He strolled through its streets alone, wondering in which one of the big old-fashioned mansions lived the remarkable Southern woman to whom his Government had referred him for orders. He must await the arrival of the messenger who would deliver to him in person its description. In the meantime with tireless eye he was studying the physical formation of every street and alley. He must know it, every crook and turn.

Until the advent of the troops, Richmond had been one of the quietest of all the smaller cities of America. Barely forty thousand inhabitants, one third of whom were negro slaves, it could boast none of the displays or excitements of a metropolis. Its vices were few, its life orderly and its society the finest type of the genuine American our country had developed.

Rowdyism was unknown. The police department consisted of a dozen "watchmen" whose chief duty was to round up a few straggling negroes who might be found on the streets after nine o'clock at night and put them in "the Cage" until morning. "The Cage" was a ramshackle wooden building too absurd to be honored by the name of prison.

The quiet, shady streets were suddenly transformed into the throbbing, tumultuous avenues of a crowded Capital—already numbering more than one hundred thousand inhabitants.

Its pulse beat with a new and fevered life. Its atmosphere was tense with the electric rumble of the coming storm—everywhere bustle, hurry and feverish preparations for war. The Tredegar Iron Works had doubled its force of men. Day and night the red glare of the furnaces threw its sinister glow over the yellow, turbulent waters of the James. With every throb now of its red heart a cannon was born destined to slay a thousand men.

Every hill was white with the tents of soldiers, their camps stretching away into the distant fields and forests.

Every street was thronged. Couriers on blooded horses dashed to and fro bearing the messages of imperious masters. From every direction came the crash of military bands. And over all the steady, low rumble of artillery and the throbbing tramp of soldiers. In every field and wood for miles around the city could be heard the neighing of horses, the bugle call of the trooper, the shouts of gay recruits and the sharp command of drilling officers.

The rattle of the ambulance and the long, red trenches of the uncoffined dead had not come yet. They were not even dreamed in the hearts of the eager, rollicking, fun-loving children of the South.

There were as yet no dances, no social festivities. The town was soldier mad. Few men not in uniform were to be seen on the streets.

A man in citizen's clothes was under suspicion as to his principles.

With each train, new companies and regiments arrived. Day and night the tramp of soldiers' feet, the throb of drum, the scream of fife, the gleam of bayonets.

Everywhere soldiers were welcomed, fêted, lionized. The finest ladies of Richmond vied with one another in serving their soldier guests. Society turned out en masse to every important review.

Southern society was melted into a single pulsing thought—the fight in defense of their homes and their liberty. In the white heat of this mighty impulse the barriers of class and sex were melted.

The most delicately reared and cultured lady of society admitted without question the right of any man who wore a gray uniform to speak to her without introduction and escort her anywhere on the streets. In not a single instance was this high privilege abused by an insult, indignity or an improper word.

Socola saw but one lady who showed the slightest displeasure. A dainty little woman of eight, delicately trained in the ways of polite society, was shocked at the familiarity of a soldier who had dared to caress her.

She turned to her elderly companion and gasped with indignation: "Auntie! Did you ever! Any man who wears a stripe on his pantaloons now thinks he can speak to a lady!"

Socola laughed and passed on to inspect the camp of the famous Hampton Legion of South Carolina.

His heart went out in a sudden wave of admiration for these Southern people who could merge thus their souls and bodies into the cause of their country.

The Hampton Legion was recruited, armed and equipped and led by Wade Hampton. Its private soldiers were the flower of South Carolina's society. The dress parades of this regiment of gentlemen were the admiration of the town. The carriages that hung around their maneuvers were as gay and numerous as the assemblage on a fashionable race course.

Each member of this famous legion went into Richmond with his trunks and body servant. They, too, were confident of a brief struggle.

A kind fate held fast the dark curtains of the future. The camp was a picnic ground, and Death was only a specter of the dim unknown.

Just as Socola strolled by the grounds, the camp spied the handsome figure of young Preston Hampton in a pair of spotless yellow kid gloves. They caught and rolled him in the dust and spoiled his gloves.

He laughed and took it good-naturedly.

The hardier sons of the South held the attention of the keen, observing eyes with stronger interest. He knew what would become of those trunks and fine clothes. The thing he wished most to know was the quality and the temper of the average man in the Southern ranks.

Socola met Dick Welford suddenly face to face, smiled and bowed. Dick hesitated, returned his recognition and offered his hand.

"Mr. Welford—"

"Signor Socola."

Dick's greeting was a little awkward, but the older man put him at once at ease with his frank, friendly manners.

"A brave show your Champ de Mars, sir!"

"Does look like business, doesn't it?" Dick responded with pride. "Would you like to go through the camps and see our men?"

"Very much."

"Come, I'll show you."

Two hundred yards from the camp of the Hampton Legion they found the Louisiana Zouaves of Wheat's command, small, tough-looking men with gleaming black eyes.

"Frenchmen!" Dick sneered. "They'll fight though—"

"Their people in the old world have that reputation," Socola dryly remarked.

Beyond them lay a regiment of fierce, be-whiskered countrymen from the lower sections of Mississippi.

"Look out for those fellows," the young Southerner said serenely. "They're from old Jeff's home. You'll hear from them. Their fathers all fought in Mexico."

Socola nodded.

Beside the Mississippians lay a regiment of long-legged, sinewy riflemen from Arkansas.

A hundred yards further they saw the quaint coon-skin caps of John B. Gordon's company from Georgia.

Socola watched these lanky mountaineers with keen interest.

"The Raccoon Roughs," Dick explained. "First company of Georgia volunteers. They had to march over two or three States before anybody would muster them in. They're happy as June bugs now."

They passed two regiments of quiet North Carolinians. The young Northerner observed their strong, muscular bodies and earnest faces.

"And these two large regiments, Mr. Welford?" Socola asked.

"Oh," the Virginian exclaimed with a careless touch of scorn in his voice, "they're Tarheels—not much for looks, but I reckon they'll stick."

"I've an idea they will," was the serious reply.

Dick pointed with pride to a fine-looking regiment of Virginians.

"Good-looking soldiers," Socola observed.

"Aren't they? That's my regiment. You'll hear from them in the first battle."

"And those giants?" Socola inquired, pointing to the right at a group of tall, rude-looking fellows.

"Texas Rangers."

"I shouldn't care to meet them in a row—"

"You know what General Taylor said of them in the Mexican War?"

"No—"

"They're anything but gentlemen or cowards."

"I agree with him," Socola laughed.

"What chance has a Yankee got against such men?" Dick asked with a wag of his big blond head.

"Let me show you what they think—"

Socola drew a leaf of *Harper's Magazine* from his pocket and spread it before the young trooper's indignant gaze.

The cartoon showed a sickly-looking Southerner carrying his musket under an umbrella accompanied by a negro with a tray full of mint juleps.

"That's a joke, isn't it!" Dick roared. "Will you give me this paper?"

"Certainly, Monsieur!"

Dick folded the sheet, still laughing. "I'll have some fun with this in camp tonight. Come on—I want to show you just one more bunch of these sickly-looking mint-julipers—"

Again the Southerner roared.

They quickened their pace and in a few minutes were passing through the camps of the Red River men from Arkansas and Northern Louisiana.

"Aren't you sorry for these poor fellows?" Dick laughed.

"I have never seen anything like them," Socola admitted, looking on their stalwart forms with undisguised admiration. Scarcely a man was under six feet in height, with broad, massive shoulders and chests and not an ounce of superfluous flesh. Their resemblance to each other was remarkable. Nature had cast each one in the same heroic mold. The spread of giant unbroken forests spoke in their brawny arms and legs. The look of an eagle soaring over great rivers and fertile plains flashed in their fearless eyes.

"What do you think of them?" Dick asked with boyish pride.

"I'd like to send their photographs to *Harper's*—"

"For God's sake, don't do that!" Dick protested. "If you do, we'll never get a chance to see a Yankee. I want to get in sight of 'em anyhow before they run. All I ask of the Lord is to give me one whack at those little, hump-backed, bow-legged shoemakers from Boston!"

Socola smiled dryly.

"In five minutes after we meet—there won't be a shoe-string left fit to use."

The dark face flashed with a strange light from the depths of the somber eyes—only for an instant did he lose self-control. His voice was velvet when he spoke.

"Your faith is strong, M'sieur!"

"It's not faith—we know. One Southerner can whip three Yankees any day."

"But suppose it should turn out that he had to whip five or six or a dozen?"

"Don't you think these fellows could do it?"

Socola hesitated. It was a shame to pull down a faith that could remove mountains. He shrugged his slender shoulders and a pensive look stole over his face. He seemed to be talking to himself.

"Your President tells me that his soldiers will do all that pluck and muscle, endurance and dogged courage, dash and red-hot patriotism can accomplish. And yet his view is not sanguine. A sad undertone I caught in his voice. He says your war will be long and bloody—"

"Yes—I know," Dick broke in, "but nobody agrees with him. We'll show old Jeff what we can do, if he'll just give us one chance—that's all we ask—just one chance. Read that editorial in the *Richmond Examiner*—"

He thrust a copy of the famous yellow journal of the South into Socola's hand and pointed to a marked paragraph:

"From mountain top and valleys to the shores of the seas there is one wild shout of fierce resolve to capture Washington City at all and every human hazard!"

The North was marching southward with ropes and handcuffs with which to end in triumph their holiday excursion on July 4. The South was marching to meet them with eager pride, each man afraid the fight would be over before he could reach the front to fire a single shot. And behind each gay regiment of scornful men marched the white silent figure of Death.

15: THE HOUSE ON CHURCH HILL

As Socola left his room at the Spotswood the following night, a stranger met him at the turn of the dimly lighted corridor.

"Signor Socola, I believe?"

"At your service."

"I know some mutual friends in Washington connected with the Sardinian Ministry—"

"I'm just starting for a stroll through the city," Socola interrupted. "Will you join me?"

"With pleasure. As I am well acquainted with the streets of Richmond, allow me to be your guide."

Socola followed with a nod of approval. Their walk led to the highest of the city's seven hills. But few were stirring at this hour—half-past seven. The people were busy at supper.

The two men paused at the gate of a stately, old-fashioned mansion in the middle of a spacious lawn. The odor of sweet pinks filled the air. The rose trellis and elaborate scheme of flower beds and the boxwood hedges told the story of wealth and culture and high social position.

"I wish to introduce you to one of the most charming ladies of Richmond," the stranger said in quick, business-like tones, opening the gate as if he were used to the feel of the latch.

"Certainly," was the short reply.

In answer to the rap of the old-fashioned brass knocker, a quaint little woman of forty opened the door and showed them into the parlor. The blinds were closed, and the room lighted by a single small kerosene lamp.

With quick precision the stranger presented his companion.

"Miss Van Lew, permit me to introduce to you Signor Henrico Socola of the Sardinian Ministry. He is the duly accredited but unofficial agent of his Majesty, Victor Emmanuel, and is cultivating friendly relations with the new Government of the South."

Miss Van Low extended her hand and took the outstretched one with a warmth that surprised her visitor beyond measure. "I recognized him at once," she said with emotion.

"Recognized me?"

"Your dear mother, sir, was my schoolmate in Philadelphia. I loved her. How alike you are!"

"Then we shall be friends—"

"We shall be more than friends—we shall be comrades—"

She paused and turned to the stranger: "You can leave us now."

With a bow the man turned and left the room.

Socola studied the little woman who had deliberately chosen to lay her life, her fortune and her home on the altar of her Country. He saw with a glance at her delicate but commanding figure the brilliant, accomplished, resolute woman of personality and charm.

She took the young man's hand again in hers and led him to a high-backed mahogany settee. She stroked the hands with her thin, cold fingers.

"How perfect the image of your mother! I would have known you anywhere. You must know and trust me. I was sent North to school. I came back to Virginia a more determined Abolitionist than ever. Our people have always hated Slavery. I made good my faith by freeing mine. We're not so well-to-do now, my mother and I."

She paused and looked wistfully about the stately room.

"This house could tell the story of gay and beautiful scenes—of balls—receptions and garden parties in bowers of roses—of coaches drawn by six snow-white horses standing at our door for the start to the White Sulphur Springs—"

She stopped suddenly, mastered her emotions and went on dreamily: "Of great men and distinguished families our guests from the North and the South—Bishop Mann, Chief Justice John Marshall, the Lees, the Robinsons, Wickhams, Adams, Cabells,—the Carringtons—Fredrika Bremer, the Swedish novelist, visited us and wrote of us in her *Homes in the New World*. Jennie Lind in the height of her glory sang in this room. Edgar Allan Poe read here aloud his immortal poem, 'The Raven.' You must realize what it means to me to become an outcast in Richmond—"

She drew from her bosom a newspaper clipping and handed it to Socola. "Read that paragraph from this morning's editorial columns—"

The young man scanned the marked clipping.

"One of the City papers contained on Monday a word of exhortation to certain females of Southern residence (and perhaps birth) but of decidedly Northern and Abolition proclivities. The creatures, though specially alluded to, are not named. If such people do not wish to be exposed and dealt with as alien enemies to the country they would do well to cut stick while they can do so with safety to their worthless carcasses—"

"And you will not 'cut stick'?"

"It's not the way of our breed. I've been doing what I could for the past year. I have sent the Government at Washington letter after letter giving them full and accurate accounts of men and events here. I have made no concealment of my principles. We are Abolitionists and Unionists and they know it. These Southern men will not lift their hands against two helpless women unless they discover the deeper plans I've laid. I've stopped them on the streets and openly flung my sentiments into their faces. As the excitement has increased I have grown more violent and more incoherent. They have begun to say that I am insane—"

Socola lifted his hand in a quiet gesture. "Good. You can play the part."

A look of elation overspread the thin, intellectual features. "True—I'll do it. I see it in a flash. 'Crazy old Bet,' they'll call me—"

She sprang to her feet. "Come upstairs."

He followed her light step up three flights of stairs into the attic. She pushed aside an old-fashioned wardrobe and opened a small door of plain pine boards about four feet in height which led to the darkened space beneath the roof.

She stooped and entered and he followed. A small, neat room was revealed eight feet high beside the inner wall, with ceiling sloping to three feet on the opposite side. An iron safe was fitted into the space beside the chimney and covered skillfully by a door completely cased in brick. The device was so perfect it was impossible to detect the fact that it was not a part of the chimney, each alternate layer of bricks fitted exactly into the place chiseled out for it in the wall of the chimney itself.

Socola examined the arrangement with care.

"A most skillful piece of work!" he exclaimed.

"I laid those bricks in that door casing with my own hand. The old safe has been there since my grandfather's day. This is your room, sir. That safe is for your important papers. You can spend the night here in safety when necessary. My house has been offered to the Government as the headquarters of its secret service. I have in this safe an important document for you."

She opened it and handed Socola a sealed envelope addressed:

"Signor Henrico Socola,

Richmond, Virginia."

He broke the seal and read the order from the new Bureau of Military Information placing him in command of its Richmond office. He offered the paper to the little woman who held the candle for him to read.

"I know its contents," she said, observing him keenly. "The Government has chosen wisely. You can render invaluable service—"

She paused and looked at Socola with a curious smile.

"You know any girls in Richmond?"

"But one and she has just arrived with the Presidential party—Miss Jennie Barton—"

"The Senator's daughter?"

"The same."

"Wonderful!" the little woman went on eagerly. "Her father is on the staff of Jefferson Davis. Old Barton is a loud-mouthed fool who can't keep a secret ten minutes. You must make love to his daughter—"

Socola laughed. "Is it necessary?"

"Absolutely. You can't remain in Richmond indefinitely without a better excuse than your unofficial connection with the Ministry of Sardinia. You are young. You are handsome. All Southern girls have sweethearts—all Southern boys. They can't understand the boy who hasn't. You'll be suspected at once unless you comply with the custom of the country."

"Of course. I needn't actually make love to her—"

"That's exactly what you must do. Make love to her with all your might—as if your life depends on her answer and your stay in

Richmond can be indefinite."

"I don't like the idea," he protested.

"Neither do I like this—" She swept the little attic room with a wave of her slender hand. "Come, my comrade, you must—"

He hesitated a moment, laughed, and said: "All right."

16: THE FLOWER-DECKED TENT

When Socola rose the following morning he determined to throw every scruple to the winds and devote himself to Jennie Barton with a zeal and passion that would leave to his Southern rivals no doubt as to the secret of his stay.

At the first informal reception at the White House of the Confederacy Jennie had been pronounced the most fascinating daughter of the new Republic, as modest and unassuming as she was brilliant and beautiful.

After the manner of Southern beaux he addressed a note to her on a sheet of exquisitely tinted foreign paper, at the top of which was the richly embossed coat of arms of the Socola family of North Italy.

He asked of her the pleasure of a horseback ride over the hills of Virginia. He was a superb horseman, and she rode as if born in the saddle.

He sealed the note with a piece of tinted wax and stamped it with the die which reproduced his coat of arms. He smiled with satisfaction as he addressed the envelope in his smooth and perfectly rounded handwriting.

He read the answer with surprise and disappointment. The Senator had replied for his daughter. A slight accident to her mother had caused her to leave on the morning train for the South. She would probably remain at Fairview for two weeks.

There was no help for it. He must await her return. In the meantime there was work to do. The army of the South was slowly but surely shaping itself into a formidable engine of war.

The mastermind at the helm of the new Government had laid the foundations of one of the most efficient forces ever sent into the arena of battle. It was as yet only a foundation but one which inspired in his mind not only a profound respect for his judgment, but a feeling of deep foreboding for the future.

Jefferson Davis had received a training of peculiar fitness for his task. The first work before the South was the organization, equipment and handling of its army of defense. The President they had called to the leadership had spent four years at West Point and seven years in the army on our frontiers, pushing the boundaries of the Republic into the West. He had led a regiment of volunteers in the conquest of Mexico, and in the battle of Buena Vista, not only saved the day in the moment of supreme crisis, but had given evidence of the highest order of military genius. On his return from the Mexican War he had been appointed a Brigadier General by the President of the United States but had declined the honor.

For four years as Secretary of War in the Cabinet of Franklin Pierce he had proven himself a master of military administration, had reorganized and placed on a modern basis of the highest efficiency the army of the Union and in this work has proven himself a terror to weakness, tradition and corruption.

He knew personally every officer of the first rank in the United States Army. His judgment of these men and their ability as commanders was marvelous in its accuracy. His genius as an army administrator undoubtedly gave to the South her first advantage in the opening of the conflict.

From the men who had resigned from the old army to cast their fortunes with the South his keen eye selected without hesitation the three men for supreme command whose abilities had no equal in America for the positions to which they were assigned. And these three men were patriots of such singleness of purpose, breadth of vision and greatness of soul that neither of them knew he was being considered for the highest command until handed his commission.

Samuel Cooper had been Adjutant General of the United States Army since 1852. Davis knew his record of stern discipline and uncompromising efficiency, and although a man of Northern birth, he appointed him Adjutant General of the Confederate Army without a moment's hesitation.

Albert Sidney Johnston was his second appointment to the rank of full General. and Robert E. Lee his third—each destined to immortality. His fourth nomination for the rank of full General he made with hesitation. Joseph E. Johnston under the terms of the law passed by the Provisional Congress of the Confederacy was entitled to a position in the first rank as acting Commissary General of the old army. The keen intuition of the President had perceived from the first the evidences of hesitation and of timidity in crisis which was the chief characteristic of Joseph E. Johnston. His sense of fairness under the terms of the law required that this man be given his chance. With misgivings but with high hopes the appointment was made.

Robert E. Lee he made military chieftain of the Government with headquarters in Richmond.

From four points the Northern forces were threatening the South. From the West by a flanking movement which might open the Mississippi River; from the mountains of Western Virginia whose people were in part opposed to secession; from Washington by a direct movement on Richmond; and from Fortress Monroe on the Virginia Peninsula.

The first skirmish before Fortress Monroe, led by B.F. Butler, had been repulsed with such ease no serious danger was felt in that quarter. The ten thousand men under Holmes and McGruder could hold Butler indefinitely.

Davis had seen from the first that one of the supreme dangers of the South lay in the long line of exposed frontier in the West. If a commander of military genius should succeed in turning his flank here, the heart of the lower South would be pierced.

For this important command he reserved Albert Sidney Johnston. The Northern army under George B. McClellan and Rosecrans had defeated the troops in Western Virginia. In a series of small fights they had lost a thousand men and all their artillery. General Lee was dispatched from Richmond to repair if possible this disaster.

The first two clashes had been a draw. The South had won first blood on the Peninsula—the North in Western Virginia. The main army of the South was now concentrated to oppose the main army of the North from Washington.

Brigadier General Beauregard, the widely acclaimed hero of Fort Sumter, was in command of this army near Manassas Station on the road to Alexandria.

Beauregard's position was in a measure an accident of fortune. The first shot had been fired by him at Sumter. He was the first paper-made hero of the war. He had led the first regiment into Virginia to defend her from invasion.

He was the man of the hour. His training and record, too, gave promise of high achievements. He had graduated from West Point in 1838, second in a class of forty-five men. His family was of high French extraction, having settled in Louisiana in the reign of Louis XV. He had entered the Mexican War a lieutenant and emerged from the campaign a major. He was now forty-five years old, in the prime of life. His ability had been recognized by the National Government in the beginning of the year by his appointment as Superintendent of the Military Academy at West Point. His commission had been revoked at the last moment by the vacillating Buchanan because his brother-in-law, Senator Slidell of Louisiana, had made a secession speech in Washington.

Jefferson Davis was not enthusiastic in his confidence in the new hero. He was too much given to outbursts of a public kind to please the ascetic mind of the Southern leader. He had written some silly letters to the public deriding the power of the North. No one could know better than Davis how silly these utterances were. He "hated and despised the Yankees." Davis feared and recognized their power. Beauregard's assertion that the South could whip the North even if her only arms were flintlocks and pitchforks had been often and loudly repeated.

Of the army marshaling in front of him under the command of the venerable Winfield Scott he wrote with the utmost contempt. "The enemies of the South," he declared, "are little more than an armed rabble, gathered together hastily on a false pretense and for an unholy purpose, with an octogenarian at its head!"

In spite of his small stature, Beauregard was a man of striking personal appearance—small, dark, thin, hair prematurely gray, his manners distinguished and severe.

It was natural that, with the fame of his first victory, itself the provoking cause of the conflict, his distinguished foreign name and courtly manners, he should have become the toast of the ladies in these early days of the pomp and glory of war. He was the center of an ever widening circle of fair admirers who lavished their attentions on him in letters, in flags, and a thousand gay compliments. His camp table was filled with exquisite flowers which flanked and sometimes covered his maps and plans. He used his bouquets for paper weights.

It was not to be wondered at, therefore, that the cold intellectual standard by which Davis weighed men should have found Beauregard wanting in the qualifications of supreme command.

The President turned his eye to the flower-decked tent of his general with grave misgivings. Yet he was the man of the hour. It was fair that he should have his chance.

17: THE FATAL VICTORY

On the banks of the Potomac General Scott had massed against Beauregard the most formidable army which had ever marched under the flag of the Union. Its preparation was considered thorough, its numbers all that could he handled, and its artillery was the best in the world. All the regular army east of the Rockies, seasoned veterans of Indian campaigns, were joined with the immense force of volunteers from the Northern States—fifty full regiments of volunteers, eight companies of regular infantry, four companies of marines, nine companies of regular cavalry and twelve batteries of artillery with forty-nine big guns.

In command of this army of invasion was General McDowell, held to be the most scientific general in the North.

To supplement Beauregard's weakness as a commanding General in case of emergency, Joseph E. Johnston was placed at Harper's Ferry to guard the entrance of the Shenandoah Valley, secure the removal of the invaluable machinery saved from the Arsenal, and form a junction with Beauregard the moment he should be threatened.

The movement of General Patterson's army against Harper's Ferry had been too obviously a feint to deceive either Davis or Lee, his chief military adviser. Johnston was given ten thousand men and able assistants including General Jackson.

On the tenth of July Beauregard, anxiously awaiting information of the Federal advance, received an important message from an accomplished Southern woman, Mrs. Rose O'Neal Greenhow. She had remained in Washington as Miss Van Lew had in Richmond, to lay her life on the altar of her country. During the administration of Buchanan she had been a leader of Washington society. She was now a widow, noted for her wealth, beauty, wit and forceful personality. Her home was the meeting place of the most brilliant men and women of the old regime. Buchanan was her personal friend, as was William H. Seward. Her niece, a granddaughter of Dolly Madison, was the wife of the Little Giant of the West, Stephen A. Douglas.

Before leaving Washington to become the Adjutant General of

Beauregard's army, Colonel Thomas Jordan had given her the cipher code of the South and arranged to make her house the Northern headquarters of the Southern secret service.

Her first messenger was a girl carefully disguised as a farmer's daughter returning from the sale of her vegetables in the Washington market. She passed the lines without challenge and delivered her message into Beauregard's hands.

With quick decision Beauregard called his aide and dispatched the news to the President at Richmond:

> "I have positive information direct from Washington that the enemy will move in force across the Potomac on Manassas via Fairfax Court House and Centreville. I urge the immediate concentration of all available forces on my lines."

The Southern commander began his preparations to receive the attack. The house on Church Hill had not been idle. Richmond swarmed with Federal spies under the skillful guidance of Socola.

General Scott knew in Washington within twenty-four hours that Beauregard was planting his men behind the Bull Run River in a position of great strength and that the formation of the ground was such with Bull Run on his front that his dislodgment would be a tremendous task.

The advance of the Federal army was delayed—delayed until the last gun and scrap of machinery from Harper's Ferry had been safely housed in Richmond and Fayetteville and Johnston had withdrawn his army to Winchester in closer touch with Beauregard.

And still the Union army did not move. Beauregard sent a trusted scout into Washington to Mrs. Greenhow with a scrap of paper on which was written in cipher the two words:

"Trust Bearer—"

He arrived at the moment she had received the long sought information of the date of the army's march. She glanced at the stolid masked face of the messenger and hesitated a moment.

"You are a Southerner?"

Donellan smiled. "I've spent most of my life in Washington, Madam," he said frankly. "I was a clerk in the Department of the Interior. I cast my fortunes with the South."

It was enough. Her keen intuitions had scented danger in the man's manner, his walk and personality. He was not a typical Southerner. The officials of the Secret Service Bureau had already given her evidence of their suspicions. She could not be too careful.

She seized her pen and hastily wrote in cipher: *"Order issued for McDowell to move on Manassas tonight."* She handed the tiny scrap of paper to Donellan.

"My agents will take you in a buggy with relays of horses down the Potomac to a ferry near Dumfries. You will be ferried across."

The man touched his hat. "I'll know the way from there, Madam."

The scout delivered his message into Beauregard's hands that night before eight o'clock.

At noon the next day Colonel Jordan had placed in her hands his answer: "Yours received at eight o'clock. Let them come. We are ready. We rely upon you for precise information. Be particular as to description and destination of forces and quantity of artillery."

She had not been idle. She was able to write a message of almost equal importance to the one she had dispatched the day before. With quick nervous hand she wrote on another tiny scrap of paper:

> "The Federal commander has ordered the Manassas railroad to be cut to prevent the junction of Johnston with Beauregard."

The moment the first authentic information reached President Davis of the purpose to attack Beauregard, he immediately urged General Johnston to make his preparations for the juncture of their forces.

And at once the President received confirmation of his fears of his General-in-Chief. Johnston delayed and began a correspondence of voluminous objections.

July 17, on receipt of the dispatch to Beauregard announcing the plan to cut the railroad, the President was forced to send Johnston a positive order to move his army to Manassas. The order was obeyed with a hesitation which imperiled the issue of battle. And while on the march, Beauregard's pickets exchanging shots with McDowell's skirmish line, Johnston began the first of his messages of complaint and haggling to his Chief at Richmond. Jealous of Beauregard's popularity and fearful of his possible insubordination, Johnston telegraphed Davis demanding that his relative rank to Beauregard should be clearly defined before the juncture of their armies.

The question was utterly unnecessary. The promotion of Johnston to the full grade of general could leave no conceivable doubt on such a point. The President realized with a sickening certainty the beginning of a quarrel between the two men, dangerous to the cause of the South. Their failure to act in harmony would make certain the defeat of the raw recruits on their first field of battle.

He decided at the earliest possible moment to go in person and prevent this threatened quarrel. Already blood had flowed. With a strong column of infantry, artillery and cavalry McDowell had attempted to force the approaches to one of the fords of Bull Run. They were twice driven back and withdrew from the field. Longstreet's brigade had lost fifteen killed and fifty-three wounded in holding his position.

The President hastened to telegraph his sulking general the explicit definition of rank he had demanded:

> Richmond, July 20, 1861.
>
> "General J. E. Johnston,
>
> "Manassas Junction, Virginia.
>
> "You are a General of the Confederate Army possessed of the power attached to that rank. You will know how to make the exact knowledge of Brigadier General Beauregard, as well of the ground as of the troops and preparation avail for the success of the object for which you cooperate. The zeal of both assures me of harmonious action.
>
> "Jefferson Davis."

As a matter of fact the President was consumed with painful anxiety lest there should not be harmonious action if Johnston should reach the field in time for the fight. His own presence was required by law at Richmond on July 20, for the delivery of his message to the assembled Congress. It was impossible for him to leave for the front before Sunday morning the 21st.

The battle began at eight o'clock.

General McDowell's army had moved to this attack hounded by the clamor of demagogues for the immediate capture of Richmond by his "Grand Army." Every Northern newspaper had dinned into his ears and the ears of an impatient public but one cry for months:

"*On to Richmond!*"

At last the news was spread in Washington that the army would move and bivouac in Richmond's public square within ten days. The march was to be a triumphal procession. The Washington politicians filled wagons and carriages with champagne to celebrate the victory. Tickets were actually printed and distributed for a ball in Richmond. The army was accompanied by long lines of excited spectators to witness the one grand struggle of the war—Congressmen, toughs from the saloons, gaudy ladies from questionable resorts, a clamoring, perspiring rabble bent on witnessing scenes of blood.

The Union General's information as to Beauregard's position and army was accurate and full. He knew that Johnston's command of ten thousand men had begun to arrive the day before. He did not know that half of them were still tangled up somewhere on the railroad waiting for transportation. Even with Johnston's entire command on the ground his army outnumbered the Southerners and his divisions of seasoned veterans from the old army and his matchless artillery gave him an enormous advantage.

With consummate skill he planned the battle and began its successful execution. His scouts had informed him that the Southern line was weak on its left wing resting on the Stone Bridge across the river. Here the long-drawn line of Beauregard's army thinned to a single regiment supported at some distance by a battalion. Here the skillful Union General determined to strike.

At two-thirty before daylight his dense lines of enthusiastic men swung into the dusty moonlit road for their movement to flank the Confederate left.

Swiftly and silently the flower of McDowell's army, eighteen thousand picked men, moved under the cover of the night to their chosen crossing at Sudley's Ford, two miles beyond the farthest gray picket of Beauregard's left.

Tyler's division was halted at the Stone Bridge on which the lone regiment of Col. Evans lay beyond the stream. He was ordered to feign an attack on that point while the second and third divisions should creep cautiously along a circuitous road two miles above, cross unopposed and slip into the rear of Beauregard's long-drawn left wing, roll it up in a mighty scroll of flame, join Tyler's division as it should sweep across the Stone Bridge and together the three divisions in one solid mass could crush the ten-mile battle line into hopeless confusion.

The plan was skillfully and daringly conceived.

Tyler's division halted at the Stone Bridge and silently formed as the first glow of dawn tinged the eastern hills.

The dull red of the July sun was just coloring the sky with its flame when the second and third divisions crossed Bull Run at Sudley's Ford and began their swift descent upon the rear of the unsuspecting Southern army.

As the sun burst above the hills, a circle of white smoke suddenly curled away from a cannon's mouth above the Stone Bridge and slowly rose in the still, clear morning air. Its sullen roar echoed over the valley. The gray figures on the hill beyond leaped to their feet and looked. Only the artillery was engaged and their shots were falling short.

The Confederates appeared indifferent. The action was too obviously a feint. Colonel Evans was holding his regiment for a clearer plan of battle to develop. From the hilltop on which his men lay he scanned with increasing uneasiness the horizon toward the west. In the far distance against the bright Southern sky loomed the dark outline of the Blue Ridge. The heavy background brought out in vivid contrast the woods and fields, hollows and hills of the great Manassas plain in the foreground.

Suddenly he saw it—a thin cloud of dust rising in the distance. As the rushing wall of sixteen thousand men emerged from the "Big Forest," through which they had worked their way along the crooked track of a rarely used road, the dust cloud flared in the sky with ominous menace. Colonel Evans knew its meaning. Beauregard's army had been flanked and the long thin lines of his left wing were caught in a trap. When the first rush of the circling host had swept his little band back from the Stone Bridge Tyler's army would then cross and the three divisions swoop down on the doomed men.

Evans suddenly swung his regiment and two field pieces into a new line of battle facing the onrushing host and sent his courier flying to General Bee to ask that his brigade be moved instantly to his support.

When the shock came there were five regiments and six little field pieces in the Southern ranks to meet McDowell's sixteen thousand troops.

With deafening roar their artillery opened. The long dense lines of closely packed infantry began their steady firing in volleys. It sounded as if some giant hand had grasped the hot Southern skies and was tearing their blue canvas into strips and shreds.

For an hour Bee's brigade withstood the onslaught of the two Federal divisions—and then began to slowly fall back before the resistless wall of fire. The Union army charged and drove the broken lines a half mile before they rallied.

Tyler's division now swept across the Stone Bridge and the shattered Confederate left wing was practically surrounded by overwhelming odds.

Again the storm burst on the unsupported lines of Bee and drove them three quarters of a mile before they paused.

The charging Federal army had struck something they were destined to feel again on many a field of blood.

General T. J. Jackson had suddenly swung his brigade of five regiments into the breach and stopped the wave of fire.

Bee rushed to Jackson's side.

"General," he cried pathetically, "they are beating us back!"

The somber blue eyes of the Virginian gleamed beneath the heavy lashes: "Then sir, we will give them the bayonet!"

Bee turned to his hard-pressed men and shouted:

"See Jackson and his Virginians standing like a stone wall! Let us conquer or die!"

The words had scarcely passed his lips when Bee fell, mortally wounded.

Four miles away on the top of a lonely hill sat Beauregard and Johnston befogged in a series of pitiable blunders.

The flanking of the Southern army was a complete and overwhelming surprise. Johnston, unacquainted with the ground, had yielded the execution of the battle to his subordinate.

While the two puzzled generals were waiting on their hill top for their orders of battle to be developed on the right, they looked to the left and the whole valley was a boiling hell of smoke and dust and flame. Their left flank had been turned and the triumphant enemy was rolling their long line up in a shroud of flame and death.

The two Generals put spurs to their horses and dashed to the scene of action, sending their couriers flying to countermand their first orders.

They reached the scene at the moment Bee's and Evans' shattered lines were taking refuge in a wooded ravine and Jackson had moved his men into a position to breast the shock of the enemy's avalanche.

In his excitement Johnston seized the colors of the fourth Alabama regiment and offered to lead them in a charge.

Beauregard leaped from his horse, faced the troops and shouted: "I have come to die with you!"

The first of the reserves were rushing to the front in a desperate effort to save the day. But in spite of the presence of the two Commanding Generals, in spite of the living stone wall Jackson had thrown in the path of the Union hosts, a large part of the crushed left wing could not be stopped and in mad panic broke for the rear toward Manassas Junction.

The fate of the Southern army hung on the problem of holding the hill behind Jackson's brigade. On its bloody slopes his men crouched with rifles leveled and from them poured a steady flame into the ranks of the charging Union columns.

Beauregard led the right wing of his newly formed battle line and Jackson the center in a desperate charge. The Union ranks were pierced and driven, only to re-form instantly and hurl their assailants back to their former position. Charge and counter-charge followed in rapid and terrible succession.

The Confederates were being slowly overwhelmed. The combined Union divisions now consisted of an enveloping battle line of twenty thousand infantry, seven companies of cavalry and twenty-four pieces of artillery, while behind them yet hung ten thousand reserves eager to rush into action.

Beauregard's combined forces defending the hill were scarcely seven thousand men. At two o'clock the desperate Southern commander succeeded in bringing up additional regiments from his right wing. Two brigades at last were thrown into the storm center and a shout rose from the hard-pressed Confederates. Again they charged, drove the Union hosts back and captured a battery of artillery.

The hill was saved and the enemy driven across the turnpike into the woods.

McDowell now hurried in a division of his reserves and re-formed his battle line for the final grand assault. Once more he demonstrated his skill by throwing his right wing into a wide circling movement to envelop the Confederate position on its left flank.

The scene was magnificent. As far as the eye could reach the glittering bayonets of the Union infantry could be seen sweeping steadily through field and wood flanked by its cavalry. Beauregard watched the cordon of steel draw around his hard-pressed men and planted his regiments with desperate determination to hurl them back.

Far off in the distance rose a new cloud of dust in the direction of the Manassas railroad. At their head was lifted a flag whose folds drooped in the hot, blistering July air. They were moving directly on the rear of McDowell's circling right wing.

If they were Union reserves the day was lost.

The Southerner lifted his field glasses and watched the drooping flag now shrouded in dust—now emerging in the blazing sun. His glasses were not strong enough. He could not make out its colors.

Beauregard turned to Colonel Evans, whose little regiment had fought with sullen desperation since sunrise.

"I can't make out that flag. If it's Patterson's army from the valley—God help us—"

"It may be Elzey and Kirby Smith's regiments," Evans replied. "They're lost somewhere along the road from Winchester."

Again Beauregard strained his eyes on the steadily advancing flag. It was a moment of crushing agony.

"I'm afraid it's Patterson's men. We must fall back on our last reserve—" He quickly lowered his glasses.

"I haven't a courier left, Colonel. You must help me—"

"Certainly, General."

"Find Johnston, and ask him to at once mass the reserves to support and protect our retreat—"

Evans started immediately to execute the order.

"Wait!" Beauregard shouted.

His glasses were again fixed on the advancing flag. A gust of wind suddenly flung its folds into the bright Southern sky line—the Stars and Bars of the Confederacy!

"Glory to God!" the commander exclaimed. "They're our men!"

The dark face of the little General flashed with excitement as he turned to Evans: "Ride, Colonel—ride with all your might and order General Kirby Smith to press his command forward at double quick and strike that circling line in the flank and rear!"

There were but two thousand in the advancing column but the moral effect of their sudden assault on the rear of the advancing victorious men, unconscious of their presence, would be tremendous. A charge at the same moment by his entire army confronting the enemy might snatch victory out of the jaws of defeat.

Beauregard placed himself at the head of his hard-pressed front, and waited the thrilling cry of Smith's men. At last it came, the heaven-piercing, hell-quivering, Rebel yell—the triumphant cry of the Southern hunter in sight of his game!

Jackson, Longstreet and Early with sudden rush of tigers sprang at the throats of the Union lines in front.

The men had scarcely gripped their guns to receive the assault when from the rear rose the unearthly yell of the new army swooping down on their unprotected flank.

It was too much for the raw recruits of the North. They had marched and fought with dogged courage since two o'clock before day—without pause for food or drink. It was now four in the afternoon and the blazing sun of July was pouring its merciless rays down on their dust-covered and smoke-grimed faces without mercy.

McDowell's right wing was crumpled like an eggshell between the combined charges front and rear. It broke and rushed back in confusion on his center. The whole army floundered a moment in tangled mass. In vain their officers shouted themselves hoarse proclaiming their victory and ordering them to rally.

Wild, hopeless, senseless, unreasoning panic had seized the Union army. They threw down their guns in thousands and started at breakneck speed for Washington. With every jump they cursed their idiotic commanders for leading them blindfolded into the jaws of hell. At least they had common sense enough left to save what was left.

The fields were covered with black swarms of flying soldiers. They cut the horses from the gun carriages, mounted them and dashed forward trampling down the crazed mobs on foot.

As the shouting, screaming throng rushed at the Cub Run bridge, a well-directed shot from Kemper's battery smashed a team of horses that were crossing. The wagon was upset and the bridge choked.

In mad efforts to force a passage mob piled on mob until the panic enveloped every division of the army that thirty minutes before was sweeping with swift, sure tread to its final victorious charge.

Across every bridge and ford of Bull Run the panic-stricken thousands rushed pellmell, horse, foot, artillery, wagons, ambulances, excursion carriages, red-jowled politicians mingling with screaming women whose faces showed death white through the rouge on their lips and cheeks.

For three miles rolled the dark tide of ruin and confusion—with not one Confederate soldier in sight.

It was three o'clock before the train bearing the anxious Confederate President and his staff drew into Manassas Junction. He had heard no news from the front and feared the worst. The long deep boom of the great guns told him that the battle was raging.

From the car window he saw rising an ominous cloud of dust rapidly approaching the Junction. To his trained eye it could mean but one thing—retreat.

He sprang from the car and asked its meaning of a pale trembling youth in disheveled, torn gray uniform.

Billy Barton turned his bloodshot eyes on the President. His teeth were chattering.

"M-m-eaning of w-what?" he stammered.

"That cloud of dust coming toward the station?"

Billy stared in the direction the President pointed.

"Why, that's the—the—w-w-wagoners—they're trying to save the pieces I reckon—"

"The army has been pushed back?" the President asked.

"No, sir—they—they never p-p-ushed 'em back! They—they just jumped right on top of 'em and made hash out of 'em where they stood! Thank God a few of us got away."

The President turned with a gesture of impatience to an older man, dust-covered and smoke-smeared.

"Can you direct me to General Beauregard's headquarters?"

"Beauregard's dead!" he shouted, rushing toward the train to board it for home. "Johnston's dead. Bee's dead. Bartow's dead. They're all dead—piled in heaps—fur ez ye eye kin see. Take my advice and get out of here quick."

Without waiting for an answer he scrambled into the coach from which the President had alighted.

The station swarmed now with shouting, gesticulating, panic-stricken men from the front. They crowded around the conductor.

"Pull out of this!"

"Crowd on steam!"

"Save your engine and your train, man!"

"And take us with you for God's sake!"

The President pushed his way through the crowd.

"I must go on, Conductor—the train is the only way to reach the field—"

"I'm sorry, sir," the conductor demurred. "I'm responsible for the property of the railroad—"

The panic-stricken men backed him up.

"What's the use?"

"The battle's lost!"

"The whole army's wiped off the earth."

"There's not a grease spot left!"

The President confronted the trembling conductor:

"Will you move your train?"

"I can't do it, sir—"

"Will you lend me your engine?"

The conductor's face brightened.

"I might do that."

The engine was detached to the disgust of the panic-stricken men and the cool-headed engineer nodded to the President, pulled his lever and the locomotive shot out of the station and in five minutes Davis alighted with his staff near the battle field. By the guidance of stragglers they found headquarters.

Adjutant General Jordan sent for horses and volunteered to conduct the President to the front.

While they were waiting he turned to Mr. Davis anxiously:

"I think it extremely unwise, sir, for you to take this risk."

The thin lips smiled: "I'll take the responsibility, General."

The President and his staff mounted and galloped toward the front. The stragglers came now in droves. They were generous in their warnings.

"Say, men, do ye want to die?"

"You're ridin' straight inter the jaws er death."

"Don't do it, I tell ye!"

The President began to rally the men. As they neared the front he was recognized and the wounded began to cheer.

A big strapping soldier was carrying a slender wounded boy to the rear.

The boy put his trembling hand on the man's shoulder, snatched off his cap and shouted: "Three cheers for the President! Look, boys, he's here—we'll lick 'em yet!"

The President lifted his hat to the stripling, crying: "To a hero of the South!"

The storm of battle was now rolling swiftly to the west—its roar growing fainter with each cannon's throb.

The President, sitting his horse with erect tense figure, dashed up the hill to General Johnston:

"How goes the battle, General?"

"We have won, sir," was the sharp curt answer.

The President wheeled his horse and rode rapidly into the front lines until stopped by the captain of a command of cavalry.

"You are too near the front, sir, without an escort—"

The President rode beside the captain and watched him form his men for their last charge on the enemy. He inspected the field with growing amazement. For miles the earth was strewn with the wreck of the Northern army—guns, knapsacks, blankets, canteens—and Brooklyn-made handcuffs! Their defeat had been so sudden, so complete, so overwhelming, it was impossible at first to grasp its meaning.

He passed the rugged figure of Jackson who had won his immortal title of "Stonewall." An aide was binding a cloth about his wounded arm.

The grim General pushed aside his surgeon, raised his battered cap and shouted: "Hurrah for the President! Ten thousand fresh men and I will be in Washington tonight!"

The President lifted his hat and congratulated him.

The victory of the South was complete and overwhelming. Jefferson Davis breathed a sigh of relief for deliverance. Within two hours he knew that this victory had not been won by superior generalship of his commanding officers. They had been outwitted at every turn and overwhelmed by the plan of battle their wily foe had forced upon them. It had not been won by the superior courage of his men in the battle which raged from sunrise until four o'clock. The broken and disorganized lines of the South and the panic-stricken mob he had met on the way were eloquent witnesses of Northern valor.

His army had been saved from annihilation by the quick wit and daring courage of a single Brigadier General who had moved his five regiments on his own initiative in the nick of time and saved the Confederates from utter rout.

Victory had been snatched at last from the jaws of defeat by an accident. The misfortune of a delayed regiment of Johnston's army was suddenly turned into an astounding piece of luck. The sudden charge of those two thousand men on the flank of the victorious army had produced a panic among tired raw recruits. McDowell was at this moment master of the field. In a moment of insane madness his unseasoned men had thrown down their guns and fled.

The little dark General in his flower-decked tent had made good his boasts. And worse—the Northern army had proven his wildest assertions true. They were a rabble. The star of Beauregard rose in the Southern sky, and with its rise Disaster stalked grim and silent toward the hilarious Confederacy.

The South had won a victory destined to prove itself the most fatal calamity that ever befell a nation.

18: THE AFTERMATH

Socola dismissed his hope of a speedy end of the war and devoted himself with new enthusiasm to his work. His eyes were sleepless—his ear to the ground. The information on conditions and public sentiment in Richmond and the South which he had dispatched to Washington were of incalculable service to his government. One of the immediate effects of the battle was the return of Jennie Barton to the Capital. Her mother was improving and Jimmie had been wounded. Her coming was most fortunate. It was of the utmost importance that he secure a position in the Civil Service of the Confederacy. It could be done through her father's influence.

Socola watched the first division of Northern prisoners march through the streets amid the shouts and laughter of a crowd of urchins black and white. A feeling of blind rage surged within him. That the tables would be shortly turned, he was sure. He would play his part now without a scruple. He would use pretty Jennie Barton as any other pawn on the chessboard of Life and Death over which he bent.

Jefferson Davis watched the effects of the battle on the North with breathless interest and increasing dismay.

His worst fears were confirmed.

He had hoped that a decisive victory would place his Government in a position to make overtures for a peaceful adjustment of the conflict.

The victory had been too decisive. The disgraceful rout of the Northern army had stung twenty-three million people to the quick. Defeat so overwhelming and surprising had roused the last drop of fighting blood in their veins.

Boasting and loud talk suddenly ceased. There was no lying about the results. In all their bald hideous reality the Northern mind faced them and began with steady purpose their vast preparations to wipe that disgrace out in blood.

Abraham Lincoln suddenly found himself relieved of all embarrassment in the conduct of the war. His critics had threatened to wreck his administration unless he forced their "Grand Army" to march on Richmond and take it without a day's delay.

In obedience to this idiotic clamor he was forced to order the army to march. They came home by a shorter route than they marched and they came quicker.

They returned without baggage.

Incompetent men and hungry demagogues had clamored for high positions in the army. Their influence had been so great he had been forced to find berths for many incompetent officers.

He had suddenly become the actual Commander-in-Chief of the Army and Navy and his word was law. Fools and incompetents were relegated to the rear. Men who knew how to fight and how to organize armies marched to the front.

His administration had been embarrassed for funds. It was found next to impossible to float a loan of a paltry seven million dollars for war purposes. He borrowed one hundred and fifty million dollars next day at a fraction above the legal rate of interest in New York. He asked Congress for 400,000 more men and $400,000,000 to support them. Congress voted a half million men and five hundred millions of dollars—a hundred million more than he had asked.

While Washington's streets were thronged with the mud-smeared, panic-stricken rabble that was once an army, the Federal Congress eagerly began the task of repairing the disaster. When they had done all and much more than their President had asked, they calmly and unanimously passed this resolution:

> "Resolved, That the maintenance of the Constitution, the preservation of the Union, and the enforcement of the laws, are sacred trusts which must be executed; that no disaster shall discourage us from the most ample performance of this high duty; and that we pledge to the Country and the world the employment of every resource, national and individual, for the suppression, overthrow and punishment of rebels in arms."

To the dismay of the far-seeing Southern leader in Richmond the press and people of the South received this resolution with shouts of derision. In vain did he warn his own Congress that the North was multiplying its armies, and building two navies with furious energy.

The people of the South went mad over their amazing victory. Davis saw their deliverance suddenly develop into the most appalling disaster.

The decisive battle of the war was fought and won. The European powers must immediately recognize the new Nation. In this hope their President could reasonably share. Their other delusions he knew to be madness.

The Southern press without a dissenting voice proclaimed that the question of manhood between the North and South was settled and settled forever. From the hustings the demagogue shouted:

"One Southerner is the equal anywhere of five Yankees."

Manassas, with its insignificant record of killed and wounded, was compared with the decisive battles of the world. The war was over. There might still be fought a few insignificant skirmishes before peace was proclaimed but that auspicious event could not be long delayed.

The fatal victory was followed by a period of fancied security and deadly inactivity. Exertions ceased. Volunteers were few. The volatile, sanguine people laughed at the fears of their croaking President.

So firmly had they established the new Nation that politicians began to plot and scheme for control of the Confederate Government on the expiration of the Davis term of office.

R.M.T. Hunter, the foremost statesman of Virginia, resigned his position in the Cabinet to be unembarrassed in his fight for the presidency.

Beauregard had been promoted to the full rank of general and his tent was now a bower of roses. Around the figure of the little fiery, impulsive, boastful South Carolinian gathered a group of ambitious schemers who determined to make him President. They filled the newspapers with such fulsome praise that the popular nominee for an honor six years in the distance, and shrouded in the smoke of battle, sought to add fuel to the flame by waving the Crown aside! In a weak bombastic letter which deceived no one, dated, "Within Hearing of the Enemies' Guns," he emphatically declared:

> "I am not a candidate, nor do I desire to be a candidate, for any civil office in the gift of the people or Executive!"

Controversies began between different Southern States, as to the location of the permanent Capital of the Confederacy. The contest developed so rapidly and went so far, that the Municipal Council of the City of Nashville, Tennessee, voted an appropriation of $750,000 for a residence for the President as an inducement to remove the Capital.

A furious controversy broke out in the yellow journals of the South as to why the Southern army had not pursued the panic-stricken mob into the City of Washington, captured Lincoln and his Congress and ended the war next day in a blaze of glory.

It was inconceivable that it was the fault of the two heroes of the battle, Joseph E. Johnston and Peter G.T. Beauregard. The President had rushed to the battlefield for some purpose. The champions of the heroes insinuated that his purpose was not to prevent their quarreling, but to take command of the field and rob them of their glory.

They made haste to find a scapegoat on whose shoulders to lay the failure to pursue. They seized on Jefferson Davis as the man. They declared in the most positive terms that Johnston and Beauregard, flushed with victory, were marshaling their hosts to sweep into Washington when they were stopped by the Confederate Chief and had no choice but to bivouac for the night.

Three men alone knew the truth: Davis, Beauregard and Johnston. The two victorious generals remained silent while their friends made this remarkable accusation against the President.

The President remained silent to save his generals from the wrath of a fickle public which might end their usefulness to the country.

As a matter of fact, Davis' trained eye had seen the enormous advantage of quick merciless pursuit the moment he was convinced that McDowell's army had fled in panic.

He had finally written a positive order commanding pursuit but was persuaded by the continued pleas of both commanders not to press it.

The reptile press of the South began on the President a bitter, malignant and unceasing vilification for this, his first fatal and inexcusable blunder!

Defeat had freed Abraham Lincoln of fools and incompetents

and armed him with dictatorial powers. Victory had saddled on the Confederacy two heroes destined to cripple its efficiency with interminable controversy, sulking bitterness and personal ambitions. The halo of supreme military genius which encircled the brows of Johnston and Beauregard with the lifting of the smoke from the field of Bull Run grew quickly into two storm clouds which threatened the life of the new Republic.

Johnston's contempt for Beauregard had from the beginning been outspoken to his intimate friends. The battle had raised this little upstart to his equal in rank! He claimed that the President had robbed him of his true position in the Southern army through favoritism in the appointment of Albert Sidney Johnston and Robert E. Lee to positions of seniority to which they were not entitled.

Johnston began a series of bitter insulting letters to the Confederate President, complaining of his injustice and demanding his rights. Not content with his letters to the Executive, Johnston poured his complaints into the ears of his friends and admirers in the Confederate Congress and began a systematic and determined personal campaign to discredit and ruin the administration.

Among his first recruits in his campaign against Jefferson Davis was the fiery, original Secessionist, Roger Barton. Barton had never liked Davis. Their temperaments were incompatible. He resigned his position on the staff of the President, allied himself openly with Johnston and became one of the bitterest and most uncompromising enemies of the government. His position in the Confederate Senate would be a powerful weapon with which to strike.

The substance of Johnston's claim on which was founded this malignant clique in Richmond was the merest quibble about the date of his commission to the rank of full general. Because its date was later than that of Robert E. Lee he felt himself insulted and degraded.

When the President mildly and good-naturedly informed him that his position of Quartermaster General in the old army did not entitle him to a field command and that Lee's rank as field commander was higher, he replied in a letter which became the text of his champions. Its high-flown language and bombastic claims showed only too plainly that a consuming ambition had destroyed all sense of proportion in his mind.

With uncontrolled passion he wrote to the President:

> Human power cannot efface the past. Congress may vacate my commission and reduce me to the ranks. It cannot make it true that I was not a general before July 4, 1861.
>
> The effect of the course pursued is this:
>
> It transforms me from the position first in rank to that of fourth. The relative rank of the others among themselves *(Cooper, Albert Sidney Johnston and Robert E. Lee)* is unaltered. It is plain that this is a blow aimed at me only. It reduces my rank in the grade I hold. This has never been done heretofore in the regular service in America but by the sentence of a court-martial as a punishment and as a disgrace for some military offense.
>
> It seeks to tarnish my fair name as a soldier and as a man, earned by more than thirty years of laborious and perilous service. I have but this—the scars of many wounds all honestly taken in my front and in the front of battle, and my father's revolutionary sword. It was delivered to me from his venerable hand without stain of dishonor. Its blade is still unblemished as when it passed from his hand to mine. I drew it in the war not for rank or fame (sic!), but to defend the sacred soil, the homes and hearths, the women and children, aye, and the men of my mother, Virginia—my native South. It may hereafter be the sword of a general leading armies, or of a private volunteer. But while I live and have an arm to wield it, it shall never be sheathed until the freedom, independence, and full rights of the South are achieved. When that is done, it then will be a matter of small concern to the Government, to Congress, or to the Country, what my rank or lot may be.

What has the aspect of a studied indignity is offered me. My noble associate with me in the battle has his preferment connected with the victory won by our common trials and dangers. His commission bears the date of July 21, 1861, but care seems to be taken to exclude the idea that I had any part in winning that triumph.

My commission is made to bear such a date that my once inferiors in the service of the United States and of the Confederate States (Cooper, Albert Sidney Johnston and Robert E. Lee) shall be above me.

But it must not be dated as of July 21, nor be suggestive of the victory of Manassas!

If the action against which I have protested is legal, it is not for me to question the expediency of degrading one who has served laboriously from the commencement of the war on this frontier, and borne a prominent part in the only great event of that war, for the benefit of persons, neither of whom has yet struck a blow for this Confederacy.

These views and the freedom with which they are presented may be unusual, so likewise is the occasion which calls them forth. "I have the honor to be, most respectfully,

Your obedient servant,

J. E. Johnston, General.

With a curve of his thin lips and a look of mortal weariness on his haggard face, the man on whose shoulders rested the burden of the lives of millions of his people seized his pen and wrote this brief note:

Richmond, Va., September 14, 1861.

General J. E. Johnston:

Sir:

I have just received and read your letter of the 12 instant. Its language is, as you say, unusual; its arguments and statements utterly one-sided, and its insinuations as unfounded as they are unbecoming.

I am, etc.,

Jefferson Davis.

While the Commander of the victorious Confederacy was sulking in his tent on the field of Manassas, playing this pitiful farce about the date of a commission, and allowing his army to go to pieces, George B. McClellan with tireless energy and matchless genius as an organizer was whipping into shape Lincoln's new levy of five hundred thousand determined Northern men.

To further add to his embarrassment and cripple his work, the Vice President of the Confederacy, Alexander H. Stephens, developed early into a chronic opponent of the administration. Much of this opposition was due to dyspepsia but it was none the less effective in undermining the influence of the Executive. Mr. Stephens' theories were the outgrowth of the most radical application of the dogma of States' Rights.

Before secession he had bitterly opposed the withdrawal of Georgia from the Union. His extreme advocacy of the Sovereignty of the States now threatened the unity and integrity of the Confederacy as a Republic.

He proclaimed the remarkable doctrine that as the war was one in which the people had led the politicians into a struggle for their rights, therefore the people could be absolutely relied on by the administrators of the Government to properly conduct the war. The people could always be depended on when a battle was to be fought. When no fighting was to be done they should be at home attending to their families and their business. The people were intelligent. They were patriotic. And they were as good judges of the necessity of their presence with the colors as the commanders of the armies. The generals were professional soldiers. They fought for rank and pay and most of them had no property in the South!

In the face of such doctrines proclaimed from so high a source it was not to be wondered at if thousands of men obtained furloughs on long leaves of absence. In the judgment of the intelligent and patriotic people of the South the war was practically over. Why should they swell the ranks of great armies to augment the power of military lords? While these comfortable doctrines were being proclaimed in the South, the North was drilling five hundred thousand soldiers who had enlisted for three years.

The soreheads, theorists, and chronic kickers now had their supreme opportunity to harass the President. They rallied behind the sulking General and his friends and established a vigilant and malignant opposition to Jefferson Davis in the Confederate Congress.

They centered their criticism naturally on the weakest spot in the new Government—the weakest spot in all new nations—its financial policy. They demanded the immediate purchase of all the cotton in the South and its exportation to England as a basis of credit. They blithely ignored two facts—that the Government had no money with which to purchase this enormous quantity of the property of its people and the still more important fact that the ports of the South had been blockaded, that this blockade was becoming more and more effective and that blockade-runners could not be found with sufficient tonnage to move one-tenth of the crop if they were willing to risk capture and confiscation.

If the President could have met the members of his Congress in daily social intercourse much of the opposition could have been cleared by his close reasoning and the magnetism of his powerful personality. But under the strain of his official life his health forbade the attempt at social amenities.

He ceased to entertain except at formal receptions, gave himself body and soul to his duties as President and allowed his critics full swing with their tongues.

The *Richmond Examiner* early developed into the leader of the reptile press of the South which sought by all means fair or foul to break down and destroy the President. This sheet was made the organ of all the bickering, backbiting, complaining and sulking in the army and the civil life of the new Republic.

Because the President could not spare the time for social entertainments, he was soundly abused for the stinginess of his administration. Because the young people of Richmond could not be received at the White House of the Confederacy on every evening in the week. The *Examiner* sneered at the assumption of "superior dignity by the satraps."

This scurrilous newspaper at last made the infamous charge that Davis was getting rich on his savings from a salary of twenty-five thousand dollars in Confederate money! Every politician who had been overlooked rushed into these friendly columns and aired his grievances. The old secession leaders who had been thrust aside for the presidency by the people who had forced the office on Jefferson Davis now pressed forward to put their knives into the sensitive soul of the man they envied. Wm. L. Yancey, Barnwell Rhett and Robert Toombs joined his foes in a chorus of criticism and abuse. Every man who had been slighted in high positions bestowed on rivals rushed now to the attack.

Davis was never a man who could hedge and trim and lie and be all things to all men. He was totally lacking in the patience that can flatter a fool. He was too sincere, too downright in his honesty for such demagoguery.

He was abused for a thousand things for which he was in no sense responsible and made no effort to defend himself. He merely took refuge in dignified silence. And when his enemies could not provoke him into angry outbursts they accused him of contempt for public opinion. In this hour of his sore trial he lacked the sense of broad humor which saved Abraham Lincoln. His rival in Washington was abused with far more savage cruelty—but it always reminded him of a funny story. He told the story, roared with laughter himself, and turned again to his work.

Not so with Jefferson Davis. He was keenly and painfully sensitive to the approval or condemnation of the people about him. The thoughtless word of a child could cut him to the quick. To have explained many of the difficulties on which he was attacked would have been to endanger the usefulness of one of his generals or expose the army to danger.

He steadfastly remained silent and accepted as inevitable the accusation that his manner was cold and repellent. But once did his soul completely break down under the strain.

An officer whom he loved had been censured by one of his commanding generals who demanded his removal. This censure was conveyed to the President in a letter marked "Private."

The officer was removed. Hard as the duty was, he felt that as the servant of his country he had no other choice.

Flushed and indignant, his old friend called. "You know me, Mr. President," he cried passionately. "How can I ever hold my head up again under censure from you—one of my oldest and best friends?"

The muscles of the drawn face twitched with nervous agony. He could not with his high sense of honor as President tell this man that he loved him and found no fault with him. To make his acceptance of the situation easier, his only course was to rouse his friend's anger.

He turned and said curtly: "You have, I believe, received your orders. I can suggest nothing but obedience."

Too angry to ask an explanation, he strode from the room without a word.

The President closed his desk, climbed the steep hill of the Capitol Square, walked home in brooding silence, and locked himself in his room without eating his dinner.

Alarmed at his absence, Mrs. Davis at last gently rapped on his door. With tender tact she drew from his reluctant lips the story.

Turning his dimmed eyes on hers, he burst out in tones of quivering anguish:

"Oh, my Winnie dear, how could any man with a soul write a letter like that, mark it private and force me to plunge a knife into the heart of my best friend and leave it there without a word—"

"You should have told your friend the whole truth!"

"No—he could have made trouble in the army. His commander knew that I could bear it best."

"You must try to mingle more with those men, dear," his wife pleaded. "Use your brains and personality to win them. You can do it."

"At the cost of precious hours I can give to better service for my country. No. I've given my life to the South. I'll eat my heart out in silence if I must—"

He paused and looked at her tenderly.

"Only your friendly eyes shall see, my dear. After all, what does it matter what men think of me now? If we succeed, we shall hear no more of malcontents. If we do not succeed, I shall be held accountable by both friend and foe. It's written so in the book of life. I must accept it.

I'll just do my best and God will give me strength to bear what comes." And so while the South was gayly celebrating the end of the war and every crow was busy pecking at the sensitive heart of their leader, the ominous shadow of five hundred thousand Northern soldiers, armed with the best weapons and drilled by the masters of military science, was slowly but surely drawing near.

19: SOCOLA'S PROBLEM

Socola found his conquest of Jennie beset with unforeseen difficulties. His vanity received a shock. His success with girls at home had slightly turned his head.

His mother was largely responsible for his conceit. She honestly believed that he was the handsomest man in America. For more than six years—in fact, since his eighteenth birthday—his mother's favorite pet name was "Handsome." He had heard this repeated so often he had finally accepted it philosophically as one of the fixed phenomena of nature.

From the moment he made up his mind to win Jennie he considered the work done—until he had set seriously about it.

The first difficulty he encountered was the discovery that a large number of Southern boys apparently considered the chief business of life going to see the girls—this girl in particular.

The first day he called he found five young men who had lingered beyond their appointed hours and were encroaching on his time without the slightest desire to apologize. He could see that she was trying to get rid of them but they hung on with a dogged, quiet persistence that was annoying beyond measure.

War seemed to have precipitated an epidemic of furious love-making. He watched Jennie twist these enterprising young Southerners around her slender fingers with an ease that was alarming. They were fine-looking, wholesome fellows, too—a little given to boyish boasting of military prowess, but for all that genuine, serious, big-hearted boys.

The matter-of-fact way in which she ruled them, as if she were a queen born to the royal purple and they were so many lackeys, was something new under the sun.

For a moment the thought was cheering. Perhaps it was her way of serving notice on his rivals that her real interests lay in another direction. But the disconcerting thing about it was that it seemed to be a habit of mind.

For the life of him he couldn't make out her real attitude. The one encouraging feature was that she certainly treated him with more seriousness than these home boys. It might be, of course, because she thought him a foreigner. And yet he didn't believe it. She had a way of looking frankly and inquiringly into his eyes with a deep, serious expression. Such a look could not mean idle curiosity.

And yet the problem he could not solve was how far he dared as yet to presume on that interest. A single false step might imperil his enterprise. His plan was of double importance since the break between her impulsive father and the President of the Confederacy. Barton was now the spokesman for the Opposition. His tongue was one that knew no restraint. An engagement with his daughter might mean the possession of invaluable secrets of the Richmond Government. Barton's championship of the quarrelsome commanders, who, in the first flood tide of their popularity as the heroes of Manassas, gave them the position of military dictators, would also place in his hands information of the army which would be priceless. The Confederate Congress sat behind closed doors. On the right footing in the Barton household he could put himself in possession of every scheme of the Southern law-makers from the moment of its conception.

The trait of the girl's character which astounded him was the sudden merging of every thought in the cause of the South. Even the time she spent laughing and flirting with those soldier boys was a sort of holy service she was rendering to her country. The devotion of these Southern women to the Confederacy was remarkable.

It had already become an obsession. From the moment blood had begun to flow, the soul and body of every Southern woman was laid a living offering on the altar of her country.

He watched this development with awe and admiration. It was an ominous sign. It meant a reserve power in the South on which statesmen had not counted. It might set at nought the weight of armies.

The moment he began to carefully approach the inner citadel of the girl's heart he found the figure of a gray soldier clad in steel on guard. What he said didn't interest her. He was a foreigner. She listened politely and attentively but her real thoughts were not there.

He had not believed it possible that patriotism could so obsess the soul of a beautiful girl of nineteen. The devotion of the Southern women, young and old, to the cause of the South was fast developing into a mania.

They were displaying a wisdom, too, which Southern men apparently did not possess. While the hot-headed, fiery masters of men were busy quarreling with one another, criticising and crippling the administration of their Government, the women were supporting the President with a unanimity and enthusiasm that was amazing.

Jennie Barton refused to listen to her father's abuse. Socola found them in the middle of a family quarrel on the subject so intense he could not help hearing the conversation from the adjoining room before Jennie entered.

"The President hates Johnston, I tell you," stormed the Senator. "He doesn't like Beauregard either. He's jealous of him!"

"Father dear, how can you be so absurd!" the girl protested. "A few months ago Beauregard was a captain of artillery. The President has made him a general of equal rank with Lee and Johnston—"

"He's doing all he can now to spite him!"

"So General Beauregard says—the conceit of it! This little general but yesterday a captain to dare to say that the President who had honored him with such high command would sacrifice the country and injure himself just to spite the man he has promoted!"

"That will do, Jennie," the Senator commanded. "Women don't understand politics!"

"Thank God I don't understand that kind. I just know enough to be loyal to my Chief, when our life and his may depend on it—"

With a stamp of his heavy foot the Senator ended the discussion by leaving the room.

Jennie smiled sweetly as she extended her hand to Socola.

"I hope you were not alarmed, Signor. We never fight—"

"The President of the Confederacy is a very fortunate leader, Miss Jennie—"

"Why?"

"He has invincible champions—"

The girl blushed. "I'm afraid we don't know much. We just feel things."

"I think sometimes we only know that way—"

He paused and looked at her hat with a gesture of dismay. "You're not going out?"

"I must," she said apologetically. "I've bought a whole carriage load of peaches and grapes. I went to the Alabama hospital yesterday with a little basket full and made some poor fellows glad. They gave out too quickly. Those who got none looked so wistfully at me as I passed out. I couldn't sleep last night. For hours and hours their deep-sunken eyes followed and haunted me with their pleading. And so I've got a whole load to take today. You'll go with me—won't you?"

He had come to declare his love and make this beautiful girl his conquest. She was ending the day by making him her lackey and errand boy.

It couldn't be helped. There was no mistaking the tones of her voice. She would certainly go. The only way to be with her was to dance attendance on wounded Confederate soldiers.

It was all in the day's work. Many a scout engulfed in the ranks of his enemy must charge his own men to save his life. He would not only make the best of it, he would take advantage of it to press his way a step closer to her heart.

"Are all of the girls of the South like you, Miss Jennie?" he asked with a quizzical smile.

"You mean insulting to their fathers?" she laughed.

"If you care to put it so—I mean, is their loyalty to the Confederacy a mania?"

"Is mine a mania?"

"Perhaps I should say a divine passion—are all your Southern women thus inspired?"

"Yes."

"In the far South and the West?"

"Everywhere!"

"It's wonderful."

"Perhaps because we can't fight we try to make up for it."

He watched her keenly.

"It's something bigger than that. Somehow it's a prophecy to me of a new future—a new world. Maybe after all political wisdom shall not begin and end with man."

Jennie blushed again under the admiring gaze with which Socola held her. The carriage stopped at the door of the Alabama hospital. Socola leaped to the ground and extended his hand for Jennie's. He allowed himself the slightest pressure of the slender fingers as he lifted her out. It was his right in just that moment to press her hand. He put the slightest bit more than was needed to firmly grasp it, and the blood flamed hotly in her cheeks.

He hastened to carry her baskets and boxes of peaches and grapes inside. For an hour he followed her with faithful dog step in her ministry of love. His orderly Northern mind shuddered at the sight of the confusion incident to the sudden organization of this hospital work. He had heard it was equally bad in the North. Two armed mobs had rushed into battle with scarcely a thought of what might be done with the mangled men who would be borne from the field.

Jennie bent low over the cot of a dying boy from her home county. He clung to her hand piteously. The waters were too swift and deep for speech. Before she could slip her hand from his and pass on the man on the next cot died in convulsions.

Socola watched his agonized face with a strange sense of exaltation. It was the law of progress—this way of death and suffering. The voice within kept repeating the one big faith of his life:

"Not one drop of human blood shed in defense of truth and right is ever spilled in vain!"

Through all the scenes of death and suffering beautiful Southern women moved with soft tread and eager hands.

A pretty girl of sixteen, with wistful blue eyes, approached a rough, wounded soldier. She carried a towel and tin basin of water.

"Can't I do something for you?" she asked the man in gray.

He smiled through his black beard into her sweet young face:

"No'm, I reckon not—"

"Can't I wash your face?" the girl pleaded.

The wounded man softly laughed.

"Waal, hit's been washed fourteen times today, but I'll stand it again, if you say so!"

The girl laughed and blushed and passed quickly on.

When all the grapes and peaches had been distributed save in one basket Socola looked at these enquiringly.

"And these, Miss Jennie—they're the finest of the lot?"

The girl smiled tenderly.

"They're for revenge—"

"Revenge?"

"Yes. The next ward is full of Yankees. I'm going to heap coals of fire on their heads—come—"

The last luscious peach and bunch of grapes had been distributed and the last soldier in blue had murmured:

"God bless you, Miss!"

Jennie paused at the door and waved her hand in friendly adieu to the hungry, homesick eyes that still followed her.

She brushed a tear from her cheek and whispered: "That's for my Big Brother. I'll tell him about it some day. He's still in the Union—but he's mine!"

She drew her lace handkerchief from her belt, dried her tears and looked up with a laugh.

"I'm not so loyal after all—am I?"

"No. But I've seen something bigger than loyalty," he breathed softly, "something divine—"

"Come," said the girl lightly. "I wish you to meet the most wonderful woman in Richmond. She's in charge of this hospital—"

Socola laughed skeptically.

"I've already seen the most wonderful woman in Richmond, Miss Jennie—"

"But she is—really—the most wonderful woman in all the South—I think in the world—Mrs. Arthur Hopkins—"

"Really?"

"She has done what no man ever has anyhow—sold all her property for two hundred thousand dollars and given it to the Confederacy. And not satisfied with giving all she had—she gave herself."

Socola followed the girl in silence into the little office of the hospital and found himself gasping with astonishment at the sight of the delicate woman who extended her hand in friendly greeting.

She was so perfect an image of his own mother it was uncanny—the same straight, firm mouth, the strong, intellectual forehead with the heavy, straight-lined eyebrows, the waving rich brown hair, with a strand of silver here and there—the somber dress of black, the white lace collar and the dainty white lace cap on the back of her beautiful hair—it took his breath.

The more he saw of these Southern people, men and women,

the more absurd became the stuff he had read so often about the Puritan of New England and the Cavalier of the South. He was more and more overwhelmed with the conviction that the Americans were one people racially and temperamentally. The only difference on earth between them was that some settled in the bleak hills and rock-bound coast of the North and others in the sunlit fields and along the shining shores of the South.

He returned with Jennie Barton to her home with the deepening conviction that he was making no progress. He must use this girl's passionate devotion to her country as the lever by which to break into her heart or he would fail.

He paused on the doorstep and spoke with quick decision:

"Miss Jennie, your Southern women have fired my imagination. I'm going to resign my commission with the Sardinian Ministry and enter the service of the South—"

"You mean it?"

"I was never in more deadly earnest."

He looked straight into her brown eyes until she lowered them.

"I need not tell you that you have been my inspiration. You understand that without my saying it."

Before Jennie could answer he had turned and gone with quick, firm step.

She watched his slender, graceful figure with a new sense of exhilaration and tenderness.

20: THE ANACONDA

While General Joseph E. Johnston was devoting his energies to a campaign to change the date of his commission and his friends organizing their opposition to the President at Richmond, Gideon Welles, the quiet, unassuming Secretary of the Navy at Washington, was slowly but surely drawing the mighty coil, the United States Navy, about the throat of the South. He made little noise but the work he did was destined to become the determining factor of the war.

The first blow was struck at North Carolina.

On August 26, 1861, at one o'clock the fleet quietly put to sea from Fortress Monroe. On Tuesday they arrived at Hatteras Inlet, opened fire on the two forts guarding its entrance and on the twenty-ninth a white flag was raised. Seven hundred and fifteen prisoners were surrendered, one thousand stand of arms, and thirty pieces of cannon. At a single blow the whole vast inland water coast of North Carolina on her Sounds was opened to the enemy with communications from Norfolk, Virginia, to Beaufort. A garrison of a thousand men could hold those forts for all time with the navy in command of the sea.

Burnside followed with his expedition into the Sounds, captured Roanoke Island and the fall of Newbern was inevitable. Every river-mouth and inlet of the entire coast of North Carolina was now in the hands of the Federal Government save the single port of Wilmington.

The moral effect of this blow by the navy was tremendous in the North. It was the first token of renewed power since the defeat at Bull Run.

The navy had not only turned the tide of defeat in the imagination of the people, the achievement was one of vast importance to the North and the most sinister import to the South.

The Federal Government had gained the first important base on the Southern coast for her blockading squadron and given a foothold for the military invasion of North Carolina.

The President at Richmond was compelled to watch this tragedy in helpless sorrow. The South had no navy with which to dispute the command of the sea and yet she had three thousand miles of coast line! With swift, remorseless sweep the navy struck Port Royal, South Carolina, and established the second secure base for the blockading squadrons.

The Beaufort district of South Carolina captured by this expedition was one of the richest and most thickly settled of the State, containing fifteen hundred square miles. It produced annually fifty million pounds of rice and fourteen thousand bales of cotton. And in its population were thirty thousand slaves suddenly brought under the power of the Federal Government.

The coast of Florida was next pierced. The blockade of the enormous coast line of the South was declared at first an impossibility. Within less than a year the United States Navy had established bases within striking distance of every port. New ships were being launched, purchased or chartered daily and the giant Anaconda was slowly winding its terrible coil about the commerce of the Confederacy.

Jefferson Davis was not the man to accept this ominous situation without a desperate struggle. The man who had substituted iron gun carriages for wood in the army consulted his Secretary of the Navy on the possibility of revolutionizing the naval-warfare of the world by the construction of an iron-clad ship of first-class power. In his report to the Confederate Naval Committee, Secretary Mallory had developed this possibility two months before the subject had been broached in the report of Gideon Welles in Washington.

"I regard the possession of an iron-armored ship," Mallory urged, "as a matter of the first necessity. Such a vessel at this time could traverse the entire coast of the United States, prevent all blockade, and encounter with a fine prospect of success their entire navy. Inequality of numbers may be overcome by invulnerability, and thus not only does economy but naval success dictate the wisdom and expediency of fighting with iron against wood, without regard to first cost."

The President of the Confederacy gave his hearty endorsement to this plan—and summoned the genius of the South to the task. At the bottom of the harbor of Norfolk lay the half-burned hull of the steam frigate Merrimac which the Government had set on fire and sunk on destroying the Navy Yard.

The Merrimac was raised. A board was appointed to draw plans and estimate the cost of the conversion of the vessel into a powerful, floating, iron-clad battery. In the crippled condition of the Norfolk Navy Yard the task was tremendous and the expense would be great. The President ordered the work prosecuted with the utmost vigor. Day and night the ring of hammers on heavy iron echoed over the quiet harbor of Norfolk. Blacksmiths were forging the most terrible ship of war that ever sailed the seas. If the hopes of her builders should be realized, the navy of the North would be swept from the ocean and the proudest ships of the world be reduced to junk in a day.

21: THE GATHERING CLOUDS

Disaster followed disaster for the South now in swift succession. The United States Navy, not content with the supremacy of the high seas, set to work with determination to build a war fleet on the great rivers of the West which could pierce the heart of the lower South.

Before the South could possibly secure arms and ammunition with which to equip the army of Albert Sidney Johnston, these gunboats were steaming down the Ohio and Mississippi bearing thousands of troops armed, drilled and led by stark, game-fighting generals from the West.

By the end of November the Federal troops threatening Tennessee numbered fifty thousand and they were rapidly reinforced until they aggregated a hundred thousand.

General Albert Sidney Johnston sent the most urgent appeals for arms to the Governors of Georgia and Alabama, to General Bragg at Pensacola and to the Government at Richmond. He asked for thirty thousand muskets and got but one thousand. The guns were not in the South. They could not be manufactured. Fully one-half his men had no arms at all. Whole brigades remained without weapons for months. The entire force at his command never numbered more than twenty-two thousand during this perilous fall.

And yet, by the masterly handling of his little army, its frequent and rapid expeditions, he kept his powerful opponents in constant expectations of an attack and produced the impression that he commanded an enormous force.

In the meantime the sensational newspapers were loud in their demands. The Richmond yellow Journal shouted:

"Let Johnston muster his forces, advance into Kentucky, capture Louisville, push across the Ohio and carry the war into Africa."

Swift and terrible the blow fell.

And always the navy's smoke on the horizon. From the Ohio, the Tennessee and Cumberland rivers could be navigated for hundreds of miles into Tennessee and Alabama. But two forts guarded the rivers and protected these States.

Early in February, 1862, the gunboats under Admiral Foote slowly steamed up the Tennessee and attacked Fort Henry. The array they covered was commanded by General Grant. The Federal fleet and army hurled twenty thousand men and fifty-four cannon against the little fort of eleven guns. With but forty men General Tilghman fought this host and held them at bay for two hours and ten minutes, until the main body of his garrison of twenty-five hundred troops had marched out and were safely on their way to Fort Donelson, twelve miles across the country on the banks of the Cumberland. Fort Henry was of small importance. Fort Donelson commanded the approach to Nashville.

There was not a moment's delay. Grant telegraphed Halleck that he would capture Fort Donelson two days later. Admiral Foote sent three light gunboats up the Tennessee to clear the river into Alabama, swept down stream with his heavier craft to the Ohio and turned into the Cumberland. Grant pressed directly across the strip of twelve miles with his army bearing on Fort Donelson.

The commander at Fort Donelson had at first but six thousand men including the garrison from Fort Henry which had just arrived. Had Grant been able to strike on the eighth of February, the day he had wired to Halleck he would capture the fort, its fall would have been sure. But high water delayed him, and Albert Sidney Johnston hastened to pour in reinforcements. Every available soldier at his command was rushed to the rescue. He determined to fight for Nashville at Donelson. General Buckner's command of Kentuckians, General Pillow's Tennesseeans and General Floyd's brigade of Virginia troops were all poured into the fort before the thirteenth. This force, approximating twenty thousand men, properly commanded should hold Donelson indefinitely.

The fortification was magnificently placed on a bluff commanding the river for two miles. Its batteries consisted of eight thirty-two-pounders, three thirty-two-pound carronades, one ten-inch Columbiad and one thirty-two-pounder rifle. A line of entrenchments stretched for two miles around the fort enclosing it.

Into these trenches the newly arrived troops were thrown. Dick Welford, with Floyd's Virginians, gripped his musket with eager enthusiasm for his first real battle. His separation from Jennie had been a bitter trial. In his eagerness to get to the front he had the misfortune to serve in the ill fated campaign in West Virginia, which preceded Bull Run. Beauregard and J. E. Johnston were in easy touch with Richmond. His unlucky brigade had been transferred to Albert Sidney Johnston's command.

The men had been in the trenches through the long miserable night expecting an attack at any moment.

Half waking, half dreaming, he lay on the cold ground wondering what Jennie was doing—and always with the nightmare of that foreign snake winding his way into her favor. Well, his chance would come in this battle. He would lead his men in a charge. He was a corporal now. He would come out of it with straps on his shoulders, he could see Jennie's eyes flash with tears of pride as she read the story of his heroism and his promotion.

"I'll show that reptile what a man can do!" he muttered. The tired body relaxed and his big blond head sank on his arms. A sudden crash of thunder and he sprang to his feet, his hand tight on his gun. There they were in the gray light of the chill February morning—the fleet of Federal gunboats under Foote, their big black funnels pouring clouds of smoke into the sky, darkening the dull red glow of the rising sun. He counted six of them—Carondalet, Pittsburgh, Louisville, St. Louis, Tyler and Conestoga.

A white breath of smoke flashed from the Carondalet's bow, and Dick watched the shell rise with a shriek and fall short of the fort. The fleet moved closer and another shell screamed through the sky and again fell short. They moved again, found the range, and for four hours the earth trembled beneath the steady roar of their forty-six guns.

At eleven o'clock Dick saw the long lines of men in blue deploy for an assault on the entrenchments. They moved with quick sure step, these men under Grant. He was sorry for them. They were marching to certain death.

On the blue waves rolled, pouring volley after volley into the heaps of earth behind which the Southerners lay.

They were close enough now and the quick command rang along the trenches. "Fire!"

A storm of death swept the ranks in the open fields. They stood their ground stubbornly, those dogged western fighters. Dazed and cut to pieces, they rallied and pressed forward again only to be mowed down in heaps.

They gave it up at last and sullenly withdrew, leaving the dead piled high and the wounded slowly freezing to death where they lay. The artillery kept the earth quivering with the steady roar of their guns and the Federal sharpshooters harassed the trenches without a moment's respite. It was impossible to move for food or water until nightfall.

At dawn next day Dick once more gripped his gun and peered over the embankment. The morning passed without attack. What could it mean? They saw at last—another fleet. Clouds of black smoke on the river told the story. Reinforcements had arrived.

At half-past two o'clock the fleet formed in line of battle—threw their big flags to the breeze and dashed squarely on the fort. They swept now within point blank range of three hundred yards, pouring in a storm of shot.

But the Confederate batteries were too heavy and too well manned. Fifty-seven shells struck the flagship and more than a hundred took effect on the five boats leading the assault. The fleet was crushed and put out of commission. Every boat was disabled except one and that withdrew beyond the range of the batteries.

Dick watched the magnificent spectacle with thrilling pride. He could have enjoyed the show but for the bitter cold. It was twenty degrees below the freezing point, and while the battle raged between the fleet and fort it began to sleet and snow. When the crippled boats at last drifted down the yellow tide and out of range, he found to his amazement that a thick coat of ice had formed on the hand in which he held his musket. His clothes were frozen stiff on his body.

He leaped to his feet and beat his arms fiercely, and glanced over the embankment toward those ominous-looking piles of blue. The sleet was sheathing their bodies in crystal shrouds now. No flag of truce was allowed and the wounded lay freezing and dying where they fell. He could hear the stronger ones still crying for help. Their long piteous moans rang above the howl of the wind through the breaking boughs of the trees.

It was hideous. Why didn't they rescue those men? Why didn't they proclaim a truce to bury the dead and save the wounded? Grant must be a fiend! Far off on the river another black smudge was seen in the sky.

More reinforcements were coming.

The three Confederate generals suddenly waked with a shock to realize that their foe had landed a second army, cutting their communications with Nashville.

A council of war was hastily called on the night of the fourteenth. It was a discordant aggregation. Floyd, the former Secretary of War in Buchanan's administration, was the senior officer in command. He was regarded more as a politician than a soldier and his exploits in West Virginia had not added to his fame. The men around him had little respect for his capacity as a commander. Besides quarreling had become the fashion in the armies of the victorious South since the affair at Bull Run. The example of Joseph E. Johnston and Beauregard was contagious.

There was but one thing to do. The wrangling generals were unanimous on that point. They must make a desperate assault next morning on Grant's right wing and reestablish their communications with Nashville at all hazards.

Under cover of the darkness on the morning of the fifteenth, the men were marched from their trenches and massed on the Federal right. But a handful were left to guard the entrenchments on the Confederate right. At the first streak of dawn, the concentrated lines of the Confederates were hurled on the division of McClernand. Before two o'clock Grant's right wing had been crushed into a shapeless mass with the loss of his artillery. The way was open to Nashville and the discordant commanding generals of the Confederacy paused.

Buckner ordered up his artillery and reserves to pursue the enemy or hold his newly-won position. Pillow flatly refused to allow a single gun to be withdrawn from the entrenchments and sent peremptory orders to his victorious subordinate to return to the trenches on the right.

As Buckner was reluctantly returning to the old lines he encountered Floyd.

"Where are you going?" the Commander-in-Chief demanded.

"I am ordered back to the entrenchments—"

"You think it wise to walk back into the trap we've just escaped from?"

"I do not!" was the short answer. "We are outnumbered three to one. We cannot hold our connections open in the face of such an army backed by gunboats and transports which can bring reinforcements daily. The road is open, we should save our army by an immediate juncture with Albert Sidney Johnston before Nashville."

"I agree with you," Floyd replied. "Hold your troops until I consult with Pillow."

While Floyd and Pillow wrangled, Grant dashed on the scene. He had not been present during the battle. The wounded Commodore had begged him for a consultation on board his flagship five miles below.

When Grant reached the field he met a sight that should have dismayed him and sent his shattered army to the shelter of the gunboats and a hasty retreat down the Cumberland to a place of safety.

McClernand had been crushed and his disorganized troops thrown back in confusion in front of the entrenchments of the Confederate right. His troops had been on the field for five days and five nights drenched in snow, sleet, mud, ice and water. The field was strewn with the dead and wounded. Great red splotches of frozen blood marked the ground in all directions. Beneath the sheltering pines where the white, smooth snow lay unbroken by the tramp of heavy feet and the crush of artillery, crimson streams could be seen everywhere. For two miles the ground was covered with the mangled dead, dying, and freezing. Smashed artillery and dead horses lay in heaps. In the retreat the heavy wheels of the artillery had rolled over the bodies of the dead and wounded, crushing and mangling many beyond recognition.

No general ever gazed upon a more ghastly scene than that which greeted the eye of U. S. Grant in this moment of his life's supreme crisis. The suffering of his wounded who had fought with the desperation of madness to save themselves from the cold, had left its mark on their stark, white faces. The ice had pressed a death mask on the convulsed features and held them in the moment of agony. They looked up into his face now, the shining eyes, gaping mouths, clenched fists, and crooked twisted limbs.

McClernand's raw troops retreating over this field of horrors were largely beyond control. Grant knew the enemy had been reinforced. He could reasonably assume from the evidence before him of the terrific slaughter in the open field that his own army was in peril. The transports were in sight ready to move his army to a place of safety where he might re-form his broken ranks.

His decision was instantaneous and thoroughly characteristic. He turned to C. F. Smith in command of his left wing whose division had been but slightly engaged.

"General Smith, the enemy does not follow up their advantage. They are probably in a worse condition than I am. Mass your men and charge their entrenchments on the right—never let up for a minute—drive—drive—drive them!"

The charging hosts swept the thin lines of the half abandoned trenches with the fury of a cyclone. The Confederate right was broken and rolled back in confusion, fresh troops were rushed from the Federal reserves and a new cordon of death thrown round the fort.

On the night of this fatal fifteenth of February Dick Welford was detailed for guard duty at the door of General Floyd's tent. He heard their council of war with sinking heart.

General Pillow favored a second desperate assault on the enemies' right to re-open the way to Nashville. Buckner faced him with rage:

"It was possible today, sir, and we did it. Now the enemy has been reinforced for the third time. If you had sent my guns as I ordered the way would still be open—"

"We can yet cut our way out," Pillow growled.

"Yes, with the sacrifice of three fourths of our brave men to save one fourth. I'll not be a party to such butchery. We're caught now in a death trap. The only rational thing to do is to surrender."

Floyd rose nervously.

"I'm not going to surrender, gentlemen. The North has accused me of treachery in Buchanan's Cabinet. I couldn't expect decent treatment from them. A steamer with recruits has just arrived from Nashville. I shall make my escape on it with as many men as can be carried."

"And I'll accompany you," Pillow declared.

"Go if you like, gentlemen," Buckner replied. "I'll stand by my men and share their fate."

Floyd and Pillow hastily began their preparations to go.

Buckner quietly asked: "Am I to consider the command turned

over to me?"

"Certainly," Floyd answered. "I turn over the command."

"I pass it, too," Pillow quickly added.

General Buckner called for pen, ink and paper and dispatched a courier immediately to General Grant. The reply was in two words: "Unconditional surrender."

Pillow crossed the river under cover of the night and made his way into the country.

Floyd offered to take Dick Welford on board the little steamer.

"No, thank you," the young Virginian answered curtly.

"You prefer to surrender?"

"I'm not going to surrender. I'm going to join Col. Forrest's cavalry and fight my way out."

With a wave of his arm Floyd hurried on board the steamer and fled to Nashville.

Dick had seen Forrest lead one of his matchless charges of cavalry in their fight that day. With a handful of men he had cut his way through a solid mass of struggling infantry and thrown them into confusion. He had watched this grave, silent, unobtrusive man of humble birth and little education with the keenest interest. He felt instinctively that he was a man of genius. From today he knew that as a leader of cavalry he had few equals. He had pointed out to his superiors in their council of war a possible path of escape by a road partially overflowed along the river banks. It was judged impracticable.

In the darkness of the freezing night Dick rode behind his silent new commander along this road with perfect faith. Forrest threw his command into Nashville and saved the city from anarchy when the dreaded news of the fall of Donelson precipitated a panic.

The South had met her first crushing defeat—a defeat more disastrous than the North had suffered at Bull Ran. Grant had lost three thousand men but the Confederate garrisons had been practically wiped out with the loss of more than fifteen thousand muskets, every big gun and thirteen thousand prisoners of war.

When Grant met Buckner, the victor and vanquished quietly shook hands. They had been friends at West Point.

"Why didn't you attack me on Friday?" the Northerner asked.

"I was not in command."

"If you had, my reinforcements could not possibly have reached me in time."

Buckner smiled grimly.

"In other words a little more promptness on one side, a little less resolute decision on the other—and the tables would have been turned!"

"That's just it," was the short answer.

It was an ominous day for the South. Bigger than the loss of the capital of Tennessee which Johnston evacuated the next day, bigger than the loss of fifteen thousand men and their guns loomed the figure of a new Federal commander. Out of the mud, and slush, ice and frozen pools of blood—out of the storm cloud of sleet and snow and black palls of smoke emerged the stolid, bulldog face of Ulysses S. Grant. Lincoln made him a major general.

22: JENNIE'S RECRUIT

Socola lost no time in applying for a position. The one place of all others he wished was a berth in the War Department. It was useless to try for it. No foreigner had ever been admitted to tiny position of trust in this wing of the Confederate Government.

He would try for a position in the Department of State. His supposed experience in the Diplomatic Service and his mastery of two languages besides the English would be in his favor. The struggle for recognition from the powers of Europe was the card he could play. Once placed in the Department of State he would make the acquaintance of every clerk and subordinate who possessed a secret of the slightest value to his cause.

He wished to enter the Department of State for another reason. He had learned from absolutely reliable sources that Judah P. Benjamin, the present Secretary of War, was slated for Secretary of State in the new Cabinet which would be named when Jefferson Davis was inaugurated as permanent President. He knew Benjamin to be the ablest man in the Cabinet, the one man on whose judgment Davis leaned with greatest confidence. It would he of immense value to his cause to be in daily touch with this man.

Fortunately he had mastered shorthand the last year of his stay in Washington. This accomplishment, rare in the South, would be an additional argument with which to secure his appointment. Jennie had promised to accompany him to the office of the President and add her voice to his plea. She had quite won the heart of the badgered chieftain of the Confederacy by her steady loyalty to his administration. The malignant opposition of Senator Barton was notorious. This opposition at the moment had become peculiarly vindictive and embarrassing. The fall of Fort Donelson and the loss of Nashville had precipitated a storm of hostile criticism. The fierce junta of malcontents in the Confederate Congress were eager to seize on any excuse to attack the President. They were now demanding the removal of Albert Sidney Johnston from his command. Davis knew that his commanding general in Tennessee was the greatest soldier of his time—and that all he needed was a single opportunity to demonstrate his genius. He refused with scorn to sacrifice such a man to public clamor.

At the White House reception the night before he had heard Jennie Barton stoutly defending him against his accusers who demanded the head of General Johnston.

He had passed her later in the evening, pressed her hand and whispered: "If our men were only as loyal! Ask anything you will of me—to the half of my kingdom."

Jennie wished to put this impulsive promise to the test. She would see that Socola secured his appointment. This brilliant young recruit for the South was her gift to her country and she was proud of him. It had all come about too quickly for her to analyze her feelings. She only realized that she felt a sense of tender proprietary interest in him. That he could render valuable service she did not doubt for a moment.

She had told him to meet her at the statue of Washington in the Capitol Square. They would wait there for the appearance of the President and follow him. His habits were simple and democratic. He walked daily from the Confederate White House to the Capitol grounds, crossed the Square and at the foot of the hill entered his office in the Custom House on Main Street, unaccompanied by an escort of any kind.

Anybody on earth could approach and speak to him. The humbler the man or woman, the easier the approach was always made.

Socola was waiting at the big group of statuary contemplating the lines of its fine workmanship with curious interest.

Jennie startled him from a reverie:

"You like him?"

The white teeth gleamed in pleasant surprise.

"The father of his country?—Yes—I like him. It's going to be my country, too, you know."

They strolled through the grounds and watched the squirrels leap from the limbs of a great tree to the swaying boughs of the next.

A tall awkward trooper on whose hat was the sign of a North Carolina regiment toiled painfully up the hill slightly under the influence of whisky. Socola saw that he was navigating the steep with difficulty and turned into a by-path to give him a free passage.

It was never pleasant to meet a man under the influence of liquor in the presence of ladies.

They had taken but a few steps along the little path when the quick firm military tread of the President was heard.

They turned just in time to see him encounter the toiling trooper from North Carolina.

The soldier's jaw suddenly dropped and his eyes kindled with joy. He stood squarely in the President's way and laughed good naturedly. "Say—Mister!"

"Well, sir?"

"Say—now—ain't yo' name Jeff'son Davis?"

The President nodded in a friendly way.

"It is."

"I knowed it," the trooper laughed. "By Gum, I knowed it, the minute I laid my eyes on ye—"

He moved closer with insinuating joy.

"I bet ye could never guess how I knowed it—could ye?"

"Hardly—"

"Ye want me ter tell ye?" The trooper laughed again. "I knowed ye the very minute I seed ye—'cause ye look thez ezactly like a Confederate postage stamp! I know 'em 'cause I've licked 'em!"

The President laughed and passed on his way without looking back. They found a crowd of cranks and inventors waiting to see him. He had the same weakness as Abraham Lincoln for this class of men. He never allowed a clerk to turn one way without his personal attention. His interest in all scientific problems was keen, and he had always maintained the open mind of youth to all inventions.

Socola and Jennie strolled through the city for an hour until the crank levee was over. The President's secretary, Burton Harrison, promised them an interview at the end of that time. He ushered them into the room under the impression that all the callers had gone. He had overlooked a modest, timid youth who had quietly approached the Chief Executive's desk.

They paused until he was at leisure. The moment was one of illumination for Socola. He saw a trait of character in the Southern leader whose existence he had not suspected.

"My name is Ashe—Mr. President, S. A. Ashe," the youth began.

Davis bowed gravely.

"Have a seat, sir."

The boy sat down and twiddled his cap nervously.

"I've come to ask an appointment of some kind in the regular army of the Confederacy. I'm an officer of the North Carolina militia. I wish to enter the regular army."

The Confederate chieftain looked at the peculiarly youthful, beardless face. He couldn't be more than eighteen from appearances.

"I'm afraid you're too young, sir," he said slowly, shaking his head.

The boy drew himself up with a touch of wounded pride.

"Why, Mr. Davis, I voted for you for President last November."

Instantly the Chief Executive rose, blushing his apology. He laid his hand on the boy's shoulder and spoke with the utmost deference. "I beg your pardon, sir. I should have been more observant and thoughtful. I was very much like you when I was a boy. It was a long time before I had any whiskers myself."

With a friendly smile he touched his thin beard.

He sent the young man away happy with his promise of consideration. That he should have asked this beardless boy's pardon in so pointed a manner Socola thought remarkable. That the Chief Executive of nine million people should blush suddenly over such a trifle was the flash that revealed a great soul.

The President advanced and gave Jennie both his hands in cordial greeting.

"I've brought you a recruit, sir," the girl cried with a merry laugh.

"Indeed?"

"I have resigned my commission with the Sardinian Ministry, Mr. President, and wish to offer my services to the South."

"We need every true friend the world can send us, Signor—I thank you—"

"I wish, sir," Socola hastened to say, "to render the most efficient service possible. I have no training as a soldier. I have experience as a diplomat. I speak three languages and I am an expert stenographer—"

"I'm sorry, Signor," the President interrupted, "that I have no vacancy in my office—or I should be pleased to have you here."

"Perhaps your State Department may find me useful?"

"No doubt they can. I'll give you a letter to the Secretary recommending your appointment."

He seated himself at once, wrote the letter and handed it to

Socola.

Jennie thanked him and, with a warm pressure of his hand, passed into the hall with Socola.

At the outer door Burton Harrison overtook them:

"Just a moment, Miss Barton. The President wishes to ask you a question."

Davis drew her to the window.

"I should have been more careful of the credentials of our friend perhaps, Miss Jennie. You can vouch for his loyalty?"

"Absolutely."

She had scarcely uttered the word in tones of positive conviction before she realized the startling fact that she had spoken under the impulse of some strange intuition and not from her knowledge of the man's character and history.

In spite of her effort at self-control she blushed furiously. Mr. Davis apparently did not observe it.

"I have been much impressed with his poise and culture and intelligence. You met him in Washington, of course?"

"Yes—"

"You know positively that he was the Secretary of the Sardinian Minister?"

"Positively, Mr. President—"

"Thank you, my dear. I'll take your word for it."

Jennie walked home on air. She had made history. How tragic its sequel was destined to be, a kind Providence concealed.

23: THE FATAL BLUNDER

On February 22, 1862, Jefferson Davis committed the one irretrievable mistake of his administration. He consented to his inauguration as permanent President of the Confederacy under the strict forms of Constitutional law.

The South was entering the shadows of the darkest hour of her new life.

A military dictator clothed with autocratic power could have subdued the discordant elements and marshaled the resources of the country to meet the crisis. A constitutional President would bind himself hand and foot with legal forms. A military dictator might ride to victory and carry his country with him.

His two Commanding Generals had allowed the victorious army of Manassas to drift into a rabble while they wrangled for position, precedence and power.

The swift and terrible blows which the navy had dealt the South, delivered so silently and yet with such deadly effect that the people had not yet realized their import, had convinced the President that the war would be one of the bloodiest in history.

The fall of Fort Henry and Fort Donelson with the evacuation of Nashville had been a sword thrust into the heart of the lower South. The extent of these disasters had not been realized by the public. The South was yet a sleeping lioness. She could be roused and her powers wielded with certainty by one man. But his hand must be firm.

There was one man in the Cabinet of the Confederacy who clearly saw this from the first dawn of the new year—Judah P. Benjamin, the astute Secretary of War. His keen logical mind had brushed aside the fog of sentiment and saw one thing—the need of success and the way in which to attain it.

The morning of February twenty-second was Washington's birthday, and for that reason fixed by the South as the day of the inauguration of their President. Nothing could have shown more clearly the tenacity with which the Southern people were clinging to their old forms. The day slowly dawned through lowering storm clouds.

The President went early to his office for a consultation with the members of his new Cabinet. Judah P. Benjamin, his chosen chief counselor as Secretary of State, was unusually reticent. The details of the inauguration were quickly agreed on and Davis hastened to return to his room at the White House to complete his preparations for the ceremony.

Benjamin followed his Chief thirty minutes later with the most important communication he had ever decided to make.

As the most trusted adviser of the President he had long had the freedom of the house.

The resolute Hebrew features of the Secretary were set with resolution.

He pushed his way to the door of Mr. Davis' room, rapped for admission and without waiting for an answer softly and swiftly entered. His mission was too important to admit of delay.

He paused at the threshold in surprise.

Jefferson Davis was on his knees in prayer so deep and earnest he had not heard.

He waited with head bowed in silent sympathy for five minutes and looked with increasing amazement at the white face of the man who prayed. This agony of soul before the God of his fathers was a revelation to the Minister of State.

His lips were moving now in audible words.

"Thou alone art my refuge, O Lord! Without Thee I shall fail. Have pity on Thy servant—with Thy wisdom guide!"

The time was swiftly passing. The Minister could not wait. "I beg your pardon, Mr. President," he began in low tones, "but I have most important communications to make to you—"

The voice of prayer softly died away and slowly the look of earth came back to the tired face. He turned his hollow cheeks to Benjamin with no attempt to mask the agony of his spirit, slowly rose and motioned him to a chair.

The Secretary lifted his hand.

"I'm restless. If you don't mind, I'll stand. I have marked three editorial attacks on you and your administration in three of the most powerful newspapers in the South—the Richmond Examiner, the Raleigh Standard and the Charleston Mercury—read them please—and then I have something to say!"

The President seated himself and read each marked sentence with care. "The same old thing, Benjamin—only a little more virulent this time—what of it?"

"This! The success of our cause demands the suppression of these reptile sheets and the imprisonment of their editors—"

"Would success be worth having if we must buy it at the cost of the liberties of our people?"

Benjamin stopped short in his tracks. He had been walking back and forth with swift panther-like tread.

"We are at war, Mr. President—fierce, savage, cruel, it's going to be. You have realized this from the first. The world will demand of us just one thing—success in arms. With this we win all. Lose this and we lose all—our liberties and a great deal more. Our coast is pierced now at regular intervals to the mouth of the Mississippi River—at Fortress Monroe in Virginia—the entire inland waters of North Carolina, Port Royal, South Carolina, Florida's line has been broken. Grant's army is swarming into Tennessee. McClellan is drilling three hundred thousand men in Washington to descend on Richmond. It's no time to nurse such reptiles in our bosom—"

"I can't play the petty tyrant—"

"They'll sting you to death—I warn you—no administration on earth can live in times of war and endure such infamous abuse as these conspirators are now heaping on your head. And mark you—they have only begun. The junta of disgruntled generals which they have organized will strangle the cause of the South unless you grip the situation today with a hand of steel. They are laying their plans in the new Congress to paralyze your work and heap on your head the scorn of the world."

The President moved with a gesture of impatience.

"I've told you, Benjamin, that I will not suppress these papers nor sign your order for the arrest of the editors. I am leading the cause of a great people to preserve Constitutional liberty. Freedom of speech is one of their rights—"

"In times of peace, yes—but not in the crisis of war when the tongue of a fool may betray the lives of millions. I am not here merely to ask you to suppress these three treacherous rags—I'm here to ask a bigger and far more important thing. I want you to stop this inaugural ceremony today—"

Davis rose with a quick excited movement.

"What do you mean?"

"Just what I say. Stop in time. We inaugurated a Provisional Government at Montgomery to last one year. Why one year? Because we believed the war would be over before that year expired. It would have been madness to provide for the establishment of the elaborate and clumsy forms of a Constitutional Government during the progress of war. Why set up a Constitution until you have won by the sword the power to maintain it?"

"But," Davis interrupted, "if we delay the adoption of a Constitution we confess to the world our want of confidence in the success of our cause. Such a permanent Constitution will be to our people the supreme sign of faith—"

"With these jackals and hyenas of the press yelping and snarling and snapping at your heels? These men will destroy the faith of our best men and women if you only allow them to repeat their lies often enough. They will believe them at last, themselves. You have the confidence today of the whole South. Your bitterest enemy could not name a candidate to oppose your election last November. Give these traitors time and they will change all—"

"Not with military success—"

"Granted. But if these jackals break down the confidence of the people in the administration, volunteering ceases and we have no army."

"We must use the Conscription. It is inevitable—"

"Exactly!" the Secretary cried triumphantly. "And Conscription is the reductio ad absurdum of your dream of Constitutional Law. Why set up a Constitution at all today?"

"Congress must pass a Conscript law when necessity demands it."

"In their own way, yes—with ifs and ands and clauses which defeat its purpose."

"They must respond to the demands of our people when their patriotism is aroused."

"Our people have patriotism to spare if we can only guide it in the right direction. If it goes to seed in the personal quarrels of generals, if it exhausts itself in abuse of the Executive, while an overwhelming enemy marches on us—What then?"

The President lifted his head.

"And you recommend?"

"Stop this ceremony. Refuse the position of permanent President and use your powers as Provisional President in a Military Dictatorship until the South wins—"

"Never!" was the quick reply. "I'll go down in eternal defeat sooner than win an empire by such betrayal of the trust imposed in me—"

"You're not betraying the trust imposed in you by assuming these powers!" Benjamin exclaimed with passion. "You're fulfilling that trust. You're doing what the people have called you to do—establishing the independence of the South! The Government at Washington has been compelled to exercise despotic powers from the first—"

"Exactly—and that's why we can't afford to do it. We are fighting the battle of the North and the South for Constitutional liberty."

"Even so, if we lose and they win, the cause is lost. Seward is now imprisoning thousands of Northern men who have dared to sympathize with us—"

"An act of infamous tyranny!"

"But if he wins—who will dare to criticise the wisdom of his policy fifty years from today? If we lose, who will give us credit for our high ideals of Civil Law in times of war? You have the chance today to win. Leap into the saddle and command the obedience of every man, woman and child in the South! Your Congress which assembles today is a weak impossible body of men. They have nothing to do except to make foolish speeches and hatch conspiracies against your administration. We have muzzled them behind closed doors. The remedy is worse than the disease. The rumors they circulate through the reptile press do more harm than the record of their vapid talk could possibly accomplish. Why tie these millstones around your neck? They came yesterday to demand the head of Albert Sidney Johnston. They are organizing to drive Lee out of the army. They allow no opportunity to pass to sneer at his position as your chief military adviser since his return from Western Virginia. You know and I know that Albert Sidney Johnston and R. E. Lee are our greatest generals—"

"I'll protect them from the chatter of fools—never fear—"

"To what end if you allow them to break down the faith of our people in their Government? The strong arm, alone, can save us. It's no time to haggle about the forms of law. Your duty is clear. Stop this foolish ceremony of Inauguration today and assume in due time the Dictatorship—"

Davis threw both arms up in a gesture of impatient refusal. "It's a waste of breath, Benjamin. I'll die first!"

The elastic spirit of the younger man recovered its poise at once and accepted the decision.

With a genial smile he slipped one arm around the tall figure.

"Brave, generous, big-hearted, foolish—my captain! Well, I've done my duty as your chief counselor. Now I'll obey orders—one thing more I must add in warning. Richmond swarms with spies. It will be impossible to defend the Capital on the approach of McClellan's army without a proclamation of martial law."

The President looked up sharply.

"We'll compromise on that. I'll proclaim martial law and suspend the writ in Richmond—"

"And a radius of ten miles."

"All right—I'll do that."

It was the utmost concession the wily minister of State could wring from his Chief. But it was important. The Secretary had his eye on a certain house on Church Hill. It might be necessary to expel its owners.

"By the way," the President added, as his Secretary stood with his hand on the door. "I wrote a recommendation to your new department for the appointment of a young friend of Miss Barton to a position in your office. He's a man of brilliant talents—a foreigner who has cast his fortunes with us. Do what you can for him—"

"I'll remember—" the Secretary nodded and hurried to his office to issue his proclamation of martial law for the city and district of Richmond.

At ten o'clock the rain began to pour in torrents. The streets were flooded. Rushing rivers of muddy water roared over its cobble stones and leaped down its steep hills into the yellow tide of the James.

Every flag drooped and flapped in dismal weeping against its staff. The decorations of the houses and windows outside were ruined. The bunting swayed and sagged in deep curves across the streets, pouring a stream of water from the folds.

At twelve o'clock, the procession formed in the Hall of the Virginia Legislature and marched through the pouring rain to the platform erected around the statue of Washington. In spite of the storm an immense crowd packed the space around the speaker's stand, presenting the curious spectacle of a sea of umbrellas.

Socola watched this crowd stand patiently in the downpour with a deepening sense of the tragedy it foreshadowed. The people who could set their teeth and go through an inauguration ceremony scheduled in the open air on such a day might be defeated in battle, but the victor would pay his tribute of blood. He had not dared to ask Jennie to accept his escort on such a day and yet they drifted to each other's side by some strange power of attraction.

The scene was weird in its utter depression of all enthusiasm, and yet the sullen purpose which held the people was sublime in its persistence. An awning covered the speaker's stand and beneath this friendly cover the ceremony was performed down to the last detail.

The President rose and faced his audience under the most trying conditions. Oratory was beyond human effort. He did not attempt it. He read his frank dignified address in simple, clear, musical tones which rang with strange effect over the crowd of drenched men and women. Not a single cheer broke the delivery of his address. He sought in no way to apologize for the disasters which had befallen his people. He faced them bravely and summoned his followers to be equally brave.

The close of his address caught the morbid fancy of Socola with peculiar fascination. Clouds of unusual threatening depths were rolling across the heavens, against which the canopied platform was sharply outlined. The thin form of the President rose white and ghost-like against this black background of clouds. He was extremely pale, his cheeks hollowed deep, his head bared regardless of the chill mists which beat through the canopy.

His tall figure stood tense, trembling, deathlike—the emblem of sacrificial offering on the altar of his country.

Socola whispered to Jennie: "Where have I witnessed this scene before?"

"Surely not in America—"

"No"—he mused thoughtfully—"I remember now—on a lonely

hill outside Jerusalem the Roman soldiers were crucifying a man on a day like this—that's where I saw it!"

He had scarcely spoken the uncanny words in a low undertone when the speaker closed his address with a remarkable prayer.

Suddenly dropping his manuscript on the table he lifted his eyes into the darkened heavens and cried with deep passion:

"With humble gratitude and adoration, to Thee, O God, I trustingly commit myself, and prayerfully invoke Thy blessing on my country and its cause!"

24: THE SLEEPING LIONESS

Again the smoke of the navy shadowed the Southern skies. Two expeditions were aiming mortal blows at the lower South.

The Confederacy had concentrated its forces of the upper waters of the Mississippi on Island Number 10 near New Madrid. The work of putting this little Gibraltar in a state of perfect defense had been rushed with all possible haste. New Madrid had been found indefensible and evacuated on March thirteenth.

On the seventeenth, Commodore Foote's fleet steamed into position and the first shell from his guns shrieked its message of death across the island. The gunboats concentrated their fire on the main battery which was located on low ground, almost submerged by the high water and separated from the others by a wide slough. Their gun platforms were covered with water—the men in gray must work their pieces standing half-leg deep in mud and slush. Five iron-clad gunboats led the attack. Three of them were lashed together in midstream and one lay under the shelter of each shore. Their concentrated fire was terrific. For nine hours they poured a stream of shot and shell on the lone battery with its beaver gunmen.

At three o'clock Captain Rucker in charge of the battery called for reinforcements to relieve his exhausted men. Volunteers rushed to his assistance and his guns roared until darkness brought them respite. It had been done. A single half-submerged battery exposed to the concentrated fire of a powerful fleet had held them at bay and compelled them to withdraw at nightfall. Rucker fired the last shot as twilight gathered over the yellow waters. His battery had mounted five guns at sunrise. Three of them were dismantled. Two of them still spoke defiance from their mud-soaked beds.

On April the sixth, the fleet reinforced succeeded in slipping past the batteries in a heavy fog. A landing was effected above and below the island in large force, and its surrender was a military necessity. Foote and Pope captured MacKall, the commander, two brigadier generals, six colonels, a stand of ten thousand arms, two thousand soldiers, seventy pieces of siege artillery, thirty pieces of field artillery, fifty-six thousand solid shot, six transports and a floating battery of sixteen guns.

A cry of anguish came from the heart of the Confederate President. The loss of men was insignificant—the loss of this enormous store of heavy guns and ammunition with no factory as yet capable of manufacturing them was irreparable.

But the cup of his misery was not yet full. The greatest fleet the United States Navy had gathered, was circling the mouth of the Mississippi with its guns pointing toward New Orleans. Gideon Welles had selected for command of this important enterprise the man of destiny, Davis Glasgow Farragut, a Southerner whose loyalty to the Union had never been questioned.

Eighty-two ships answered Farragut's orders in his West Gulf squadron at their rendezvous. His ships were wood, but no braver men ever walked the decks of a floating battery.

In March he managed to crawl across the bar and push his fleet into the mouth of the Mississippi. The Colorado was too deep and was left outside. The Pensacola and the Mississippi he succeeded in dragging through the mud.

His ships inside, the Commander ordered them stripped for the death grapple.

New Orleans had been from the first considered absolutely impregnable to attack from the sea. Forts Jackson and St. Phillip, twenty miles below the city, were each fortifications of the first rank mounting powerful guns which swept the narrow channel of the river from shore to shore. The use of steam, however, in naval warfare was as yet an untried element of force in the attacking fleet against shore batteries. That steam in wooden vessels could overcome the enormous advantage of the solidity and power of shore guns had been considered preposterous by military experts.

Jefferson Davis had utilized every shipbuilder in New Orleans to hastily construct the beginnings of a Southern navy. Two powerful iron-clad gunboats, Louisiana and Mississippi, were under way but not ready for service. Eight small vessels had been bought and armed.

To secure the city against the possibility of any fleet passing the forts at night or through fog, the channel of the river between Forts Jackson and St. Phillip was securely closed. Eleven dismasted schooners were moored in line across the river and secured by six heavy chains.

These chains formed an unbroken obstruction from shore to shore. This raft was placed immediately below the forts. There was no serious alarm in the city on the appearance of the fleet in the mouth of the river. For months they had been cruising about the Gulf of Mexico without apparent decision.

The people laughed at their enemy. There was but one verdict:

"They'll think twice before attempting to repeat the scenes of 1812." Not only were the two great forts impregnable but the shores were lined with batteries. What could wooden ships do with such forts and guns? It was a joke that they should pretend to attack them. Their only possible danger was from the new iron-clad gunboats in the upper waters of the river. They were building two of their own kind which would be ready long before the enemy could break through the defenses from the North.

When Farragut stripped his fleet for action and moved toward the forts on the sixteenth of April, New Orleans was the gayest city in America. The spirit of festivity was universal. Balls, theaters, operas were the order of the day. Gay parties of young people flocked down the river and swarmed the levees to witness the fun of the foolish attempt of a lot of old wooden ships to reduce the great forts.

The guns were roaring now their mighty anthem. Ships and forts—forts and ships. The batteries of Farragut's mortar schooners were hurling their eleven-inch shells with harmless inaccuracy.

The people laughed again.

For six days the earth trembled beneath the fierce bombardment. The fleet had thrown twenty-five thousand shells and General Duncan reported but two guns dismantled, with half a dozen men killed and wounded. The forts stood grim and terrible, their bristling line of black-lipped guns unbroken, their defenses as strong as when the first shot was fired. On the evening of April twenty-third, the fire of the fleet slackened. Farragut had given up the foolish attempt, of course. He had undertaken the impossible and at last had accepted the fact.

But the people of New Orleans had not reckoned on the character of the daring commander of the Federal fleet. He coolly decided that since he could not silence the guns of the forts he would run past them with his swift steam craft and take the chances of their batteries sending him to the bottom.

Once past these forts and the city would be at his mercy.

He must first clear the river of the obstruction placed below the forts. Farragut ordered two gunboats to steal through the darkness without lights and clear this raft. The work was swiftly done. The task was rendered unexpectedly easy by a break caused by a severe storm. At three o'clock in the morning of the twenty-fourth, the lookout on the ramparts of the forts saw the black hulls of the fleet, swiftly and silently steaming up the river straight for the mouths of their guns.

The word was flashed to the little nondescript fleet of the Confederacy lying in the smooth waters above and they moved instantly to the support of the forts.

The night was one of calm and glorious beauty. The Southern skies sparkled with jeweled stars. The waning moon threw its soft, mellow light on the shining waters, revealing the dark hulls of the fleet with striking clearness. The daring column was moving straight for Fort Jackson. They must pass close under the noses of her guns.

They were in for it now.

The dim star-lit world with its fading moon suddenly burst into sheets of blinding, roaring flame. The mortar batteries moored in range, opened instantly in response—their eleven-inch shells, glowing with phosphorescent halo, circled and screamed and fell.

The black hulls belched their broadsides of yellow flame now. From battlement and casemate of forts rolled the thunder of their batteries, sending their heavy shots smashing into the wooden hulls. Through the flaming jaws of hell, the fleet, with lungs throbbing with every pound of steam, dashed and passed the forts!

Farragut led in the Hartford. But his work had only begun. He had scarcely reckoned on the little Confederate fleet. He found them a serious proposition.

Suddenly above the flash and roar and the batteries of the forts and over the broadsides of the ships leaped a wall of fire straight into the sky.

Slowly but surely the flaming heavens moved down on the attacking fleet lighting the yellow waters with unearthly glare. The Confederates had loosed a fleet of fire ships loaded with pitch pine cargoes. Farragut's lines wavered in the black confusion of rolling clouds of impenetrable smoke, lighted by the glare of leaping flames.

The daring little fleet of the Confederacy moved down through the blinding vapors of their own fires and boldly attacked the on-coming hosts. Friend could scarcely be told from foe. A game little Confederate tug stuck her nose into a fire-ship, pushed it squarely against Farragut's Hartford and slipped between his guns in the smoke and flame unharmed. The Flagship ran aground. Her sailors bravely stuck to their post and from their pumps threw a deluge of water on the flames and extinguished them. The engines of the Hartford, working with all their might, pulled her off the shore under her own steam. The Louisiana, the new gunboat of the Confederacy, had been pressed into service with but two of her guns working—but she was of little use and became unmanageable.

Captain Kennon, the gallant Confederate commander of the Governor Moore, found that the bow of his ship interfered with the aim of his gunners.

"Lower your muzzle and blow the bow of your ship away!"

The big gun dipped its black mouth and blew the bow of his own ship to splinters and through the opening poured shot after shot into the Federal fleet. Kennon fired his last shot at point-blank range, turned the broken nose of his ship ashore and blew her up.

For an hour and a half the two desperate foes wrestled with each other amid flame and smoke and darkness. As the first blush of dawn mantled the eastern sky the conflict slowly died away.

Three of Farragut's gunboats had been driven back and one sunk, but his fleet had done the immortal deed. Battered and riddled with shots, they had passed the forts successfully. As the sun rose on the beautiful spring morning he lifted his battle flags and steamed up the river.

New Orleans, the commercial capital of the South, the largest export city of the world, lay on the horizon in silent shimmering beauty, a priceless treasure, at his mercy.

Speechless crowds of thousands thronged the streets. The small garrison had been withdrawn and the city left to its fate. The marines stood statue-like before the City Hall, their bayonets glittering in the sunlight. Not a breath of wind stirred. In dead, ominous silence the flag of the South was lowered from its staff and the flag of the Union raised in its old place.

There was one man among the thousands who saw this flag with a cry of joy. Judge Roger Barton, Jr., had braved the scorn of his neighbors through good report and evil report, holding their respect by the sheer heroism of his undaunted courage. His aged grandfather was in the city at the moment, having come on a visit from Fairview. Baton Rouge must fall at once. There was nothing to prevent Farragut's fleet from steaming up the river now for hundreds of miles. The old Colonel was furious when informed that he could not return to Fairview. But there was no help for it.

"Don't worry, Grandfather," the judge pleaded; "you can depend on it, Senator Barton will save Fairview if it's within human power—" "But your grandmother is there, sir!" thundered the old man, "helpless on her back. There's no one to protect her from the damned Yankees—"

The Judge smiled.

"Maybe the Yankees will not be so bad after all, grandfather. Anyhow there's no help for it. I've got you here with me safe and sound and I'm going to keep you—"

The fall of New Orleans sent a dagger into the heart of the South. Ft. Donelson had broken the center. The fall of New Orleans had smashed the left wing of the far-flung battle line. The power of the Confederacy was crushed in the rich and powerful State of Louisiana at a single stroke. The route to Texas was cut. The United States Navy had established a base from which to send their fleets into the interior by the great rivers and by the gulf from the Rio Grande to the Keys of Florida.

The sleeping lioness stirred at last. The delusion of Bull Run had passed. It took six months of disasters to do for the South what Bull Run did for the North in six days. The South began now to rise in her might and gird her loins for the fight she had foolishly thought won on the plains of Manassas.

Senator Barton was in bed so ill from an attack of influenza it was impossible for him to travel.

Jennie hastily packed her trunk and left on the first train for the South. She must reach her helpless grandmother before the Federal army could attack Baton Rouge.

The tenderness with which Socola helped her on board the train had brought the one ray of sunlight into her heart. She had expected to go in tears and terror for what the future held in store in the stricken world at home.

A smile on the lips of a stranger had set her heart to beating with joy. She was ashamed of herself for being so happy. But it was impossible to make her heart stop beating and laughing. He had not yet spoken a word of love but she knew. She knew with a knowledge sweet and perfect because she had suddenly realized her own secret. She might have gone on for months in Richmond without knowing that she cared any more for him than for a dozen other boys who were as attentive. In this hour of parting it had come in a blinding flash as he bent over her hand to say goodbye. It made no difference when he should speak. Love had come into her own heart full, wonderful, joyous, maddening in its glory. She could wait in silence until in the fullness of time he must speak. It was enough to know that she loved.

"May I write to you occasionally, Miss Jennie?" he asked with a timid, hesitating look.

She laughed.

"Of course, you must write and tell me everything that happens here." Socola wondered why she laughed. It was disconcerting. He hadn't faced the question of loving Jennie. She was just a charming, beautiful child whose acquaintance he could use for great ends. His depression came from the tremendous nerve strain of his work. The early movement of McClellan's army had kept him in that darkened attic on Church Hill continuously every hour of the past night. He was feeling the strain. He would throw it off when he got a good night's rest.

It was not until twenty-four hours after Jennie's departure that he waked with a dull ache in his heart that refused to go. And so while he dragged himself about his task with a sense of sickening loneliness, a girl was softly singing in the far South.

25: THE BOMBARDMENT

Baton Rouge seethed with excitement on the day of Jennie's arrival. Every wagon and dray was pressed into service. The people were hauling their cotton to be burned on the commons. Negroes swarmed over the bales, cutting them open, piling high the fleecy lint and then applying the torch. The flames leaped upward with a roar and dropped as suddenly into a smoldering and smoking mass.

A crowd rushed to the wharf to see them fire an enormous flat-boat piled mountain-high with cotton. A dozen bales had been broken open and the whole floating funeral pyre stood shrouded in spotless white which leaped into flames as it was pushed into the stream.

Along the levee as far as the eye could reach negroes crawled like black ants rolling the cotton into the river. The ties were smashed, and the white bundle of cotton tumbled into the water and was set on fire. Each bale sent up its cloud of smoke until the surface of the whole river seemed alive with a fleet of war crowding its steam to run fresh batteries. Another flat-boat was piled high, its bales cut open, soaked with whiskey, and set on fire. The blue flames of burning alcohol gave a touch of weird and sinister color to the scene.

The men who owned this cotton stood by cheering and helping in its destruction. The two flat-boats with flames leaping into the smoke pall of the darkened skies led the fleet of fire down the river to greet Farragut's men in their way.

Every saloon was emptied and every gutter flowed with wines and liquors.

* * * * *

Jennie found her grandmother resting serenely in her great rocking chair, apparently indifferent to the uproar of the town. The household with its seventy-odd negro servants was running its usual smooth, careless course.

Jennie read aloud the announcement in the morning paper of Butler's order to New Orleans: "All devices, signs, and flags of the Confederacy shall be suppressed—"

She clenched her fist and sprang to her feet.

"Good! I'll devote all my red, white and blue silk to the manufacture of Confederate flags! When one is confiscated—I'll make another. I'll wear one pinned on my bosom. The man who says, 'Take it off,' will have to pull it off himself. The man who does that—well, I've a pistol ready!—"

"What are you saying, dear?" the old lady asked with her thin hand behind her ear.

"Oh, nothing much, grandma dear," was the sweet answer. "I was only wishing I were a man!"

She slipped her arms about her thin neck and whispered this in deep, tragic tones. With a bound she was off to the depot to see the last squad of soldiers depart for the front before the gunboats arrived.

They waved their hats to the crowds of women and children as the train slowly pulled out.

"God bless you, ladies! We're going to fight for you!"

Jennie drew her handkerchief, waved and sobbed the chorus in reply.

"God bless you, soldiers! Fight for us!"

Four hours later the black gunboats swung at their anchors. The proud little conquered city lay at the mercy of their guns.

Jennie watched them with shining eyes, and that without fear. The Union flag was streaming from every peak and halyard.

The girl rushed home, made a flag five inches long, pinned it to her shoulder and deliberately walked down town. Mattie Morgan joined her at the corner and drew one from the folds of her dress, emboldened by the example.

They marched straight to the State House terrace to take a good look at the Brooklyn lying close inshore. Fifteen or twenty Federal officers were standing on the first terrace, stared at by the crowd as if they were wild beasts.

"Oh, Mattie," Jennie faltered. "We didn't expect to meet these people. What shall we do?"

"Stand by your colors now. There's nothing else to do."

On they marched, hearts thumping painfully with conscious humiliation at their silly bravado. Fine, noble-looking, quiet fellows those officers in blue—refinement and gentlemanly bearing in every movement of their stalwart bodies. They had come ashore as friendly sightseers and stood admiring the beauty of the quaint old town. Jennie's eyes filled with tears of vexation.

"Let's go home, Mattie—"

"I say so, too—"

"Never again for me! I'll hang my flag on the mantel. I'll not try to wave it in the face of a gentleman again—oof—what silly fools we were!"

The Federal commander of the fleet had warned the citizens of Baton Rouge that any hostile demonstration against his ships or men would mean the instant bombardment of the town.

Jennie had just finished breakfast and helped her grandmother to find her way to the rocker. Mandy had been sent to the store for some thread with which to make a new uniform for one of the boys. Jennie resolved to turn her energies to practical account now. No more flaunting of tiny flags in the faces of brave, dignified young officers of the navy. The maid rushed through the hall wild with excitement. She had run every step back from the store without the thread.

"Lowdy, Miss Jennie," she gasped, "sumfin' awful happened!"

"What is it? What's the matter?"

Mandy stood in dumb terror, the whites of her eyes shining. She was listening apparently for the arch-angel's trumpet to sound.

Jennie seized her shoulders.

"What's the matter? Tell me before I murder you!"

"Yassam!" Mandy gasped and again her head was cocked to one side as if straining her ears for the dreaded sound of Gabriel.

"What's happened?—Tell me!" Jennie stormed.

At last poor Mandy's senses slowly returned. She stared into her young mistress' face and gasped:

"Yassam—Mr. Castle's killed a Yankee ossifer on de ship an' dey gwine ter shell—"

"Boom!"

The deep thunder peal of a great gun shook the world. There was no mistaking the sound of it or its meaning. The fleet had opened fire on the defenseless town. Mandy's teeth chattered and her voice failed.

And then pandemonium.

Poor old negroes and helpless pickaninnies swarmed into the house for shelter from the doom of Judgment Day.

"Run—run for your lives—get out of the way of those shells!" Jennie shouted.

Her three terror-stricken maids huddled by her side in helpless panic.

Her grandmother sprang to her feet and asked in subdued tones: "What is it, child?"

"The fleet's shelling the town—grandma—you'll be killed—the house'll be smashed—you must run—run for your life—"

Jennie screamed her warning into the sweet old lady's ears and seized her by the hand.

"But they can't shell a town full of helpless women and children, my dear," the grandmother protested gently. "It's impossible—"

"Boom—boom!" pealed two guns in quick succession.

"De Lawd save us!" Lucy screamed.

"You see they're doing it—come—"

Jennie grasped her grandmother's hand firmly and dragged her from the house. From the servants' quarters came one long wail of prayer and lamentation mingled with shouts and exhortation. An old bed-ridden black woman, a fervent Methodist, raised a hymn:

"Better days are coming, we'll all go right!"

Jennie had reached the gate when she suddenly remembered her canary—a present Billy had given her on her eighteenth birthday. She rushed back into the house, snatched the cage up and started on the run again.

What was the use? It was impossible to take the bird. He would starve to death.

She quickly opened the cage, took him out and kissed his yellow head.

"Goodbye, Jimmy darling!"

The tears would come in spite of all she could do.

"I hope you'll be happy!"

With quick decision she tossed him in the air.

The bird gave one helpless chirp of surprise and terror at the strange new world, fluttered in a circle, spread his wings at last and was gone.

The girl brushed her tears away and returned to her

grandmother's side. The gravel was cutting her feet. Her shoes were utterly unfit for running. She would rush back and get a pair of the boys' strong ones.

She had worn them before.

"Wait, grandma!" she shouted. "I must change my shoes!"

Back into the house she plunged and found the shoes. Seeing the house still standing, she thought of other things she might need, grasped her tooth brushes and thrust them in her corset. She would certainly need a comb. She added that—a powder bag and lace collar lying on the bureau were also saved. Her hair was tumbling down. She thought of hairpins and tucking comb and added them.

Her grandmother in alarm came back to find her. They decided between them to fill a pillow case with little things they would certainly need.

There was a lull in the shelling. Jennie's maids rushed back in terror at being left alone.

The guns again opened with redoubled fury. Still bent on saving something Jennie grabbed two soiled underskirts and an old cloak and once more dragged her grandmother to the door.

* * * * *

Five big shells sailed squarely over the house at the same moment. They seemed to swing in circles, spiral-shaped like corkscrews. The dull whiz and swish of their flight made the most blood-curdling unearthly noise.

Her grandmother fumbled at the door trying to turn the bolt of the unused lock.

"Don't fool with that door, grandma!" Jennie cried—"run—run— you'll be killed."

"I won't run!" the old lady said with firm decision. "I'll go down there and tell those cowards what I think of their firing on women and children—"

A big shell whizzed past the house and grandma jumped behind a pillar.

She was painfully deaf to human speech—but the whiz of that shell found her nerves. They ran now without looking back—ran at least for a hundred yards until the poor old lady could run no more and then walked as rapidly as possible.

They were at last on the main country road, leading out of town.

Hurrying terror-stricken people, young, old, black and white, were passing them every moment now.

A mile and a half out her grandmother broke down completely. A gentleman passing in a buggy took pity on her gray hairs and lifted her to the seat by his side while his own little ones crouched at her feet.

Jennie waved her hand as they drove off:

"I'll find you somewhere, grandma dear—don't worry!"

Another mile she trudged with Mandy and Lucy clinging to her skirts and then sat down to rest. Her nerves were slowly recovering their poise and she began to laugh at the funny sights the terror-stricken people presented at every turn.

A cart approached piled high with household goods.

"Let's ride, Mandy!" Jennie cried.

"Yassam, dat's what I says, too," the little black maid eagerly agreed.

The cart belonged to a neighbor. It was driven by an old negro man.

"Let us ride, uncle!" Jennie called.

The old man pulled his reins quickly and laughed good-naturedly.

"Dat you shall, Honey. De name er Gawd, ter see Miss Jennie Barton settin' here in dis dirty road!"

He helped them climb to seats on the top of his load. Jennie found a berth between a flour barrel and mattress, while Mandy sat astride of an enormous bundle of bed clothes. Lucy scrambled up beside the driver.

The hot sun was pouring its fierce rays down without mercy. The old negro pulled a faded umbrella from beneath his seat, raised it, and handed it to Jennie with a grand bow.

"Thank you, uncle. You certainly are good to us!"

"Yassam—yassam—I wish I could do mo', honey chile. De ve'y idee er dem slue-footed Yankees er shellin' our town an' scerin' all our ladies ter death. Dey gwine ter pay fur all dis 'fore dey git through."

Three miles out they began to overtake the main body of the fugitives who escaped at the first mad rush. Hundreds of bedraggled women and children were toiling along the dust-covered road in the blistering sun, some bare-headed, some with hats on, some with street clothes, others with their morning wrappers just as they had fled from their unfinished breakfast.

Little girls of eight and ten and twelve were wandering along through the suffocating dust alone.

Jennie called to one she knew:

"Where's your mother, child?"

The girl shook her dust-powdered head.

"I don't know, m'am."

"Where are you going?"

"To walk on till I find her."

Her mother was wandering with distracted cries among the crowds a mile in the rear looking for a nursing baby she had lost in the excitement.

Jennie's eyes kindled at the sight of faithful negroes everywhere lugging the treasures of their mistresses. She began asking them what they were carrying just to hear the answer that always came with a touch of loyal pride.

"Dese is my missy's clothes! I sho weren't gwine let dem Yankees steal dem!"

"Didn't you save any of your own things?"

"Didn't have time ter git mine!"

They came to a guerilla camp. Men and horses were resting on either side of the road. Some of them were carrying water to their horses or to the women who cooked about their camp fires. The scene looked like a monster barbecue. These irregular troops of the South were friends in time of need today.

They crowded the road, asking for news and commenting freely on the shelling of the city.

A rough-looking fellow pushed his way to Jennie's cart.

"When did they begin firin'?"

"Just after breakfast."

Yesterday she would have resented the familiar tones in which this uncouth illiterate countryman spoke without the formality of an introduction. In this hour of common peril he was a Knight entering the lists wearing her colors.

He didn't mince words in expressing his opinions.

"It's your own fault if you've saved nothing. The people in Baton Rouge must have been damned fools not to know trouble wuz comin' with them gunboats lyin' thar with their big-mouthed cannon gapin' right into the streets. If the men had had any sense women wouldn't a been drove into the woods like this—"

"But they had no warning. They began to shell us without a minute's notice—"

His rough fist closed and his heavy jaw came together with a grinding sound.

"Waal, you're ruined—so am I—and my brothers and all our people, too.

There's nothin' left now except to die—and I'll do it!"

The girl clapped her hands.

"I wish I could go with you!"

He turned back toward his camp fire with a shake of his unkempt head.

"Die fighting for us!" Jennie cried.

He waved his black powder-stained hand:

"That I will, little girl!"

The rough figure rose in the unconscious dignity with which he waved his arm and pledged his word to fight to the death. War had leveled all ranks.

The talk on the road was all of burning homes, buildings demolished, famine, murder, and death.

Jennie suddenly found herself singing a lot of Methodist Camp Meeting hymns with an utterly foolish happiness surging through her heart.

She led off with "Better days are coming." Mandy was still too scared to sing the chorus of this first hymn but she joined softly in the next.

It was one of her favorites:

"I hope to die shoutin'—the Lord will provide."

The old man driving the cart kept time with a strange undertone of interpolation all his own. The one he loved best he repeated again and again.

"I'm a runnin'—a runnin' up ter glory!"

How could she be happy amid a scene of such desolation and suffering?

She tried to reproach herself and somehow couldn't be sorry. A vision of something more wonderful than houses and land, goods and chattels, slaves and systems of government, had made her heart beat with sudden joy and her eyes sparkle with happiness. It was only the picture of a dark slender young fellow who had never spoken a word of love that flashed before her. And yet the vision had wrought a spell that transformed the world.

The guns no longer echoed behind them. A courier came dashing from the city at sunset asking the people to return to their homes.

Two old men had rowed out to the war ships during the bombardment. They called to the commander of the flagship as they pushed their skiff alongside:

"There are no men in town, sir—you're only killing women and children!"

The commander leaned over the rail of his gunboat.

"I'm sorry, gentlemen. I thought, of course, your town had been evacuated before your men were fools enough to fire on my marines. I've shelled your streets to intimidate them."

The firing ceased. The order to shell the city had been caused by four guerillas firing on a yawl which was about to land without a flag of truce. Their volley killed and wounded three.

"These four men," shouted the elders from the skiff, "were the only soldiers in town!"

One woman had been killed and three wounded. Twenty houses had been pierced by shells and two little children drowned in their flight. A baby had been born in the woods and died of the exposure.

It was three o'clock next day before Jennie reached home, her grandmother utterly oblivious of her own discomforts but complaining bitterly because she could hear nothing from the old Colonel who had found it impossible to leave New Orleans. They had not been separated so long since the Mexican war. Jennie comforted her as best she could, put her to bed, and took refuge in a tub of cold water.

The dusty road had peeled the skin off both her heels but no matter—thank God, she was at home again. Orders were issued now from the Federal commandant for the government of the town. No person was permitted to leave without a pass. All families were prohibited to leave—except persons separated by the former exodus. Cannon were planted in every street. Five thousand soldiers had been thrown into the city, General Williams commanding. Any house unoccupied by its owners would be used by the soldiers.

Jennie decided to stick to the house at all hazards until forced to go.

She walked down town to the post office in the vain hope a letter might have come through from New Orleans to her grandmother. Soldiers were lounging in the streets in squads of forty and fifty. A crowd was playing cards in the ditch and swearing as they fought the flies. Crowds of soldiers relieved from duty were marching aimlessly along the street.

Some were sleeping on the pavements, others sprawled flat on their backs in the sun, heads pillowed in each other's lap.

To her surprise a letter addressed in the familiar handwriting of her brother was handed out at the post office by the young soldier in charge.

The seal had been broken.

Jennie's eyes flashed with rage.

"How dare you open and read my letter, sir!" she cried with indignation.

"I'm sorry, Miss," he answered politely. "We're only soldiers. Our business is to obey orders."

Jennie blushed furiously.

"Of course, I beg your pardon. I wasn't thinking when I spoke." She read the letter with eager interest:

"Dearest little Sister:

"You must bring grandmother to New Orleans at the earliest possible opportunity. Grandpa can't get out. He is as restless and unhappy as a caged tiger. Do come quickly. If you need money let me know. Hoping soon to see you. With a heart full of love,

"Your big brother,

"Roger."

It would be best. Her grandmother would be safe there in any event. If our troops again captured New Orleans she would be in the house of the South. If the Federal army still held it, she was at home in her grandson's house.

The wildest rumors were flying thick. No passes would be issued to leave the city on any pretext. Beauregard was reported about to move his army from Corinth to attack Baton Rouge.

The troops were massing for the defense of the city. The Federal cavalry had scoured the country for ten miles in search of guerillas.

Through all the turmoil and confusion of the wildly disordered house Jennie kept repeating the foolish old hymn in soft monotones: "I hope to die shouting—the Lord will provide!"

General Williams sent a guard to protect the house. A file of six soldiers marched to the gate and their commander saluted:

"Madam, the pickets await your orders."

General Williams had met her brother in New Orleans. His loyalty was enough to mark the beautiful old homestead for protection.

Jennie laughed. It was a funny situation were it not so tragic. Her father and three brothers fighting these men with tooth and nail while an officer saluted and put his soldiers at her command.

Butler's men were arresting the aged citizens of Baton Rouge now.

Without charge or warrant they were hustled on the transports, hurried to New Orleans and thrown into jail. Jennie ground her white teeth with rage:

"Oh, to be ruled by such a wretch!"

From the first day he had set foot on the soil of Louisiana Butler had made himself thoroughly loathed. His order reflecting on the character of the women of New Orleans had not only shocked the South, it had roused the indignation of the civilized world.

A proud and sensitive people had no redress.

One of the first six citizens sentenced to prison in Fort Jackson was Dr. Craven, the Methodist minister. A soldier nosing about his house at night had heard the preacher at family prayers. He had asked God's blessing on the cause of the South while kneeling in prayer. When Jennie

heard of it, she cried through her tears: "Show me a dungeon deep enough to keep me from praying for my brothers who are fighting for us!"

The speech of Butler which had gone farthest and sank deepest into the outraged souls of the people of Southern Louisiana was his defiant utterance to Solomon Benjamin on the threat of England to intervene in our struggle:

"Let England or France dare to try it," Butler swore in a towering rage, "and I'll be damned if I don't arm every negro in the South and make them cut the throats of every man, woman and child in it. I'll make them lay this country waste with fire and sword and leave it desolate."

That Butler was capable of using his enormous power as the Military Governor of Louisiana to accomplish this purpose, no one who had any knowledge of the man or his methods doubted for a moment.

On the slightest pretexts he arrested whom he pleased, male and female, and threw them into prison. Aged men who had incurred his displeasure were confined at hard labor with ball and chain. Men were imprisoned in Fort Jackson, whose only offense was the giving of medicine to sick Confederate soldiers. The wife of a former member of Congress was arrested and sent to Ship Island in the Gulf of Mexico. Her only offense was that she laughed at some foolish thing that marked the progress of a funeral procession through the streets of the city.

On his office wall in the St. Charles Hotel Butler had inscribed in huge letters:

> THERE IS NO DIFFERENCE BETWEEN
> A HE AND A SHE ADDER IN THEIR VENOM.

His henchmen were allowed to indulge their rapacity at will. The homes of distinguished men and women were seized on any pretext and turned into disreputable establishments which were run for gain. They appropriated the contents of wine cellars, plundered the wardrobes and dining-rooms of ladies and gentlemen to their hearts' content. Fines were levied and collected in many cases where it could be secured. Those who refused to pay were given the choice of ball and chain. A thriving trade in cotton was opened against the positive orders of the Washington Government. Butler's own brother was the thrifty banker and broker of this corrupt transaction.

Property was "confiscated" right and left, provisions and military stores were exchanged for cotton. The chief of this regime of organized plunder lived in daily fear of assassination. It was said he wore secret armor. He never ventured out except heavily guarded. In his office several pistols lay beside him and the chair on which his visitor was seated was chained to the wall to prevent someone suddenly rising and smashing his brains out.

There were ten thousand soldiers in Baton Rouge now though the anticipated attack of the Confederates had not materialized. Perhaps they had heard of the heavy reinforcements in time. The poor fellows from the cool hills and mountains of the North were dying in hundreds in the blistering July sun of the South. They didn't know how to take care of themselves and their officers didn't seem to care. Butler was a lawyer and a politician first—a general only when the navy had done his work for him.

Jennie saw hundreds of these sick and dying men lying on their backs in the broiling sun, waiting for wagons to carry them to the hospital. One had died absolutely alone without a human being near to notice or to care. The girl's heart was sick with anguish at the sight of scores too weak to lift their hands to fight the ravenous flies swarming in their eyes and months. All day and all night Baumstark, the little undertaker, was working with half a dozen aides making coffins.

Day and night they died like dogs with no human help extended. The Catholic priest who had not been arrested as yet, passing among them in search of his own, bent for a moment over a dying soldier and spoke in friendly tones. The poor fellow burst into tears and with his last gasp cried:

"Thank God! I have heard one kind word before I die!"

The Federal pickets were driven in at last, and the guard around the house withdrawn. General Williams insisted that Jennie and her grandmother find a place of refuge more secure than the coming battlefield.

They thanked the General but decided to brave battle at home to the terrors of another flight.

The little band of twenty-five hundred Confederates struck the town like a thunderbolt and fought with desperation against the combined fleet and heavy garrison. They drove the Federals at first in panic to the water's edge and the shelter of the cannon until a Maine regiment barred the way, fighting like demons, and rallied the fleeing mob. When the smoke of battle lifted the gray army had gone with the loss of only sixty-five killed and a hundred and fifty wounded.

The worst calamity which befell Baton Rouge was the death of General Williams, the gentlemanly and considerate Federal commander.

Butler's man who took his place lacked both his soldierly training and his fine scruples as a Christian gentleman. There were no more guards placed around "Rebel" homes.

The marauder came with swift sure tread on the heels of victory. A squad of officers and men smashed in the front door at Fairview without so much as a knock for signal. To the shivering servant who stood in the hall the leader called:

"Where are the damned secesh women? We know they've hid in here and we'll make them dance for hiding—"

Jennie suddenly appeared in the library door, her face white, her hand concealed in the pocket of her dress.

"There are but two women here, gentlemen," she began steadily—"my grandmother and I. The house is at your mercy—"

The man in front gave a short laugh and advanced on the girl. He stopped short in his tracks at the sight of the glitter of her eye and changed his mind.

"All right, look out for the old hen. We'll let you know when it's time to pick up the pieces."

Jennie returned to the library and slipped her arm about her grandmother's neck standing beside her chair while she set her little jaw firmly and waited for the end.

They rushed the dining-room first and split its side-board open with axes—fine old carved mahogany pieces so hardened with age, the ax blades chipped from the blows as if striking marble. The china was smashed chests were laid open with axes, and their contents of silver removed.

They rushed the parlors and stripped them of every ornament. Jennie's piano they dragged into the center of the floor, smashed its ivory keys and split its rosewood case into splinters. An officer slashed the portrait of Mrs. Barton into shreds and hurled the frame on the floor.

Every portrait on the walls shared a similar fate. Upstairs the fun grew wild. Mrs. Barton's beautiful old mahogany armoir whose single door was a fine French mirror was shivered with a blow from a sledge hammer, emptied of every article and the shelves splintered with axes. They broke every bureau and case of drawers, scattered their contents on the floor, selecting what suited their fancy. Every rag of the boys' clothes, the old Colonel's and Senator Barton's were tied in bundles.

They entered Jennie's room, broke every mirror, tore down the rods from the bed and ripped the net into shreds. The desk was split, letters turned out and scattered over the floor. A light sewing machine was sent below for a souvenir. The heavy one was broken with an ax. From Jennie's bureau they tore a pink flowered muslin, stuck it on a bayonet and paraded the room, the officers striking it with their swords shouting their dull insults:

"I've struck the damned secesh!"

"The proud little hellion!"

"That's the time I cut her!"

One seized her bonnet, put it on, tied the ribbon under his chin and amid the shouts of his half-drunken companions, paraded the house, and wore it into the streets when he left.

When the noise had died away and the house was still at last, Jennie came forth from the little room in which she had taken refuge, leading her grandmother. Hand in hand they viewed the wreck.

The thing that hurt the girl most of all was the ruin of her desk—her letters from Dick Welford, the boys, her father and mother, the diary she had kept with the intimate secrets of her young heart—all had been opened, thumbed and thrown over the floor. The little perfumed notes she had received from her first beaux—invitations to buggy rides, concerts, and parties, and all of them beginning, "Compliments of"—had been profaned by dirty greasy fingers. Some were torn into little bits and scattered over the room, others were ground into the floor by hobnails in heavy boot heels.

Her last letter from Socola was stolen—to be turned over to the commander for inspection no doubt. And then she broke into a foolish laugh. The strain was over. What did it matter—this clutter of goods and chattels on the floor—she was young—it was the morning of life and she had met her fate!

In a sudden rush of emotion she threw her arms around her grandmother's neck and cried: "Thank the good Lord, grandma, they didn't shoot you!"

The sweet old lady was strangely quiet, and her eyes had a queer set look. She bore the strain without a break until they entered the wreck of the stately parlor. She saw the slashed portrait of the

Colonel lying on the floor and sank in a heap beside it without a word or sound. Jennie succeeded at last in obtaining a pass to New Orleans, consigning the body to Judge Roger Barton. She stepped on board the little steamer absolutely alone. Every servant had gone to the camp of the soldiers or had entered the service of the crowd of marauders who decided to return to Fairview and occupy the house.

Jennie had gone through so much the tired spirit refused to respond to further sensations. She obeyed orders in a dumb mechanical way.

The officers at New Orleans opened her baggage and searched it without ceremony, or the slightest show of interest on her part.

They were administering the "oath" of loyalty to the United States. She would have to turn Yankee to do this last duty of love. She covered her face with her hands and prayed breathlessly for the boys and for the Confederacy while the words of the oath were mumbled by the officer.

"So help you God?"

Jennie's only answer was to close her eyes and pray harder.

"So help you God?" the officer shouted again.

The girl lifted her tear-stained face and nodded, closed her eyes again and prayed.

"Help them, O God,—my brothers Tom and Jimmie and Billy and Dick Welford—and—and the man I love—save them and their cause for Jesus' sake—I don't know what they made me say—I only did it for poor grandpa's sake—I didn't mean it. Forgive me, dear Lord, and save my people!"

The Judge met them with a carriage and hearse. He slipped his strong arm around the girl, drew her close and kissed the waving brown hair again and again.

"Dear little sis—you're at home now," he said softly.

A shiver ran through her figure and she sat bolt upright.

"No, Big Brother," she answered firmly, "I'm not. New Orleans is in the hands of the enemy. I'd set it on fire and wipe it from the face of the earth tomorrow if I could sweep old Ben Butler and his men into the bottomless pit with its ashes—"

She paused at the look of pain on his face.

"Except you—dear—you're my brother, always my dear Big Brother and I'll love you forever. What you think right is right—for you. You are for the Union, because you believe it's right. I honor you for being true to your convictions—"

"You can never know what it has cost me—Honey—"

She drew him down and kissed him tenderly.

"Yes, I do know—and it's all right—even if you draw your sword and meet us in battle—you're fighting for the right as God shows it to you—but I've just one favor to ask—"

"I'll do anything on earth for you I can—you know that—"

She looked at him steadily a moment in silence and spoke in hard cold tones.

"Get me out of New Orleans inside the Confederate lines—anywhere—a guerilla camp—a swamp—anywhere, you understand. I'll find my way to Richmond—"

He pressed her hand in silence and then softly answered:

"I understand, dear—and I'll arrange it for you. I'll hire a schooner to set you across Lake Pontchartrain."

The old Colonel looked on the face of his dead wife and went to bed. He made no complaints. He asked no questions. The book of life was closed.

Within a week he died as peacefully as a child.

Ten days later Jennie had passed the Federal lines and was whirling through the Carolinas, her soul aflame with a new deathless courage.

26: THE IRREPARABLE LOSS

Jefferson Davis not only refused to remove Albert Sidney Johnston from his command in answer to the clamor of his critics, he wrote his general letters expressing such unbounded confidence in his genius that he inspired him to begin the most brilliant campaign on which the South had yet entered.

Grant, flushed with victory, had encamped his army along the banks of the Tennessee, then at flood and easily navigable for gunboats and transports. The bulldog fighter of Fort Donelson had allowed his maxim of war to lead him into a situation which the eye of Johnston was quick to see.

Grant's famous motto was:

"Never be over anxious about what your enemy is going to do to you; make him anxious about what you are going to do to him."

In accordance with this principle the Union General was busy preparing his Grand Army for a triumphant march into the far South. He was drilling and training his men for their attack on the Confederates at Corinth. His army was not in a position for defense. It was, in fact, strung out into a long line of camps for military instruction, preparing to advance on the foe he had grown to despise.

Sherman's division occupied a position near Shiloh Church. A half mile further was B. M. Prentiss with newly arrived regiments, one of which still had no ammunition. Near the river McClernand was camped behind Sherman and Hurlbert still farther back. Near them lay W. H. L. Wallace's division, and at Crump's Landing, Lew Wallace was stationed with six thousand men.

Grant himself was nine miles down the river at Savannah, a point at which he expected to form a junction with Buell's army approaching from the east.

Grant sat at breakfast on a beautiful Sunday morning quietly sipping his coffee while he planned his conquest of the vast territory which now lay at the mercy of his army the moment the juncture should be effected. With swift stealthy tread, Johnston was moving through the dense forests of the wild region to the south. His army had been rapidly recruited to approximately forty thousand effective men. Beauregard had been detached from the East and was second in command.

The night before this beautiful spring Sabbath morning the Confederate army had bivouacked within two miles of the Federal front. Johnston had so baffled the scouts and reconnoitering parties of Grant that his presence was not suspected.

In the gray mists of the dawn his divisions silently deployed and formed in line of battle. General Leonidas Polk on the left, Braxton Bragg in the center, William J. Hardee on the right and John C. Breckinridge in reserve.

The men were alert and eager to avenge the defeats of Forts Henry and Donelson. With chuckles of exhilaration they had listened that night to the rolling of the drums in Grant's camps.

A mist from the river valley hung low over the fresh budding trees. With swift elastic tread the gray lines moved forward through the shadows of the dawn.

So complete was the surprise that not a picket was encountered. Not a single company of cavalry guarded the flanks of the sleeping army. The mists lifted and the sheen of white tents could be seen through the trees.

Only a few of the blue soldiers had risen. They were washing and cooking their morning meal. Some had sat down to eat at generous mess-chests. Thousands were yet soundly sleeping in their tents.

On Prentiss' division from flank to flank with sudden fury the gray host fell. Even the camp sentinels were taken completely by surprise and barely had time to discharge their guns. On their heels rushed the Confederates cheering madly.

Officers and men were killed in their beds and many fled in confusion without their arms. Hildebrand's brigade of Sherman's division was engulfed by the cyclone and swept from existence, appearing no more in the battle.

In vain the broken lines of the Federal camps were formed and re-formed. Charge followed charge in swift and terrible succession. By half past ten o'clock the Confederates had captured and demolished three great military encampments and taken three batteries of artillery. Storehouses and munitions of war in rich profusion were captured at every turn. The demoralized Union army was retreating at every point.

When Grant reached the field, the lines both of attack and defense were lost in confusion. The battle raged in groups. Sometimes mere squads of men surged back and forth over the broken, tangled, blood-soaked arena, now in ravines and swamps, now for a moment emerging into clearings and then buried again in the deep woods.

The stolid Federal commander sat his horse, keen-eyed, vigilant and imperturbable in the storm of ruin. His early efforts counted for little in the blind confusion and turmoil of his crushed army. Lew Wallace had been ordered to the field in post haste. The bridge across Owl Creek, held by Sherman in the morning, was now in the hands of the Confederates. Wallace marched and countermarched his army in a vain effort to reach the field.

At two o'clock Johnston had brought up his reserves and ordered the entire gray army to charge and sweep the field. His fine face flushed with victory, he rose in his saddle, addressed a few eloquent words to Breckinridge's division, placed himself at the head of his army and his sword flashed in the sunlight as he shouted to the line:

"Charge!"

Dick Welford had been detached from Forrest's cavalry on staff duty by his Chief's side. Forrest had been marked by Johnston for promotion for his work at Donelson, and Dick had grown to worship his gallant Commanding General. He had watched his plan of battle grow with boyish pride. He knew his Chief was going to crush the two divisions of Grant's army in detail before they could be united. And he had done it. Such complete and overwhelming victory would lift the South from her slough of despair.

With a shout of triumph he spurred his horse neck to neck with his General. At two o'clock the blue lines were still rolling back on the river in hopeless confusion, the gray lines cheering and charging and crushing without mercy.

A ball pierced Johnston's right leg. Dick saw his hand drop the rein for an instant and a look of pain sweep his handsome face. "You're wounded, sir?" he asked.

"It's nothing, boy," he answered, "only a flesh cut—drive—drive—drive them!" Without pause he rode on and on.

He was riding the white horse of Death—an artery had been cut and his precious life was slowly but surely ebbing away.

He swayed in his saddle and Dick dashed forward: "General, your wound must be dressed!"

Governor Harris of Tennessee, his aide, observed him at the same moment and spurred his horse to his side.

The General turned his dim eyes to the Governor and gasped: "I fear I'm mortally wounded—"

He reeled in his saddle and would have fallen had not Dick caught him and tenderly lowered him to the ground.

The brave war Governor of Tennessee received the falling Commander in his arms and helped Dick bear him a short distance from the field into a deep ravine.

Dick took the flask of whiskey from his pocket and pressed it to his lips in vain. A moment and he was dead.

In a passion of grief the boy threw his arms around his beloved Chief and called through his tears and groans:

"My God, General, you can't die—you mustn't die now! Don't you hear the boys shouting? They're driving Grant's army into the river. They've avenged Donelson!—General—for God's sake speak to me—say you won't die—you can't, you can't—Oh, Lord God, save his precious life!—"

No sign or answer came. His breast had ceased to move. The Governor tenderly lifted the grief-stricken boy and sent him with his General's last message.

"Find Beauregard and tell him he is in command of the field. Not a word of the death of the Chief until his victory is complete."

Dick saluted and sprang into the saddle. "I understand, sir."

It was late in the afternoon before he located General Beauregard and delivered the fateful news.

The victorious Confederate army had furiously pressed its charge. Johnston's word had passed from command to command.

"Forward—forward—let every order be forward!"

Everything had yielded at last before them. From camp to camp, from rallying point to rallying point the Union hosts had been hurled, division piling on division in wild confusion.

Driven headlong, the broken ranks were thrown in panic on the banks of the river. Thousands crouched in ravines and sought shelter under the steep bluffs of the river banks. Trampling mobs were struggling in vain to board the transports and cross the river.

The Federal reserve line had been completely crushed, and the entire army, driven from the field they had held that morning, were huddled in a confused mass of a half mile around the Pittsburg Landing.

The next charge of the Confederates would hurl the whole army into the river or they must surrender.

The gunboats had opened in vain. They were throwing their shells a mile beyond the Confederate lines where they fell harmlessly.

The Confederate division commanders were gathering their hosts for the last charge at sunset. There was yet an hour of daylight in which to end the struggle with the complete annihilation of the Union army. Down under the steep banks of the river's edge the demoralized remnants of the shattered divisions were already stacking their arms to surrender.

They had made their last stand.

General Bragg turned to his aide:

"Tell Major Stewart of the twenty-first Alabama to advance and drive the enemy into the river!"

The aide saluted.

"And carry that order along the whole line!"

The aide put spurs to his horse to execute the command, when a courier dashed up from General Beauregard's headquarters.

"Direct me to General Bragg!"

The aide pointed to the General and rode back with Beauregard's courier.

"General Beauregard orders that you cease fighting and rest your men tonight."

Bragg turned his rugged dark face on the messenger with a scowl.

"You have promulgated this order to the army?"

"I have, sir—"

"If you had not, I would not obey it—"

He paused and threw one hand high above his head.

"Our victory has been thrown to the winds!"

The sudden and inexplicable abandonment of this complete and overwhelming success was one of the most remarkable events in the history of modern warfare.

The men bivouacked on the field.

The blunder was fatal and irretrievable. Even while the order was being given to cease firing the advance guard of Buell's army was already approaching the other bank of the river. Twenty-five thousand fresh men under cover of the darkness began to pour their long lines into position to save Grant's shattered ranks.

As night fell another misfortune was on the way to obscure the star of Beauregard. His soldiers, elated with their wonderful victory, broke into disorderly plundering of the captured Federal camps. Except for a few thousand sternly disciplined troops under Bragg's command the whole Southern army suddenly degenerated into a mob of roving plunderers, mad with folly. In the rich stores of the Federal army thousands of gallons of wines and liquors were found. Hundreds of gray soldiers became intoxicated. While scenes of the wildest revelry and disorder were being enacted around the camp fires, Buell's army was silently crossing the river under cover of the night and forming in line of battle for tomorrow's baptism of blood.

Albert Sidney Johnston's body lay cold in death—and the army of the victorious South had no head. Better had there been no second general of full rank in the field. Either of Johnston's division commanders, Bragg, Hardee, Polk or Breckinridge, would have driven Grant's panic-stricken mob into the river within an hour if let alone.

But the little hero of Bull Run of the flower-decked tent halted his men to rest for the night at the very hour of the day when Napoleon ordered his first charge on one of his immortal battlefields.

Beauregard gave his foe ample time for breakfast next morning. The sun was an hour high in the heavens before the battle was joined. The genius of Johnston had surprised Grant and rolled his army back on the river—never pausing for a moment to give him time to rally his broken ranks.

But when Beauregard leisurely led his disorganized army next morning against Grant's new lines, there was no shock, no surprise—the line was ready. His panic-stricken men had been reorganized and massed in strong defensive position and reinforced by the divisions of Generals Nelson, McCook, Crittenden, and Thomas of Buell's army—twenty-five thousand strong.

Lew Wallace's division had also effected the junction and the Federal front presented a solid wall of fifty-three thousand determined men against whom Beauregard must now throw his little army of thirty thousand effective fighters.

The assault was made with dash and courage. For four hours the battle raged with fury. The shattered regiments that had been surprised and crushed the day before, yielded at one time before the onslaughts of the Confederates. By noon Beauregard had sent into the shambles his last brigade and reserves and shortly afterwards gave his first order to withdraw his army.

Breckinridge's division covered the retreat and there was no attempt at pursuit. Grant was only too glad to save his army. The first great battle of the war had been fought and won by the genius of the South's commander and its results thrown away by the hero of Bull Run.

Never was the wisdom of a great leader more thoroughly vindicated than was Jefferson Davis in the record Albert Sidney Johnston made at Shiloh.

The men who had been loudest in demanding his removal stood dumb before the story of his genius. The death list of this battle sent a shiver of horror through the North and the South. All other battles of the war were but skirmishes to this.

The Confederate losses in killed, wounded and missing were ten thousand six hundred and ninety-nine. At Bull Run the combined armies of Joseph E. Johnston and Beauregard lost but one thousand nine hundred and sixty-four men.

Grant's army lost thirteen thousand one hundred and sixty-two in killed, wounded and prisoners. McDowell at Bull Run had lost but two thousand seven hundred, and yet was removed from his command.

The rage against Grant in the North was unbounded. The demand for his removal was so determined, so universal, so persistent, it was necessary for Abraham Lincoln to bow to it temporarily.

Lincoln positively refused to sacrifice his fighting General for his first error, but sent Halleck into the field as Commander-in-Chief and left Grant in command of his division.

The bulldog fighter of the North learned his lesson at Shiloh. The South never again caught him napping.

Great as the losses were to the North they were as nothing to the disaster which this bloody field brought to the Confederacy. Albert Sidney Johnston alive was equal to an army of a hundred thousand men—dead; his loss was irreparable.

27: THE LIGHT THAT FAILED

The struggle which Jefferson Davis was making to parry the force of the mortal blows delivered by the United States Navy at last gave promise of startling success.

The fight to establish the right of the Confederacy to arm its allies under letters of marque and reprisal had been won by the Southern President. The first armed vessel sailing under the orders of Davis which was captured by the navy had brought the question to sharp issue. The Washington Government had proclaimed the vessels flying the Confederate flag under letters of marque to be pirates and subject to the treatment of felons.

The Captain and the crew of the Savannah when captured had been put in irons and condemned to death as pirates. If the Washington Government could make good this daring assumption, the power of the Confederacy to damage the commerce of the North would be practically destroyed at a blow.

Davis met the crisis with firmness. He selected an equal number of Federal prisoners of war in Richmond and threw them into a dungeon below Libby Prison. He dispatched a letter to Washington whose language could not be misunderstood.

"Dare to execute an officer or sailor of the Savannah, and I will put to death as felons an equal number of Federal officers and men. I have placed them in close confinement and ordered similar treatment to that accorded our prisoners from the captured vessel."

Socola received a message summoning him to the house on Church Hill. A courier had arrived from Washington. The Government must know immediately if this threat were idle or genuine. If Jefferson Davis should dare to execute these thirteen officers and men, the administration could not resist the storm of indignant protest which would overwhelm it from the North.

Socola read the cipher dispatch by the dim light of the candle in his attic and turned to Miss Van Lew.

"My information in the State Department is of the most positive kind. The prisoners have been put in the dungeon set apart for condemned felons and they but wait the word of the execution of the men from the Savannah, to be led to certain death. It may be talk. We must know.

Apply for permission to visit the condemned men and minister to their comfort—"

"At once," was the prompt response. "I've made friends with Captain Todd, the Commandant of Libby Prison; I'll succeed."

Crazy Bet appeared at Libby Prison next morning with a basket of flowers for the condemned men. Captain Todd humored her mania. Poor old abolition fanatic, she could do no harm. She was too frank and outspoken to be dangerous. Besides, it was a war of brothers. His own sister was the wife of Abraham Lincoln. These condemned men were the best blood of the North. It was a pitiful tragedy.

Miss Van Lew, with a market basket on her arm, watched for Socola's appearance from the office of the Secretary of State. The young clerk was walking slowly down Main Street and turned into an unused narrow road at the foot of the hill.

Crazy Bet, swinging the basket and humming a song, passed him without turning her head.

"It's true," she whispered quickly, "all horribly true. Thirteen of the finest officers of the Union army have been condemned to death the moment the crew of the Savannah are executed—among them Colonel Cochrane of New York and Colonel Paul Revere of Massachusetts. The dispatch must go tonight."

"Tonight," was the short answer.

Within an hour Socola's courier was on his way to Washington with a message which unlocked the prison doors of the condemned men on both sides of the line.

Abraham Lincoln stoutly opposed a repetition of the effort to treat Confederate prisoners as outlaws, no matter where taken by land or sea.

Davis had established the legality of his letters of marque and reprisal beyond question.

The United States Navy in the first flood of its victories made another false step which brought to the South an hour of brilliant hope. Captain Wilkes overhauled a British steamer carrying the royal mail and took from her decks by force the Commissioners

Mason and Slidell whom Davis had dispatched to Europe to plead for the recognition of the Confederacy. The North had gone wild with joy over the act and Congress voted Wilkes the thanks of the nation as its hero.

Great Britain demanded an apology and the restoration of the prisoners, put her navy on a war footing and dispatched a division of her army to Canada to strike the North by land as well as sea.

The hard common sense of Abraham Lincoln rescued the National Government from a delicate and dangerous situation. Lincoln apologized to Great Britain, restored the Confederate Commissioners and returned with redoubled energy to the prosecution of the war. In answer to the shouts of demagogues and the reproaches of both friend and foe, the homely rail-splitter from the West had a simple answer.

"One war at a time."

Jefferson Davis watched this threat of British invasion with breathless intensity. He saw the hope of thus breaking the power of the navy fade with sickening disappointment.

There was one more hope. The hull of the Merrimac had been raised from the bottom of the harbor of Norfolk and the work of transforming her into a giant iron-clad ship capable of carrying a fighting crew of three hundred men had been completed, though her engines were slow.

But the enthusiastic men set to this task by Davis had accomplished wonders. Their reports to him had raised high hopes of a sensation. If this new monster of the sea should succeed single handed in destroying the fleet of six vessels lying in Hampton Roads, the naval warfare of the world would be revolutionized in a day and overtures for peace might be within sight.

The Norfolk newspapers, under instructions from the Confederate Commandant, pronounced the experiment of the Merrimac a stupid and fearful failure. Her engines were useless. Her steering gear wouldn't work. Her armament was so heavy she couldn't be handled. These papers were easily circulated at Newport News and Old Point Comfort among the officers and men of the Federal fleet.

The men who had built the strange craft knew she was anything but a failure. With eager, excited hands her crew finished the last touch of her preparations and with her guns shotted she slowly steamed out of the harbor of Norfolk accompanied by two saucy little improvised gunboats, the Beaufort and the Raleigh.

Her speed was not more than five knots an hour and she steered so badly the Beaufort was compelled to pull her into the main current of the channel more than once.

The Federal squadron lay off Newport News, the Congress and the Cumberland well out in the stream, the Minnesota, Roanoke and St. Lawrence further down toward Fortress Monroe. The Congress, Cumberland and St. Lawrence mounted one hundred and twenty-four guns, twenty-two of them of nine-inch caliber. Their crews aggregated more than a thousand men.

The new crack steam frigates Minnesota and Roanoke had crews of six hundred men each and carried more than eighty guns of nine and eleven-inch caliber. That any single craft afloat would dare attack such a squadron was preposterous.

It was one o'clock before the strange black looking object swung into the channel and turned her nose up stream toward Newport News. The crews of the Congress and the Cumberland were lounging on deck enjoying the balmy spring air. It was wash day and the clothes were fluttering in the breeze.

They couldn't make out the foolish-looking thing at first. It looked like the top of a long-hipped roof house that had been sawed off at the eaves and pushed into the water. The two little river steamers that accompanied the raft seemed to be towing it.

"What 'ell, Bill, is that thing?" a sailor asked his mate on the Congress.

Bill scanned the horizon.

"I give it up, sir," he admitted. "I been a sailin' the seas for forty years—but that's one on me!"

A battle signal suddenly flashed from the Cumberland and down came the wash lines.

The Beaufort with a single thirty-two-pounder rifle mounted in her bow was steaming alongside the port of the strange craft. A puff of white smoke flared from her single gun and its dull roar waked the still beautiful waters of the Virginia harbor.

The Merrimac flung her big battle flag into the sky and her tiny escorts dropped down stream to give her free play. The Congress and the Cumberland were surprised, but they slipped their anchors in a jiffy, swung their guns in haste and began pouring a storm of shot on the iron sides of the coming foe.

The Merrimac moved forward with slow, steady throb as though the shot that rained on her slanting sides were so many pebbles thrown by school boys. She passed the Congress and pointed her ugly prow for the Cumberland. The ship poured her broadside squarely into the face of the Merrimac without damage and the bow gun roared an answer that pierced her bulwarks.

Through the thick cloud of heavy smoke that hung low on the water the throbbing monster bore straight down on the Cumberland, struck her amidship and sent her to the bottom.

As the gallant ship sank in sickening lurches her brave crew cheered her to her grave and continued firing her useless guns until the waves engulfed the decks. When her keel touched the bottom her flag was still flying from her masthead. She rolled over on her beam's end and carried the flag beneath the waves.

The Confederate mosquito fleet, consisting of the little gunboats Patrick Henry, Teaser and Jamestown, swung down from the river now, ran boldly past the flaming shore batteries and joined in the attack on the Federal squadron.

The Congress had set one of her sails and with the aid of a tug was desperately working to reach shoal water before she could be sunk. Her captain succeeded in beaching her directly under the guns of the shore batteries. At four o'clock she gave up the bloody unequal contest and hauled down her colors.

The Minnesota, Roanoke and St. Lawrence, in trying to reach the scene of the battle, had all been grounded. The Minnesota was still lying helpless in the mud as the sun set and the new monarch of the seas slowly withdrew to Sewell's Point to overhaul her machinery and prepare to finish her work next day.

The Merrimac had lost twenty-one killed and wounded—among the wounded was her gallant flag officer, Franklin Buchanan. The Patrick Henry had lost fourteen, the Beaufort eight, the Raleigh seven, including two officers.

The Federal squadron had lost two ships and four hundred men. But by far the greatest loss to the United States Navy was the supremacy of the seas. The power of her fleets had been smashed at a blow. The ugly, black, powder-stained, iron thing lying under the guns of Sewell's Point had won the crown of the world's naval supremacy. The fleets of the United States were practically out of commission while she was afloat. The panic at the North which followed the startling news from Hampton Roads was indescribable. Abraham Lincoln hastily called a Cabinet meeting to consider what action it was necessary to take to meet the now appalling situation. Never before had any man in authority at Washington realized how absolute was their dependence on the United States Navy—how impossible it would be to maintain the Government without its power.

Edwin M. Stanton, the indefatigable Secretary of War, completely lost his nerve at this Cabinet meeting. He paced the floor with quick excited tread, glancing out of the window of the White House toward the waters of the Potomac with undisguised fear.

"I am sure, gentlemen," he said to the Cabinet, "that monster is now on her way to Washington. In my opinion we will have a shell from one of her big guns in the White House before we leave this room!"

Lincoln was profoundly depressed but refused to believe the cause of the Union could thus be completely lost at a single blow from a nondescript, iron raft. Yet it was only too easy to see that the moral effect of this victory would be crushing on public opinion.

The wires to Washington were hot with frantic calls for help. New York was ready to surrender at the first demand. So utter was the demoralization at Fortress Monroe, the one absolutely impregnable fort on the Atlantic coast, that the commander had already determined to surrender in answer to the first shot the Merrimac should fire.

The preparations for moving McClellan's army to the Virginia Peninsula for the campaign to capture Richmond were suddenly halted. Two hundred thousand men must rest on their arms until this crisis should pass. All orders issued to the Army of the Potomac were now made contingent on the destruction of the iron monster lying in Hampton Roads.

By one of the strangest coincidences in history the United States Navy had completed an experiment in floating iron at precisely the same moment.

While the guns of the battle were yet echoing over the waters of the harbor, this strange little craft, a floating iron cheese box, was slowly steaming into the Virginia capes.

At nine o'clock that night Ericsson's Monitor was beside the panic-stricken Roanoke. When C. S. Bushnell took the model of this strange craft to Washington, he was referred to Commander C. H. Davis by the Naval Board. When Davis had examined it he handed it back to Bushnell with a pitying smile:

"Take the little thing home, and worship it. It would not be idolatry, because it's made in the image of nothing in the heaven above or the earth beneath or in the waters under the earth."

Wiser councils had prevailed, and the floating cheese box was completed and arrived in Hampton Roads in time to put its powers to supreme test.

The Merrimac's crew ate their breakfast at their leisure and prepared to drive their ugly duckling into the battle line again and finish the work of destroying the battered Federal squadron.

The Merrimac had fought the battle of the day before under the constant pounding of more than one hundred guns bearing on her iron sides. Her armor was intact. Two of her guns were disabled by having their muzzles shot off. Her nose had been torn off and sank with the Cumberland. One anchor, her smoke stacks and steam pipes were shot away. Every scrap of her railing, stanchions, and boat davits had been swept clean. Her flag staff was gone and a boarding pike had been set up in its place.

With stern faces, and absolutely sure of victory, her crew swung her into the stream, crowded on full steam and moved down on the Minnesota.

Close under the ship's side they saw for the first time the cheese box. They had heard of the experiment of her building but knew nothing of her arrival. Her insignificant size was a surprise and the big Merrimac dashed at her with a sullen furious growl of her big guns. The game little bulldog swung out from the Minnesota and made straight for the onrushing monster.

The flotilla of gunboats had been signaled to retire and watch the duel. From the big eleven-inch guns of the Monitor shot after shot was hurled against the slanting armored walls of the Merrimac.

Broadside after broadside poured from her guns against the

iron-clad tower of the Monitor. The Merrimac, drawing twenty feet of water, was slow and difficult to handle. The game little Monitor drew but twelve feet and required no maneuvering. Her tower revolved. She could stand and fight in one spot all day.

The big black hull of the Merrimac bore down on the Monitor now to ram and sink her at a blow. The nimble craft side stepped the avalanche of iron, turned quickly and attempted to jamb her nose into the steering gear of the Southerner—but in vain.

For two solid hours the iron-clads pounded and hammered each other. The shots made no impression on either boat. Again the Merrimac tried to ram her antagonist and run her aground. The nimble foe avoided the blow, though struck a grinding, crushing side-swipe.

The little Monitor now stuck her nose squarely against the side of the Merrimac, held it there, and fired both her eleven-inch guns against the walls of the Southerner.

The charge of powder was not heavy enough. No harm was done. The impact of the shots had merely forced the sloping sides an inch or two. The captain of the Merrimac turned to his men in sharp command.

"All hands on deck. Board and capture her!"

The smoke-smeared crew swarmed to the portholes and were just in the act of springing on the decks of the Monitor, when she backed quickly and dropped down stream.

After six hours of thunder in each other's faces the Monitor drew away into the shoal waters guarding the Minnesota. The Merrimac could not follow her in the shallows and at two o'clock turned her prow again toward Sewell's Point.

The battle was a drawn conflict. But the plucky little Monitor had won a tremendous moral victory. She had rescued the navy in the nick of time. The Government at Washington once more breathed.

From the heights of rejoicing the South sank again to the bitterness of failure. For twenty-four hours her flag had been mistress of the seas. Jefferson Davis saw the hope of peace fade into the certainty of a struggle for the possession of Richmond.

The way had been cleared. McClellan's two hundred thousand men were rushing on their transports for the Virginia peninsula.

28: THE SNARE OF THE FOWLER

Long before Jennie Barton arrived in Richmond Socola had waked to the realization of the fact that he had been caught in the trap he had set for another. He had laughed at his growing interest in the slender dark little Southerner. He imagined that he had hypnotized himself into the idea that he really liked her. He had kept no account of the number of visits he had made. They were part of his program. They had grown so swiftly into the habit of his thought and life he had not stopped to question the motive that prompted his zeal in pressing his attentions. In fact his mind had become so evenly adjusted to hers, his happiness had been so quietly perfect, he had lost sight of the fact that he was pressing his attentions at all.

The day she was suddenly called South and he said goodbye with her brown eyes looking so frankly into his he was brought sharply up against the fact that he was in love.

When he took her warm hand in his to press it for the last time, he felt an almost resistless impulse to bend and kiss her. From that moment he realized that he was in love—madly, hopelessly, desperately. He had left the car and hurried back to his post in the State Department, his heart beating like a trip hammer. It was a novel experience. He had never taken girls seriously before. The last girl on earth he had ever meant to take seriously was this slip of a Southern enthusiast. For a moment he was furious at the certainty of his abject surrender. He lifted his eyes to the big columns of the Confederate Capitol and laughed:

"Come, come, man—common sense—this is a joke! Forget it all. To your work—your country calls!"

Somehow the country refused to issue but one call—the old eternal cry of love. Wherever he turned, Jennie's brown eyes were smiling into his.

He looked at the Confederate Capitol to inspire him to deeds of daring and all he could remember was that she was a glorious little rebel with three brothers fighting for the flag that floated there. All he could get out of the supreme emblem of the "Rebellion" was that it was her Capitol and her flag and he loved her.

And then he laughed for sheer joy that love had come into his heart and made the world beautiful. He surrendered himself body and soul to the madness and wonder of it all.

If he could only see his mother and tell her, she could understand. He couldn't talk to the bundle of nerves Miss Van Lew had become. Her eyes burned each day with a deeper and deeper light of fanatical patriotism.

He had yielded none of his own enthusiasm. But this secret of his heart was too sweet to be shared by a comrade in arms.

Only God's eye, or the soul of the mother who bore him, could understand what he felt. The realization of his love for Jennie brought a new fear into his heart. His nerve was put daily to supreme test in the dangerous work in which he was engaged. A single mistake would start an investigation sure to end with a rope around his neck. Love had given life a new meaning. The chatter of the squirrels in the Capitol Square was all about their homes and babies in the tree tops. The song of birds in the old flower garden on Church Hill made his heart thump with a joy that was agony. The flowers were just bursting into full bloom and their perfume filled the air with the lazy dreaming of the southern spring.

He must speak his love. His heart would burst with its beating. His mate must know. And she had returned to Richmond with a bitterness against the North that was something new in the development of her character. The newspapers of Richmond had published an elaborate account of the sacking of her father's house, the smashing of its furniture and theft of its valuables. It had created a profound sensation. There was no mistaking the passion with which she had told this story.

He had laughed at first over the fun of winning the fairest little rebel in the South and carrying his bride away a prize of war, against the combined efforts of his Southern rivals. His love and pride had not doubted for a moment that her heart would yield to the man she loved no matter what uniform he might wear at the end of this war.

He couldn't make up his mind to ask her to marry him until she should know his real name and his true principles. What would she do if the truth were revealed? His heart fairly stopped its beating at the thought. The fall of Richmond he now regarded as a practical certainty. The Merrimac had proven a vain hope to the Confederacy.

McClellan was landing his magnificent army on the Peninsula and preparing to sweep all before him. McDowell's forty thousand men were moving on his old line of march straight from Washington. Their two armies would unite before the city and circle it with an invincible wall of fire and steel. Fremont, Milroy and Banks were sweeping through the valley of the Shenandoah. Their armies would unite, break the connections of the Confederacy at Lynchburg and the South would be crushed.

That this would all be accomplished within thirty days he had the most positive assurances from Washington. So sure was Miss Van Lew of McClellan's triumphant entry into Richmond she had put her house in order for his reception. Her parlor had been scrupulously cleaned. Its blinds were drawn and the room dark, but a flag staff was ready and a Union standard concealed in one of her feather beds. Over the old house on Church Hill the emblem of the Nation would first be flung to the breeze in the conquered Capital of the Confederacy.

The certainty of his discovery in the rush of the Union army into the city was now the nightmare which haunted his imagination.

He could fight the Confederate Government on even terms. He asked no odds. His life was on the hazard. Something more than the life of a Union spy was at stake in his affair with Jennie. Her life and happiness were bound in his. He felt this by an unerring instinct. If this proud, sensitive, embittered girl should stumble on even a suspicion of the truth, she would tear her heart out of her body if necessary to put him out of her life.

For a moment he was tempted to give up his work and return to the North. It was the one sure way to avoid discovery when Richmond fell. The war over, he would have his even chance with other men when its bitterness had been softened. His work in Richmond was practically done. His men could finish it. The number of soldiers in the Southern armies had been accurately counted and reported to Washington. Why should he risk the happiness of the woman he loved and his own happiness for life by remaining another day?

The thought had no sooner taken shape than he put it out of his mind. "Bah! I've set my hand to a great task. I'm not a quitter. I'll stand by my guns. No true woman ever loved a coward!"

He would take his chances and tell her his love.

He lifted the old-fashioned brass knocker on Senator Barton's door and banged it with such force he laughed at his own foolish eagerness:

"At least I needn't smash my way in!" he muttered.

"Yassah, des walk right in de parlor, sah," Jennie's maid said, with her teeth shining in a knowing smile.

Senator Barton had recovered from his illness. There could be no doubt about it. He was in the library holding forth in eloquent tones to a group of Confederate Congressmen who made his house their rendezvous. He was enjoying the martyrdom which the outrage on his home and the death of his aged mother and father had brought. He was using it to inveigh with new bitterness against the imbecility of Jefferson Davis and his administration. He held Davis personally responsible for every defeat of the South. He was the one man who had caused the fall of New Orleans, the loss of Fort Donelson and the failure to reap the victory at Shiloh.

"But you must remember, Senator," one of his henchmen mildly protested, "that Davis did save Albert Sidney Johnston to us and that alone made a victory possible."

"And what of it, if he threw it away by appointing a fool second in Command?"

There was a good answer to this—too good for the henchman to dare use it. He had sent Beauregard west to join Albert Sidney Johnston's command because Barton's junta, supporting Joseph E. Johnston against the administration, would no longer tolerate Beauregard in the same camp with their chief. They had demanded a free field for Joseph E. Johnston in the conflict with McClellan or they had threatened his resignation and the disruption of the Confederate army.

The President, sick unto death over the wrangling of these two generals, had separated them and sent Beauregard west where the genius of Albert Sidney Johnston could use his personal popularity, and his own more powerful mind would neutralize in any council of war the little man's feeble generalship.

Socola listened to Barton's fierce, unreasoning invective with a sense of dread. It was impossible to realize that this big-mouthed, bitter, vindictive, ridiculous politician was the father of the gentle girl he loved. There must be something of his power of malignant hatred somewhere in Jennie's nature. He had caught just a glimpse of it in the story she had told the Richmond papers.

She stood in the doorway at last, a smiling vision of modest beauty. Her dress of fine old lace seemed woven of the tender smiles that played about the sensitive mouth.

He sprang to his feet and took her hand, his heart thumping with joy. She felt it tremble and laughed outright.

"So you have returned a fiercer rebel than ever, Miss Jennie?" he said hesitatingly. He tried to say something purely conventional but it popped out when he opened his mouth—the ugly thought that was gnawing at his happiness.

"Yes," she answered thoughtfully, "I never realized before what it meant to be with my own people. I could have burned New Orleans and laughed at its ruins to have smoked Ben Butler out of it—"

"President Davis has proclaimed him an outlaw I see," Socola added.

"If he can only capture and hang him, the people of Louisiana would be perfectly willing to lose all—"

"But your brother, the Judge, is still loyal to the Union—you can't hate him you know?"

Jennie's eyes flashed into Socola's.

Why had he asked the one question that opened the wound in her heart? Perhaps her mind had suggested it. She had scarcely spoken the bitter words before she saw the vision of his serious face and regretted it.

"Strange you should have mentioned my brother's name at the very moment his image was before me," the girl thoughtfully replied.

"Clairvoyance perhaps—"

"You believe in such things?" Jennie asked.

"Yes. My mother leaped from her bed with a scream one night and told me that she had seen my father's spirit, felt him bend over her and touch her lips. He had died at exactly that moment."

"Wonderful, isn't it," Jennie murmured softly, "the vision of love!"

She was dreaming of the moments of her distress in the sacking of her home when the vision of this man's smiling face had suddenly set her to laughing.

"Yes," Socola answered. "I asked you about your older brother because I don't like the idea of you poisoning your beautiful young life with hatred. Such thoughts kill—they can't bring health and strength, Miss Jennie."

"Of course," the girl responded tenderly, "you can see things more calmly. You can't understand how deep the knife has entered our hearts in the South."

"That's just what I do understand. It's that against which I'm warning you. This war can't last always you know. There must be a readjustment—"

"Between the North and South?"

"Of course—"

"Never!"

With sudden emotion she leaped to her feet her little fists clinched.

She stood trembling in silence for a moment and her face paled.

"No, Signor," she went on in cold tones. "There can be no readjustment of this war. It's to the death now. I confess myself a rebel body and soul—Confess? I glory in it! I'm proud of being one. I thought my father extravagant at first. Ben Butler has changed my views. The South can't look back now. It's forward—forward—always forward to death—or independence!"

She paused overcome with emotion.

"Yes," she went on in quick tones, "I thank God we're two different tribes! I'm proud of the South and her old-fashioned, out-of-date chivalry. The South respects and honors women. God never made the Southern white man who could issue Butler's orders in New Orleans or insult the heart-broken women who are forced to enter his office with the vile motto he has placed over his desk—"

Socola lifted his hand in gentle smiling protest.

"But you must remember, Miss Jennie, that General Butler is a peculiar individual. He probably does not represent the best that's in New England—"

"God knows I hope not for their sakes," was the answer. "I only wish I could fight in the ranks with our boys. If I can't fight at least I'm going to help our men in other ways. I'll work with my hands as a slave. I'll sew and knit and nurse. I'll breathe my soul into the souls of our men. I sing Dixie when I rise in the morning. I hum it all day. I sing it with my last thoughts as I go to sleep."

Socola moved uneasily.

She looked at him a moment with an expression of sudden tenderness.

"I can't tell you how proud and happy I am in the thought that I may have helped you to give your brilliant mind to the service of the South. It's my offering to my country and her cause!"

It was impossible to resist the glow of love in her shining face. Socola felt his soul dissolve.

With a little gesture of resignation she dropped to a seat on the lounge beside the window, her young face outlined against a mass of early roses in full bloom. Their perfume poured through the window and filled the room.

Socola seated himself deliberately by her side and held her gaze with direct purpose. She saw and understood and her heart beat in quick response.

"You realize that you are the incarnate Cause of the South for me?" She smiled triumphantly.

"I have always known it."

There was no silly boasting in her tones, no trace of the Southern girl's light mood with one of her numerous beaux. Her words were spoken with deliberate tenderness.

"And yet how deeply and wonderfully you could not know—"

"I have guessed perhaps—"

He took her hand in his.

"I love you, Jennie—"

Her voice was the tenderest whisper.

"And I love you, my sweetheart—"

He clasped her in his arms and held her in silence.

She pushed him at arm's length and looked wistfully into his face.

"For the past month my heart has been singing. Through all the shame and misery of the sacking of our home, I could laugh and be happy—foolishly happy, because I knew that you loved me—"

"How did you know?"

"You told me—"

"When?"

"With the last little touch of your hand when I went South."

He pressed it with desperate tenderness.

"It shall be forever?"

"Forever!"

"Neither life nor death, nor height nor depth can separate us?"

"What could separate us, my lover? You are mine. I am yours. You have given your life to our cause—"

"I am but a soldier of fortune—"

"You are my soldier—you have given your life because I asked it. I give you mine in return—"

"Swear to me that you'll love me always!"

She answered with a kiss.

"I swear it."

Again he clasped her in his arms and hurried from the house. The twilight was falling. Artillery wagons were rumbling through the streets. A troop train had arrived from the South. Its regiments were rushing across the city to reinforce McGruder's thin lines on the Peninsula. McClellan's guns were already thundering on the shores. He hurried to the house on Church Hill, his dark face flushed with happiness, his heart beating a reveille of fear and joy.

29: THE PANIC IN RICHMOND

Richmond now entered the shadows of her darkest hour. Three armies were threatening from the west commanded by Fremont, Milroy, and Banks, whose forces were ordered to unite. McDowell with forty thousand men lay at Fredericksburg and threatened a junction with McClellan, who was moving up the Peninsula with an effective army of 105,000.

Joseph E. Johnston had under his command more than fifty thousand with which to oppose McClellan's advance. It was the opinion of Davis and Lee that the stand for battle should be made on the narrow neck of the Peninsula which lent itself naturally to defense.

To retreat toward Richmond would not only prove discouraging to the army, and precipitate a panic in the city, it meant the abandonment of Norfolk, the loss of the navy yard, the destruction of the famous iron-clad, and the opening of the James River to the gunboats of the enemy to Drury's Bluff within twelve miles of the Confederate Capital.

In this crisis Johnston gave confirmation to the worst fears of the President. He displayed the constitutional timidity and hesitation to fight which marked every step of his military career to its tragic end. With the greatest army under his command which the Confederacy had ever brought together—with Longstreet, McGruder and G. W. Smith as his lieutenants, he was preparing to retreat without a battle.

The President called in council of war General Lee, Randolph, the Secretary of War, and General Johnston. Johnston asked that Longstreet and Smith be invited. The President consented.

After full consultation, Davis decided, with Lee's approval to hold the Peninsula, save the navy yard and keep command of the James. And Johnston received orders accordingly.

With characteristic stubbornness the Field Commander persisted in his determination to retreat without a battle.

With aching heart Davis sent him a telegram.

"Richmond, Va., May 1st, 1861.

"General Joseph E. Johnston,

"Yorktown, Va.

"Accepting your conclusion that you must soon retire, arrangements are commenced for the abandonment of the navy yard and removal of public property from Norfolk and the Peninsula.

"Your announcement today that you would withdraw tomorrow night, takes us by surprise and must involve enormous losses, including unfinished gunboats. Will the safety of your army allow more time?

"Jefferson Davis."

Johnston had retreated from his base at Manassas with absurd haste, burning enormous stores and supplies of which the Confederacy was in desperate need. The losses now occasioned by his hasty withdrawal from Yorktown were even more serious.

The destruction of the iron-clad which had smashed the Federal fleet in Hampton Roads sent a shiver of horror throughout the South.

*****

The fiery trial through which Davis was passing brought out the finest traits of his strong character.

He had received ample warning that one of the first places marked for destruction by the Federal fleet passing up the Mississippi River was his home "Briarfield." He refused to send troops to defend it. His house was sacked, his valuable library destroyed, the place swept bare of his fine blooded stock and the negroes deported by force.

To his wife he wrote:

"You will see the notice of the destruction of our home. If our cause succeeds we shall not mourn our personal deprivation; if it should not, why—'the deluge.' I hope I shall be able to provide for the comfort of the old negroes."

Uncle Bob and Aunt Rhinah had been roughly handled by Butler's men. The foragers utterly refused to believe them when they told of their master's kindness in giving them piles of blankets. They were roughly informed that they had stolen them from the house and their treasures were confiscated amid the lamentations of the aged couple. The two precious rocking chairs were left them but of blankets and linens they were stripped bare.

* * * * *

With Johnston's army in retreat toward Richmond, his rear guard of but twelve thousand men under General McGruder had demonstrated the wisdom of Davis' position that the Peninsula could be successfully defended. McGruder's little army held McClellan at bay for nearly thirty days. He was dislodged from his position with terrible slaughter of the Union forces. McClellan's army lost two thousand two hundred and seventy-five men in this encounter, McGruder less than a thousand. Had Johnston concentrated his fifty thousand men on this line McClellan would never have taken it, and the only iron-clad the South possessed might have been saved.

The daring Commander of the Merrimac, while McClellan was encamped before Yorktown, had appeared in Hampton Roads and challenged the whole Federal fleet again to fight. The Monitor had taken refuge under the guns of Fortress Monroe and refused to come out. The ugly duckling of the Confederacy, in plain view of the whole Federal fleet and witnessed by French and English vessels, captured three schooners and carried them into port as prizes of war.

When Norfolk was abandoned, the iron-clad drew so much water she could only ascend the James by lightening her until her wooden sides showed above the water line. She was therefore set on fire and blown up on Johnston's retreat uncovering the banks of the James to the artillery of McClellan.

The Federal fleet could now dash up the James.

They did this immediately on the news of the destruction of the Confederate iron-clad.

On May fifteenth, the Galena, the Aroostook, the Monitor, the Port Royal, and the Stevens steamed up the river without opposition to Drury's Bluff within twelve miles of the Capital of the South. A half-finished fort mounting four guns guarded this point. The river was also obstructed by a double row of piles and sunken vessels.

If the eleven-inch guns of the Monitor could be brought to bear on this fort, it was a problem how long the batteries could be held in action.

The wildest alarm swept Richmond. The railroads were jammed with frantic people trying to get out. The depots were piled with mountains of baggage it was impossible to move. A mass meeting was held on the night the fleet ascended the river which was addressed by Governor Letcher and Mayor Mayo.

The Governor ended his speech with a sentence that set the crowd wild with enthusiasm.

"Sooner than see our beloved city conquered today by our enemies we will lay it in ashes with our own hands!"

The Legislature of Virginia showed its grit by passing a resolution practically inviting the President of the Confederacy to lay the city in ruins if he deemed wise:

"Resolved, That the General Assembly hereby expresses its desire that the Capital of the State be defended to the last extremity, if such defense is in accordance with the views of the President of the Confederate States, and that the President be assured that whatever destruction and loss of property of the State or of individuals shall thereby result, will be cheerfully submitted to."

When the Committee handed this document to Jefferson Davis, he faced them with a look of resolution:

"Richmond will not be abandoned, gentlemen, until McClellan marches over the dead bodies of our army. Not for one moment have I considered the idea of surrendering the Capital—"

"Good!"

"Thank God!"

"Hurrah for the President!"

The Committee grasped his hand, convinced that no base surrender of their Capital would be tolerated by their leader. "Rest assured, gentlemen," he continued earnestly, "if blood must be shed, it shall be here. No soil of the Confederacy could drink it more acceptably and none hold it more gratefully. We shall stake all on this one glorious hour for our Republic. Life, death, and wounds are nothing if we shall be saved from the fate of a captured Capital and a humiliated Confederacy—"

The Government and the city had need of grim resolution. The Federal fleet moved up into range and opened fire on the batteries at Drury's Bluff. The little Confederate gunboat Patrick Henry which had won fame in the first engagement of the Merrimac steamed down into line and joined her fire with the fort.

General Lee had planted light batteries on the banks of the river to sweep the decks of the fleet with grape and cannister.

The little Monitor, the Galena, and the Stevens steamed straight up to within six hundred yards of the battery of the fort and opened with their eleven-inch guns. The Galena and the Stevens were iron-clad steamers with thin armor.

For four hours the guns thundered. The batteries poured a hail of shot on the Monitor. They bounded off her round-tower and her water-washed decks like pebbles. The rifled gun on the Stevens burst and disabled her. The Galena was pierced by heavy shot and severely crippled, losing thirty-seven of her men. As the Monitor was built, it was impossible to make effective her guns at close range against the high bluff on which the Confederate battery was placed.

At eleven o'clock the crippled fleet slowly moved down the river and Richmond was saved.

* * * * *

When Johnston in his retreat up the Peninsula reached the high ground near the Chickahominy river, he threw out his lines and prepared to give McClellan battle. He dispatched a messenger to the President at Richmond informing him of this fact. The Cabinet was in session. A spirited discussion ensued. The Secretary of War and the whole council were alarmed at the prospect of battle on such an ill chosen position. His rear would rest on an enormous swamp through which the treacherous river flowed. There were no roads or bridges of sufficient capacity to take his army rapidly if he should be compelled to retreat.

"I suggest, Mr. President," said the Secretary of War, "that you call General Johnston's attention to this fact."

Davis shook his head emphatically.

"No, gentlemen. We have entrusted the command to General Johnston. It is his business with all the facts before him to know what is best. It would be utterly unfair and very dangerous to attempt to control his operations by advice from the Capital."

Davis was too great a general and too generous and just to deny Johnston his opportunity for supreme service to his country. It was the fixed policy of the President to select the best man for the position to which he assigned him and leave the responsibility of action on the field to his judgment.

On the following morning instead of a report of battle the President received a dispatch announcing that his General had decided to cross the Chickahominy River and use its swamps and dangerous crossings as his line of defense.

The Cabinet expressed its sense of profound relief and Davis watched his commander with an increase of confidence in his judgment. If the narrow roads and weak bridges across the river were guarded, an army of half his size could hold McClellan for months. The nearest crossing was twenty-five miles from Richmond.

General Reagan of the Cabinet rode down that night to see Hood at the head of his Texas brigade.

At noon next day on returning to the city he saw the President coming out of his office.

The long arm of the Chief was lifted and Reagan halted.

"Wait a minute—"

"At your service, Mr. President."

"Get your dinner and ride down to the Chickahominy with me. I want to see General Johnston."

Reagan shouted an answer which the President failed to catch: "You won't have to go to the Chickahominy to see Johnston!"

Joining Reagan after dinner the President rode rapidly through the suburban district called "The Rockets," and had reached the high ground beyond. A half mile away stretched a vast field of white tents.

"Whose camp is that?" Davis asked in surprise.

"Hood's brigade," Reagan replied.

"Why Hood's on the Chickahominy twenty-odd miles from here—"

"I camped here with them last night, sir—"

"Impossible!"

Reagan watched the thin face of the Confederate Chieftain grow deadly pale.

"If you wish to see General Johnston, Mr. President, you'll find him in that red brick house on the right—"

Reagan pointed in the direction of the house.

The President looked at his friend a moment, a quizzical expression relieving his anxiety.

"Of course—it's a joke, Reagan."

"It's true, sir!"

Davis shook his head:

"General Johnston is on the Chickahominy guarding the crossings. I sent my aide with a dispatch to him last night."

"He hadn't returned when you left the office—"

"No—"

"I thought not. There can be no mistake, sir. I saw General Johnston and his staff enter that house and establish his headquarters there—"

"Here in the suburbs of Richmond?"

"Right here, sir—"

Davis put spurs to his horse, and waved to his aide: "Colonel Ives—come!"

Reagan turned and rode again into Hood's camp.

The President rode straight to Johnston's headquarters. He sprang to the ground with a quick decisive leap.

The ceremony between the two men was scant. No words were wasted.

"You have moved your army into the suburbs of Richmond, General Johnston?"

"I have—"

"Why?"

"I consider this better ground—"

"You have left no rear guard to contest McClellan's crossing?"

"No."

"May I ask why you chose to give up the defenses of such a river without a blow?"

"My army was out of provisions—"

"They could have been rushed to you—"

"The ground near the Chickahominy is low and marshy. The water is bad—" "And you have come to the very gates of the city?"

"Because the ground is dry, the water good, and we are near our supplies—"

The President's lips trembled with rage.

"And McClellan can now plant his guns within six miles and his soldiers hear our church bells on Sunday—"

"Possibly—"

The President's eye pierced his General.

"Richmond is to be surrendered without a battle?"

"That depends, sir, upon conditions—"

The Confederate Chief suddenly threw his thin hands above his head and faced his stubborn sulking Commander.

"If you are not going to give battle, I'll appoint a man in your place who will—"

Before Johnston could reply the President turned on his heel, waved to Colonel Ives, mounted his horse and dashed into the city.

His Cabinet was called in hasty consultation with General Lee.

Davis turned to his counselors.

"Gentlemen, I have just held a most amazing conference with General Johnston. You were afraid he would fight beyond the Chickahominy. He has crossed the river, left its natural defenses unguarded, and has run all the way to town without pause. I have told him to fight or get out of the saddle. In my judgment he intends to back straight through the city and abandon it without a blow. We must face the situation."

He turned to Lee. The question he was going to put to the man in whom he had supreme confidence would test both his judgment and his character.

On his answer would hang his career. If it should be what the Confederate Chief believed, Lee was the man of destiny and his hour had struck.

"In case Johnston abandons Richmond," the President slowly began, "where in your opinion, General Lee, is the next best line of defense?"

Lee's fine mouth was set for a moment. He spoke at first with deliberation.

"As a military engineer, my answer is simple. The next best line of defense would be at Staten River—but—"

He suddenly leaped to his feet, his eyes streaming with tears.

"Richmond must not be given up—it shall not be given up!"

Davis sprang to his side and clasped Lee's hand.

"So say I, General!"

From that moment the President and his chief military adviser lived on Johnston's battle line, Lee ready at a moment's notice to spring into the saddle and hurl his men against McClellan the moment Johnston should falter.

The Commander was forced to a decision for battle. He could not allow his arch enemy to remove him without a fight.

The retreat across the Chickahominy had given McClellan an enormous advantage which his skillful eye saw at once. He threw two grand divisions of his army across the river and pushed his siege guns up within six miles of Richmond. His engineers immediately built substantial bridges across the stream over which he could move in safety his heaviest guns in any emergency, either for reinforcements or retreat.

He swung his right wing far to the north in a wide circling movement until he was in easy touch with McDowell's forty thousand men at Fredericksburg.

McClellan was within sight of the consummation of his hopes. When this wide movement of his army had been successfully made without an arm lifted to oppose, he climbed a tall tree within sight of Richmond from which he could view the magnificent panorama.

A solid wall of living blue with glittering bayonets and black-fanged batteries of artillery, his army spread for ten miles. Beyond them here and there only he saw patches of crouching gray in the underbrush or crawling through the marshes.

The Northern Commander came down from his perch and threw his arms around his aide:

"We've got them, boy!" he cried enthusiastically. "We've got them!"

It was not to be wondered at that the boastful oratorical Confederate Congress should have taken to their heels. They ran in such haste, the people of Richmond began to laugh and in their laughter took fresh courage.

A paper printed in double leads on its first page a remarkable account of the stampede:

"For fear of accident on the railroad, the stampeded Congress left in a number of the strongest and swiftest of our new canal-boats. The boats were drawn by mules of established sweetness of temper.

To protect our law-makers from snakes and bullfrogs that infest the line of the canal, General Winder detailed a regiment of ladies to march in advance of the mules, and clear the tow-path of these troublesome pirates. The ladies are ordered to accompany the Confederate Congress to a secluded cave in the mountains of

Hepsidan, and leave them there in charge of the children of that vicinity until McClellan thinks proper to let them come forth. The ladies will at once return to the defense of their country."

The President for a brief time was free of his critics.

On May thirty-first, Johnston's army, under the direct eye of Davis and Lee on the field, gave battle to McClellan's left wing—comprising the two grand divisions that had been pushed across the Chickahominy to the environs of Richmond.

The opening attack was delayed by the failure of General Holmes to strike McClellan's rear as planned. A terrific rain storm the night before had flooded a stream and it was impossible for him to cross.

Late in the afternoon Longstreet and Hill hurled their divisions through the thick woods and marshes on McClellan.

Longstreet's men drove before them the clouds of blue skirmishers, plunged into the marshes with water two feet deep and dashed on the fortified lines of the enemy. The Southerners crept through the dense underbrush to the very muzzles of the guns in the redoubts, charged, cleared them, grappling hand to hand with the desperate men who fought like demons.

Line after line was thus carried until at nightfall McClellan's left wing had been pushed back over two miles through swamp and waters red with blood.

The slaughter had been frightful in the few hours in which the battle had raged. On the Confederate left where Johnston commanded in person the Union army held its position until dark, unbroken.

Johnston fell from his horse wounded and Davis on the field immediately appointed General Lee to command.

The appointment of Lee to be Commander-in-Chief not only intensified the hatred of Johnston for the President, it made G. W. Smith, the man who was Johnston's second, his implacable enemy for life. Technically G. W. Smith would have succeeded to the command of the army had not Davis exercised his power on the field of battle to appoint the man of his choice.

In no act of his long, eventful life did Davis evince such clearness of vision and quick decision, under trying conditions. Lee had failed in Western Virginia and McClellan had out-generaled him, the yellow journals had declared. They called Lee "Old Spade." So intense was the opposition to Lee that Davis had sent him to erect the coast defenses of South Carolina. The Governor of the State protested against the appointment of so incompetent a man to this important work. Davis sent the Governor an emphatic message in reply:

"If Robert E. Lee is not a general I have none to send you."

Davis now called the man whom McClellan had defeated to the supreme command against McClellan at the head of his grand army in sight of the housetops of Richmond. Only a leader of the highest genius could have dared to make such a decision in such a crisis.

Davis made it without a moment's hesitation and in that act of individual will gave to the world the greatest commander of the age.

30: THE DELIVERANCE

From the moment Davis placed Lee in the saddle, order slowly emerged from chaotic conditions and the first rays of light began to illumine the fortunes of the Confederacy.

Modest and unassuming in his personality, he demonstrated from the first his skill as an organizer and his power in the conception and execution of far-reaching strategy.

From the moment he breathed his spirit into the army he made it a rapid, compact, accurate and terrible engine of war. The contemptible assault of the Richmond Examiner fell harmless from the armor of his genius.

Davis was bitterly denounced for his favoritism in passing G. W. Smith and appointing Governor Letcher's pet. He was accused of playing a game of low politics to make "a spawn of West Point" the next Governor of Virginia. But events moved with a pace too swift to give the yellow journals or the demagogues time to get their breath.

Lee had sent Jackson into the Valley of the Shenandoah to make a diversion which might hold the armies moving on the Capital from the west and at the same time puzzle McDowell at Fredericksburg.

Lee, Jackson and Davis were three men who worked in perfect harmony from the moment they met in their first council of war at the White House of the Confederacy. So perfect was Lee's confidence in Jackson, he was sent into the Valley unhampered by instructions which would interfere with the execution of any movement his genius might suggest.

Left thus to his own initiative, Jackson conceived the most brilliant series of engagements in the history of modern war. He determined to use his infantry by forced marches to cover in a day the ground usually made by cavalry and fall on the armies of his opponents one by one before they could form a juncture.

On May 23, by a swift, silent march of his little army of fifteen thousand men, he took Banks completely by surprise, crushed and captured his advance guard at Fort Royal, struck him in the flank and drove him back into Strassburg, through Winchester, and hurled his shattered army in confusion and panic across the Potomac on its Washington base.

Desperate alarm swept the Capital of the Union. Stanton, the Secretary of War, issued a frantic appeal to the Governors of the Northern States for militia to defend Washington. Panic reigned in the cities of the North. Governors and mayors issued the most urgent appeals for enlistments.

Fremont was ordered to move with all possible haste and form a juncture with a division of McDowell's army and cut off Jackson's line of retreat.

The wily Confederate General wheeled suddenly and rushed on Fremont before Shields could reach him. On June 8, at Cross Keys, he crushed Fremont, turned with sudden eagle swoop and defeated Shields at Port Republic.

Washington believed that Jackson commanded an enormous army, and that the National Capital was in danger of his invading host. The defeated armies of Milroy, Banks, Fremont and Shields were all drawn in to defend the city.

In this campaign of a few weeks Jackson had marched his infantry six hundred miles, fought four pitched battles and seven minor engagements. He had defeated four armies, each greater than his own, captured seven pieces of artillery, ten thousand stands of arms, four thousand prisoners and enormous stores of provisions and ammunition. It required a train of wagons twelve miles long to transport his treasures—every pound of which he saved for his Government.

He was never surprised, never defeated, never lost a train or an organized piece of his army, put out of commission sixty thousand Northern soldiers under four distinguished generals and in obedience to Lee's command was now sweeping through the mountain passes to the relief of Richmond.

While Jackson was thus moving to join his forces with Lee, Washington was shivering in fear of his attack.

On the day Jackson was scheduled to fall on the flank of McClellan's besieging army Lee moved his men to the assault. The first battle which Johnston had joined at Seven Pines had only checked McClellan's advance.

The Grand Army of the Potomac still lay on its original lines, and

McClellan had used every day in strengthening his entrenchments. Lee had built defensive works to enable a part of his army to defend the city while he should throw the flower of his gray soldiers on his enemy in a desperate flank assault in coöperation with Jackson.

On the arrival of his triumphant lieutenant from the Shenandoah Valley Lee suddenly sprang on McClellan with the leap of a lion. The Northern Commander fought with terrible courage, amazed and uneasy over the discovery that Jackson had suddenly appeared on his flank.

Within thirty-six hours McClellan's right wing was crushed and in retreat. Within seven days Lee drove his Grand Army of more than a hundred thousand men from the gates of Richmond thirty-five miles and hurled them on the banks of the James at Harrison's Landing under the shelter of the Federal gunboats.

Instead of marching in triumph through the streets of the Confederate Capital, McClellan congratulated himself and his Government on his good fortune in saving his army from annihilation. His broken columns had reached a place of safety after a series of defeats which had demoralized his command and resulted in the loss of ten thousand prisoners and ten thousand more in killed and wounded. He had been compelled to abandon or burn stores valued at millions. The South had captured thirty-five thousand stand of arms and fifty-two pieces of artillery.

Lee in his report modestly expressed his disappointment that greater results had not been achieved.

"Under ordinary circumstances," he wrote, "the Federal army should have been destroyed. Its escape was due to causes already stated. Prominent among them was the want of correct and timely information. The first, attributable chiefly to the character of the country, enabled General McClellan skillfully to conceal his retreat and to add much to the obstructions with which nature had beset the way of our pursuing column.

But regret that more was not accomplished gives way to gratitude to the Sovereign Ruler of the Universe for the results achieved."

Jackson, the grim soldier, whose habit was to pray all night before battle, wrote with the fervor of the religious enthusiast.

"Undying gratitude is due to God for this great victory—by which despondency increases in the North, hope brightens in the South and the Capital of Virginia and the Confederacy is saved."

A wave of exultation swept the South—while Death stalked through the streets of Richmond.

Instead of the tramp of victorious hosts, their bayonets glittering in the sunlight, which Socola had confidently expected, he watched from the windows of the Department of State the interminable lines of ambulances bearing the wounded from the fields of McClellan's seven-days' battle.

The darkened room on Church Hill was opened. Miss Van Lew had watched the glass rattle under the thunder of McClellan's guns, and then with sinking heart heard their roar fade in the distance until only the rumble of the ambulances through the streets told that he had been there. She burned the flag. It was too dangerous a piece of bunting to risk in her house now. It would be many weary months before she would need another.

Through every hour of the day and night since Lee sprang on McClellan, those never-ending lines of ambulances had wound their way through the streets. Every store and every home and every public building had been converted into a hospital. The counters of trade were moved aside and through the plate glass along the crowded streets could be seen the long rows of pallets on which the mangled bodies of the wounded lay. Every home set aside at least one room for the wounded boys of the South.

The heart-rending cries of the men from the wagons as they jolted over the cobble stones rose day and night—a sad, weird requiem of agony, half-groan, half-chant, to which the ear of pity could never grow indifferent.

Death was the one figure now with which every man, woman and child was familiar. The rattle of the dead-wagons could be heard at every turn.

They piled them high, these uncoffined bodies of the brave, and hurried them under the burning sun to the trenches outside the city. They piled them in long heaps to await the slow work of the tired grave-diggers. The frail board coffins in which they were placed at last would often burst from the swelling corpse. The air was filled with poisonous odors. The hospitals were jammed with swollen, disfigured bodies of the wounded and the dying. Gangrene and erysipelas did their work each hour in the weltering heat of mid-summer.

But the South received her dead and mangled boys with a majesty of grief that gave no cry to the ear of the world. Mothers lifted their eyes from the faces of their dead and firmly spoke the words of resignation:

"Thy will, O Lord, be done!"

Her houses were filled with the wounded, the dying and the dead, but Richmond lifted up her head. The fields about her were covered with imperishable glory.

The Confederacy had won immortality.

The women of the South resolved to wear no mourning for their dead. Their boys had laid their lives a joyous offering on their country's altar. They would make no cry.

Johnston had lost six thousand and eighty-four men, dead, wounded and missing at Seven Pines, and Lee had lost seventeen thousand five hundred and eighty-three in seven days of continuous battle. But the South was thrilled with the joy of a great deliverance.

Jefferson Davis in his address to the army expressed the universal feeling of his people:

> "Richmond, July 5, 1862.
>
> "To the Army of Eastern **Virginia**:
>
> "Soldiers:
>
> "I congratulate you upon the series of brilliant victories which, under the favor of Divine Providence, you have lately won; and as President of the Confederate States, hereby tender to you the thanks of the country, whose just cause you have so skillfuly and heroically saved.
>
> "Ten days ago an invading army, vastly superior to yours in numbers and the material of war, closely beleaguered your Capital and vauntingly proclaimed our speedy conquest. You marched to attack the enemy in his entrenchments. With well-directed movements and death-defying valor you charged

upon him in his strong positions, drove him from field to field over a distance of more than thirty-five miles, and, despite his reinforcements, compelled him to seek safety under the cover of his gunboats, where he now lies cowering before the army so lately despised and threatened with utter subjugation.

"The fortitude with which you have borne trial and privation, the gallantry with which you have entered into each successive battle, must have been witnessed to be fully appreciated. A grateful people will not fail to recognize you and to bear you in loved remembrance. Well may it be said of you that you have 'done enough for glory,' but duty to a suffering country and to the cause of Constitutional liberty claims for you yet further effort. Let it be your pride to relax in nothing which can promote your future efficiency; your one great object being to drive the invader from your soil, and, carrying your standards beyond the outer borders of the Confederacy, to wring from an unscrupulous foe the recognition of your birthright and independence."

Within the year from the fatal victory at Bull Run the South had through bitterness, tears and defeat at last found herself. Under the firm and wise leadership of Davis, her disasters had been repaired and her army brought to the highest standard of efficiency. At the head of her armies now stood Robert E. Lee and Stonewall Jackson. Their fame filled the world. In the west, Braxton Bragg, a brilliant and efficient commander, was marshaling his army to drive the Union lines into Kentucky.

From the depths of despair the South rose to the heights of daring assurance. For the moment the junta of politicians led by Senator Barton were compelled to halt in their assaults on the President. The people of the South had forgotten the issue of the date on Joseph E. Johnston's commission as general.

With characteristic foolhardiness, however, Barton determined that they should not forget it. He opened a series of bitter attacks on Davis for the appalling lack of management which had permitted McClellan to save what was left of his army. He boldly proclaimed the amazing doctrine that the wounding of Johnston at Seven Pines was an irreparable disaster to the South.

"Had Johnston remained in command," he loudly contended, "there can be no doubt that he would have annihilated or captured McClellan's whole army and ended the war."

On this platform he gave a banquet to General Johnston on the occasion of his departure from Richmond for his new command in the west. The Senator determined to hold his faction together for future assaults. Lee's record was yet too recent to permit the politicians to surrender without a fight.

The banquet was to be a love feast at which all factions opposed to Davis should be united behind the banner of Johnston. Henry S. Foote had quarreled with William L. Yancey. These two fire-eaters were enthusiastic partisans of his General.

Major Barbour, Johnston's chief quartermaster, presided at the head of the banquet table in Old Tom Griffin's place on Main Street. Foote was seated on his right, Governor Milledge T. Bonham of South Carolina next. Then came Gustavus W. Smith, whose hatred of Davis was implacable for daring to advance Robert E. Lee over his head. Next sat John U. Daniel, the editor of Richmond's yellow journal, the Examiner. Daniel's arm was in a sling. He had been by Johnston's side when wounded at Seven Pines.

At the other end of the table sat Major Moore, the assistant quartermaster, and by his side on the left, General Joseph E. Johnston, full of wounds in the flesh and grievances of soul. On his right was John B. Floyd of Fort Donelson fame whom Davis had relieved of his command. And next William L. Yancey, the matchless orator of secession, whose hatred of Davis was greater than this old hatred of Abolition.

The feast was such as only Tom Griffin knew how to prepare. Johnston as usual was grave and taciturn, still suffering from his unhealed wound. Yancey and Foote, the reconciled friends who had shaken hands in a common cause, were the life of the party.

Daniel, the editor of the organ of the Soreheads and Irreconcilables, was even more taciturn than his beloved Chief. General Bonham sang a love song. Yancey and Foote vied with each other in the brilliancy of their wit.

When the banquet had lasted for two hours, Yancey turned to Old Tom Griffin and said:

"Fresh glasses now and bumpers of champagne!"

When the glasses were filled the Alabama orator lifted his glass.

"This toast is to be drunk standing, gentlemen!"

Every man save Johnston sprang to his feet. Yancey looked straight into the eye of the General and shouted:

"Gentlemen! We drink to the health of the only man who can save the Southern Confederacy—General Joseph E. Johnston!"

The glasses were emptied and a shout of applause rang from every banqueter save one. The General had not yet touched his glass. Without rising, Johnston lifted his eyes and said in grave tones:

"Mr. Yancey, the man you describe is now in the field—his name is Robert E. Lee. I drink to his health."

Yancey's quick wit answered in a flash:

"I can only reply to you, sir, as the Speaker of the House of Burgesses did to General Washington—'Your modesty is only equaled by your valor!'"

Johnston's tribute to Lee was genuine, and yet nursing his grudge against the President with malignant intensity he left for the west, encouraging his friends to fight the Chieftain of the Confederacy with tooth and nail and that to the last ditch.

31: LOVE AND WAR

Captain Richard Welford reached Richmond from the Western army two days after Lee had driven McClellan under the shelter of the navy. He had been wounded in battle, promoted to the rank of Captain for gallantry on the field and sent home on furlough for two months.

He used his left hand to raise the knocker on Jennie's door. His right arm was yet in a sling. His heart was beating a wild march as he rushed from the hotel to the Senator's house. He had not heard from Jennie in two months but the communications of the Western army had been cut more than once and he thought nothing of the long silence. It had only made his hunger to see the girl he loved the more acute. He had fairly shouted his joy when a piece of shell broke his right arm and hurled him from his horse. He never thought of promotion for gallantry. It came as a surprise. The one hope that leaped when he scrambled to his feet and felt the helpless arm hanging by his side was to see the girl he had left behind.

"Glory to God!" he murmured fervently, "I'll go to her now!"

He was just a little proud of that broken arm as he waited for her entrance. The shoulder straps he wore looked well, too. She would be surprised. It had all happened so quickly, no account had yet reached the Richmond papers.

Jennie bounded into the room with a cry of joy.

"Oh, Dick, I'm so glad to see you!"

He smiled and extended his left hand.

"Jennie!" was all he could say.

"You are wounded?" she whispered.

Dick nodded.

"Yep—a shell toppled me over but I was on my feet in a minute laughing—and I'll bet you couldn't guess what about?"

"No—"

"Laughed because I knew I'd get to see you—"

"I'm so proud of you!" she cried through her tears.

"Are you?" he asked tenderly.

"Of course I am—don't you think I know what those shoulder straps mean?"

"Well, I just care because you care, Jennie—"

"You're a brave Southern boy fighting for our rights—you care for that, too."

"Oh yes, of course, but that's not the big thing after all, little girl—"

He paused and seized her hand.

She blushed and drew it gently away.

"Please—not that now—"

"Why—not now?"

He asked the question in tones so low they were almost a gasp. He felt his doom in the way she had withdrawn her hand.

"Because—" she hesitated just a moment to strike the blow she knew would hurt so pitifully and then went on firmly, "I've met my fate, Dick—and pledged him my heart."

The Captain lifted his shoulders with a little movement of soldierly pride, held himself firmly, mastered the first rush of despair and then spoke with assumed indifference:

"Socola?"

Jennie smiled faintly.

"Yes."

He rose awkwardly and started to the door. Jennie placed her hand on his wounded arm with a gesture of pathetic protest.

"Dick!"

"I can't help it, I must go—"

"Not like this!"

"I can't smile and lie to you. It means too much. I hate that man. He's a scoundrel, if God ever made one—"

Jennie's hand slipped from his arm.

"That will do now—not another word—"

"I beg your pardon, Jennie," he stammered. "I didn't think what I was saying, honey. It just popped out because it was inside. You'll forgive me?"

The anger died in her eyes and she took his outstretched hand. "Of course, I understand—and I'm sorry. I appreciate the love you've given me. I wish in my heart I could have returned it. You deserve it—"

The Captain lifted his left hand.

"No pity, please. I'm man enough to fight—and I'm going to fight.

You're not yet Signora Socola—"

The girl laughed.

"That's more like a soldier!"

"We'll be friends anyhow, Jennie?"

"Always."

The Captain left the Senator's house with a grim smile playing about his strong mouth. He had made up his mind to fight for love and country on the same base. He would ask for his transfer to the Secret Service of the Confederacy.

32: THE PATH OF GLORY

Jefferson Davis had created the most compact and terrible engine of war set in motion since Napoleon founded the Empire of France. It had been done under conditions of incredible difficulty, but it had been done. The smashing of McClellan's army brought to the North the painful realization of this fact. Abraham Lincoln must call for another half million soldiers and no man could foresee the end.

Davis had begun in April, 1861, without an arsenal, laboratory or powder mill of any capacity, and with no foundry or rolling mill for iron except the little Tredegar works in Richmond.

He had supplied them.

Harassed by an army of half a million men in blue led by able generals and throttled by a cable of steel which the navy had drawn about his coast line, he had done this work and at the same time held his own defiantly and successfully. Crippled by a depreciated currency, assaulted daily by a powerful conspiracy of sore-head politicians and quarreling generals, strangled by a blockade that deprived him of nearly all means of foreign aid—he had still succeeded in raising the needed money. Unable to use the labor of slaves except in the unskilled work of farms, hampered by lack of transportation even of food for the army, with no stock of war material on hand,—steel, copper, leather or iron with which to build his establishments—yet with quiet persistence he set himself to solve these problems and succeeded.

He had created, apparently out of nothing, foundries and rolling mills at Selma, Richmond, Atlanta and Macon, smelting works at Petersburg, a chemical laboratory at Charlotte, a powder mill superior to any of the United States and unsurpassed by any in Europe,—a mighty chain of arsenals, armories, and laboratories equal in their capacity and appointments to the best of those in the North, stretching link by link from Virginia to Alabama.

He established artificial niter beds at Richmond, Columbus, Charleston, Savannah, Mobile and Selma of sufficient capacity to supply the niter needed in the powder mills.

Mines for iron, lead and copper were opened and operated. Manufactories for the production of sulphuric and nitric acid were established and successfully operated.

Minor articles were supplied by devices hitherto unheard of in the equipment of armies. Leather was scarce and its supply impossible in the quantities demanded.

Knapsacks were abolished and haversacks of cloth made by patriotic women with their needles took their places. The scant supply of leather was divided between the makers of shoes for the soldiers and saddles and harness for the horses. Shoes for the soldiers were the prime necessity.

To save leather the waist and cartridge-box belts were made of heavy cotton cloth stitched in three or four thicknesses. Bridle reins were made of cotton in the same way. Cartridge boxes were finally made thus—with a single piece of leather for the flap. Even saddle skirts for the cavalry were made of heavy cotton strongly stitched.

Men to work the meager tanneries were exempt from military services and transportation for hides and leather supplies was free.

A fishery was established on the Cape Fear River in North Carolina from which oil was manufactured. Every wayside blacksmith shop was utilized as a government factory for the production of horseshoes for the cavalry.

To meet the demands for articles of prime necessity which could not be made in the South, a line of blockade runners was established between the port of Wilmington, North Carolina, and Bermuda. Vessels capable of storing in their hold six hundred bales of cotton were purchased in England and put into this service. They were long, low, narrow craft built for speed. They could show their heels to any ship of the United States Navy. Painted a pale grayish-blue color, and lying low on the water they were sighted with difficulty in the day and they carried no lights at night. The moment one was trapped and sunk by the blockading fleet, another was ready to take her place.

Depots and stores were established and drawn on by these fleet ships both at Nassau and Havana.

By the fall of 1862, through the port of Wilmington, from the arsenals at Richmond and Fayetteville, and from the victorious fields of Manassas and the Seven Days' Battle around Richmond, sufficient arms had been obtained to equip two hundred thousand soldiers and supply their batteries with serviceable artillery.

On April 16, 1862, Davis asked of his Congress that every white man in the South between the ages of 18 and 35 be called to the colors and all short term volunteer contracts annulled. The law was promptly passed in spite of the conspirators who fought him at every turn. Camps of instruction were established in every State, and a commandant sent from Richmond to take charge of the new levies.

Solidity was thus given to the military system of the Confederacy and its organization centralized and freed from the bickerings of State politicians.

With her loins thus girded for the conflict the South entered the second phase of the war—the path of glory from the shattered army of McClellan on the James to Hooker's crushed and bleeding lines at Chancellorsville.

The fiercest clamor for the removal of McClellan from his command swept the North. The position of the Northern General was one of peculiar weakness politically. He was an avowed Democrat. His head had been turned by flattery and he had at one time dallied with the idea of deposing Abraham Lincoln by the assumption of a military dictatorship.

Lincoln knew this. The demand for his removal would have swayed a President of less balance. Lincoln refused to deprive McClellan of his command but yielded sufficiently to the clamor of the radicals of his own party to appoint John Pope of the Western army to the command of a new division of troops designed to advance on Richmond.

The generals under McClellan who did not agree with his slow methods were detached with their men and assigned to service under Pope. McClellan did not hesitate to denounce Pope as an upstart and a braggart who had won his position by the lowest tricks of the demagogue. He declared that the new commander was a military impostor, a tool of the radical wing of the Republican party, a man who mistook brutality in warfare for power and sought to increase the horrors of war by arming slaves, legalizing plunder and making the people of the South irreconcilable to a restored Union by atrocities whose memory could never be effaced.

Pope's first acts on assuming command did much to justify

McClellan's savage criticism. He issued a bombastic address to his army which brought tears to Lincoln's eyes and roars of laughter from Little Mac's loyal friends.

He issued a series of silly general orders making war on the noncombatant population of Virginia within his line. If citizens refused to take an oath of allegiance which he prescribed they were to be driven from their homes and if they dared to return, were to be arrested and treated as spies.

His soldiers were given license to plunder. Houses were robbed and cattle shot in the fields. Against these practices McClellan had set his face with grim resolution. He fought only organized armies. He protected the aged, and all noncombatants. It was not surprising, therefore, when Lincoln ordered him to march his army to the support of Pope, McClellan was in no hurry to get there.

Pope had boldly advanced across the Rappahannock and a portion of his army had reached Culpeper Court House. He had determined to make good the proclamation with which he had assumed command.

In this remarkable document he said:

"By special assignment of the President of the United States, I have assumed command of this army. I have come to you from the West where we have always seen the backs of our enemies—from an army whose business it has been to seek the adversary and to beat him when found, whose policy has been attack not defense. Let us study the probable lines of retreat of our opponents and leave ours to take care of themselves. Let us look before us and not behind."

While his eyes were steadily fixed before him Jackson, moving with the stealthy tread of a tiger, slipped in behind his advance guard, sprang on it and tore his lines to pieces before he could move reinforcements to their rescue.

When his reinforcements reached the ground Jackson had just finished burying the dead, picking up the valuable arms left on the field and sending his prisoners to the rear.

Before Pope could lead his fresh men to an attack the vanguard of Lee's army was in sight and the general who had just issued his flaming proclamation took to his heels and fled across the Rappahannock where he called frantically for the divisions of McClellan's army which had not yet joined him.

While Lee threatened Pope's front by repeated feints at different points along the river, he dispatched Jackson's corps of twenty-five thousand "foot cavalry" on a wide flanking movement through the Blue Ridge to turn the Federal right, destroy his stores at Manassas Junction and attack him in the rear before his reinforcements could arrive.

With swiftness Jackson executed the brilliant movement. Within twenty-four hours his men had made the wide swing through the low mountain ranges and crouched between Pope's army and the Federal Capital. To a man of less courage and coolness this position would have been one of tragic danger. ShOuld Pope suddenly turn from Lee's pretended attacks and spring on Jackson he might be crushed between two columns. Franklin and Sumner's corps were at Alexandria to reinforce his lines.

Jackson had marched into the jaws of death and yet he not only showed no fear, he made a complete circuit of Pope's army, struck his storehouses at Manassas Junction and captured them before the Federal Commander dreamed that an army was in his rear. Eight pieces of artillery and three hundred prisoners were among the spoils. Fifty thousand pounds of bacon, a thousand barrels of beef, two thousand barrels of pork, two thousand barrels of flour, and vast quantities of quartermaster's stores also fell into his hands.

Jackson took what he could transport and burned the rest. Pope rushed now in frantic haste to destroy Jackson before Lee's army could reach him.

Jackson was too quick for the eloquent commander. He slipped past his opponent and took a strong position west of the turnpike from Warrenton where he could easily unite with Longstreet's advancing corps.

Pope attempted to turn Jackson's left with a division of his army and the wily Southerner fell on his moving columns with sudden savage energy, fought until nine o'clock at night and drove him back with heavy loss.

When Pope moved to the attack next day at two o'clock Longstreet had reached Jackson's side. The attack failed and his men fell back through pools of blood. The Federal Commander was still sending pompous messages to Washington announcing his marvelous achievements while his army had steadily retreated from

Culpeper Court House beyond the Rappahannock, back to Manassas where the first battle of the war was fought.

At dawn on August 30, the high spirited troops of the South were under arms standing with clinched muskets within a few hundred yards of the pickets of Pope. Their far flung battle line stretched for five miles from Sudley Springs on the left to the Warrenton road and on obliquely to the southwest.

The artillery opened the action and for eight hours the heavens shook with its roar. At three o'clock in the afternoon Pope determined to hurl the flower of his army against Jackson's corps and smash it. His first division pressed forward and engaged the Confederates at close quarters. A fierce and bloody conflict followed, Jackson's troops refusing to yield an inch. The Federal Commander brought up two reserve lines to support the first but before they could be of any use, Longstreet's artillery was planted to rake them with a murderous fire and they fell back in confusion.

As the reserves retreated Jackson ordered his men to charge and at the same moment Longstreet hurled his division against the Federal center, and the whole Confederate army with piercing yell leaped forward and swept the field as far as the eye could reach.

No sublimer pageant of blood and flame and smoke and shrouded Death ever moved across the earth than that which Lee now witnessed from the hilltop on which he stood. For five miles across the Manassas plains the gray waves rolled, their polished bayonets gleaming in the blazing sun.

They swept through the open fields, now lost a moment in the woods, now flashing again in the open. They paused and the artillery dashed to the front, spread their guns in line and roared their call of death to the struggling, fleeing, demoralized army. Another shout and the charging hosts swept on again to a new point of vantage from which to fire.

Through clouds of smoke and dust the red tongues of flame from a hundred big-mouthed guns flashed and faded and flashed again. The charging men slipped on the wet grass where the dead lay thickest.

Waves of white curling smoke rose above the tree-tops and hung in dense clouds over the field lighted by the red glare of the sinking sun. The relief corps could be seen dashing on, with stretchers and ambulances following in the wake of the victorious army.

The hum and roar of the vast field of carnage came now on the ears of the listener—the groans of the wounded and the despairing cry of the dying. And still the living waves of gray-tipped steel rolled on in relentless sweep.

Again the fleeing Federal soldiers choked the waters of Bull Run. Masses of struggling fugitives were pushed from the banks into the water and pressed down. Here and there a wounded man clung to the branch of an overhanging tree until exhausted and sank to rise no more.

The meadows were trampled and red. Hundreds of weak and tired men were ridden down by cavalry and crushed by artillery. On and on rushed the remorseless machine of the Confederacy, crushing, killing, scarring, piling the dead in heaps.

It was ten o'clock that night before the army of Lee halted and Pope's exhausted lines fell into the trenches around Centreville for a few hours' respite. At dawn Jackson was struggling with his tired victorious division to again turn Pope's flank, get into his rear and cut off his retreat.

A cold and drenching rainstorm delayed his march and the rabble that was once Pope's army succeeded in getting into the defenses of Washington. Davis' army took seven thousand prisoners and picked up more than two thousand wounded soldiers whom their boastful commander had left on the field to die. Thirty pieces of artillery and twenty thousand small arms fell into Lee's hands.

Pope's losses since Jackson first struck his advance guard at Culpeper Court House had been more than twenty thousand men and his army had been driven into Washington so utterly demoralized it was unfit for further service until reorganized under an abler man.

For the moment the North was stunned by the blow. Deceived by Pope's loud dispatches claiming victory for the first two days it was impossible to realize that his shattered and broken army was cowering and bleeding under the shadow of the Federal Capitol.

Even on the night of August thirtieth, with his men lying exhausted at Centreville where they had dropped at ten o'clock when Lee's army had mercifully halted, poor Pope continued to send his marvelous messages to the War Department.

He reported to Halleck:

"The enemy is badly whipped, and we shall do well enough. Do not be uneasy. We will hold our own here. We have delayed the enemy as long as possible without losing the army. We have damaged him heavily, and I think the army entitled to the gratitude of the country."

To this childish twaddle Halleck replied:

"My dear General, you have done nobly!"

Abraham Lincoln, however, realized the truth quickly. He removed Pope and in spite of the threat of his Cabinet to resign called McClellan to reorganize the dispirited army.

The North was in no mood to listen to the bombastic defense of General Pope. They were stunned by the sudden sweep of the Confederate army from the gates of Richmond on June first, to the defenses at Washington within sixty days with the loss of twenty thousand men under McClellan and twenty thousand more under Pope.

The armies of the Union had now been driven back to the point from which they had started on July 16, 1861. It had been necessary to withdraw Burnside's army from eastern North Carolina and the forces of the Union from western Virginia. The war had been transferred to the suburbs of Washington and the Northern people who had confidently expected McClellan to be in Richmond in June were now trembling for the safety of Pennsylvania and Maryland, to say nothing of the possibility of Confederate occupation of the Capital.

An aggressive movement of all the forces of the South under Lee in the East and Bragg and Johnston in the West was ordered. In spite of the fact that Lee's army could not be properly shod—the supply of army shoes being inadequate and the lack of shoe factories a defect the Confederacy had yet been unable to remedy, the Southern Commander threw his army of barefooted veterans across the Potomac and boldly invaded Maryland on September the fifth.

The appearance of Stonewall Jackson on his entrance into Frederick City, Maryland, was described by a Northern war correspondent in graphic terms:

"Old Stonewall was the observed of all observers. He was dressed in the coarsest kind of homespun, seedy, and dirty at that. He wore an old hat which any Northern beggar would consider an insult to have offered him. In his general appearance he was in no respect to be distinguished from the mongrel barefoot crew who followed his fortunes. I had heard much of the decayed appearance of rebel soldiers,—but such a looking crowd!

Ireland in her worst straits could present no parallel, and yet they glory in their shame!"

Lee's army was now fifty miles north of Washington, within striking distance of Baltimore. His strategy had completely puzzled the War Department of the Federal Government. McClellan was equally puzzled. Lincoln and his Cabinet believed Lee's movement into Maryland a feint to draw the army from the defense of the Capital, and, when this was accomplished, by a sudden swoop the Southern Commander would turn and capture the city.

While McClellan was thus halting in tragic indecision one of the unforeseen accidents of war occurred which put him in possession of Lee's plan of campaign and should have led to the annihilation of the Southern army. A copy of the order directing the movement of the Confederates from Frederick, Maryland, was thrown to the ground by a petulant officer to whom it was directed. It fell into the hands of a Federal soldier who hurried to McClellan's headquarters with the fateful document.

Jackson's corps had been sent on one of his famous "foot cavalry" expeditions to sweep the Federal garrison from Martinsburg, surround and capture Harper's Ferry. McClellan at once moved a division of his army to crush the small command Lee had stationed at South Mountain to guard Jackson's movement.

McClellan threw his men against this little division of the Confederates and attempted to force his way to the relief of Harper's Ferry. The battle raged with fury until nine o'clock at night. Their purpose accomplished Lee withdrew them to his new position at Sharpsburg to await the advent of Jackson.

The "foot cavalry" had surrounded Harper's Ferry, assaulted it at dawn and in two hours the garrison surrendered. Thirteen thousand prisoners with their rifles and seventy-three pieces of artillery fell into Jackson's hands. Leaving General A. P. Hill to receive the final surrender of the troops Jackson set out at once for Sharpsburg to join his army with Lee's.

The Southern Commander had but forty thousand men with

which to meet McClellan's ninety thousand, but at sunrise on September seventeenth, his batteries opened fire and the bloodiest struggle of the Civil War began. Through the long hours of this eventful day the lines of blue and gray charged and counter-charged across the scarlet field. When darkness fell neither side had yielded. The dead lay in ghastly heaps and the long pitiful wail of the wounded rose to Heaven.

Lee had lost two thousand killed and six thousand wounded. McClellan had lost more than twelve thousand. His army was so terribly shattered by the bloody work, he did not renew the struggle on the following day. Lee waited until night for his assault and learning that reinforcements were on the way to join McClellan's command withdrew across the Potomac.

It was a day later before Lee's movements were sufficiently clear for McClellan to claim a victory.

On September nineteenth, he telegraphed Washington:

"I do not know if the enemy is falling back or recrossing the river. We may safely claim the victory as ours."

Abraham Lincoln hastened to take advantage of McClellan's claim to issue his Emancipation Proclamation. And yet so utter had been the failure of his general to cope with Lee and Jackson, the President of the United States relieved McClellan of his command.

While Lee's invasion had failed of the larger purpose, its moral effect on the North had been tremendous. He carried back into Virginia fourteen thousand prisoners, eighty pieces of artillery and invaluable equipment for his army.

In the meantime the Western army under Bragg had invaded Kentucky, sweeping to the gates of Cincinnati and Louisville and retiring with more than five thousand prisoners, five thousand small arms and ten pieces of artillery.

The gain in territory by the invasion of Maryland and Kentucky had been nothing but the moral effect of these movements had been far reaching. The daring valor of the small Confederate armies fighting against overwhelming odds had stirred the imagination of the world. In the west they had carried their triumphant battle flag from Chattanooga to Cincinnati, and although forced to retire, had shown the world that the conquest at the southwestern territory was a gigantic task which was yet to be seriously undertaken.

The London Times, commenting on these campaigns, declared: "Whatever may be the fate of the new nationality or its subsequent claims to the respect of mankind, it will assuredly begin its career with a reputation for genius and valor which the most famous nations may envy."

On McClellan's fall he was succeeded by General Burnside who found a magnificently trained army of veteran soldiers at his command. It was now divided into three grand divisions of two corps each, commanded by three generals of tried and proven ability, Sumner, Hooker and Franklin.

Burnside quickly formed and began the execution of an advance against Richmond. He moved his army rapidly down the left bank of the Rappahannock River to Fredericksburg, and ordered pontoon bridges to cross the stream. His army could thus defend Washington while moving in force on the Confederate Capital.

When Burnside led his one hundred and thirteen thousand men across the river and occupied the town of Fredericksburg, Lee and Jackson were ready to receive him. Lee had entrenched on the line of crescent-shaped hills behind the town. When the new Northern Commander threw his army, with its bands playing and its thousand flags flying, against these hills on the morning of December 13, 1862, he plunged headlong and blindfolded into a death trap.

Charge after charge was repulsed with unparalleled slaughter. Lee's guns were planted to cross fire on each charging line of blue. Burnside's men were mowed down in thousands until their sublime valor won the praise and the pity of their foe.

When night at last drew the veil over the awful scene the shattered masses of the charging army were huddled under the shelter of the houses in Fredericksburg leaving the field piled high with the dead and the wounded. The wounded were freezing to death in the pitiless cold.

Burnside had lost thirteen thousand men—the flower of his troops—the bravest men the North had ever sent into battle.

Jackson's keen eye was quick to see the shambles into which this demoralized army had been pushed. The river behind them could be crossed only on a narrow pontoon bridge. A swift and merciless night attack would either drive the bleeding lines into the freezing river, annihilate or capture the whole army. He urged Lee to this attack.

Lee demurred. He could not know the extent of the enemy's losses. It was inconceivable to the Southern Commander that Burnside with his one hundred and thirteen thousand picked soldiers, could be repulsed with such slight losses to the South. Only a small part of the army under his command had been active in the battle and their losses were insignificant in comparison with the records of former struggles.

Burnside would renew the attack with redoubled vigor. He refused to move his men from their entrenchments into the open field where they would be exposed to the batteries beyond the river.

Jackson turned his somber blue eyes on Lee:

"Send my corps into Fredericksburg alone tonight. Hold the hills with the rest of the army. I'll do the work."

"You cannot distinguish friend from foe, General Jackson—"

"I'll strip my men to the waist and tie white bands around their right arms."

"In this freezing cold?"

"They'll obey my orders, General Lee—"

"It's too horrible—"

"It's war, sir," was Jackson's reply. "War means fighting—fighting to kill, to destroy—fighting with tooth and nail—"

Lee shook his head. He refused to take the risk. Jackson returned to his headquarters with heavy heart. His chief of medical staff was busy preparing bandages for his men. He had been sure of Lee's consent. He countermanded the order and Burnside's army was saved from annihilation. When the sun rose next morning half his men were safely across the river—and the remainder quickly followed.

Again the North was stunned. Another wave of horror swept its homes as the lists of the dead and wounded were printed.

Burnside resigned his command and "Fighting" Joe Hooker was placed at the head of the Northern troops. Since June first, Lee and Jackson had destroyed four blue armies and driven their commanders from the field,—McClellan twice, John Pope and now Burnside.

The political effects of these brilliant achievements of Davis' army had been paralyzing on the administration of Lincoln. The Proclamation of Emancipation which he had issued immediately after the bloody battle in Maryland had not only fallen flat in the North, it had created a reaction against his policies and the conduct of the war. The November elections had gone against him and his party had been all but wiped out.

The Democrats in New York had reversed a majority of one hundred and seven thousand against them in 1860 and swept the State, electing their entire ticket. The administration was defeated in New Jersey, Pennsylvania, Ohio, Indiana and Illinois.

The voters of the North not only condemned the administration for declaring the slaves free, but they assaulted the war policy of their Government with savage fury. They condemned the wholesale arrest of thousands of citizens for their political opinions and arraigned the Government for its incompetence in conducting the military operations of an army of more than twice the numbers of the triumphant South.

The Emancipation Proclamation and the victories of Davis' army had not only divided and demoralized the North, they had solidified Southern opinion.

Even Alexander H. Stephens, the Vice-President of the Confederacy, who had been a thorn in the flesh of Davis from the beginning in his advocacy of foolish and impossible measures of compromise now took his position for war to the death. In a fiery speech in North Carolina following Lincoln's proclamation Stephens said:

"As for any reconstruction of the Union—such a thing is impossible—such an idea must not be tolerated for an instant. Reconstruction would not end the war, but would produce a more horrible war than that in which we are now engaged. The only terms on which we can obtain permanent peace is final and complete separation from the North. Rather than submit to anything short of that, let us resolve to die as men worthy of freedom."

A few days after the defeat of Burnside's army at Fredericksburg the South was thrilled by the feat of General McGruder in Galveston harbor. The daring Confederate Commander had seized two little steamers and fitted them up as gun boats by piling cotton on their sides for bulwarks. With these two rafts of cotton coöperating on the water, his infantry waded out into the waters of Galveston Bay and attacked the Federal fleet with their bare hands.

When the smoke of battle lifted the city of Galveston was in Confederate hands, the fleet had been smashed and scattered and the port opened to commerce. Commodore Renshaw had blown up his flag ship to prevent her falling into McGruder's hands and gone down with her. The garrison surrendered.

Jackson had invented a "foot cavalry." McGruder had supplemented it by a "foot navy."

At Murfreesboro, Tennessee, on the same day General Bragg had engaged the army of Rosecrans and fought one of the bloodiest engagements of the war. Its net results were in favor of the Confederacy in spite of the fact that he permitted Rosecrans to move into Murfreesboro. The Northern army had lost nine thousand men, killed and wounded, and Bragg carried from the field six thousand Federal prisoners, thirty pieces of artillery, sixty thousand stand of small arms, ambulances, mules, horses and an enormous amount of valuable stores.

His own losses had been great but far less than those he inflicted on Rosecrans. He had lost one thousand two hundred and ninety-two killed, seven thousand nine hundred and forty-five wounded and one thousand twenty-seven missing.

At Charleston a fleet of iron-clads on the model of the Monitor had been crushed by the batteries and driven back to sea with heavy loss. The Keokuk was left a stranded wreck in the harbor.

A second attack on Vicksburg had failed under Sherman. A third attack by Grant had been repulsed. Farragut's attack on Port Hudson had failed with the loss of the Richmond.

The Federal Government now put forth its grandest effort to crush at a blow the apparently invincible army of Davis' still lying in its trenches on the heights behind Fredericksburg.

Hooker's army was raised to an effective force of one hundred and thirty thousand and his artillery increased to four hundred guns. Lee had been compelled to detach Longstreet's corps, comprising nearly a third of his army for service in North Carolina. The force under his command was barely fifty thousand.

So great was the superiority of the Northern army Hooker divided his forces for an enveloping movement, each wing of his being still greater than the whole force under Lee.

Sedgwick's corps crossed the river below Fredericksburg and

began a flanking movement from the south while Hooker threw the main body across the Rappahannock at three fords seven miles above.

On April thirtieth, he issued an address to his men. His forces were all safely across the river without firing a shot. He had Lee's little army caught in a trap between his two grand divisions.

In his proclamation he boldly announced:

"The operations of the last three days have determined that our enemy must ingloriously fly, or come out from behind their defenses and give us battle on our own ground, where certain destruction awaits him."

His enemy was not slow in coming out from behind his defenses. With quick decision Lee divided his little army by planting ten thousand men under Early on Marye's Heights to stop Sedgwick's division and moved swiftly with the remainder to meet Hooker in the dense woods of the Wilderness near Chancellorsville.

With consummate daring and the strategy of genius he again divided his army. He detached Jackson's corps and sent his "foot cavalry" on a swift wide detour of twenty-odd miles to swing around Hooker's right and strike him in the flank while he pretended an attack in force on his front.

It was nearly sundown when Jackson's tired but eager men saw from the hill top their unsuspecting foe quietly cooking their evening meal.

When the battle clouds lifted at the end of three days of carnage, Hooker's army of one hundred and thirty thousand men had been cut to pieces and flung back across the Rappahannock, leaving seventeen thousand killed and wounded on the field.

In the face of his crushing defeat Hooker issued another address to his army.

He boldly announced from his safe retreat beyond the banks of the river:

"The Major-General commanding tenders to the army his congratulations on its achievements of the last seven days. If it has not accomplished all that was expected the reasons are well known to the army. It is sufficient to say, that they were of a character not to be foreseen or prevented by human sagacity or resources.

"In withdrawing from the south bank of the Rappahannock

before delivering a general battle to our adversaries, the army has given renewed evidence of its confidence in itself and its fidelity to the principles it represents.

"Profoundly loyal and conscious of its strength, the Army of the Potomac will give or decline battle whenever its interests or honor may command it.

"By the celerity and secrecy of our movements, our advance and passage of the river was undisputed, and on our withdrawal not a rebel dared to follow us. The events of the last week may well cause the heart of every officer and soldier of the army to swell with pride!"

The heart of the North quickly swelled with such pride that the President was forced to remove General Hooker and appoint General George Meade to his command.

While the South was celebrating the wonderful achievement of their now invincible army, Lee's greatest general lay dying at a little farm house a few miles from the scene of his immortal achievement. Jackson had been accidentally wounded by a volley from his own men fired by his orders.

His wound was not supposed to be fatal and arrangements were made for his removal to Richmond when he was suddenly stricken with pneumonia and rapidly sank. He lifted his eyes to his physician and calmly said:

"If I live, it will be for the best—and if I die, it will be for the best; God knows and directs all things for the best."

His last moments were marked with expressions of his abiding faith in the wisdom and love of the God he had faithfully served.

Yet his spirit was still on the field of battle. In the delirium which preceded death his voice rang in sharp command:

"Tell Major Hawkes to send forward provisions to the men!"

His head sank and a smile lighted his rugged face. In low tender tones be gasped his last words on earth:

"Let us cross over the river and rest under the shade of the trees."

So passed the greatest military genius our race has produced—the man who never met defeat. His loss was mourned not only by the South but by the world. His death extinguished a light on the shores of Time.

The leading London paper said of him:

"That mixture of daring and judgment which is the mark of

heaven-born generals distinguished him beyond any man of his age. The blows he struck at the enemy were as terrible and decisive as those of Bonaparte himself."

Thousands followed him in sorrow to the grave. The South was bathed in tears.

Lee realized that he had lost his right arm and yet, undaunted, he marshaled his legions and girded his loins for an invasion of Northern soil.

33: THE ACCUSATION

Captain Welford had entered the Secret Service of the Confederacy believing firmly that Socola was a Federal spy. He would not make known his suspicions until he had secured evidence on which to demand his arrest.

This evidence he found most difficult to secure. For months he had watched the handsome foreigner with the patience of a hound. He had taken particular pains to hold Jennie's friendship in order to be thrown with Socola on every possible occasion. His men from the Secret Service Department had followed Socola's every movement day and night with no results.

He pretended the most philosophic acceptance of the situation and bantered the lovers with expressions of his surprise that an early marriage had not been announced.

Socola received the Captain's professions of friendship with no sign of suspicion. He read Dick's mind as an open book. He saw through his pretentions and the tragic purpose which underlay his good-natured banter. He knew instinctively that his movements were watched and moved with the utmost caution. For a time he found it impossible to visit the house on Church Hill. Detectives were on his heels the moment he turned his steps to that hill.

The boarding house in which he lived was watched day and night. And yet so carefully had he executed his work the men who were hounding him were completely puzzled. They could not know, of course, that Socola had chosen as his secretary a man in the Department of State. This man he had involved in his conspiracy so completely and hopelessly from the first interview that there was no retreat. He had risked his own life on his judgment of character the day he made his first proposition. But his estimate had proven correct. The fellow blustered and then accepted the bribe and entered with enthusiasm into his service.

Through this clerk the wily director of the Federal Bureau of Information was compelled now to communicate with Miss Van Lew. Socola had secured his services in the nick of time. He had been an old friend of the Van Lew family before the war, their people were distantly related and no suspicion could attach to his visits to her house unless made at an unusual hour.

It was nearly a year from the day he began his watch before Captain Welford succeeded in connecting the stenographer in the Department of State with the woman on Church Hill.

He had been quietly studying "Crazy Bet" for months. From the first he had accused this woman of being a spy. The older men in the Department laughed. Miss Van Lew was the standard joke of the amateurs who entered the Service. The older men all knew that she was a harmless fool whose mind had been unbalanced by her love for negroes and her abolition ideas.

With characteristic stubbornness Dick refused to accept their decision and set about in his own way to watch her. She was in the habit now of making more and more frequent trips to Libby Prison, carrying flowers and delicacies to the Northern prisoners. Dick had observed the use of an old fashioned French platter with an extremely thick bottom. He called the attention of the guard to this platter.

The keen ears of the woman had heard it mentioned. The double bottom at that moment was harmless. The messages she had carried to the prisoners had all been taken from their hiding place and the platter returned to her through the bars.

She hurried home before the guard could make up his mind to examine the contrivance. The next day Dick was on the watch. The Captain whispered to the guard who halted "Crazy Bet" at the door.

"I'll have to examine that thing," he said sharply.

"Take it then!" she said with a foolish laugh.

She slipped the old shawl from around it and suddenly plumped the platter squarely into the guard's hands. The double bottom that day was filled with boiling water.

"Hell fire!" the guard yelled, dropping the platter with a crash.

He blew on his fingers and let her pick it up and pass on.

The woman had fooled the guard completely, but she had not been so successful with Dick. The trick was too smoothly done. No woman with an unbalanced mind would have been capable of it.

With extraordinary care the Captain followed her through the crowded streets and saw her pass Socola in front of the Custom

House. No sign of recognition was made by either, but he saw the stenographer stoop and pick up something from the edge of the sidewalk.

He would have thought nothing of such an act had he not been following this woman on whom his suspicions had been fixed. He leaped at once to the truth.

Miss Van Lew had dropped a cypher message and Socola had taken it.

He watched her again the next day, and, suddenly turning the corner of an obscure street, saw Socola speak to her in low quick tones, raising his voice on his appearance to an idle conventional greeting.

He passed them without apparently noticing anything unusual and hurried to his office with his suspicions now a burning certainty. He had only to wait his opportunity to trap his quarry in the possession of a dispatch that would send him to the gallows.

His evidence was not yet sufficient to ask for his arrest. It was sufficient to convince Jennie Barton whose loyalty to the South was so intense she would not walk on the same side of the street with Miss Van Lew.

He rushed to the Barton house.

Jennie saw before he spoke that he bore a message of tragic import.

"What is it, Dick?" she asked under her breath. "Why do you look at me so?"

"Jennie," he began seriously, "you are sure that you love the South?"

"Don't ask me idiotic questions," she answered sternly; "what are you driving at?"

"If I prove to you that the man to whom you have pledged your love is an impostor—"

She lifted her head in a gesture of cold protest.

"I thought we had settled that question."

"But you must listen to me," he went on with calm persistence. "If I prove to you that this man is a Federal spy—"

Jennie broke into a laugh.

"I can't get mad at you—you're such a big clumsy goose—"

"I said if I prove it—"

There was no mistaking the fact that he was in dead earnest.

The girl's face went white and her eyes took on a hard glitter.

"Now, Dick Welford, that you've said it—you've got to prove it—"

The Captain lifted his hand solemnly.

"I'll prove it. You know Miss Van Lew, the old abolitionist on Church

Hill?—"

"I don't know that such a creature walks the earth."

"You've heard of her?"

"Yes."

"You know that she is a traitor to her own people?"

"I've heard it."

The Captain paused and looked straight at her with searching gaze.

"I just ran into Socola talking to this woman—"

"Is that all?"

"No."

"What else?"

"Yesterday I saw them pass each other on Main Street. Socola stooped and picked up something from the pavement—"

"Something she dropped?"

"I'm sure of it—"

"But you didn't see her drop it?"

"No—"

"How can you be so absurd!"

"You don't believe what I tell you?"

"But it proves nothing—"

"To me, it's as plain as day—"

"Because you hate him. I'm ashamed of you, Dick."

"Mark my words, I'll prove it before I'm through."

"I'll give you the chance now—that's his knock on the front door—"

"I'd rather not make my accusation today—"

"You've made it to me."

"You're a loyal Southern girl. I had the right to make it to you."

The girl laughed.

"And I'll demand of him an explanation—"

Before he could protest Socola walked into the room and grasped Jennie's hand.

"Captain Welford," she laughed, "has just accused you of hobnobbing with the enemy on the streets—what explanation can you offer?"

"Need I explain?" he asked lightly.

"Miss Van Lew is a suspicious character."

"That's my excuse, I fear. She is a character. I've been curious to know if she is really sane. I stopped her on the street and asked her a question. Is it forbidden in Richmond?"

He spoke with easy convincing carelessness.

Jennie smiled.

"Captain Welford evidently thinks so—"

"And you?"

"I am quite satisfied with your explanation—"

Dick took a step closer and faced his enemy.

"Well, I'm not Signor Socola—if that's your name—"

"Dick!" Jennie interrupted angrily.

The Captain ignored the interruption, holding the eye of the man he hated.

"You spoke to that woman in low quick tones—"

"Your imagination is vivid, Captain—"

Dick squared his jaw into Socola's face.

"It's vivid enough to see through you. I'm going to wring your neck before we're through with this thing—"

Jennie thrust her trembling figure between the two men and confronted Dick.

"How dare you insult the man I love in my presence, Dick Welford?"

"Because I love the South better than my life and you do, too, Jennie Barton—"

The girl's eyes flashed with rage.

"Leave this room, sir!"

Dick still faced Socola.

"Get out of this town tonight—or I'll wring your neck, you damned spy!"

"Leave this room, Dick Welford!" Jennie repeated.

The Captain turned and left without even a glance over his broad shoulders.

"I couldn't strike him in your presence, dear," Socola apologized.

"You behaved splendidly. I'm proud of your perfect poise and mastery of yourself. Our Southern men splutter easily."

Socola took her hand and pressed it.

"You don't believe this?"

"I'd sooner doubt my own heart—I'd sooner doubt God—"

"I'll prove to you that I'm worthy of your love," he murmured gently.

He knelt that night and tried to ask God to show him the way. His heart was rising in fierce rebellion at the deception into which he had entrapped himself. And yet never had his country's need been so bitter and the service he was rendering so priceless. He rose at last with face stern and pale. He would fight to the end.

34: THE TURN OF THE TIDE

The death of Jackson was to Jefferson Davis an appalling disaster. He had never seriously believed the Southern people could win their unequal struggle against the millions of the North backed by their inexhaustible resources until the achievements of Lee and Jackson had introduced a new element into the conflict. So resistless and terrible had become the effective war power of Southern soldiers led by these two men whose minds moved in such harmony with each other and with their Chief in Richmond that the South at last was in sight of success.

The impossible had been accomplished. Anything now seemed possible. Jackson's death had destroyed this new equation of war.

Davis' faith in Jackson was in every way equal to Lee's and Lee but once refused to follow Jackson's lead in his veto on his Lieutenant's plan to annihilate Burnside's army at Fredericksburg.

When the report reached Richmond that Jackson was dying Davis was inconsolable.

The whole evening the President of the Confederacy shut himself in his room—unable to think of anything save the impending calamity. When the end was sure he sent with his own hand the handsomest flag in Richmond in which to wrap his body.

When Davis gazed on the white, cold, rugged features, the tears were streaming down his hollow cheeks. He bent low and the tears fell on the face of the dead.

When an officer of the Government came to the President's Mansion where the body lay in state to consult him on a matter of importance, the Confederate Chieftain stared at his questioner in a dazed sort of way and remained silent.

Lifting his haggard face at last he said in pathetic tones:

"You must excuse me, my friend, I am staggering from a dreadful blow—I cannot think—"

Three days and nights the endless procession passed the bier and paid their tribute of adoration and love. And when he was borne to his last resting place through the streets of the city, the sidewalks, the windows and the housetops were a throbbing mass of weeping women and men.

Jefferson Davis was perhaps the only man in the South in a position to realize the enormous loss which the Confederacy had sustained in the death of Lee's great lieutenant.

The Southern people who gloried in Jackson's deeds had as yet no real appreciation of the services he had rendered. They could not realize their loss until events should prove that no man could be found to take his place.

The brilliant victory of Chancellorsville, following so closely on Fredericksburg, had lifted the Confederacy to the heights.

In the West the army had held its own. The safety of Vicksburg was not seriously questioned. General Bragg confronted Rosecrans with an army so strong he dared not attack it and yet not strong enough to drive Rosecrans from Tennessee.

Two campaigns were discussed with Davis.

The members of his Cabinet, who regarded the possession of Vicksburg and the continued grip on the Mississippi River vital to the life of the Confederacy, were alarmed at Grant's purpose to fight his way to this stronghold and take it.

They urged that Lee's army be divided and half of it sent immediately to reinforce Bragg. With this force in the West Rosecrans could be crushed and Grant driven from his design of opening the Mississippi.

Lee, flushed with his victories, naturally objected to the weakening of his army by such a division. He proposed a more daring and effective way of relieving Vicksburg.

He would raise his army to eighty-five thousand men, clear Virginia of the enemy and sweep into Pennsylvania, carry the war into the North, forage on its rich fields, capture Harrisburg and march on Washington.

Davis did not wish to risk this invasion of Northern soil. But his situation was peculiar. His relations with Lee had been remarkable for their perfect accord. They had never differed on an essential point of political or military strategy. Davis' pride in Lee's genius was unbounded, his confidence in his judgment perfect.

Lee was absolutely sure that his army raised to eighty-five thousand effective men could go anywhere on the continent and do anything within human power. He had crushed McClellan's army of two hundred thousand with seventy-five thousand men, and driven him from his entrenchments at Richmond down the Peninsula. With sixty thousand he had crushed Pope and hurled his army into the entrenchments at Washington, a bleeding, disorganized mob. With sixty-two thousand he had cut to pieces Burnside's hundred and thirteen thousand. With fifty thousand he had rolled up Hooker's host of one hundred and thirty thousand in a scroll of flame and death and flung them across the Rappahannock.

His fame filled the world. His soldiers worshiped him. At his command they would charge the gates of hell with their bare hands. His soldiers were seasoned veterans in whose prowess he had implicit faith. His faith was not a guess. It was founded on achievements so brilliant there was scarcely room for a doubt.

Lee succeeded in convincing Davis that he could invade the North, live on its rich fields and win a battle which would open the way, not only to save Vicksburg from capture, but secure the peace and independence of the South.

A single great victory on Northern soil with his army threatening Washington would make peace a certainty. Davis was quick to see the logic of Lee's plan. It was reasonable. It was a fair risk. And yet the dangers were so enormous he consented with reluctance.

Reagan, the Western member of his Cabinet, urged with all the eloquence of his loyal soul the importance of holding intact the communications with the territory beyond the Mississippi. He begged and pleaded for the plan to reinforce Bragg and play the safe game with Vicksburg. Davis listened to his advice with the utmost respect and weighed each point with solemn sense of his responsibility.

The one point he made last he tried to drive home in a sharp personal appeal.

"You cannot afford, Mr. President," he urged with vehemence, "to further expose your own people of Mississippi to the ravages of such men as now control the invading army. They have laid your own home waste. The people of Vicksburg are your neighbors. They know you personally. The people of this territory have sent their sons and brothers into Virginia by thousands. There are no soldiers left to defend them—"

The President lifted his thin hand in protest.

"I can't let the personal argument sway me, Reagan. Our own people must endure what is best for the cause. All I wish to know is what is best—your plan or General Lee's."

Lee persuaded him against his personal judgment to consent to the daring scheme of Northern invasion.

So intent was Reagan on the plan of direct relief to Vicksburg that after Lee had begun his preparations for the advance, Davis called a Cabinet meeting and reconsidered the whole question. Reagan pleaded with tears at last for what he knew his Chief felt to be best. Davis weighed for the second time each point with care and again decided that Lee's plan promised the greater end—peace.

The moment his final decision was made Davis at once commissioned Vice President Alexander H. Stephens, who knew Lincoln personally, to go to Washington to make the proposition for an armistice and begin the negotiations for a permanent peace on the day Lee should make good his promise.

The letter with which Stephens started to Washington asked on its face that the President of the United States arrange for an exchange of prisoners which would be prompt and effective and prevent all suffering by Northern men in Southern climates and Southern men in Northern prisons. Davis had asked again and again that all prisoners be exchanged. The Federal War Department had obstructed this exchange until thousands of Northern soldiers crowded the prisons of the South and it was impossible for the Confederate authorities to properly care for them. Medicine had been made contraband of war by the North and the simplest remedies could not be had for the Confederate soldiers or their prisoners. Behind this humane purpose of Stephens' mission lay the bigger proposition, which was a verbal one, to propose peace on Lee's victory on Northern soil.

Lee's army lay on the plains of Culpeper during the beautiful month of May. The vast field was astir with the feverish breath of preparations for the grand march. Trains rushed to the front loaded with munitions of war. New batteries of artillery with the finest equipment ever known were added to his army. The ordnance trains were packed to their capacity. His troops were better equipped than ever before in the history of the war. Every department of the huge, pitiless machine was running like clockwork.

Fifteen thousand cavalry were reviewed at Brandy Station led by Stuart's waving plume—Stuart, the matchless leader who had twice ridden round a hostile army of a hundred thousand men. Crowds of cheering women watched this wonderful pageant and waved their handkerchiefs to the handsome young cavalier as he passed on his magnificent horse draped with garlands of flowers.

It required an entire week to review the cavalry, infantry, and artillery.

On June the first, the advance began.

Ewell's corps, once commanded by Jackson, led the way. They swung rapidly through the Blue Ridge Mountains, into the Valley and suddenly pounced on General Milroy at Winchester. Milroy with a few of his officers escaped through the Confederate lines at night and succeeded in crossing the Potomac at Harper's Ferry. Ewell captured three thousand prisoners, thirty pieces of artillery, a hundred wagons and great stores. Seven hundred more men were taken at Martinsburg.

On June twenty-seventh, the whole of Lee's army was encamped at Chambersburg in Pennsylvania in striking distance of the Capital of the State.

The execution of this march had been a remarkable piece of strategy. He had completely baffled the Northern Commanders, spread terror through the North and precipitated the wildest panic in Washington.

Within twenty-odd days the Southern General had brought his forces from Fredericksburg, Virginia, confronted by an army of one hundred thousand men, through the Blue Ridge, and the Shenandoah Valley into Pennsylvania. He had done this in the face of one of the most powerful and best equipped armies the North had put into the field. He had swept the hostile garrisons at Winchester, Martinsburg and Harper's Ferry into his prisons and camped in Pennsylvania without his progress being once arrested or a serious battle forced upon him. He had cleared Virginia of the army which threatened Richmond and they were rushing breathlessly after him in a desperate effort to save the Capital of Pennsylvania.

So far Lee had made good every prediction on which he had based his plan of campaign.

Davis felt so sure that he would make good his promised victory that he hurriedly dispatched Stephens to Fortress Monroe under a flag of truce and asked for a safe conduct for his Commissioner to Washington.

In alarm the Governors of Ohio, Pennsylvania, New York, Maryland, and West Virginia called out their militia. Lee was not deterred by their panic. He knew that those raw troops would cut no figure in the swift and terrible drama which was being staged among the ragged crags around Gettysburg. The veteran armies of the North and South would decide the issue. If he won, he would brush aside the militia as so many school boys and march into Washington.

Meade was rushing his army after his antagonist with feverish haste. His advance guard struck Lee before the town of Gettysburg on July first, 1863. A desperate struggle ensued. Neither Meade nor Lee had yet reached the field.

Within a mile of the town the Confederates made a sudden and united charge and smashed the Federal line into atoms. General Reynolds, their Commander, was killed and his army driven headlong into the streets of Gettysburg. Ewell, charging through the town, swept all before him and took five thousand prisoners.

The crowded masses of fugitives, fleeing for their lives, passed out of the town and rushed up the slopes of the hills beyond.

At five o'clock Lee halted his men until the rest of his army should reach the field.

During the night General Meade rallied his disorganized men, poured his fresh troops among them and entrenched his army on the heights where his defeated advance guard had taken refuge.

Had Lee withdrawn the next morning when he scanned those hills which looked down on him through bristling brows of brass and iron the history of the Confederacy might have been longer. It could not have been more illustrious.

His reasons for assault were sound. To his council of war he was explicit.

"I had not intended, gentlemen," he said, "to fight a general battle at such distance from our base, unless attacked by the enemy. We find ourselves confronted by the Federal army. It is difficult to withdraw through the mountains with our large trains. The country is unfavorable for collecting supplies while in the presence of the main body of the enemy as he can restrain our foraging parties by occupying the mountain passes. The battle is in a measure unavoidable. We have won a great victory today. We can defeat Meade's army in spite of these hills."

When Lee surveyed the heights of Gettysburg again on the morning of the second of July, he saw that the Northerners held a position of extraordinary power. Yet his men were flushed with victory after victory. They had swept their foe before them in the first encounter as chaff before a storm. They were equal to anything short of a miracle.

He ordered Longstreet to hurl his corps against Cemetery Ridge and drive the enemy from his key position before the entrenchments could be completed.

Longstreet was slow. Jackson would have struck with the rapidity of lightning. On this swift action Lee had counted. The blow should have been delivered before eight o'clock. It was two o'clock in the afternoon before Longstreet made the attack and Meade's position had been made stronger each hour.

From two o'clock until dark the long lines of gray rolled and dashed against the heights and broke in red pools of blood on their rocky slopes.

Three hundred pieces of artillery thundered their message in an Oratorio of Death. The earth shook. Hills and rocks danced and reeled before the excited vision of the onrushing men. For two hours the guns roared and thundered without pause. The shriek of shell, the crash of falling trees, the showers of flying rocks ripped from cliffs by solid shot, the shouts of charging hosts, the splash of bursting shrapnel, the neighing of torn and mangled horses, transformed the green hills of Pennsylvania into a smoke-wreathed, flaming hell. The living lay down that night to sleep with their heads pillowed on the dead.

On this second day Lee's men had gained a slight advantage. They had taken Round Top and held it for two hours. They had at least proven that it could be done. They had driven in the lines on the Federal left. The Southern Commander still believed his men could do the impossible. Longstreet begged his Chief that night to withdraw and choose another field. Lee ordered the third day's fight.

On his gray horse he watched Pickett lead his immortal charge and fall back down the hill.

He rode quietly to the front, rallying the broken lines. He made no speech. He uttered no bombast.

He calmly lifted his hand and cried:

"Never mind—boys!"

To his officers he said:

"It's all my fault. We'll talk it over afterward. Let every good man rally now."

His army had never known a panic. The men quietly fell into line and cheered their Commander.

To an English officer on the field Lee quietly said:

"This has been a sad day for us, Colonel—a sad day; but we can't expect always to gain victories."

Lee had lost twenty thousand men and fourteen generals. Meade had lost twenty-three thousand men and seventeen generals. Lee withdrew his army across the swollen Potomac, carrying away his guns and all the prisoners he had taken.

General Meade had saved the North, but Lee's army was still intact, on its old invincible lines in Virginia, sixty-five thousand strong.

The news from Gettysburg crushed the soul of Davis. He had hoped with this battle to end the war, and stop the frightful slaughter of our noblest men, North and South. His Commissioner, Alexander H. Stephens, was halted at Fortress Monroe and sent back to Richmond with an insulting answer.

So bitter was Lee's disappointment that he offered his resignation to Davis.

The President at once wrote a generous letter in which he renewed the expressions of his confidence in the genius of his Commanding General and begged him to guard his precious life from undue exposure.

Gettysburg was but one of the appalling calamities which crushed the hopes of the Confederate Chieftain on this memorable fourth of July, 1863.

On the recovery of Joseph E. Johnston from his wound at Seven Pines he was assigned to the old command of Albert Sidney Johnston in the West. His department included the States of Tennessee,

Mississippi, Alabama, Georgia and North Carolina.

He entered on the duties of his new and important field—complaining, peevish, sulking.

On the day before his departure Mrs. Davis visited his wife and expressed to General Johnston the earnest wish of her heart for her husband's success.

"I sincerely hope, General," she said cordially, "that your campaign will be brilliant and successful."

The General pursed the hard lines of his mouth.

"I might succeed if I had Lee's chances with the army of Northern Virginia."

From the moment Johnston reached his field he began to quarrel with his generals and complain to the Government at Richmond. He made no serious effort to unite his forces for the defense of Vicksburg and continuously wrote and telegraphed to the War Department that his authority was inadequate to really command so extended a territory. He made no effort to throw the twenty-four thousand men he commanded into a juncture with Pemberton who was struggling valiantly against Grant's fifty thousand closing in on the doomed city.

On May eighteenth, Johnston sent a courier to Pemberton and advised him to evacuate Vicksburg without a fight! Pemberton held a council of war and refused to give up the Mississippi River without a struggle. Johnston sat down in his tent and left him to his fate.

Grant closed in on Vicksburg and the struggle began. Pemberton could not believe that Johnston would not march to his relief.

Women and children stood by their homes amid the roar of guns and the bursting of shells. Caves were dug in the hills and they took refuge under the ground.

A shell burst before a group of children hurrying from their homes to the hills. The dirt thrown up from the explosion knocked three little fellows down, but luckily no bones were broken. They jumped up, brushed their clothes, wiped the dirt from their eyes, and hurried on without a whimper.

When the dark days of starvation came, the women nursed the sick and wounded, lived on mule and horse meat and parched corn.

Johnston continued to send telegrams to the War Department

saying he needed more troops and didn't know where to get them. Yet he was in absolute command of all the troops in his department and could order them to march at a moment's notice in any direction he wished. He hesitated and continued to send telegrams and write letters for more explicit instructions.

He got them finally in a direct peremptory order from the War Department.

On June fifteenth, he telegraphed his Government:

"I consider saving Vicksburg hopeless."

Davis ordered his Secretary of War to reply immediately in unmistakable language:

"Your telegram grieves and alarms us, Vicksburg must not be lost without a struggle. The interest and honor of the Confederacy forbid it. I rely on you to avert this loss. If better resource does not offer you must hazard attack. It may be made in concert with the garrison, if practicable, but otherwise without. By day or night as you think best."

The Secretary of War, brooding in anxiety over the possibility of Johnston's timidity in the crisis, again telegraphed him six days later:

"Only my convictions of almost imperative necessity for action induced the official dispatch I have sent you. On every ground I have great deference to your judgment and military genius, but I feel it right to share, if need be to take the responsibility and leave you free to follow the most desperate course the occasion may demand. Rely upon it, the eyes and hopes of the whole Confederacy are upon you, with the full confidence that you will act, and with the sentiment that it were better to fail nobly daring, than through prudence even to be inactive. I rely on you for all possible to save Vicksburg."

On June twenty-seventh, Grant telegraphed Washington:

"Joe Johnston has postponed his attack until he can receive ten thousand reinforcements from Bragg's army. They are expected early next week. I feel strong enough against this increase and do not despair of having Vicksburg before they arrive."

Pemberton's army held Vicksburg practically without food for forty-seven days. His brave men were exposed to blistering suns and drenching rains and confined to their trenches through every hour of the night. They had reached the limit of human endurance and were now physically too weak to attempt a sortie. Johnston still sat in his tent writing letters and telegrams to Richmond.

Pemberton surrendered his garrison to General Grant on July fourth, and the Mississippi was opened to the Federal fleet from its mouth to its source.

Grant telegraphed to Washington:

> The enemy surrendered this morning. General Sherman will face immediately on Johnston and drive him from the State.

But the great letter writer did not wait for Sherman to face him. He immediately abandoned the Capital of Mississippi and retreated into the interior.

In the fall of Vicksburg, the Confederacy had suffered a most appalling calamity—not only had the Mississippi River been opened to the Federal gunboats, but Grant had captured twenty-four thousand prisoners of war, including three Major Generals and nine Brigadiers, ninety pieces of artillery and forty thousand small arms.

The Johnston clique at Richmond made this disaster the occasion of fierce assaults on Jefferson Davis and fresh complaints of the treatment of their favorite General. The dogged persistence with which this group of soreheads proclaimed the infallibility of the genius of the weakest and most ineffective general of the Confederacy was phenomenal. The more miserable Johnston's failures the louder these men shouted his praises. The yellow journals of the South continued to praise this sulking old man until half the people of the Confederacy were hoodwinked into believing in his greatness.

The results of this Johnston delusion were destined to bear fatal fruit in the hour of the South's supreme trial.

35: SUSPICION

Jennie Barton had refused to listen to Captain Welford's accusation of treachery against her lover but the seed of suspicion had been planted. It grew with such rapidity her peace of mind was utterly destroyed.

In vain she put the ugly thought aside.

"It's impossible!" she murmured a hundred times only to come back to the idea that would not down.

Night after night she tossed on her pillow unable to sleep. The longer she faced the problem of Socola's character and antecedents the more probable became the truth of Dick's suspicions. She had made his present position in the State Department possible.

Again her love rose in rebellion. "It's a lie—a lie!" she sobbed. "I won't believe it. Dick's crazy jealousy's at the bottom of it all—"

Why had Socola buried himself in the Department of State so completely since the scene with Dick? His calls had been brief. Their relations had been strained in spite of her honest effort to put them back on the old footing.

He gave as his excuse for not calling oftener the enormous pressure of work which the crisis of the invasion of Pennsylvania had brought to his office. The excuse was valid. But perfect love would find a way. It should need no excuse.

There was something wrong. She realized it now with increasing agony. Unable to endure the strain she sent for Socola.

Their meeting was awkward. She made no effort to apologize or smooth things over. Her attitude was instinctive. She gave her feelings full rein.

She fixed on him a steady searching gaze.

"It's useless for me to try to pretend, my love. There's something wrong between us."

"Your mind has been poisoned," was the quick, serious answer. "Thoughts are things. They have the power to kill or give life. A poisonous idea has been planted in your soul. It's killing your love for me. I feel it—and I'm helpless."

"You can cast it out," she answered tenderly.

"How?"

"Tell me frankly and honestly the whole story of your life—"

"You believe me an impostor?"

"I love you—"

"And that is not enough?"

"No. Make suspicion impossible. You can do this—if you are innocent as I believe you are—"

She paused and a sob caught her voice.

"Oh, my love, it's killing me—I can neither eat nor sleep. Show me that such a thing is impossible—"

He took her hand.

"How foolish, my own, to ask this of me—we love right or wrong. Love is the fulfillment of the law. You call me here to cross-examine me—"

"No—no—dear heart—just to have you soothe my fears and make me laugh again—"

"But how is it possible—once this thought has found its way into your mind? If I am a spy, as your Captain Welford says, it is my business to deceive the enemy. I couldn't tell the truth and live in Richmond. I would swing from the nearest limb if I should be discovered—"

Jennie covered her face with her hands:

"Don't—don't—please—"

"Can't you see how useless such a question?"

"You can't convince me?" she asked pathetically.

"I won't try," he said firmly. "You must trust me because you love me. Nothing I could say could convince you—"

He paused and held her hands in a desperate clasp—

"Trust me, dear—I promise in good time to convince you that I am all your heart has told you—"

"You must convince me now—or I'll die," she sobbed.

"You're asking the impossible—"

He stroked her hand with tender touch, rose and led her to the door.

"You'll try to trust me?"

There was an unreal sound in her voice as Jennie slowly replied:

"Yes—I'll try."

Socola hurried to the house on Church Hill and dispatched a

courier on a mission of tragic importance. Kilpatrick and Dahlgren were preparing to capture Richmond by a daring raid of three thousand cavalrymen.

Jennie watched him go with the determination to know the truth at all hazards.

36: THE FATAL DEED

The battle of Gettysburg and the disaster of the fall of Vicksburg once more gave to the Johnston junta in the Confederate Congress their opportunity to harass the President.

Their power for evil had been greatly diminished by the pressure of the swiftly moving tragedy of the war.

The appearance of this Congress was curiously plain and uninteresting. With the exception of J. L. M. Curry of Alabama and Barksdale of Mississippi there was not a man among them of constructive ability as a statesman. Foote of Tennessee was noted for his high-flown English, his endless harangues and his elaborate historical illustrations. Had his ability been equal to the intensity of his hatred for Davis he would have been a dangerous man to the administration. James Lyons of Virginia stood six feet three in his stockings, had fine, even, white teeth, and was considered the handsomest man in the assembly.

Yancey, the fierce, uncompromising agitator of secession, was too violent to command the influence to which his genius entitled him.

Senator Barton, fierce, impatient, bombastic, had long ago exhausted the vocabulary of invective and could only repeat himself in descending anti-climax.

Hill of Georgia was a young man of ability who gave promise of greater things under more favorable conditions.

The real business of this Congress was transacted in secret executive sessions. When the public was admitted, the people of Richmond generally looked on with contempt. They sneeringly referred to them as "the College Debating Society, on Capitol Hill."

The surroundings of their halls added to the impression of inefficiency—dingy, dirty and utterly lacking in the luxuries which the mind associates with the exercise of sovereign power.

The Senate was forced to find quarters in the third story of the "State House." There was no gallery and the spectators were separated from the members by an improvised railing. The only difference noticeable between the Senators and the spectators was that the members had seats and the listeners and loafers had standing room only behind the rail.

The House of Representatives had a better chamber. But its walls were bare of ornament or paintings, its chairs were uncushioned, its desks dingy and slashed with pocket knives. Its members sat with their heels in the air and their bodies sprawled in every conceivable attitude of ugly indifference.

The heart and brains of the South were on the field of battle—her noblest sons destined to sleep in unmarked graves.

The scenes of personal violence which disgraced the sittings of this nondescript body of law makers did much to relieve the President of the burden of their hostility.

Foote of Tennessee provoked an encounter with Judge Dargan of Alabama which came near a tragic ending. The Judge was an old man of eccentric dress, much given to talking to himself—particularly as he wandered about the streets of Richmond. The gallery of the House loved him from the first for his funny habit of scratching his arm when the itch of eloquence attacked him. And he always addressed the Speaker as "Mr. Cheerman." They loved him particularly for that. The eccentric Judge had a peculiarly fierce antipathy to Foote. Words of defiance had passed between them on more than one occasion. The House was in secret night session. The Judge was speaking.

Foote sitting near, glanced up at his enemy and muttered:

"Damned old scoundrel—"

The Judge's gray head suddenly lifted, he snatched a bowie knife from his pocket and dashed for the man who had insulted him.

From every direction rose the shouts and cries of the excited House.

"Stop him!"

"Hold him!"

"Great God!"

"Judge—Judge!"

The wildest uproar followed. Half a dozen members threw themselves on the old man, dragged him to the floor, pinned him down and wrested the knife from his grasp.

When the eloquent gentleman from Tennessee saw that his assailant was disarmed and safely guarded by six stalwart men he struck an attitude, expanded his chest, smote it with both hands and exclaimed with melodramatic gusto:

"I defy the steel of the assassin!"

The House burst into shouts of uncontrollable laughter, and adjourned for the night.

Another scene of more tragic violence occurred in the Senate—a hand to hand fight between William L. Yancey and Ben Hill. The Senator from Georgia threw his antagonist across a desk, held him there in a grip of steel and pounded his face until dragged away by friends. Yancey's spine was wrenched in the struggle, and it was rumored that this injury caused his death. It possibly hastened the end already sure from age, disease and careless living.

Committees from this assembly of law makers who attempted to instruct the conscientious, hard-working man of genius the Southern people had made their President found little comfort in their efforts.

Davis received them with punctilious ceremony. His manners were always those of a gentleman—but he never allowed them to return to their onerous work in the Debating Society without a clear idea of his views. They were never expressed with violence. But the ice sometimes formed on the window panes if he stood near while talking.

A Congressional Committee were demanding the restoration of Beauregard to command.

"General Beauregard asked me to relieve him, gentlemen—"

"Only on furlough for illness," interrupted the Chairman.

"And you have forced him into retirement!" added a member.

The President rose, walked to the window, gazed out on the crowded street for a moment and turned, suddenly confronting his tormentors. He spoke with quiet dignity, weighing each word with cold precision:

"If the whole world asked me to restore General Beauregard to the command which I have given to Braxton Bragg, I would refuse."

He resumed his seat and the Committee retired to Senator Barton's house where they found a sympathetic ear.

Bragg was preparing to fight one of the greatest battles of the war. At Chickamauga, the "River of Death," he encountered Rosecrans. At the end of two days of carnage the Union army was totally routed, right, left, and center and hurled back from Georgia into Chattanooga. Polk's wing captured twenty-eight pieces of artillery and Longstreet's twenty-one. Eight thousand prisoners of war were taken, fifteen thousand stand of arms and forty regimental colors.

Rosecrans' army of eighty thousand men was literally cut to pieces by Bragg's fifty thousand Southerners. No more brilliant achievement of military genius illumines history. Chickamauga was in every way as desperate a battle as Arcola—and in all Napoleon's Italian campaigns nothing more daring and wonderful was accomplished by the Man of Destiny.

Bragg had justified the faith of Davis. Rosecrans was hemmed in in Chattanooga, his supplies cut off and his army facing starvation when he was relieved of his command, Thomas succeeding him. Grant was hurried to Chattanooga with two army corps to raise the siege.

With his reinforcements Grant raised the siege, surprised and defeated Bragg's army which had been weakened by the detachment of Longstreet's corps for a movement on Knoxville.

Bragg withdrew his army again into Georgia and resigned his command. The stern, irritable Confederate fighter was disgusted with the constant attacks on him by peanut politicians and refused to hear Davis' plea that he remain at the head of the Western army. The President called him to Richmond and made him his Chief of Staff.

The disaster to the Confederacy at Chattanooga which gave General Grant supreme command of the Union forces, brought to the Johnston junta at Richmond its opportunity to once more press their favorite to the front. Since his Vicksburg fiasco the President had isolated him. Davis resisted this appointment with deep foreboding of its possible disaster to the South.

In the midst of this bitter struggle over the selection of a Western Field Commander, the President of the Confederacy received the first and only recognition of his Government accorded by any European power.

His early education at the St. Thomas Monastery had given the Southern leader a lofty opinion of the Roman Catholic Church. Davis had always seen in the members of this faith in America friends who could not be alienated from the oppressed.

Failing to receive recognition from the great powers of Europe, he dispatched his diplomatic representative to Rome with a carefully worded letter to the Pope in which he expressed his gratitude to Pius IX for his efforts in behalf of peace. The Pope had urged his bishops in New Orleans and New York to strive to end the war.

The Vatican received the Confederate diplomat with every mark of courtesy and every expression of respect accorded the most powerful nations of the world. The Dominican friars had not forgotten the wistful, eager boy they had taught, and loved in Kentucky.

The Pope replied to this communication in an official letter which virtually recognized the Confederacy—both in his capacity as a temporal sovereign and as the head of the Roman Catholic Church.

The President read this letter with renewed hope of favorable action abroad.

"ILLUSTRIOUS AND HONORABLE PRESIDENT:

"Salutation:

"We have just received with all suitable welcome the persons sent by you to place in our hands your letter dated twenty-third of September last.

"Not slight was the pleasure we experienced when we learned from those persons and the letter, with what feelings of joy and gratitude you were animated, illustrious and honorable President, as soon as you were informed of our letters to our venerable brother John, Archbishop of New York, and John, Archbishop of New Orleans, dated the eighteenth of October of last year, and in which we have with all our strength excited and exhorted these venerable brothers, that in their episcopal piety and solicitude, they should endeavor, with the most ardent zeal, and in our name, to bring about the end of the fatal civil war which has broken out in those countries, in order that the American people may obtain peace and concord, and dwell charitably together.

"It is particularly agreeable to us to see that you, illustrious and honorable President, and your good people, are animated with the same desire of peace and tranquillity which we have in our letters inculcated upon our venerable brothers. May it please God at the same time to make the other people of America and their ruler, reflecting seriously how terrible is civil war, and what calamities it engenders, listen to the inspiration of a calm spirit, and adopt resolutely the part of peace.

"As for us, we shall not cease to offer up the most fervent prayers to God Almighty that He may pour out upon all the people of America the Spirit and peace and charity, and that He will stop the great evils which afflict them. We at the same time beseech the God of pity to shed abroad upon you the light of His countenance and attach you to us by a perfect friendship.

"Given at Rome, at St. Peter's, the third of December, 1863, of our Pontificate 18.

"(Signed) Pius IX."

The dark hour was swiftly approaching when the South and her leader would need the prayers of all God's saints.

Failing to persuade Bragg to reconsider his resignation, Davis appointed General Hardee as his successor to command the Western army. Hardee declared the responsibility was more than he could assume.

Under the urgent necessity of driving the Union army back from its position at Chattanooga and heartsick with eternal wrangling of the opposition, Davis reluctantly ordered Joseph E. Johnston personally to assume command of the Army of Tennessee—and the fatal deed was done.

37: THE RAIDERS

In February, 1864, both North and South were straining every nerve for the last act of the grand drama of blood and tears. The Presidential election would be held in November to choose a successor to Abraham Lincoln. At this moment Lincoln was the most unpopular, the most reviled, the most misunderstood and the most abused man who had ever served as President of the United States. The opposition to him inside his own party was fierce, malignant, vindictive and would stop short of nothing to encompass his defeat in their nominating convention. They had not hesitated even to accuse his wife of treason.

Military success and military success alone could save the administration at Washington. George B. McClellan, the most popular general of the Union army, was already slated to oppose Lincoln on a platform demanding peace.

If the South could hold her own until the first Monday in November, the opposition to the war in the North would crush the administration and peace would be had at the price of Southern independence.

No man in America understood the tense situation more clearly than Jefferson Davis. His agents in the North kept him personally informed of every movement of the political chess board. Personally he had never believed in the possibility of the South winning in a conflict of arms since the death of Jackson had been given its full significance in the battle of Gettysburg. He had however believed in the possibility of the party of the North which stood for the old Constitution winning an election on the issue of a bloody and unsuccessful war and, on their winning, that he could open negotiations for peace and gain every point for which the war had been fought. It all depended on the battles of the coming spring and summer.

Grant, the new Commander-in-Chief of the armies of the Union, had been given a free hand with unlimited resources of men and money. He was now directing the movements of nearly a million soldiers in blue.

Sherman was drilling under his orders an army of a hundred thousand with which to march into Georgia—while Grant himself would direct the movement of a quarter of a million men in his invasion of Virginia.

The Confederate President saw at once that Lee's army must be raised to its highest point of efficiency and that it was of equal importance that Joseph E. Johnston should be given as many or more men with which to oppose Sherman.

To allow for Johnston's feeble strategy, Davis sent him 68,000 soldiers to Dalton, Georgia, to meet Sherman's 100,000 and gave Lee 64,000 with which to oppose Grant's 150,000 threatening to cross the Rapidan and move directly on Richmond.

Socola had informed the War Department at Washington that the Confederate Capital had been stripped of any semblance of an effective garrison to fill the ranks of Lee and Johnston.

General Judson Kilpatrick was authorized to select three thousand picked cavalry, dash suddenly on Richmond, capture it and release the 15,000 Union prisoners confined in its walls and stockades.

These prisoners Grant steadily refused to receive in exchange. In vain Davis besought the Federal Government to take them home in return for an equal number of Confederate prisoners who were freezing and dying in the North.

Grant's logic was inexorable. Every Confederate prisoner exchanged and sent back home meant a recruit to Lee's army. It was cruel to leave his men to languish in beleaguered Richmond whose citizens were rioting in the streets for bread, but he figured these prisoners as soldiers dying in battle. The Confederate Government had no medicine for them. The blockade was drawn so tight scarcely an ounce of medicine could be obtained for the Confederate army. Davis offered the Washington Government to let their own surgeons come to Richmond and carry medicine and food to their prisoners. His request was refused.

The only thing Grant conceded was his consent to Kilpatrick's attempt to free and arm these 15,000 prisoners and loose them with fire and sword in the streets of the Confederate Capital.

Little did the men, women and children of Richmond dream that they were lying down each night to sleep on the thin crust of a volcano.

Captain Welford in the pursuit of Socola and Miss Van Lew had found that the woman on Church Hill persisted in her visits to the prisons. Libby, which contained a number of Union officers of rank, was her favorite.

On the last day of February his patient watch was rewarded. He had placed a spy in Libby disguised as a captive Union soldier.

This man had sent the Captain an urgent message to communicate with him at once. Within thirty minutes Welford confronted him in the guardroom of the prison.

The Captain spoke in sharp nervous tones:

"Well?"

"I've something big—"

He paused and glanced about the room.

"Go on!"

"There's a plot on foot inside to escape—"

"Of course. They're always plotting to escape—we've no real prison system—no discipline. Hundreds have escaped already. It's nothing new—"

"This is new," the spy went on eagerly, "They let me into their councils last night. There's going to be a big raid on Richmond—the men inside are going to fight their way out, arm themselves and burn the city. When they get the signal from the outside they'll batter down the walls and rush through—"

"Batter down the walls?"

"Yes, sir—"

"How?"

"They've loosed two big rafters and have them ready to use as battering rams—"

"You're sure of this?"

"Sure's God's in heaven. Go in and see for yourself—"

Captain Welford gave a low whistle.

"This is big news. There are enough prisoners in Richmond to make an army corps—eleven hundred in here—twenty-five hundred at Crew and Pemberton's—at Belle Isle and the other stockades at least fifteen thousand in all. They are guarded by a handful of men. If they realize their power, they can batter their way out in five minutes and sweep the city with blood and fire—"

He stopped suddenly, drew a deep breath and turned again to the man.

"That'll do for you here. Take a little rest. You'd as well go back into a lion's den when they find out that I know. They'd spot you sure and tear you limb from limb."

The spy saluted.

"Report to me a week from today at the office. You've earned a vacation."

The man saluted again and passed quickly out.

Captain Welford asked the Superintendent to call his prisoners together.

"I have something to say to them."

A thousand silent men in blue were gathered in the assembly room of the old warehouse.

Captain Welford boldly entered the place carrying a box in his hand. He placed it on the floor, sprang on it and lifted his hand over the crowd:

"I've an announcement to make, gentlemen," he began quietly amid a silence that was death like. "The Department which I represent has learned that you are planning to batter down the walls and join a force of raiders who are on the way to capture Richmond—"

He paused and a murmur of smothered despair, inarticulate, bitter, crept through the crowd.

"To forestall this little scheme, I have planted a thousand pounds of powder under this building. I have mined every other prison. The first one of you that lifts his finger to escape gives the signal that will blow you into Eternity—"

Dick stepped from the box and made his way out without another word. He could feel the wild heart beat of baffled hope as they followed him to the door with despairing eyes.

A murmur of sickening rage swept the prison. An ominous silence fell where hope had beat high.

The same strategic announcement was made in every prison in Richmond. No mines had been laid. But the story served its purpose. Fifteen thousand men were bound hand and foot by fear. Three hundred soldiers guarded them successfully. Not a finger was lifted to help their bold rescuers who were already dashing toward the city.

Colonel Ulric Dahlgren was crossing the James above Richmond to strike from the south side, while General Kilpatrick led the attack direct from the north, Dahlgren crossed the river at Ely's Ford, passed in the rear of Lee's army, captured a Confederate court martial in session, but missed a park of sixty-eight pieces of artillery which had been left unguarded.

When they again reached the James at Davis' Mill, where a ford was supposed to be, none could be found. Stanton had sent from Washington a negro guide. They accused the negro of treachery and hung him from the nearest limb without the formality of a drumhead court martial.

At dawn on March first, Bradley Johnson's cavalry, guarding Lee's flank, struck one of Kilpatrick's parties and drove them in on the main body. They pursued Kilpatrick's men through Ashland and down to the outer defenses of Richmond.

Here the raiders dismounted their twenty-five hundred men and prepared to attack the entrenchments. Wade Hampton immediately moved out to meet him. Bradley Johnson's Marylanders drew up in Kilpatrick's rear at the same moment, and captured five men bearing dispatches from Dahlgren. He would attack on the rear at sunset. He asked Kilpatrick to strike at the same moment.

Johnson boldly charged Kilpatrick's rear with his handful of men and drove him headlong down the Peninsula to the York River. The Confederate leader had but seventy-five men and two pieces of artillery but he hung on Kilpatrick's division of twenty-five hundred and captured a hundred and forty prisoners.

Dahlgren at night with but four hundred men boldly attacked the defenses on the north side of the city. He was met by a company of Richmond boys under eighteen years of age. The youngsters gave such good account of themselves that he withdrew from the field, leaving forty of his men dead and wounded.

In his retreat down the Peninsula, he failed to find Kilpatrick's division. His command was cut to pieces and captured and Dahlgren himself killed.

The part which Socola had played in this raid was successfully accomplished without a hitch. He was compelled to answer the drum which called every clerk of his Department to arms for the defense of the city. In the darkness he succeeded in pressing into Dahlgren's lines and on his retreat made his way back to his place in the ranks of the Confederates.

It was a little thing which betrayed him after the real danger was past and brought him face to face with Jennie Barton.

38: THE DISCOVERY

From the moment Captain Welford had discovered the plot of the prisoners to cooperate with Kilpatrick and Dahlgren he was morally sure that Miss Van Lew had been their messenger. He was equally sure that Socola had been one of her accomplices.

On the day of the announcement of his powder plant to the prisoners he set a guard to watch the house on Church Hill, and report to him the moment "Crazy Bet" should emerge.

Within two hours he received the message that she was on her way down town with her market basket swinging on her arm. Dick knew that this woman could not recognize him personally. He was only distantly related to the Welfords of Richmond.

Miss Van Lew was in a nervous agony to deliver her dispatch to Kilpatrick, warning him that the purpose of the raid had been discovered and that he must act with the utmost caution. She had no scout at hand and Kilpatrick's was expected every moment at her rendezvous near the market.

Dick turned the corner, circled a block, and met her. She was childishly swinging the basket on her arm and humming a song. She smiled vacantly into his face. He caught the look of shrewd intelligence and saw through her masquerade. A single word from her lips now would send her to the gallows and certainly lead to Socola's arrest.

The Captain was certain that she carried dispatches on her person at that moment. If he could only induce her to drop them, the trick would be turned.

He turned, retraced his steps, overtook her and whispered as he passed:

"Your trusted messenger—"

She paid no attention. There was not the slightest recognition—no surprise—no inquiry. Her thin face was a mask of death.

Was this man Kilpatrick's scout? Or was he a Secret Service man on her trail? The questions seethed through her excited soul. Her life hung on the answer. It was a question of judgment of character and personality. The man was a stranger. But the need was terrible. ShOuld she take the chance?

She quickened her pace and passed Dick.

Again she heard him whisper:

"Your messenger is here. I am going through tonight."

In her hand clasped tight was her dispatch torn into strips and each strip rolled into a tiny ball. ShOuld she commence to drop them one by one?

Perplexed, she stopped and glanced back suddenly into Dick's face. Her decision was instantaneous. The subtle sixth sense had revealed in a flash of his eager eyes her mortal danger. She turned into a side street and hurried home.

The Captain was again baffled by a woman's wit. His disappointment was keen. He had hoped to prove his accusation to Jennie Barton before the sun set. She had ceased to fight his suspicions of Socola. His name was not mentioned. She was watching her lover with more desperate earnestness even than he.

The Captain had failed to entrap the wily little woman with her market basket, but through her he struck the trail of the big quarry he had sought for two years. Socola was imperiled by a woman's sentimental whim—this woman with nerves of steel and a heart whose very throb she could control by an indomitable will.

Heartsick over her failure to get through the lines her warning to Kilpatrick, she had felt the responsibility of young Dahlgren's tragic death. Woman-like she determined, at the risk of her life and the life of every man she knew, to send the body of this boy back to his father in the North.

In vain Socola pleaded against this mad undertaking.

The woman's soul had been roused by the pathetic figure of the daring young raider whose crutches were found strapped to his saddle. He had lost a leg but a few months before.

He had been buried at the cross-roads where he fell—the roads from Stevensville and Mantua Ferry. In pity for the sorrow of his distinguished father Davis had ordered the body disinterred and brought into Richmond. It was buried at night in a spot unknown to anyone save the Confederate authorities. Feeling had run so high on the discovery of the purpose of the raiders to burn the city that the Confederate President feared some shocking indignity might be offered the body.

The night Miss Van Lew selected for her enterprise was cold and dark and the rain fell in dismal, continuous drizzle. The grave had been discovered by a negro who saw the soldiers bury the body. It was identified by the missing right leg.

The work was done without interruption or discovery.

Socola placed the body in Rowley's wagon which was filled with young peach trees concealing the casket. The pickets would be deceived by the simple device. ShOuld one of them thrust his bayonet into the depths of those young trees more than one neck would pay the penalty. But they wouldn't. He was sure of it.

At the picket post Rowley sat in stolid indifference while he heard the order to search his wagon. He engaged the guard in conversation. Wagons entered and passed and still he talked lazily to his chosen friend.

The Lieutenant looked from his tent and yelled at last:

"What 'ell's the matter with you—search that man and let him go—"

"It would be a pity to tear up all those fruit trees!" the guard said with a yawn.

"I didn't think you'd bother 'em," Rowley answered indifferently, "but I know a soldier's duty—"

Another wagon dashed up in a hurry. The guard examined him and he passed on.

Again the Lieutenant called:

"Search that man and let him go!"

Rowley's face was a mask of lazy indifference.

The guard glanced at him and spoke in low tones:

"Your face is guarantee enough, partner—go on—"

Socola flanked the picket and joined Rowley. Near Hungary, on the farm of Orrick the German, a grave was hurriedly dug and the casket placed in it. The women helped to heap the dirt in and plant over it one of the peach trees.

Three days later in response to a pitiful appeal from Dahlgren's father, Davis ordered the boy's body sent to Washington. The grave had been robbed. The sensation this created was second only to the raid itself.

It was only too evident to the secret service of the Confederate Government that an organization of Federal spies honeycombed the city. The most desperate and determined efforts were put forth to unearth these conspirators.

Captain Welford had made the discovery that the conspirators who had stolen Dahlgren's body had cut his curling blond hair and dispatched it to Washington. The bearer of this dispatch was a negro. He had been thoroughly searched, but no incriminating papers were found. The Captain had removed a lock of this peculiarly beautiful hair and allowed the messenger of love to go on his way determined to follow him on his return to Richmond and locate his accomplices.

Dick's report of this affair to Jennie had started a train of ideas which again centered her suspicions on Socola. The night this body had been stolen she had sent for her lover in a fit of depression. The rain was pouring in cold, drizzling monotony. Her loneliness had become unbearable.

He was not at home and could not be found. Alarmed and still more depressed she sent her messenger three times. The last call he made was long past midnight.

Her suspicion of his connection with the service of the enemy had become unendurable. She had not seen or heard from him since the effort to find him that night. He was at his desk at work as usual next morning.

She wrote him a note and begged that he call at once. He came within half an hour, a wistful smile lighting his face as he extended his hand:

"I am forgiven for having been born abroad?"

"I have sent for you—"

"I've waited long."

"It's not the first time I've asked you to call," she cried in strained tones.

"No?"

She held his gaze with steady intensity.

"I sent for you the night young Dahlgren's body was stolen—"

"Really?"

"It was raining. I was horribly depressed. I couldn't endure the strain. I meant to surrender utterly and trust you—"

"I didn't get your message—"

"I know that you didn't—where were you?"

"Engaged on important business for the Government—"

"What Government?"

"How can you ask such a question?"

"I do ask it. I sent for you three times—the third time after midnight. It wasn't very modest, perhaps, I was so miserable I didn't care. I just wanted to put my arms around your neck and tell you to love me always—that nothing else mattered—"

"Nothing else does matter, dearest—"

"Yes—it does. It matters whether you have used me to betray my people. Where were you at twelve o'clock night before last?"

"I'd rather not tell you—"

"I demand it—"

A quizzical smile played about Socola's handsome mouth as he faced her frankly.

"I was in a gambling establishment—"

"Whose?"

"Johnnie Worsham's—"

"What were you doing there? You neither drink nor gamble."

Again the dark face smiled.

"I was asked by my Chief to report on the habits of every man in my Department—particularly to report every man who frequents the gambling hells of Richmond—"

Jennie watched him nervously, her hands trembling.

"It's possible of course—"

Her eyes suddenly filled with tears and she threw herself into his arms.

And then it happened—the little thing, trivial and insignificant, that makes and unmakes life.

For a long while no words were spoken. With gentle touch he soothed her trembling body, bending to kiss the waves of rich brown hair.

She pushed him at arm's length at last and looked up smiling.

"I can't help it—I love you!"

"When will you learn that we must trust where we love—"

He stopped suddenly. Her brown eyes were fixed with terror on a single strand of curling blond hair caught on the button of his waistcoat.

"What is it?" he asked in alarm.

She drew the hair from his coat carefully and held it to the light in silence.

"You can't be jealous?"

She looked at him curiously.

"Yes. I have a rival—"

"A rival?"

Her eyes pierced him.

"Your love for the Union! I've suspected you before. You've evaded my questions. Our love has been so big and sweet a thing that you have always stammered and hesitated to tell me a deliberate lie. It's not necessary now. I know. Ulrich Dahlgren is the age of my brother Billy. They used to play together in Washington at Commodore Dahlgren's home and at ours. He had the most peculiarly beautiful blond hair I ever saw on a man. I'd know it anywhere on earth. That strand is his, poor boy! Besides, Dick Welford captured your messenger with that pathetic little bundle on his way to Washington—"

Socola started in spite of his desperate effort at self-control and was about to speak when Jennie lifted her hand.

"Don't, please. It's useless to quibble and argue with me longer. We face each other with souls bare. I don't ask you why you have deceived me. Your business as a Federal spy is to deceive the enemy—"

"You are not my enemy," he interrupted in a sudden burst of passion. "You are my mate! You are mine by all the laws of God and nature. I love you. I worship you. We are not enemies. We never have been—we never shall be. With the last breath I breathe your name shall be on my lips—"

"You may speak your last word soon—"

"What do you mean?"

"I am going to surrender you to the authorities—"

"And you have just been sobbing in my arms—the man you have sworn to love forever?"

"It's the only atonement I can make. Through you I have betrayed my country and my people. I would gladly die in your place. The hard thing will be to do my duty and give you up to the death you have earned."

"You can deliver me to execution?"

"Yes—" was the firm answer. "Listen to this—"

She seized a copy of the morning paper.

"Colonel Dahlgren's instructions to his men. This document was found on his person when shot. There is no question of its genuineness—"

She paused and read in cold hard tones:

"Guides, pioneers (with oakum, turpentine and torpedoes), signal officer, quarter master, commissary, scouts, and picket men in rebel uniform—remain on the north bank and move down with the force on the south bank. If communications can be kept up without giving an alarm it must be done. Everything depends upon a surprise, and no one must be allowed to pass ahead of this column. All mills must be burned and the canal destroyed. Keep the force on the southern side posted of any important movement of the enemy, and in case of danger some of the scouts must swim the river and bring us information. We must try to secure the bridge to the city (one mile below Belle Isle) and release the prisoners at the same time. If we do not succeed they must then dash down, and we will try to carry the bridge from each side. The bridges once secured, and the prisoners loosed and over the river, the bridges will be secured and the city destroyed—"

Jennie paused and lifted her eyes burning with feverish light.

"Merciful God! How? With oakum and turpentine. A city of one hundred thousand inhabitants, under the cover of darkness—men, women and children, the aged, the poor, the helpless!"

Socola made no answer. A thoughtful dreamy look masked his handsome features.

Jennie read the next sentence from the Dahlgren paper in high quivering tones:

"The men must be kept together and well in hand, and once in the city, it must be destroyed and Jeff Davis and his Cabinet killed—"

The girl paused and fixed her gaze on Socola.

"The man who planned that raid came with the willful and deliberate murder of unarmed men in his soul. The man who helped him inside is equally guilty of his crime—"

She resumed her reading without waiting for reply.

"Prisoners will go along with combustible material. The officer must use his discretion about the time of assisting us. Pioneers must be prepared to construct a bridge or destroy one. They must have plenty of oakum and turpentine for burning, which will be rolled in soaked balls, and given to the men to burn when we get into the city—"

Socola lifted his hand.

"Please, dear—these instructions are not mine. I do not excuse or palliate them. The daring youngster who conceived this paid the penalty with his life. It's all that any of us can give for his country. There's something that interests me now far more than this sensation—far more than the mere fact that my true business here has been discovered by you and my life forfeited to your Government—"

"And that is?"

"That the woman I love can deliver me to death—"

"You doubt it?"

"I had not believed it possible."

"I'll show you."

Jennie stepped to the door and pulled the old-fashioned bell-cord.

A servant appeared.

In strained tones the girl said:

"Go to Captain Welford's office and ask him to come here immediately with two soldiers—"

"Yassam—"

The negro bowed and hurried from the house, and Jennie sat down in silence beside the door.

Socola confronted her, his hands gripped in nervous agony behind his back, his slender figure erect, his breath coming in deep excited draughts.

"You think that I'll submit to my fate without a fight?"

"You've got to submit. Your escape from Richmond is a physical impossibility—"

He searched the depths of her heart.

"I was not thinking of my body just then. I have no desire to live if you can hand me to my executioner—"

He paused and a sob came from the girl's distracted soul.

He moved a step closer.

"I'm not afraid to die—you must know that—I'm not a coward—"

"No. I couldn't have loved a coward!"

"The thing I can't endure is that you, the woman to whom I have surrendered my soul, should judge me worthy of death. Come, my own, this is madness. We must see each other as God sees now. You must realize that only the highest and noblest motive could have sent a man of my character and training on such a mission. We differ in our political views for the moment—even as you differ from the older brother whom you love and respect—"

"I am not responsible for my brother's acts. I am for yours—"

"Nonsense, dear heart. My work was ordained of God from the beginning. It was fate. Nothing could have stopped me. I came under a mighty impulse of love for my country—bigger than the North or the South. God sent me. You have helped me. But if you had not I would still have succeeded. Can't you forget for the moment the details of this blood-stained struggle—the maimed lad with his crutches strapped to his saddle, lost in the black storm night in the country of his enemies and shot to pieces—the mad scheme his impulsive brain had dreamed of wiping your Capital from the earth and leading fifteen thousand shouting prisoners back into freedom and life—surely he paid for his madness. Forget that I have deceived you, and see the vision of which I dream—a purified and redeemed Nation—united forever—no North, no South—no East, no West—the inheritance of our children and all the children of the world's oppressed! I am fighting for you and yours as well as my own. The South is mine. I love its beautiful mountains and plains—its rivers and shining seas—Oh, my love, can't you see this divine vision of the future? The Union must be saved. The stars in their courses fight its battles. Nothing is surer in the calendar of time than that the day is swiftly coming when the old flag your fathers first flung to the breeze will be again lifted from your Capitol building. You can't put me out of your life as a criminal worthy of death! I won't have it. I am yours and you are mine. I am not pleading for my life. I'm pleading for something bigger and sweeter than life. I'm pleading for my love. I can laugh at death. I can't endure that you put me out of your heart—"

Jennie rose with determination, walked to the window and laughed hysterically.

"Well, I'm going to put you out. Captain Welford and his men are coming. They've just turned the corner!"

The man's figure slowly straightened, and his eyes closed in resignation.

"Then it's God's will and my work is done."

With a sudden cry Jennie threw herself in his arms.

"Forgive me, dear Lord. I can't do this hideous thing! It's my duty, but I can't. My darling—my own! You shall not die. I was mad. Forgive me! Forgive me! My own—"

"Halt!"

The sharp command of the Captain rang outside the door.

"Get into this room—quick—" the girl cried, pushing Socola into the adjoining room and slamming the door as Dick entered the hall.

She faced the Captain with a smile.

"It's all right, now, Dick. I thought I had discovered an important secret. It was a mistake—"

The Captain smiled.

"You don't mind my looking about the house?"

"Searching the house?"

"Just the lower floor?"

"I do mind it. How dare you suggest such a thing, sir—"

"Because I've made a guess at the truth. You discovered important evidence incriminating Socola. Your first impulse was to do your duty—you weakened at the last moment—"

"Absurd!" she gasped.

"I happened to hear a door slam as I entered. I'll have to look around a little."

He started to the door behind which Socola had taken refuge. Jennie confronted him.

"You can't go in there—"

"It's no use, Jennie—I'm going to search that room—the whole house if necessary."

"Why?"

"I know that Socola is here—"

"And if he is?"

"I'll arrest him—"

"On what charge?"

"He is a Federal spy and you know it—"

"You can't prove it."

"I've found the evidence. I have searched his rooms—"

"Searched his rooms?"

"Your servant told me that he was here. I leaped to a conclusion, forced his door and found this—"

He thrust a well-thumbed copy of the cipher code of the Federal Secret Service into her hand.

"You—you—can't execute him, Dick," Jennie sobbed.

"I will."

"You can't. I love him. He can do no more harm here."

"He's done enough. His life belongs to the South—"

She placed her trembling hand on his arm.

"You are sure that deep down in your heart there's not another motive?"

"No matter how many motives—one is enough. I have the evidence on which to send him to the gallows—"

The girl's head drooped.

"And I gave it to you—God have mercy!"

The tears began to stream down her cheeks. Dick moved uneasily and looked the other way.

"I've got to do it," he repeated stubbornly.

Her voice was the merest whisper when she spoke.

"You're not going to arrest him, Dick. He will leave Richmond never to enter the South again. I'll pledge my life on his promise. His death can do us no good. It can do you no good—I—I—couldn't live and know that I had killed the man I love—"

"You haven't killed him. He has forfeited his life a thousand times in his work as a spy."

"I sent for you. I caused his betrayal. I shall be responsible if he dies—"

Again the little head drooped in pitiful suffering. She lifted it at last with a smile.

"Dick, you're too big and generous for low revenge. You hate this man. But you love me. I know that. I'm proud and grateful for it. I appeal to the best that's in you. Save my life and his—"

"You couldn't live if he should die, Jennie?" the man asked tenderly.

"Not if he should die in this way—"

The Captain struggled and hesitated.

Again her hand touched his arm.

"I ask the big divine thing of you, Dick?"

"It's hard. I've won and you take my triumph from me. For two years I've given body and soul to the task of unmasking this man."

"I'm asking his life—and mine—" the pleading voice repeated.

"I'll give him up on one condition—"

"What?"

The Captain held her gaze in silence a moment.

"That you send him back to the North and put him out of your life forever!"

Jennie laughed softly through her tears.

"You big, generous, foolish boy—you might have left that to me—"

"All right," he hastened to agree. "I'll leave it to you. Forgive me. I can't deny you anything—"

"You're a glorious lover, Dick!" she cried tenderly. "Why didn't I love you?"

"I don't know, honey," he replied chokingly. "We just love because we must—there's no rhyme or reason to it—"

He paused and laughed.

"Well, it's all over now, Jennie. I've given him back to you—goodbye—"

She grasped his hand and held it firmly.

"Don't you dare say goodbye to me, sir—you've got to love me, too—as long as I live—my first sweetheart—brave, generous, kind—"

She drew his blond head low and kissed him.

He looked at her through dimmed eyes and slowly said:

"That makes life worth living, Jennie."

He turned and quickly left the house.

She heard his low orders to his men and watched them pass up the street with their rifles on their shoulders.

She opened the door and Socola entered, his face deathlike in its pallor.

"Why did he stay so long?"

"He has searched your room and found your cipher code—"

"And you have saved my life?"

"It was I who put it in peril—"

"No—I gave my life in willing sacrifice when the war began—"

"You are to leave," Jennie went on evenly—"leave at once—"

"Of course—"

"And give me your solemn parole—never again during this war

to fight the South—"

"It is your right to demand it. I agree."

She gently took his hand.

"I know that I can trust you now—" She paused and looked wistfully into his face. "One last long look into your dear eyes—"

"Not the last—"

"One last kiss—"

She drew his lips down to hers.

"One last moment in your arms." She clung to him desperately and freed herself with quick resolution.

"And now you must go—from Richmond—from the South and out of my life forever—"

"You can't mean this!" he protested bitterly.

"I do," was the firm answer. "Goodbye."

He pressed her hand and shook his head.

"I refuse to say it—"

"You must."

"No—"

"It is the end—"

"It is only the beginning."

With a look of tenderness he left her standing in the doorway, the hunger of eternity in her brown eyes.

39: THE CONSPIRATORS

The raid of Dahlgren and Kilpatrick had sent a thrill of horror through Richmond. The people had suddenly waked to the realization of what it meant to hold fifteen thousand desperate prisoners in their city with a handful of soldiers to guard them.

The discovery on the young leader's body of the remarkable papers of instructions to burn the city and murder the Confederate President and his Cabinet produced a sharp discussion between Jefferson Davis and his councilors.

Not only did the people of Richmond demand that such methods of warfare be met by retaliation of the most drastic kind but the Cabinet now joined in this demand. Hundreds of prisoners had been captured both from Dahlgren's and Kilpatrick's division.

It was urged on Davis with the most dogged determination that these prisoners—in view of the character of their instructions to burn a city crowded with unarmed men, women and children and murder in cold blood the civil officers of the Confederate Government—should be treated as felons and executed by hanging.

The President had refused on every occasion to lend his power to brutal measures of retaliation. This time his Cabinet was persistent and in dead earnest in their purpose to force his hand.

Davis faced his angry council with unruffled spirit.

"I understand your feelings, gentlemen," he said evenly. "You have had a narrow escape. The South does not use such methods of warfare. Nor will I permit our Government to fall to such level by an act of retaliation. The prisoners we hold are soldiers of the enemy's army. Their business is to obey orders—not plan campaigns—"

"We have captured officers also," Benjamin interrupted.

"Subordinate officers are not morally responsible for the plans of their superiors."

No argument could move the Confederate Chieftain. He was adamant to all appeals for harsh treatment. Even Lee had at last found it impossible to maintain discipline in his army unless he prevented the review of his court martial by Davis. The President was never known to sign the death warrant of a Confederate soldier. Lincoln was a man of equally tender heart and yet the Northern President did sign the death warrants of more than two hundred Union soldiers during his administration.

The only action Davis would permit was the removal of the fifteen thousand prisoners further south to places of safety where such raids would be impossible. The prisons of Richmond were emptied and the stockades at Salisbury and Andersonville overcrowded with these men.

Davis renewed his urgent appeal to the Federal Government for the exchange of these men. His request was treated with discourtesy and steadily refused. When the hot climate of Georgia caused the high death rate at Andersonville he released thousands of those men without exchange and notified the Washington Government to send transportation for them to Savannah.

Lincoln had given Grant a free hand in assuming the command of all the armies of the Union. But he watched his cruel policy of refusal to exchange prisoners with increasing anguish. In every way possible, without directly opposing his commanding general, the bighearted President at Washington managed to smuggle Southern prisoners back into the South unknown to Grant and take an equal number of Union soldiers home.

A crowd of Southern boys from the prison at Elmira, New York, were announced to arrive in Richmond on the morning train from Fredericksburg. Among them Jennie expected her brother Jimmie who had been captured in battle six months ago. She hurried to the station to meet them.

A great crowd had gathered. A row of coffins was placed on the ground at the end of the long platform awaiting the train going south. A dozen men were sitting on those rude caskets smoking, talking, laughing, their feet drawn up tailor-fashion to keep them out of the mud.

With a shiver the girl hurried to the other gate.

Her eager eyes searched in vain among the ragged wretches who shambled from the cars. A man from Baton Rouge, whom she failed to recognize, lifted his faded hat and handed her a letter.

She read it through her tears and hurried to the Confederate White House to show it to the President. Davis scanned the scrawl with indignant sympathy:

"Dear Little Sis:

"This is the last message I shall ever send. Before it can reach you I shall be dead—for which I'll thank God. I'm sorry now I didn't take my chances with the other fellows, bribe the guard and escape from Camp Douglas in Chicago. A lot of the boys did it. Somehow I couldn't stoop. Maybe the fear of the degrading punishment they gave McGoffin, the son of the Governor of Kentucky, when he failed, influenced me, weak and despondent as I was. They hung him by the thumbs to make him confess the name of his accomplices. He refused to speak and they left him hanging until the balls of his thumbs both burst open and he fainted. "The last month at Camp Douglas was noted for scant rations. Hunger was the prevailing epidemic. At one end of our barracks was the kitchen, and by the door stood a barrel into which was thrown beef bones and slops. I saw a starving boy fish out one of these bones and begin to gnaw it. A guard discovered him. He snatched the bone from the prisoner's hand, cocked his pistol, pressed it to his head and ordered him to his all-fours and made him bark for the bone he held above him— "We expected better treatment when transferred to Elmira. But I've lost hope. I'm too weak to ever pull up again. I've made friends with a guard who has given me the list of the men who have died here in the five months since we came. In the first four months out of five thousand and twenty-seven men held here, one thousand three hundred and eleven died—six and one-half per cent a month—"

Davis paused and shook his head—

"The highest rate we have ever known at Salisbury or Andersonville during those spring months was three per cent!"

He finished the last line in quivering tones.

"There's not a chance on earth that I'll live to see you again. See the President and beg him for God's sake to save as many of the boys as he can. With a heart full of love.

"Jimmie."

The President took both of Jennie's hands in his.

"I need not tell you, my dear, that I have done and am doing my level best. The policy of the new Federal Commander is to refuse all offers of exchange. You understand my position?"

"Perfectly," was the sorrowful answer. "I only came as a duty to bear his dying message—"

"Express to your father and mother my deepest sympathy."

With a gentle pressure of the Chieftain's hand the girl answered:

"I need not tell you I appreciate it—"

The President watched her go with a look of helpless anguish. His troubles for the moment had only begun. The returned prisoners had marched in a body to his office to thank their Chief for his sympathy and help and asked him to say something to them.

Jennie paused and stared in a dazed way into the poor shrunken faces. When the President appeared every ragged hat was in the air and they cheered with all the might of the strength that was left in them. The girl burst into tears. These men, so forlorn, so dried up with a strange, half-animal, hunted look in their eyes—others restless and wild-looking—others calmly vacant in their stare as if they had been dead for years!

A poor mother was rushing in and out among them hunting for her son.

"He was coming with you boys, you know!" she cried.

She stopped suddenly and laughed at her own anxiety and confusion.

"He's here somewhere—I just can't find him—help me, men!"

She hadn't spoken his name, in her eager search for his loved face. She kept lifting the cloth from a basket of provisions which she had cooked that morning.

"I've got his breakfast here—poor boy—I expect he's hungry."

She had lost all consciousness of the crowd now.

She was talking to herself, trying to keep her courage up.

The President looked into the emaciated faces before him and lifted his long arm in solemn salutation.

"Soldiers of the South:

"I thank you from the bottom of my heart for this tribute of your loyalty. You were offered your freedom in prison at any moment if you would take the oath and forswear your allegiance to the South. You deliberately chose the living death to the betrayal of your faith. I stand with uncovered head before you. I am proud to be the Chief Executive of such men!"

Again they cheered.

The old mother with her basket was searching again for her boy.

Jennie slipped an arm gently around her and led her away.

On the day Lee left Richmond for the front to meet Grant's invading host, the Confederate President was in agony over a letter from General Winder portraying the want and suffering among the prisoners confined at Andersonville.

"If we could only get them across the Mississippi," Davis cried, "where beef and supplies of all kind are abundant—but what can we do for them here?"

"Our men are in the same fix," Lee answered quickly, "except that they're free. These sufferings are the result of our necessity, not of our policy. Do not distress yourself."

The South was entering now the darkest hours of her want. The market price of food was beyond the reach of the poor or even the moderately well-to-do. Turkeys sold for $60 each. Flour was $300 a barrel, corn meal $50 a bushel. Boots were $200 a pair. A man's coat cost $350—his trousers $100. He could get along without a vest. Wood was $50 a cord. It took $1,800 to buy $100 in gold.

In the midst of this universal suffering the yellow journals of the South, led by the Richmond Examiner, made the most bitter and determined assaults on Davis to force him to a policy of retaliation on Northern prisoners.

"Hoist the black flag!" shrieked the Examiner. "Retaliate on these Yankee prisoners for the starvation and abuse of our men in the North—a land teeming with plenty." The President was held up to the scorn and curses of the Southern people because with quiet dignity he refused to lower the standard of his Government to a policy of revenge on helpless soldiers in his power.

To a Committee of the Confederate Congress who waited on him with these insane demands he answered with scorn:

"You dare ask me to torture helpless prisoners of war! I will resign my office at the call of my country. But no people have the right to demand such deeds at my hands!"

In answer to this brave, humane stand of the Southern President the Examiner had the unspeakable effrontery to accuse him of clemency to his captives that he might curry favor with the North and shield himself if the South should fail.

No characteristic of Davis was more marked than his regard for the weak, the helpless and the captive. His final answer to his assailants was to repeat with emphasis his orders to General Winder to see to it that the same rations issued to Confederate soldiers in the field should be given to all prisoners of war, though taken from a starving army and people.

Enraged by the defeat of their mad schemes, the conspirators drew together now to depose Davis and set up a military dictatorship.

40: IN SIGHT OF VICTORY

When Grant crossed the Rapidan with his army of one hundred forty-one thousand one hundred and sixty men Lee faced him with sixty-four thousand. The problem of saving Richmond from the tremendous force under the personal command of the most successful general of the North was not the only danger which threatened the Confederate Capital. Butler was pressing from the Peninsula with forty thousand men along the line of McClellan's old march, supported again by the navy.

Jefferson Davis knew the task before Lee to be a gigantic one yet he did not believe that Grant would succeed in reaching Richmond.

The moment the Federal general crossed the Rapidan and threw his army into the tangled forest of the Wilderness, Lee sprang from the jungles at his throat.

Battle followed battle in swift and terrible succession. At Cold Harbor thirty days later the climax came. Grant lost ten thousand men in twenty minutes. The Northern general had set out to hammer Lee to death by steady, remorseless pounding. At the end of a month he had lost more than sixty thousand men and Lee's army was as strong as when the fight began.

Grant's campaign to take Richmond was the bloodiest and most tragic failure in the history of war. The North in bitter anguish demanded his removal from command. Lincoln stubbornly refused to interfere with his bulldog fighter. He sent him word to hold on and chew and choke.

As Grant in his whirl of blood approached the old battle grounds of McClellan, Davis rode out daily to confer with Lee. He was never more cheerful—never surer of the safety of his Capital. His faith in God and the certainty that he would in the end give victory to a cause so just and holy grew in strength with the report from each glorious field. No doubt of the right or justice of his cause ever entered his mind. Day and night he repeated the lines of his favorite hymn:

"I'll strengthen thee, help thee and cause thee to stand,
Upheld by my righteous omnipotent hand."

Again and again he said to his wife half in soliloquy, half in exalted prayer:

"We can conquer a peace against the world in arms and keep the rights of freemen if we are worthy of the privilege!"

The spirit which animated the patriotic soldiers who followed their commander in this bloody campaign was in every way as high as that which inspired their President.

Jennie spent an hour each day ministering to the sick prisoners who had returned from the North and were unable to go further than Richmond. It was her service of love for Jimmie's friends and comrades.

A poor fellow was dying of the want he had endured in prison. He lifted his dimmed eyes to hers:

"Will you write to my wife for me, Miss?"

"Yes—yes—I will."

"And give her my love—"

He paused for breath and fumbled in his pocket.

"I've a letter from her here—read it before you write. Our little girl had malaria. She tried willow tea and everything she could think of for the chills. The doctor said nothin' but quinine could save her. She couldn't get it, the blockade was too tight, and so our baby died—and now I'm dyin' and my poor starvin' girl will have nothin' to comfort her—but—"

He gasped and lifted himself on his elbow.

"If our folks can just quit free men, it's all right. It's all right!"

The women and children of Richmond were suffering now for food. The Thirteenth Virginia regiment sent Billy Barton into the city with a contribution for their relief.

Billy delivered it to Jennie with more than a boy's pride. There was something bigger in the quiet announcement he made.

"Here's one day's rations from the regiment, sis," he said—"all our flour, pork, bacon and meal. The boys are fasting today. It's their love offering to those we've left at home—"

Jennie kissed him.

"It's beautiful of you and your men, boy. Give my love to them all and tell them I'm proud to be their countrywoman—"

"And they're proud of their country and their General, too—maybe you wouldn't believe it—but every regiment in Lee's army has reenlisted for the war."

She seized Billy's hand.

"Come with me—I want you to see the President and tell him what your regiment has done. It'll help him."

As they approached the White House a long, piercing scream came through the open windows.

"What on earth?" Jennie exclaimed.

"An accident of some kind," the boy answered, seizing her arm and hurrying forward. Every window and door of the big lonely house set apart on its hill swung wide open, the lights streaming through them, the wind blowing the curtains through the windows. The lights blazed even in the third story.

Mrs. Burton Harrison, the wife of the President's Secretary, met them at the door, her eyes red with weeping.

She pressed Jennie's hand.

"Little Joe has been killed—"

"Mrs. Davis' beautiful boy—impossible!"

"He climbed over the bannisters and fell to the brick pavement and died a few minutes after his mother reached his side—"

The girl could make no answer. She had come on a sudden impulse to cheer the lonely leader of her people. Perhaps his need in this dark hour had called her. She thought of Socola's story of his mother's vision and wondered with a sudden pang of self-pity where the man she loved was tonight.

This beautiful child, named in honor of his favorite brother, was the greatest joy of the badgered soul of the Confederate leader.

Suddenly his white face appeared at the head of the stairs. A courier had come from the battlefield with an important dispatch. Grant and Lee were locked in their death grapple in the Wilderness. He would try even

in this solemn hour to do his whole duty.

He passed the sympathetic group murmuring a sentence whose pathos brought the tears again to Jennie's eyes.

"Not my will, O Lord, but thine—thine—thine!"

He took the dispatch from the courier's hand and held it open for some time, staring at it with fixed gaze.

He searched the courier's face and asked pathetically:

"Will you tell me, my friend, what is in it—I—I—cannot read—"

The courier read the message in low tones. A great battle was joined. The fate of a nation hung on its issue. The stricken man drew from his pocket a tiny gold pencil and tried to write an answer—stopped suddenly and pressed his hand on his heart.

Billy sprang to his side and seized the dispatch:

"I'll take the message to General Cooper—Mr. President—"

The white face turned to the young soldier and looked at him pitifully:

"Thank you, my son—thank you—it is best—I must have this hour with our little boy—leave me with my dead!"

Jennie stayed to help the stricken home.

She took little Jeff in her arms to rock him to sleep. He drew her head down and whispered:

"Miss Jennie, I got to Joe first after he fell. I knelt down beside him and said all the prayers I know—but God wouldn't wake him!"

The girl drew the child close and kissed the reddened eyes. Over her head beat the steady tramp of the father's feet, back and forth, back and forth, a wounded lion in his cage. The windows and doors were still wide open, the curtains waving wan and ghost-like from their hangings.

Two days later she followed the funeral procession to the cemetery—thousands of children, each child with a green bough or bunch of flowers to pile on the red mound.

A beautiful girl pushed her way to Jennie's side and lifted a handful of snowdrops.

"Please put these on little Joe," she said wistfully. "I knew him so well."

With a sob the child turned and fled. Jennie never learned her name. She turned to the grave again, her gaze fixed on the striking figure of the grief-stricken father, bare-headed, straight as an arrow, his fine face silhouetted against the shining Southern sky. The mother stood back amid the shadows, in her somber wrappings, her tall figure drooped in pitiful grief.

The leader turned quickly from his personal sorrows to those of his country, his indomitable courage rising to greater heights as dangers thickened.

Two weeks later General Sheridan attempted what Dahlgren tried and failed to accomplish.

The President hurried from his office to his home, seized his pistols, mounted his horse and rode out to join Generals Gracie and Ransom who were placing their skeleton brigades to repulse the attack.

The crack of rifles could be distinctly heard from the Executive Mansion.

The mother called her children to prayers. As little Jeff knelt he raised his chubby face and said with solemn earnestness:

"You had better have my pony saddled, and let me go out and help father—we can pray afterwards!"

In driving Sheridan's cavalry back from Richmond General Stuart fell at Yellow Tavern mortally wounded—the bravest of the brave—a full Major General who had won immortal fame at thirty-one years of age. His beautiful wife, the daughter of a Union General, Philip St. George Cooke, could not reach his bedside before he breathed his last.

The President reverently entered the death chamber and stood for fifteen minutes holding the hand of his brilliant young commander.

They told him that he could not live to see his wife.

"I should have liked to have seen her," he said gently, "but God's will be done."

The doctor felt his fast fading pulse.

"Doctor, I suppose I'm going fast now," Stuart said. "It will soon be over. I hope I have fulfilled my duty to my country and my God—"

"Your end is near, General Stuart," the doctor responded softly.

"All right," was the even answer. "I'll end my little affairs down here. To Mrs. Robert E. Lee I give my gold spurs, in eternal memory of the love I bear my glorious Chief. To my staff, my horses—"

He paused and turned to the heavier officer who stood with bowed head.

"You take the larger one—he'll carry you better. To my son I leave my sword—"

He was silent a moment and then said with an effort:

"Now I want you to sing for me the song I love best:

"Rock of ages cleft for me
 Let me hide myself in thee"—

With his fast-failing breath he joined in the song, turned and murmured:

"I'm going fast now—God's will be done—"

So passed the greatest cavalry leader our country has produced—a man whose joyous life was one long feast of good will toward his fellow men.

* * * * *

In spite of all losses, in spite of four years of frightful carnage, in spite of the loss of the Mississippi, the States of Louisiana and Tennessee, the Confederacy was in sight of victory.

Lee had baffled Grant's great army at every turn and now held him securely at bay before Petersburg. The North was mortally tired of the bloody struggle. The party which demanded peace was greater than any political division—it included thousands of the best men in the party of Abraham Lincoln.

The nomination of General McClellan for President on a platform declaring the war a failure and demanding that it end was a foregone conclusion. Jefferson Davis knew this from inside information his friends had sent from every section of the North.

The Confederacy had only to hold its lines intact until the first Monday in November and the Northern voters would end the war.

The one point of mortal danger to the South lay in the mental structure of Joseph E. Johnston, the man whom Davis had been persuaded, against his better judgment, to appoint to the command of one of the greatest armies the Confederacy had ever put into the field.

Johnston had been sent to Dalton, Georgia, and placed in command of sixty-eight thousand picked Confederate soldiers with which to attack and drive Sherman out of the lower South.

Lee with sixty-four thousand had defeated Grant's one hundred and forty thousand. Richmond was safe, and the North was besieging Washington with an army of heart-broken mothers and fathers who demanded Grant's removal.

No effort was spared by Davis to enable Johnston to stay Sherman's advance and assume the offensive. The whole military strength of the South and West was pressed forward to him. His commissary and ordnance departments were the best in the Confederacy. His troops were eager to advance and retrieve the disaster at Missionary Ridge—the first and only case of panic and cowardice that had marred the brilliant record of the Confederacy.

The position of Johnston's army was one of commanding strength. Long mountain ranges, with few and difficult passes, made it next to impossible for Sherman to turn his flank or dislodge him by direct attack. Sherman depended for his supplies on a single line of railroad from Nashville.

Davis confidently believed that Johnston could crush Sherman in the first pitched battle and render his position untenable.

And then began the most remarkable series of retreats recorded in the history of war.

Without a blow and without waiting for an attack, Johnston suddenly withdrew from his trenches at Dalton and ran eighteen miles into the interior of Georgia. He stopped at Resaca in a strong position on a peninsula formed by the junction of two rivers fortified by rifle pits and earthworks.

He gave this up and ran thirteen miles further into Georgia to Adairsville. Not liking the looks of Adairsville he struck camp and ran to Cassville seventeen miles.

He then declared he would fight Sherman at Kingston. Sherman failing to divide his army, as Johnston had supposed he would, he changed his mind and ran beyond Etowah. He next retreated to Alatoona. Here Sherman spread out his army, threatened Marietta and Johnston ran again.

On July fifth he ran from Kenesaw Mountain and took refuge behind the Chattahoochee River.

From Dalton to Resaca, from Resaca to Adairsville, from Adairsville to Alatoona (involving the loss of Kingston and Rome with their mills, foundries and military stores), from Alatoona to Kenesaw, from Kenesaw to the Chattahoochee and then tumbled into the trenches before Atlanta.

Retreat had followed retreat for two months and a half over one hundred and fifty miles to the gates of Atlanta without a single pitched battle!

Davis watched this tragedy unfold its appalling scenes with increasing bitterness, disappointment and alarm.

The demand for Johnston's removal was overwhelming in the State of Georgia whose gate city was now besieged by Sherman. The people of the whole South had watched this retreat of a hundred and fifty miles into their territory with sickening hearts.

Again Johnston began his nagging and complaining to the Richmond authorities. His most important message was an accusation of disloyalty against Joseph E. Brown. He telegraphed in blunt plain English:

"The Governor of Georgia refuses me provisions and the use of his roads."

Brown answered:

"The roads are open to him and in capital condition. I have furnished him abundantly with provisions."

The President of the Confederacy now faced the most dangerous and tragic decision of his entire administration. The removal of Johnston from his command before Sherman's victorious army in the heart of Georgia could be justified only on the grounds of the sternest necessity. The Commanding General not only had the backing of his powerful junta in Richmond who were now busy with their conspiracy to establish a dictatorship and oust the President from his office, but he was immensely popular with his army. His care for his soldiers was fatherly. His painful efforts to save their lives, even at the cost of the loss of his country, were duly appreciated by the leaders of opinion in the army. Johnston had the power to draw and hold the good will of the men who surrounded him. He had the power, too, of infecting his men with his likes and dislikes. His hatred of Davis had been for three years the one mania of his sulking mind.

To remove him from command in such a crisis was to challenge a mutiny in his army which might lead to serious results. Yet if he should continue to retreat, and back out of Atlanta without a fight as he had backed out of every position for the one hundred and fifty miles from Dalton, the results would be still more appalling.

The loss of Atlanta at this moment meant the defeat of the peace party of the North, and the reelection of Lincoln. If Lincoln should be elected it was inconceivable that the South could continue the unequal struggle for four years more.

If Johnston would only hold his trenches and save Atlanta for a few days the South would win. Lee could hold Grant indefinitely.

The thought which appalled Davis was the suspicion which now amounted to a practical certainty that his retreating General would evacuate Atlanta as he had threatened to abandon Richmond when confronted by McClellan, and had abandoned Vicksburg without a blow.

He must know this with absolute certainty before yielding to the demand for his removal. That no possible mistake could be made, he dispatched his Chief of Staff, General Braxton Bragg, to Atlanta for conference with Johnston and make a personal report.

Bragg reported that Johnston was arranging to abandon Atlanta without a battle and the President promptly removed him from command and appointed Hood in his place.

When Hood assumed command of the disgruntled army, it was too late to save Atlanta. Had Johnston delivered battle with his full force at Dalton, Sherman might have been crushed as Rosecrans was overwhelmed at Chickamauga.

Hood's army was driven back into their trenches. Sherman threw his hosts under cover of night on a wide flanking movement and Atlanta fell.

Under the mighty impulse of this news Lincoln was reelected, the peace party of the North defeated and the doom of the Confederacy sealed.

41: THE FALL OF RICHMOND

The conspirators who had complained most bitterly of Davis for the appointment of Lee to the command of the army before Richmond when McClellan was thundering at its gates, now succeeded in passing through the Confederate Congress a bill to create a military dictatorship which they offered to the man for whose promotion they had condemned the President.

Lee treated this attempt to strike the Confederate Chieftain over his head with the contempt it deserved. Davis laughed at his enemies by the most complete acceptance of their plans.

His answer to Senator Barton's committee was explicit.

"I have absolute confidence in General Lee's patriotism and military genius. I will gladly cooperate with Congress in any plan to place him in supreme command."

Lee refused to accept the responsibility except with the advice and direction of the President, and the conspiracy ended in a fiasco.

From the moment Sherman's army pierced the heart of the South the Confederate President saw with clear vision that the cause of Southern independence was lost. Lee's army must slowly starve. His one supreme purpose now was to fight to the last ditch for better terms than unconditional surrender which would mean the loss of billions in property and the possible enfranchisement of a million slaves.

That Lincoln was intensely anxious to stop the shedding of blood he knew from more than one authentic source. It was rumored that the Northern President was willing to consider compensation for the slaves. An army of a hundred thousand determined Southern soldiers led by an indomitable general could fight indefinitely. That it was of the utmost importance to the life of the South to secure a surrender which would forbid the enfranchisement of the slaves and the degradation of an electorate to their level, Davis saw with clear vision. From the North now came overtures of peace. Francis P. Blair asked for permission to visit Richmond.

Blair proposed to end the war by uniting the armies of the

North and South for an advance on Mexico to maintain the Monroe Doctrine against the new Emperor whom Europe had set upon a throne in the Western Hemisphere.

The Confederate President received his proposals with courtesy.

"I have tried in vain, Mr. Blair," he said gravely, "to open negotiations with Washington. How can the first step be taken?"

"Mr. Lincoln, I am sure, will receive commissioners—though he would give me no assurance on that point. We must stop this deluge of blood. I cherish the hope that the pride and honor of the Southern States will suffer no shock in the adjustment."

The result of this meeting was the appointment by Davis of three Commissioners to meet the representatives of the United States. Alexander H. Stephens, R.M.T. Hunter and Judge John A. Campbell were sent to this important conference. For some unknown reason they were halted at Fortress Monroe and not allowed to proceed to Washington. A change had been suddenly produced in the attitude of the National Government. Whether it was due to the talk of the men in Richmond who were trying to depose Davis or whether it was due to the fall of Fort Fisher and the closing of the port of Wilmington, the last artery which connected the Confederacy with the outside world, could not be known.

The Confederate Commissioners were met by Abraham Lincoln himself and his Secretary of State, William H. Seward, in Hampton Roads. The National Government demanded in effect, unconditional surrender.

Davis used the indignant surprise with which this startling announcement was received in Richmond and the South to rouse the people to a last desperate effort to save the country from the deluge which the Radical wing of the Northern Congress had now threatened—the confiscation of the property of the whites and the enfranchisement of the negro race. In his judgment this could only be done by forcing the National Government through a prolongation of the war to pledge the South some measure of protection before they should lay down their arms.

Mass meetings were held and the people called to defend their cause with their last drop of blood. The President made a speech that night to a crowd in the Metropolitan Hall on Franklin Street in Richmond which swept them into a frenzy of patriotic passion. Even his bitterest enemy, the editor of the Examiner, was spellbound by his eloquence.

When he first appeared on the speakers' stand and lifted his tall thin figure, gazing over the crowd with glittering eye, a tremendous cheer swept the assembly. In that moment, he was the incarnate Soul of the South. The Chieftain of the men who wore the gray in this hour of solemn trial, stood before them with countenance like the lightning. Cheer on cheer rose and fell with throbbing passion.

A smile of strange prophetic sweetness lighted his pale haggard face. The ovation he received was the sure promise to his tired soul that when the passions and prejudices, the agony and madness of war had passed the people would understand all he had tried to do in their service. In that moment of divine illumination he saw his place in the hearts of his countrymen and was content.

He spoke with even restrained flow of words, with a mastery of himself and his audience that is the mark of the orator of the highest genius. His gestures were few. His low, vibrant, musical voice found the heart of his farthest listener. He swayed them with indescribable passion.

Into the faces of the foe who had demanded unconditional surrender he hurled the defiance of an unconquered and unconquerable soul. He closed with an historical illustration which lifted his audience to the highest reach of emotion. Kossuth had abandoned Hungary with an army of thirty thousand men in the field. The friends of liberty had never forgiven nor could forgive this betrayal.

"What shall we say," he cried, "of the disgrace beneath which we should be buried if we surrender with an army in the field more numerous than that with which Napoleon achieved the glory of France, an army standing among its homesteads, an army in which each individual is superior in warlike quality to the individual who opposes him!"

When the tumult and applause had died away did he realize in the secret places of his heart that the spirit of the South had been broken by the terrible experiences of four years of blood and fire and death? His iron will gave no sign. To him the manhood of the Southern soldier was unconquerable, his courage dauntless forever.

Six months after Sherman's sword had pierced the heart of the

South from Atlanta, Lee's army in the trenches before Petersburg had reached the end of their endurance. Lee wired Davis that his thin line could hold back Grant's hosts but a few days and that Richmond must fall. His men were living on parched corn.

The President hurried to the White House and slipped his arm around his wife.

"You must leave the city, my dear."

"Please let me stay with you," she pleaded.

"Impossible," he answered firmly. "My headquarters must be in the saddle. Your presence here could only grieve and distress me. You can take care of our babies. I know you wish to help and comfort me. You can do this in but one way—go and take the children to a place of safety—"

He paused, overcome with emotion.

"If I live," he continued slowly, "you can come to me when the struggle is over, but I do not expect to survive the destruction of our liberties."

He drew his small hoard of gold from his pocket, removed a five-dollar piece for himself, and gave it all to his wife together with the Confederate money he had on hand.

"You must take only your clothing," he said after a moment's silence. "The flour and supplies in your pantry must be left. The people are in want."

He had arranged for his family to settle in North Carolina. The day before his wife left, he gave her a pistol and taught her trembling hands to load, aim and fire it.

"The danger will be," he warned, "that you may full into the hands of lawless bands of deserters from both armies who are even now pillaging and burning. You can at least, if you must, force your assailants to kill you. If you cannot remain undisturbed in your own land make for the coast of Florida and take a ship for a foreign country."

Their hearts dumb with despair, his wife and children boarded the train—or the thing that once had been a train—the roof of the cars leaked and the engine wheezed and moved with great distress.

The stern face of the Southern leader was set in his hour of trial. He felt that he might never again look on the faces of those he loved. His little girl clung convulsively to his neck in agonizing prayer that she might stay. The boy begged and pleaded with tears raining down his chubby face.

Just outside of Richmond the engine broke down and the heartsick family sat in the dismal day-coach all night. Sleepers had not been invented. They were twelve hours getting to Danville—a week on the way to Charlotte.

The reign of terror had already begun.

The President's wife avoided seeing people lest they should be compromised when the invading army should sweep over the State.

They found everything packed up in the house that had been rented, but Weill, the big-hearted Jew who was the agent, sent their meals from his house for a week, refusing every suggestion of pay. He offered his own purse or any other service he could render.

When Burton Harrison had seen them safely established in Charlotte he returned at once to his duties with the President in Richmond.

On the beautiful Sunday morning of April 2, 1865, a messenger hurriedly entered St. Paul's Church, walked to the President's pew and handed him a slip of paper. He rose and quietly left.

Not a rumor had reached the city of Lee's broken lines. In fact a false rumor had been published of a great victory which his starving army had achieved the day before.

The report of the evacuation of Richmond fell on incredulous ears. The streets were unusually quiet. Beyond the James the fresh green of the spring clothed the fields in radiant beauty. The rumble of no artillery disturbed the quiet. Scarcely a vehicle of any kind could be seen. The church bells were still ringing their call to the house of God.

The straight military figure entered the Executive office. A wagon dashed down Main Street and backed up in front of the Custom House door. Boxes were hurried from the President's office and loaded into it.

A low hum and clatter began to rise from the streets. The news of disaster and evacuation spread like lightning and disorder grew. The streets were crowded with fugitives making their way to the depot—pale women with disheveled hair and tear-stained faces leading barefooted children who were crying in vague terror of something they could not understand. Wagons were backed to the doors of every department of the Confederate Government. As fast as they could be loaded they were driven to the Danville depot.

All was confusion and turmoil. Important officers were not to be seen and when they were found would answer no questions. Here and there groups of mean-visaged loafers began to gather with ominous looks toward the houses of the better class.

The halls of the silent Capitol building were deserted—a single footfall echoed with hollow sound.

The Municipal Council gathered in a dingy little room to consider the surrender of the city. Mayor Mayo dashed in and out with the latest information he could get from the War Department. He was slightly incoherent in his excitement, but he was full of pluck and chewed tobacco defiantly. He announced that the last hope was gone and that he would maintain order with two regiments of militia.

He gave orders to destroy every drop of liquor in the stores, saloons and warehouses and establish a patrol.

The militia slipped through the fingers of their officers and in a few hours the city was without a government. Disorder, pillage, shouts, revelry and confusion were the order of the night. Black masses of men swayed and surged through the dimly-lighted streets, smashing into stores and warehouses at will. Some of them were carrying out the Mayor's orders to destroy the liquor. Others decided that the best way to destroy it was to drink it. The gutters ran with liquor and the fumes filled the air.

To the rear guard of Lee's army under Ewell was left the task of blowing up the vessels in the James, and destroying the bridges across the river. The thunder of exploding mines and torpedoes now shook the earth. The ships were blown to atoms and the wharves fired.

In vain the Mayor protested against the firing of the great warehouses. Orders were orders, and the soldiers obeyed. The warehouses were fired, the sparks leaped to the surrounding buildings and the city was in flames.

As day dawned a black pall of smoke obscured the heavens. The sun's rays lighted the banks of rolling smoke with lurid glare. The roar of the conflagration now drowned all other sounds.

The upper part of Main Street was choked with pillagers— men with drays, some with bags, some rolling their stolen barrels painfully up the hills.

A small squadron of Federal cavalry rode calmly into the wild scene. General Weitzel, in command of the two divisions of Grant's army on the north side, had sent in forty Massachusetts troopers to investigate conditions.

At the corner of Eleventh Street they broke into a trot for the Square and planted their guidons on the Capitol of the Confederacy.

Long before this advance guard could be seen in the distance the old flag of the Union had been flung from the top of the house on Church Hill. Foreseeing the fall of the city Miss Van Lew had sent to the Federal Commander for a flag. Through his scouts he had sent it. As Weitzel's two grand divisions swung into Main Street this piece of bunting eighteen feet long and nine feet wide waved from the Van Lew mansion on the hill above them.

Stretching from the Exchange Hotel to the slopes of Church Hill, down the hill, through the valley, and up the ascent swept this gorgeous array of the triumphant army, its bayonets gleaming in the sunlight, every standard, battle flag and guidon streaming in the sky, every band playing, swords flashing, and shout after shout rolling from end to end of the line.

To the roar of the flames, the throb of drum, the scream of fife, the crash of martial music, and the shouts of marching hosts, was added now the deep thunder of exploding shells in the burning arsenals.

A regiment of negro cavalry swept by the Exchange Hotel and as they turned the corner drew their sabers with a savage shout.

An old Virginian with white locks standing in the doorway of the hotel gazed on these negro troops a moment, threw his hands on high, and solemnly cried:

"Blow, Gabriel! Blow your trumpet—for God's sake blow!"

For hours the fire raged unchecked—burned until the entire business section of the city lay a smoldering heap of ashes. Crowds of men, women and children crowded the Capitol Square fighting with smoke and flying cinders for a breath of fresh air. Piles of furniture lay heaped on its greensward. Terror-stricken, weeping women had dragged it from their homes. In improvised tents made of broken tables and chairs covered with sheets and bedding hundreds of homeless women and children huddled.

As night fell the pitiful reaction came from the turmoil and excitement of the day. The quiet of a great desolation brooded over the smoking ruins.

In the rich and powerful North millions were mad with joy. In New York twenty thousand people gathered in Union Square and sang the Doxology.

Jennie Barton was in Richmond through it all and yet the tragedy made no impression on her heart or mind. A greater event absorbed her. Dick Welford had hurried to Lee's army on the day following Socola's departure from Richmond. He wanted to fight once more. Through all the whirlwind of death and blood from the first crash with Grant in the Wilderness to his vain assaults on Petersburg he had fought without a scratch. His life was charmed. And then in the first day of the final struggle which broke the lines of Lee's starving army he fell, leading his men in a glorious charge. He reached the hospital in Richmond the day before the city's evacuation.

Jennie had watched by his bedside every hour since his arrival. But few words passed between them. She let him hold her hand for hours in silence, always looking, looking and smiling his deathless love.

He had not spoken Socola's name nor had she.

"It's funny, Jennie," he said at last, "I don't hate him any more—"

The girl's head drooped and the tears streamed down her checks.

"Please, Dick—don't—"

"Yes," he insisted, "I want to talk about it and you must hear me—won't you?"

"Of course, if you wish it," she answered tenderly.

"You see I don't hate these Yankee soldiers any more—anyhow. I saw too many of them die from the Wilderness to Petersburg—brave manly fellows. The fire of battle has burned the hate out of me. Now I just want you to be happy, Jennie dear, that's all—goodbye—"

His hand slipped from hers and in a moment his spirit had passed.

42: THE CAPTURE

At midnight on the day of the evacuation the President and his Cabinet left Richmond for Danville. He still believed that Lee might cut his way through Grant's lines and join his army with Johnston's in North Carolina. Lee had restored Johnston to command of the small army that yet survived in opposition to Sherman. He had hopes that Johnston's personal popularity with the soldiers might in a measure restore their spirits.

The President established his temporary Capital at Danville. G. W. Sutherlin placed his beautiful home at his disposal. Communications with Lee had been cut and the wildest rumors were afloat. Davis wrote his last proclamation urging his people to maintain their courage.

In this remarkable document he said:

"I announce to you, my fellow countrymen, that it is my purpose to maintain your cause with my whole heart and soul. I will never consent to abandon to the enemy one foot of the soil of any of the States of the Confederacy.

"If by stress of numbers, we should be compelled to a temporary withdrawal from the limits of Virginia or any other border State, we will return until the baffled and exhausted enemy shall abandon in despair his endless and impossible task of making slaves of a people resolved to be free.

"Let us, then, not despair, my countrymen, but, relying on God, meet the foe with fresh defiance, and with unconquered and unconquerable hearts."

So Washington spoke to his starving, freezing little army at Valley Forge in the darkest hour of our struggle for independence against Great Britain. With the help of France Washington succeeded at last.

Davis was destined to fail. No friendly foreign power came to his aid. His courage was none the less sublime for this reason.

Lee's skeleton army surrendered to Grant at Appomattox, and Davis hurried to Greensboro where Johnston and Beauregard were encamped with twenty-eight thousand men. Two hundred school girls marched to the house in Danville and cheered him as he left.

Mrs. Sutherlin in the last hour of his stay asked for a moment of his time.

He ushered her into his room with grave courtesy.

"Dear Madam," he began smilingly, "you have risked your home and the safety of your husband to honor me and the South. I thank you for myself and the people. Is there anything I can do to show how much I appreciate it?"

"You have greatly honored us by accepting our hospitality," was the quick cheerful answer. "We shall always be rich in its memory. I have but one favor to ask of you—"

"Name it—"

She drew a bag from a basket and handed it to him.

"Accept this little gift we have saved. It will help you on your journey. It's only a thousand dollars in gold—I wish it were more."

The President's eyes grew dim and he shook his head.

"No—no—dear, dear Mrs. Sutherlin. Your needs will be greater than mine. Besides, I have asked all for the cause—nothing for myself—nothing!"

He left Danville with heart warmed by the smiles and cheers of two hundred beautiful girls and the offer of every dollar a patriotic woman possessed.

He had need of its memory to cheer him at Greensboro. Here he felt for the first time the results of the malignant campaign which Holden's Raleigh Standard had waged against him and his administration. So great was the panic and so bitter the feeling which Holden's sheet had roused that it was impossible for the President and his Cabinet to find accommodations in any hotel or house. He was compelled to camp in a freight car.

It remained for a brave Southern woman to resent this insult to the Chieftain. When Mrs. C. A. L'Hommedieu learned that the President was in town, housed in a freight car and shunned by the citizens, she sent him a note and begged him to make her house his home and to honor her by commanding anything in it and all that she possessed.

The leader was at this moment preparing to leave for Charlotte and had to decline her generous and brave offer. But he was deeply moved. He stopped his work to write her a beautiful letter of thanks.

His interview with Johnston and Beauregard was strained and formal. Johnston's army in its present position in the hands of a resolute and daring commander could have formed a light column of ten thousand cavalry and cut its way through all opposition to the Mississippi River. Knowing the character of his General so well he had small hopes.

After receiving the report of the condition of the army the President called his Cabinet to consider what should be done.

Johnston sat at as great a distance from Davis as the room would permit.

The President reviewed briefly the situation and turned calmly to Johnston:

"General, we should like now to hear your views."

The reply was given with brutal brevity and in tones of unconcealed defiance and hatred.

"Sir," the great retreater blurted out, "my views are that our people are tired of war, feel themselves whipped and will not fight."

A dead silence followed.

The President turned in quiet dignity to Beauregard:

"And what do you say, General Beauregard?"

"I agree with what General Johnston has said," he replied.

There was no appeal from the decision of these two commanders in such an hour. The President dictated a letter to General Sherman suggesting their surrender and outlining the advantageous terms which the Northern Commander accepted.

And then the Confederate Chieftain received a message so amazing he could not at first credit its authority.

A courier from Sherman conveyed the announcement to Johnston that Davis might leave the country on a United States vessel and take whoever and whatever he pleased with him.

The answer of Jefferson Davis was characteristic.

"Please thank General Sherman for his offer and say that I can do no act which will put me under obligations to the Federal Government."

Sherman had asked Lincoln at their last interview whether he should capture Davis or let him go.

A sunny smile overspread the rugged features of the National

President:

"That reminds me," he said, "of a temperance lecturer in Illinois. Wet and cold he stopped for the night at a wayside inn. The landlord, noting his condition, asked if he would have a glass of brandy.

"No—no—' came the quick reply. 'I am a temperance lecturer and do not drink—' he paused and his voice dropped to a whisper—'I would like some water however—and if you should of your own accord, put a little brandy in it unbeknownst to me—why, it will be all right.'"

Sherman was trying to carry out the wishes of the man with the loving heart.

At Charlotte Davis was handed a telegram announcing the assassination of Abraham Lincoln. His thin fate went death white. Handing the telegram to his Secretary, he quietly said:

"I am sorry. We have lost our noblest and best friend in the court of the enemy."

He immediately telegraphed the news to his wife who had fled further south to Abbeville, South Carolina. Mrs. Davis burst into tears on reading the fatal message. Her woman's intuition saw the vision of horror which the tragedy meant to her and to her stricken people.

The President left Charlotte with an escort of a thousand cavalrymen for Abbeville. His journey was slow. The wagons were carrying all that remained of the Confederate Treasury with the money in currency from the Richmond banks which had been entrusted to the care of the Secretary of the Treasury.

Davis stopped at a little cabin on the roadside and asked the lady who stood in the doorway for a drink of water.

She turned to comply with his request.

While he was drinking a baby barely able to walk crawled down the steps and toddled to him.

The mother smiled.

"Is this not President Davis?" she asked tremblingly.

"It is, Madam," he answered with a bow.

She pointed proudly to the child:

"He's named for you!"

The President drew a gold coin from his pocket and handed it to the mother.

"Please keep it for my little namesake and tell him when he is old enough to know."

As he rode away with Reagan, his faithful Postmaster General, he said:

"The last coin I had on earth, Reagan. I wouldn't have had that but for the fact I'd never seen one like it and kept it for luck."

"I reckon the war's about finished us," the General replied.

"Yes," Davis cheerfully answered. "My home is a wreck. Benjamin's and Breckinridge's are in Federal hands. Mallory's fine residence at Pensacola has been burned by the enemy. Your home in Texas has been wrecked and burned—"

He paused and drew from his pocketbook a few Confederate bills.

"That is my estate at the present moment."

He received next day a letter from his wife which greatly cheered him:

> "Abbeville, S. C., April 28, 1865.
>
> "My dear old Husband:
>
> "Your very sweet letter reached me safely by Mr. Harrison and was a great relief. I leave here in the morning at 6 o'clock for the wagon train going to Georgia. Washington will be the first place I shall unload at. From there we shall probably go on to Atlanta or thereabouts, and wait a little until we hear something of you. Let me beseech you not to calculate upon seeing me unless I happen to cross your shortest path toward your bourne, be that what it may.
>
> "It is surely not the fate to which you invited me in the brighter days. But you must remember that you did not invite me to a great hero's home but to that of a plain farmer. I have shared all your triumphs, been the only beneficiary of them, now I am claiming the privilege for the first time of being all to you, since these pleasures have passed for me.
>
> "My plans are these, subject to your approval. I think I shall be able to procure funds enough to enable me

to put the two eldest to school. I shall go to Florida if possible and from thence go over to Bermuda or Nassau, from thence to England, unless a good school offers elsewhere, and put them to the best school I can find, and then with the two youngest join you in Texas—and that is the prospect which bears me up, to be once more with you if need be—but God loves those who obey Him and I know there is a future for you.

"Here they are all your friends and have the most unbounded confidence in you. Mr. Burt and his wife have urged me to live with them—offered to take the chances of the Yankees with us—begged to have little Maggie—done everything in fact that relatives could do. I shall never forget all their generous devotion to you.

"I have seen a great many men who have gone through—not one has talked fight. A stand cannot be made in this country! Do not be induced to try it. As to the trans-Mississippi, I doubt if at first things will be straight, but the spirit is there, and the daily accretions will be great when the deluded of this side are crushed between the upper and nether millstones. But you have not tried the 'strict construction' fallacy. If we are to require a Constitution, it must be much stretched during our hours of outside pressure if it covers us at all.

"Be careful how you go to Augusta. I get rumors that Brown is going to seize all Government property, and the people are averse and mean to resist with pistols. They are a set of wretches together, and I wish you were safe out of their land. God bless you, keep you. I have wrestled with Him for you. I believe He will restore us to happiness.

"Devotedly,

"Your Wife."

"Kindest regards to Robert, and thanks for faithful conduct. Love to Johnson and John Wood. Maggie sends you her best love."

The President and his party reached Abbeville on May first, only to find that his wife had left for Washington, Georgia.

At Abbeville, in the home of Armistead Burt, Davis called his last Cabinet meeting and council of war.

There were present five brigade commanders, General Braxton Bragg, his Chief-of-Staff, Breckinridge, Benjamin and Reagan of his Cabinet. The indomitable spirit made the last appeal for courage and the continuance of the fight until better terms could be made that might save the South from utter ruin and the shame of possible negro rule.

He faced them with firm resolution, his piercing eye undimmed by calamity.

"The South, gentlemen," he declared, "is in a panic for the moment. We have resources to continue the war. Let those who remain with arms in their hands set the example and others will rally. Let the brave men yet with me renew their determination to fight. Around you reinforcements will gather."

The replies of his discouraged commanders were given in voices that sank to whispers. Each man was called on for his individual opinion.

Slowly and painfully each gave his answer in the negative. The war was hopeless, but they would not disband their men until they had guarded the President to a place of safety.

"No!" Davis answered passionately. "I will listen to no proposition for my safety. I appeal to you for the cause of my country. Stand by it, men—stand by it!"

His appeal was received in silence. His councilors could not agree with him. The proud old man drew his slender body to its full height, lifted his hands and cried pathetically:

"The friends of the South consent to her degradation!"

He attempted to pass from the meeting, his emaciated face white with anger. His step tottered and his body swayed and would have sunk to the floor had not General Breckinridge caught him in his arms and led him from the room.

Benjamin parted from the President when they crossed the Savannah River and he had dropped the Seal of the Confederate Government in the depths of its still, beautiful waters.

"Where are you going?" Reagan asked.

"To the farthest place from the United States," was the quick reply, "if it takes me to China."

He made his way successfully to England and won fame and fortune in the old world.

On hearing that the Federal cavalry were scouring the country, Breckinridge and Reagan proposed that Davis disguise himself in a soldier's clothes, a wool hat and brogan shoes, take one man with him and go to the coast of Florida, ship to Cuba.

His reply was firm:

"I shall not leave Southern soil while a Confederate regiment is on it. Kirby Smith has an army of 25,000 men. He has not surrendered. General Hampton will cut his way across the Mississippi. We can lead an army of 60,000 men on the plains of Texas and fight until we get better terms than unconditional surrender."

Breckinridge was left at Washington to dispose of the small sum yet left in the Treasury and turn over to their agent the money of the Richmond banks.

Robert Toombs lived in Washington. General Reagan called on the distinguished leader.

He invited his guest into his library and closed the door.

"You have money, Reagan?"

"Enough to take me west of the Mississippi—"

"You are well mounted?"

"One of the best horses in the country."

"I am at home," he added generously. "I can command what I want, and if you need anything, I can supply you—"

"Thank you, General," Reagan responded heartily.

Toombs hesitated a moment, and then asked suddenly:

"Has President Davis money?"

"No, but I have enough to take us both across the Mississippi."

"Is Mr. Davis well mounted?"

"He has his fine bay, 'Kentucky,' and General Lee sent him at Greensboro by his son Robert, his gray war horse 'Traveler,' as a present. He has two first class horses."

Again Toombs was silent.

"Mr. Davis and I," he went on thoughtfully, "have had our quarrels. We have none now. I want you to say to him that my men are around me here, and if he desires it I will call them together and see him safely across the Chattahoochee River at the risk of my life—"

"I'll tell him, General Toombs," Reagan cordially responded. "And I appreciate your noble offer. It differs from others who have pretended to be his best friends. They are getting away from him as fast as they can. Some are base enough to malign him to curry favor with the enemy. I've known Jefferson Davis intimately for ten years. The past four years of war I've been with him daily under every condition of victory and defeat, and I swear to you that he's the truest, gentlest, bravest, tenderest, manliest man I have ever known—"

"Let me know," Toombs urged, "if I can serve him in any possible way."

When Reagan delivered the message to the President he responded warmly:

"That's like Toombs. He was always a whole souled man. If it were necessary I should not hesitate to accept his offer."

He was slowly reading his wife's last letters which had been delivered to him by scouts who were still faithful.

They were riding in a wagon with picked Mississippi teamsters twenty miles below Washington:

"All well, with Winnie sweet and smiling. Billy plenty of laughter and talk with the teamsters keeps quiet. Jeff is happy beyond expression. Maggie one and two quite well.

"I have $2,500, something to sell, and have heart and a hopeful one, but above all, my precious only love, a heartful of prayer. May God keep you and have His sword and buckler over you. Do not try to make a stand on this side. It is not in the people. Leave your escort and take another road often. Alabama is full of cavalry, fresh and earnest in pursuit. May God keep you and bring you safe to the arms of

"Your devoted,
"Winnie."

He opened and read another:

"My own precious Banny:

"May God give us both patience against this heavy trial. The soldiers are very unruly and have taken almost all the mules and horses from the camp. Do not try to meet me. I dread the Yankees getting news of you so much. You are the country's only hope and the very best intentions do not advise a stand this side of the river. Why not cut loose from your escort? Go swiftly and alone with the exception of two or three.

"Oh, may God in His goodness keep you safe, my own. Maggie says she has your prayer book safe. May God keep you, my old and only love, as ever, devotedly,

"Your own,

"Winnie."

He had not seen his wife and babies since they left Richmond. The conduct of the soldiers determined his course. He turned to Reagan:

"This move will probably cause me to be captured or killed. You are not bound to go with me—but I must protect my family."

"I go with you, sir—" was the prompt response.

The soldiers were dismissed and the money still remaining in the Treasury divided among them. A picked guard of ten men rode with the fallen Chieftain in search of his loved ones.

They joined Mrs. Davis after a hard ride and found her camp threatened by marauders. He traveled with her two days and, apparently out of danger, she begged him to leave her and make good his escape. He finally agreed to do this and with Reagan, the members of his staff and Burton Harrison, his Secretary, started for the Florida coast.

The day was one of dismal fog and rain and the party lost the way, turning in a circle, and at sunset met Mrs. Davis and her company at the fork of the road near the Ocmulgee River.

The President and staff traveled with his wife next day and made twenty-eight miles. At Irwinsville their presence was betrayed to the Federal cavalry, his camp surrounded by Colonel Pritchard, and the Confederate President and party arrested.

The soldiers plundered his baggage, tore open his wife's trunks and scattered her dresses. In one of these trunks they found a pair of new hoopskirts which Mrs. Davis had bought but never worn. An enterprising newspaper man immediately invented and sent broadcast the story that he had been captured trying to escape in his wife's hoopskirts. His enemies refused to hear any contradiction of this invention. It was too good not to be true. They clung to it long after Colonel Pritchard and every man present had given it the lie.

They had traveled a day's journey toward Macon, the headquarters of General Wilson, when an excited man galloped into the camp waving over his head a printed slip of paper.

"What is it?" Davis asked of his guard.

The guard seized and read the slip and turned to the Confederate Chieftain and his wife.

"Andrew Johnson's proclamation offering a reward of $100,000 for the capture of Jefferson Davis as the murderer of Abraham Lincoln!"

A cry of anguish came from the faithful wife.

The leader touched her shoulder gently.

"Hush, my dear. The miserable scoundrel who wrote that proclamation knew that it is false. He is the one man in the United States who knows that I preferred Abraham Lincoln in the White House to him or any other man the North might elect. Such an accusation must fail—"

The wife was not comforted.

"These men may assassinate you!"

The soldiers crowded about their defenseless prisoner and heaped on him the vilest curses and insults. He made no answer. The far-away look in his eagle eye told them only too plainly that he did not hear.

Colonel Pritchard in his manly way made every effort to protect him from insult. Within a short distance of Macon, the prisoners were halted and their escort drawn up in line on either side of the road. Colonel Pritchard had ridden into Macon for a brigade to escort his captives through the streets of the city.

The soldiers again cursed and jeered. The children climbed into their father's arms, kissed and hugged him tenderly and put their little hands over his ears that he should not hear what they said.

He soothed their fears and comforted them with beautiful lines from the Psalms which he quoted in tones of marvelous sweetness.

General Wilson received his distinguished prisoner with the deference due his rank and character. His guard in silence opened their lines and presented arms as Davis entered the building.

43: THE VICTOR

Socola hurried into Richmond three days after its fall in the desperate hope that he might be of service to Jennie.

He was two days finding her. She had offered her services to Mrs. Hopkins in the Alabama hospital. He sent in his card and she refused to see him. He asked an interview with Mrs. Hopkins and begged her to help. Her motherly heart went out to him in sympathy. His utter misery was so plainly written in his drawn face.

"You're so like my own mother, madame," he pleaded. "I'm an orphan today. Our army has conquered, but I have lost. I find myself repeating the old question, what shall it profit a man if he gain the whole world and forfeit his life? She is my life—I can't—I won't give her up. Tell her she must see me. I will not leave Richmond until I see her. If she leaves, I'll follow her to the ends of the world. Tell her this."

The gentle hand pressed his.

"I'll tell her."

"And try to help me?" he begged.

"All the world loves a lover," the fine thin lips slowly repeated—"yes, I'll try."

At the end of ten minutes she returned alone. Her face gave no hope.

"I'm afraid it's useless. She positively refuses."

"You gave her my message?"

"Yes."

"I'll wait a day and try again—"

"You knew of Captain Welford's death, I suppose?"

Socola started and turned pale.

"No—"

"He died and was buried two days ago near the spot where General Stuart sleeps."

The lover was stunned for a moment. The hidden thought flashed through his mind that she might have married Welford in the reaction over her discovery of his deception. He opened his lips to ask the question and held his peace. It was impossible. She couldn't have done such a thing. He put the idea out of his heart.

"Thank you for the information, dear madame," he answered gravely, turned and left the building.

He walked quickly to his hotel, hired a negro to get him a wreath of roses and meet him at the cemetery gate. He had just placed them on Welford's grave as Jennie suddenly appeared.

She stopped, transfixed in astonishment—her eyes wide with excitement.

He walked slowly to meet her and stood looking into her soul, searching its depths.

"You here?" she gasped—

"Yes. I brought my tribute to a brave and generous foe. He hated me, perhaps—but for your sake he gave me my life—I never hated him—"

"With his last breath he told me that he no longer hated you," she answered dreamily.

"And you cannot forgive?"

"No. Our lives are far apart now. The gulf between us can never be passed."

He smiled tenderly and spoke with vibrant passion.

"I'm going to show you that it can be passed. I'm going to love you with such devotion I'll draw you at last with resistless power—"

"Never—"

She turned quickly and left him gazing wistfully at her slender figure silhouetted against the glow of the sunset.

44: PRISON BARS

The ship which bore the distinguished prisoner from Savannah did not proceed to Washington, but anchored in Hampton Roads at Fortress Monroe.

A little tug puffed up and drew alongside the steamer. She took off Alexander H. Stephens, General Joseph Wheeler and Burton Harrison. Stephens and Wheeler were sent to Fort Warren in Boston Harbor.

The next, day the tug returned.

Little Jeff ran to his mother trembling and sobbing:

"They say they've come for father—beg them to let us go with him!"

Davis stepped quickly forward and returned with an officer.

"It's true," he whispered. "They have come for Clay and me. Try not to weep. These people will gloat over your grief."

Mrs. Davis and Mrs. Clay stood close holding each other's hands in silent sympathy and grim determination to control their emotions. They parted with their husbands in dumb anguish.

As the tug bore the fallen Chieftain from the ship, he bared his head, drew his tall figure to its full height, and, standing between the files of soldiers, gazed on his wife and weeping children until the mists drew their curtain over the solemn scene.

Mrs. Davis' stateroom was entered now by a raiding party headed by Captain Hudson. Her trunks were again forced open and everything taken which the Captain or his men desired—among them all her children's clothes. Jeff seized his little soldier uniform of Confederate gray and ran with it. He managed to hide and save it.

Captain Hudson then demanded the shawl which Davis had thrown over his shoulders on the damp morning when he was captured.

"You have no right to steal my property," his wife replied indignantly. "Peace has been declared. The war is over. This is plain robbery."

Hudson called in another file of soldiers.

"Hand out that shawl or I'll take the last rag you have on earth. I'll pay you for it, if you wish. But I'm going to have it."

Mrs. Davis took the shawl from Mrs. Clay's shoulders and handed it to the brute.

"At least I may get rid of your odious presence," she cried, "by complying with your demand."

Hudson took the shawl with a grin and led his men away. Two of his officers returned in a few minutes and thrust their heads in the stateroom of Mrs. Davis' sister with whom Mrs. Clay was sitting.

"Gentlemen, this is a ladies' stateroom," said the Senator's wife.

One of them threw the door open violently and growled:

"There are no ladies here!"

"I am quite sure," was the sweet reply, "that there are no gentlemen present!"

With an oath they passed on. Little tugs filled with vulgar sightseers steamed around the ship and shouted a continuous stream of insults when one of the Davis party could be seen.

General Nelson A. Miles, the young officer who had been appointed jailer of Jefferson Davis and Clement C. Clay boarded the ship and proceeded without ceremony to give his orders to their wives.

"Will you tell me, General," Mrs. Davis asked, "where my husband is imprisoned and what his treatment is to be?"

"Not a word," was the short reply.

His manner was so abrupt and boorish she did not press for further news.

Miles ventured some on his own account.

"Jeff Davis announced the assassination of Abraham Lincoln the day before it happened. I guess he knew all about it—"

The wife bit her lips and suppressed a sharp answer. Her husband's life was now in this man's hands.

"You are forbidden to buy or read a newspaper," he added curtly, "and your ship will leave this port under sealed orders."

In vain Davis pleaded that his wife and children might be allowed to go to Washington or Richmond where they had acquaintances and friends.

"They will return to Savannah," Miles answered, "by the same ship in which they came and remain in Savannah under military guard."

Jefferson Davis was imprisoned in a casemate of Fortress Monroe, the embrasure of which was closed with a heavy iron grating. The two doors which communicated with the gunner's room were closed with heavy double shutters fastened with crossbars and padlocks. The side openings were sealed with fresh masonry.

Two sentinels with loaded muskets paced the floor without a moment's pause day or night. Two other sentinels and a commissioned officer occupied the gunner's room, the door and window of which were securely fastened. Sentinels were stationed on the parapet overhead whose steady tramp day and night made sleep impossible.

The embrasure opened on the big ditch which surrounds the fort—sixty feet wide and ten feet deep in salt water. Beyond the ditch, on the glacis, was a double line of sentinels and in the casemate rooms on either side of his prison were quartered that part of the guard which was not on post.

To render rest or comfort impossible a lighted lamp was placed within three feet of the prisoner's eyes and kept burning brightly all night. His jailer knew he had but one eye whose sight remained and that he was a chronic sufferer from neuralgia.

His escape from Fortress Monroe was a physical impossibility without one of the extraordinary precautions taken. The purpose of these arrangements could have only been to inflict pain, humiliation and possibly to take his life. He had never been robust since the breakdown of his health on the Western plains. Worn by privation and exposure, approaching sixty years of age, he was in no condition physically to resist disease.

The damp walls, the coarse food, the loss of sleep caused by the tramp of sentinels inside his room, outside and on the roof over his head and the steady blaze of a lamp in his eyes at night within forty-eight hours had completed his prostration.

But his jailers were not content.

On May twenty-third, Captain Titlow entered his cell with two blacksmiths bearing a pair of heavy leg irons coupled together by a ponderous chain.

"I am sorry to inform you, sir," the polite young officer began, "that I have been ordered to put you in irons."

"Has General Miles given that order?"

"He has."

"I wish to see him at once, please."

"General Miles has just left the fort, sir."

"You can postpone the execution of your order until I see him?"

"I have been warned against delay."

"No soldier ever gave such an order," was the stern reply; "no soldier should receive or execute it—"

"His orders are from Washington—mine are from him."

"But he can telegraph—there must be some mistake—no such outrage is on record in the history of nations—"

"My orders are peremptory."

"You shall not inflict on me and on my people through me this insult worse than death. I will not submit to it!"

"I sincerely trust, sir," the Captain urged kindly, "that you will not compel me to use force."

"I am a gentleman and a soldier, Captain Titlow," was the stern answer. "I know how to die—" he paused and pointed to the sentinel who stood ready. "Let your men shoot me at once—I will not submit to this outrage!"

The prisoner backed away with his hand on a chair and stood waiting.

The Captain turned to his blacksmiths:

"Do your duty—put them on him!"

As the workman bent with his chain Davis hurled him to the other side of the cell and lifted his chair.

The sentinel cocked and lowered his musket advancing on the prisoner who met him defiantly with bared breast.

The Captain sprang between them:

"Put down your gun. I'll give you orders to fire when necessary."

He turned to the officer at the door:

"Bring in four of your strongest men—unarmed—you understand?"

"Yes, sir—"

The men entered, sprang on their helpless victim, bore him to the floor, pinned him down with their heavy bodies and held him securely while the blacksmiths riveted the chains on one leg and fastened the clasp on the other with a heavy padlock.

He had resented this cowardly insult for himself and his people.

He had resisted with the hope that he might be killed before it was accomplished. He saw now with clear vision that the purpose of his jailer was to torture him to death. His proud spirit rose in fierce rebellion. He would cheat them of their prey. They might take his life but it should be done under the forms of law in open day. He would live. His will would defy death. He would learn to sleep with the tramp of three sets of sentinels in his ears. He would eat their coarse food at whatever cost to his feelings. He would learn to bury his face in his bedding to avoid the rays of the lamp with which they were trying to blind him.

He had need of all his fierce resolution.

He had resolved to ask no favors, but his suffering had been so acute, his determination melted at the doctor's kind expressions.

The physician found him stretched on his pallet, horribly emaciated and breathing with difficulty, his whole body a mere fascine of raw and tremulous nerves, his eyes restless and fevered, his head continually shifting from side to side searching instinctively for a cool spot on the hot coarse hair pillow.

"Tell me," Dr. Craven said kindly, "what I can do to add to your comfort?"

The question was asked with such genuine sympathy it was impossible to resist it.

A smile flickered about his thin mouth, "This camp mattress, Doctor," he slowly replied, "I find a little thin. The slats beneath chafe my poor bones. I've a frail body—though in my youth and young manhood, while soldiering in the West, I have done some rough camping and campaigning. There was flesh then to cover my nerves and bones."

The doctor called an attendant:

"Bring this prisoner another mattress and a softer pillow."

"Thank you," Davis responded cordially.

"You are a smoker?" the doctor asked.

"I have been all my life, until General Miles took my pipe and tobacco."

The doctor wrote to the Adjutant General and asked that his patient be given the use of his pipe.

On his visit two days later the doctor said:

"You must spend as little time in bed as possible. Exercise will be your best medicine."

The prisoner drew back the cover and showed the lacerated ankles.

"Impossible you see—the pain is so intense I can't stand erect. These shackles are very heavy. If I stand, the weight of them cuts into my flesh—they have already torn broad patches of skin from the places they touch. If you can pad a cushion there, I will gladly try to drag them about—"

Dr. Craven sought the jailer:

"General Miles," he began respectfully, "in my opinion the condition of state-prisoner Davis requires the removal of those shackles until such time as his health shall be established on a firmer basis. Exercise he must have."

"You believe that is a medical necessity?"

"I do, most earnestly."

About the same time General Miles had heard from the country. The incident had already aroused sharp criticism of the Government. Stanton had come down to Fortress Monroe and peeped through the bars at the victim he was torturing, and had extracted all the comfort possible from the incident. The shackles were removed.

His jailer persisted in denying him the most innocent books to read. He asked the doctor to get for him if possible the geology or the botany of the South. General Miles thought them dangerous subjects. At least the names sounded treasonable. He denied the request.

The prisoner asked for his trunk and clothes. Miles decided to keep them in his own office and dole out the linen by his own standards of need.

Davis turned to his physician with a flash of anger.

"It's contemptible that they should thus dole out my clothes as if I were a convict in some penitentiary. They mean to degrade me. It can't be done. No man can be degraded by unmerited insult heaped upon the helpless. Such acts can only degrade their perpetrators. The day will come when the people will blush at the memory of such treatment—"

At last the loss of sleep proved beyond his endurance. He had tried to fight it out but gave up in a burst of passionate protest to Dr. Craven. The sight of his eye was failing. The horror of blindness chilled his soul.

"My treatment here," he began with an effort at restraint, "is killing me by inches. Let them make shorter work of it. I can't sleep. No man can live without sleep. My jailers know this. I am never alone a moment—always the eye of a guard staring at me day and night. If I doze a feverish moment the noise of the relieving guard each two hours wakes me and the blazing lamp pours its glare into my aching throbbing eyes. There must be a change or I shall go mad or blind or both."

He paused a moment and lifted his hollow face to the physician pathetically.

"Have you ever been conscious of being watched? Of having an eye fixed on you every moment, scrutinizing your smallest act, the change of the muscles of your face or the pose of your body? To have a human eye riveted on you every moment, waking, sleeping, sitting, walking, is a refinement of torture never dreamed of by a Comanche Indian—it is the eye of a spy or an enemy gloating over the pain and humiliation which it creates. The lamp burning in my eyes is a form of torment devised by someone who knew my habit of life never to sleep except in total darkness. When I took old Black Hawk the Indian Chief a captive to our barracks at St. Louis I shielded him from the vulgar gaze of the curious. I have lived too long in the woods to be frightened by an owl and I've seen Death too often to flinch at any form of pain—but this torture of being forever watched is beginning to prey on my reason."

The doctor's report that day was written in plain English:

"I find Mr. Davis in a very critical state, his nervous debility extreme, his mind despondent, his appetite gone, complexion livid, and pulse denoting deep prostration of all vital energies. I am alarmed and anxious over the responsibility of my position. If he should die in prison without trial, subject to such severities as have been inflicted on his attenuated frame the world will form conclusions and with enough color to pass them into history."

Dr. Craven was getting too troublesome. General Miles dismissed him, and called in Dr. George Cooper, a physician whose political opinions were supposed to be sounder.

45: THE MASTERMIND

Socola read the story of the chaining of the Confederate Chieftain with indignation. His intimate association with Jefferson Davis had convinced him of his singular purity of character and loftiness of soul. That he was capable of conspiring to murder Abraham Lincoln was inconceivable. That the charge should be made and pressed seriously by the National Government was a disgrace to the country.

Charles O'Connor, the greatest lawyer in America, indignant at the outrage, had offered his services to the prisoner. Socola hastened to a conference with O'Connor and placed himself at his command.

The lawyer sent him to Washington to find out the master mind at the bottom of these remarkable proceedings.

"Johnson the President," he warned, "is only a tool in the hands of a stronger man. Find that man. Stanton, the Secretary of War, is vindictive enough, but he lacks the cunning. Stevens, the leader of the House, is the real ruler of the Nation at this moment. Yet I have the most positive information that Stevens sneers at the attempt to accuse Davis of the assassination of Lincoln. Stevens hated Lincoln only a degree less than he hates Davis. He is blunt, outspoken, brutal in his views. There can be no question of the honesty of his position. Sumner, the leader of the Senate, is incapable of such low intrigue. Find the man and report to me."

Socola found him within six hours after his arrival in Washington. He was morally sure of him from the moment he left O'Connor's office.

Immediately on his arrival at the Capital he sought an interview with Joseph Holt, now the Judge Advocate General of the United States Army. He was therefore in charge of the prosecution of the cases of Clay and Davis.

For five minutes he watched the crooked poisonous mouth of the ex-Secretary of War and knew the truth. This vindictive venomous old man, ambitious, avaricious, implacable in his hatreds, had organized a Board of Assassination, which he called "The Bureau of Military Justice." This remarkable Bureau had already murdered

Mrs. Surratt on perjured testimony.

Socola had given his ex-Chief no intimation of his personal feelings and no hint of his association with O'Connor.

"I've a little favor to ask of you, young man," Holt said suavely.

Socola bowed.

"At your service, Chief—"

"I need a man of intelligence and skill to convey a proposition to Wirz, the keeper of Andersonville prison. He has been sentenced to death by the Bureau of Military Justice. I'm going to offer him his life on one condition—"

"And that is?"

"If he will confess under oath that Davis ordered the starving and torturing of prisoners at Andersonville I'll commute his sentence—"

"I see—"

"I'll give you an order to interview Wirz. He has never seen you. Report to me his answer."

When Socola explained to Wirz in sympathetic tones the offer of the Government to spare his life for the implication of Davis in direct orders from Richmond commanding cruelties at Andersonville, the condemned man lifted his wounded body and stared at his visitor.

His answer closed the interview.

"Tell the scoundrel who sent you that I am a soldier. I was a soldier in Germany before I cast my fortunes with the South. I bear in my body the wounds of honorable warfare. If I hadn't time to learn the meaning of honor from my friends in the South, my mother taught me in the old world. You ask me to save my life from these assassins by swearing away the life of another. Tell my executioner that I never saw the President of the Confederacy. I never received an order of any kind from him. I did the best I could for the men in my charge at Andersonville and tried honestly to improve their conditions. I am not a perjurer, even to save my own life. A soldier's business is to die. I am ready."

Socola extended his hand through the bars and grasped the prisoner's.

The deeper he dived into the seething mass of corruption and blind passion which had engulfed Washington the more desperate he saw the situation of Davis at Fortress Monroe. After two weeks of careful work he hurried to New York and reported the situation to O'Connor.

"The master mind," he began slowly, "I found at once. His name is Holt—"

"The Judge Advocate General?"

"Yes."

"That accounts for my inability to obtain a copy of the charges against Davis. Holt drew those charges. They are in his hands and he has determined to press his prisoner to trial before his Board of Assassins without allowing me to know the substance of his accusations. It's infamous."

"There are complications which may increase our dangers or suddenly lift them—"

"Complications—what do you mean?"

"The President, who has been intensely hostile to Davis, realizes that his own term of office and possibly his life are now at stake. He has broken with the Radicals who control Congress, old Thaddeus Stevens's at their head. Stevens lives in Washington in brazen defiance of conventionalities with a negro woman whom he separated from her husband thirty odd years ago. Under the influence of this negress he has introduced a bill into the House of Representatives to confiscate the remaining property of the white people of the South and give it to the negroes—dividing the land into plots of forty acres each. He proposes also to disfranchise the whites of the Southern States, enfranchise the negroes, destroy the State lines and erect on their ruins territories ruled by negroes whom his faction can control.

"Johnson the President, a Southern born white man, has already informed the Radicals that he will fight this program to the last ditch. Stevens' answer was characteristic of the imperious old leader. 'Let him dare! I'll impeach Andrew Johnson, remove him from office and hang him from the balcony of the White House.'

"The President realizes that the Bureau of Military Justice which he allowed Holt to create may be used as the engine of his own destruction. They have already taken the first steps to impeach him—"

"Then he'll never dare allow another case to be tried before that Bureau—" O'Connor interrupted.

"It remains to be seen. He is afraid of both Stanton and Holt. The

Bureau of Military Justice is their hobby."

O'Connor sprang to his feet.

"We must smash it by an appeal to the people. Their sense of justice is yet the salt that will save the Nation. The key to the situation is in the character of the remarkable witnesses whom Holt has produced before this tribunal of assassination. In my judgment they are a gang of hired perjurers. Their leader is a fellow named Conover. There are five men associated with him. They used these witnesses against Mrs. Surratt. They used them against Wirz. They are preparing to use them against Davis. It is inconceivable that these plugs from the gutters of New York could have really stumbled on the facts to which they have sworn. Find who these men are. Get their records to the last hour of the day you track them—and report to me."

Socola organized a force of detectives and set them to work. The task was a difficult one. He found that Conover and his pals were protected by the unlimited power of the National Government.

46: THE TORTURE

While the prisoner fought to save his reason in the dungeon at Fortress Monroe, his wife was denied the right to lift her hand in his defense. No communication was allowed between them except through his jailer.

On arrival in Savannah Mrs. Davis and her children were compelled to walk through the blazing heat the long distance from the wharf uptown, the whole party trudging immigrant fashion through the streets. Her sister carried the baby. Mrs. Davis and the two little boys and Maggie followed with parcels, and Robert, her faithful black man, brought up the rear with the baggage.

The people of Savannah, on learning of their arrival, treated their prisoners with the utmost kindness. Every home in the city was thrown open to them. Her children had been robbed of all their clothing except what they wore. The neighbors hurried in with clothes.

The newspaper of Savannah of the new regime, The Republican, published and republished with gleeful comments the most sensational accounts of the brutal scene of the shackling of Davis. Maggie composed a prayer and taught her little brothers to repeat it in concert for their grace at the table morning, noon and night:

"Dear Lord, give our father something he can eat, and keep him strong, and bring him back to us with eyes that can see and in his good senses, to his little children, for Jesus' sake."

Nearly every day the child who composed the prayer was so moved by its recital she would run from the table and dry her tears in the next room before she could eat.

Hourly scenes of violence increased between the whites and the inflamed blacks. A negro sentinel leveled his gun at little Jeff and threatened to shoot him for calling him "Uncle." With prayers and tears the mother sent her children away to the home of a friend in Montreal.

A year passed before President Johnson in answer to the wife's desperate pleading permitted her to visit her husband in prison. She arrived from Montreal on the cold raw morning of May 10, 1866, at four o'clock before day. There was no hotel at the fort at that time and the mother was compelled to sit in the desolate little waiting room with her baby without a fire until ten o'clock.

General Miles called. His references to her husband were made in a manner which brutally expressed his hatred and contempt. She had been informed that his health was in so dangerous a condition that physicians had despaired of his life.

Miles hastened to say:

"Davis' is in good health—"

"I can see him at once?" she begged.

"Yes. You understand the terms of your parole that you are to take no deadly weapons into the prison?"

Suppressing a smile at the unique use of the language which a man of the rank of Miles could make she replied quickly:

"I understand. Please arrange that I can see him at once."

Without answering the jailer turned and left the room. In a few minutes an officer appeared who conducted her to the room in Carroll Hall to which Dr. Cooper had forced Miles to remove the prisoner. Dr. Cooper proved as troublesome to the General as Dr. Craven. In fact a little more so. He had a way of swearing when angered which made the General nervous. American physicians don't make good politicians when the life of a patient is involved.

They were challenged by three lines of sentries, each requiring a password, ascended a stairway, turned to the right and entered a guard room where three young officers were sitting. Through the bars of the inner room the wife gazed at her husband with streaming eyes.

His body had shrunk to a skeleton, his eyes set and glassy, his cheek bones pressing against the shining skin. He rose and tottered across the room, his breath coming in short gasps, his voice scarcely audible.

Mrs. Davis was locked in with him. She sent the baby back to her quarters by Frederick, another faithful negro servant who had followed their fortunes through good report and evil.

His room had a horse bucket for water, a basin and pitcher on an old chair whose back had been sawed off, a little iron bedstead with hard mattress, one pillow, a wooden table, and a wooden chair with one leg shorter than the others which might be used as an improvised rocker. His bed was so thick with bugs the room was filled with their odor. He was so innocent of such things he couldn't imagine what distressed him so at night—insisting that he had contracted some sort of skin disease.

His dinner was brought slopped from one dish to another and covered by a gray hospital towel sogged with the liquids. The man of fastidious taste glanced at the platter and saw that the good doctor's wife had added oysters to his menu that day and ate one. His vitality was so low even this gave him intense pain.

He was not bitter, but expressed his quiet contempt for the systematic petty insults which his jailer was now heaping on him daily. His physician had demanded that he take exercise in the open air. Miles always walked with him and never permitted an occasion of this kind to pass without directing at his helpless prisoner personal insults so offensive that Davis always cut his walks short to be rid of his tormentor. On one occasion the general was so brutal in his conversation after he had locked his prisoner in his room that he suddenly sprang at the bars, grasped them with his trembling, skeleton hands and cried:

"But for these you should answer to me—here and now!"

A favorite pastime of his jailer was to admit crowds of vulgar sightseers and permit them to gaze at his prisoner.

A woman inquired of Frederick, who was on his way to his room:
"Where's Jeff?"

The negro bowed gravely and drew his stalwart figure erect:

"I am sorry, madame, not to be able to tell you. I do not know any such person."

"Yes, you do—aren't you his servant?"

"No, madame, you are mistaken. I have the honor to serve ex-President Davis."

Only a great soul can command the love and respect of servants as did this quiet grave statesman of the old regime.

Never during the long hours of these weeks and months of torture did he lose his dignity or his lofty bearing quail before his tormentor. He was too refined and dignified to be abusive, and too proud in General Miles' delicate phraseology to "beg."

The loving wife began now her desperate fight to nurse him

back into life again.

The new Commandant of the fort, General Burton, who replaced Miles, proved himself a gentleman and a soldier of the old school. He immediately gave to the prisoner every courtesy possible and to his wife sympathy and help.

The Bishop of Montreal sent him a case of green chartreuse from his own stores. This powerful digestive stimulant helped his feeble appetite to take the nourishment needed to sustain life and slowly build his strength.

He could sleep only when read to, and many a day dawned on the worn figure of his wife still droning her voice into his sensitive ears, with one hand on his pulse praying God it might still beat. At times it stopped, and then she roused the sleeper, gave him the stimulant and made him eat something which she always kept ready. Dr. Cooper had warned that the walls of his heart were so weak even a sound sleep might prove his death if too long continued.

47: VINDICATION

When Socola had finished his work developing the history and character of Conover and his crew of professional perjurers there was a sudden collapse in the machinery of the Bureau of Military Justice. Holt was compelled not only to repudiate the wretches by whose hired testimony he had committed more than one murder through the forms of military law, but also to issue a long document defending himself as Judge Advocate General of the United States from the charge of subornation of perjury—the vilest accusation that can be brought against a sworn officer of any court. His weak defense served its purpose for the moment. He managed to cling to his office and his salary for a brief season. With the advent of restored law he sank into merited oblivion.

The charge of murder having collapsed, the Government now pressed against Davis an indictment for treason. Salmon P. Chase, the Chief Justice of the United States, warned the President and his Cabinet that no such charge could be sustained.

And still malice held the Confederate Chieftain a prisoner. Every other leader of the South had long since been released. On the public exposure of Holt and his perjurers the conscience of the North, led by Horace Greeley and Gerrit Smith, demanded the speedy trial or release of Davis.

The Radical conspirators at Washington, under the leadership of Stevens inspired by his dusky companion, were now pressing with feverish haste their program of revolution. They passed each measure over the veto of the President amid jeers, groans and curses. They disfranchised one-third of the whites of the South, gave the ballot to a million ignorant negroes but yesterday taken from the jungles of Africa, blotted out the civil governments of the Southern States, and sent the army back to enforce their decrees. Stevens introduced his bill to confiscate the property of the whites and give it to the negroes. This measure was his pet. It was the only one of his schemes which would be defeated on a two-thirds vote if Johnson should veto it. Stevens and Butler at once drew their bill of indictment against the President and set in motion the machinery to remove him from office—the grim old leader still swearing that he would hang him.

In this auspicious moment Charles O'Connor marshaled his forces and demanded the release of Davis on bail. Andrew Johnson had seen a new light. He was now in a life and death struggle with the newly enthroned mob to save the Republic from a Dictatorship. The conspirators had already selected the man they proposed to set up on his removal from office.

The President issued an order to General Burton at Fortress Monroe to produce his prisoner in the United States District Court of Richmond.

On May fourth, 1867, the little steamer from the fort touched the wharf at Richmond and Jefferson Davis and his wife once more appeared in the Capital of the Confederacy.

The South had come to greet them.

All differences of opinion were stilled before the white face of the man who had been put in irons for their sins. They came from the four corners of the country for which he had toiled and suffered.

Senator Barton, his wife and daughter and all his surviving sons had come from Fairview to do him honor. A vast crowd assembled at the wharf. No king ever entered his palace with grander welcome. The road from the wharf to the Spotswood Hotel was a living sea of humanity. His carriage couldn't move until the way was forced open by the mounted police. The windows and roofs of every house were crowded. Men and women everywhere were in tears. As the carriage turned into Main Street a man shouted:

"Hats off, Virginians!"

Every head was bared in the vast throng which stretched a mile along the thoroughfare. As he passed in triumph, the people for whom he had worked and suffered crowded to his carriage, stretched out their hands in silence and touched his garments while the tears rolled down their cheeks.

They arraigned him for trial on a charge of high treason.

The indictment had also named Robert E. Lee as guilty of the same crime. Grant lifted his mailed fist and told the Government he would fight if necessary to protect the man who had surrendered in good faith to his army. The peanut politicians dropped Lee's name.

When the tall, emaciated leader of the South stood erect before his accusers in court he faced a scene which proclaimed the advent of the new Democracy in America which must yet make good its right to live.

On the Judge's bench sat John C. Underwood, a crawling, shambling, shuffling, ignorant demagogue who had set a new standard of judicial honor and dignity. He had selected one of the handsomest homes in Virginia, ordered it confiscated as a Federal judge, and made his wife buy it in and convey it to him after warning other bidders to keep off the scene. The thief was living in his stolen mansion on the day he sat down beside the Chief Justice of the United States in this trial. When Chase had warned the Government that no charge of treason could stand against Davis, Underwood assured the Attorney General that he would fix a negro jury in Richmond which could be relied on to give the verdict necessary. He had impaneled the first grand jury ever assembled in America composed of negroes and whites. A negro petit jury now sat in the box grinning at the judge, their thick lips, flat noses and omnipotent African odor proclaiming the dawn of a new era in the history of America.

Salmon P. Chase with quiet dignity voted to quash the indictment. Underwood with a vulgar stump speech to the crowd of negroes voted to hold the indictment good. The case was sent to the Supreme Court on this disagreement and the defendant admitted to bail.

Horace Greeley and Gerrit Smith, Cornelius Vanderbilt and Augustus Schell, representing the noblest spirit in the North were among the men who signed his bail bond.

When he was released and walked out of the court room cheer after cheer swept the struggling crowd that greeted him. Senator Barton took the driver's place on the box while thousands followed to the hotel shouting themselves hoarse. For three hours he stood shaking the hands of weeping men and women. No sublimer tribute was ever paid to human worth. It came with healing to his wounded soul. The anguish of the past was as if it had never been.

Jennie Barton gazed with astonishment when Socola grasped his outstretched hand. She was standing near enough to hear his voice.

"I want to thank you, young man," he said gratefully, "for all you've done for me and mine. Mr. O'Connor tells me that your services have been invaluable. For myself, my wife and babies and my people, I thank you again. I wish I might do something to repay you—"

"I've only done my duty," was the modest response. "But I think you might help me a little—"

"If it's within my power—"

"You remember Miss Barton?"

"I've just shaken hands with her—she is here!"

"Would you mind putting in a word—"

"I'll do more, sir—I'm in command today. I'll issue positive orders—"

Jennie moved, he saw her and beckoned. She came, blushing.

"What's this, my little comrade?" he whispered, seizing her hands. "The war is over. I've shaken hands with Horace Greeley and Gerrit Smith today. There can be no stragglers in our camp, I owe my life to this young man."

He took Jennie's hand, placed it on Socola's arm, and he led her silent and blushing from the crowd to an alcove in the far corner of the hall.

She looked up into his face with tenderness.

"You've done a noble and beautiful thing in the gift of your life to our Chief for these two miserable years—"

"They've been miserable to you?"

She smiled.

"But I knew you would come—"

"You'll not send me away again?"

She slowly slipped her arms around his neck and kissed him.

They stood on the balcony hand in hand and watched the crowds surging about the carriage as the tall Chieftain left the hotel to take the train to greet his children.

Socola uncovered his head and spoke reverently.

"He belongs to the race of giants who have made our Nation what it is today. We owe a debt to the unflinching dignity and honesty of his mind. He made hedging, trimming and compromise impossible—the issues which divided us of Life and Death. A weaker man would have wavered and we should have had to fight our battles over again. They have been settled for all time."

Jennie lifted her eyes to his:

"What's your name, my sweetheart?"
He laughed softly.
"Does it matter now? Our country's one—my name is Love."

www.ingramcontent.com/pod-product-compliance
Lightning Source LLC
Chambersburg PA
CBHW020741100426
42735CB00037B/160